Pitt Series in Policy and Institutional Studies

WILLIAM O. DOUGLAS *Collection of the Supreme Court of the United States*

"He Shall Not Pass This Way Again"

The Legacy of Justice William O. Douglas

STEPHEN L. WASBY

EDITOR

University of Pittsburgh Press for the William O. Douglas Institute

Published by the University of Pittsburgh Press, Pittsburgh, Pa. 15260
Copyright © 1990 University of Pittsburgh Press
All rights reserved
Baker & Taylor International, London
Manufactured in the United States of America

Library of Congress Cataloging-in-Publication Data

"He shall not pass this way again" : the legacy of Justice William O. Douglas /
    Stephen L. Wasby, editor.
        p.   cm. — (Pitt series in policy and institutional studies)
    Includes bibliographical references (p.   ).
    ISBN 0-8229-3644-5. — ISBN 0-8229-5435-4 (pbk.)
    1. Douglas, William O. (William Orville), 1898–   . I. Wasby, Stephen L.,
    1937–   . II. Series.
KF8745.D6H4   1990
347.73′2634 — dc20
[347.3072634]
                                                                89-21544
                                                                    CIP

In Commemoration of the
Fiftieth Anniversary
of the Appointment of
WILLIAM O. DOUGLAS
to the Supreme Court
17 April 1939

Contents

CHARLES A. REICH *Foreword: "He Shall Not Pass This Way Again"*   xi

STEPHEN L. WASBY *Introduction*   xv

I. DOUGLAS AS JUSTICE

STEPHEN L. WASBY *Introduction: Douglas as Justice: The View from Political Science*   3

HOWARD BALL *Loyalty, Treason and the State: An Examination of Justice William O. Douglas's Style, Substance, and Anguish*   7

MELVIN I. UROFSKY *Getting the Job Done: William O. Douglas and Collegiality in the Supreme Court*   33

ROBERT JEROME GLENNON *Commentary: Collegialism and Change over Time: William O. Douglas as Justice*   51

DONALD W. JACKSON *Commentary: On the Correct Handling of Contradictions Within the Court*   57

II. DOUGLAS AND CIVIL LIBERTIES: THE FIRST AMENDMENT AND CIVIL RIGHTS

NORMAN DORSEN *Introduction: Douglas and Civil Liberties*   65

L. A. POWE, JR. *Justice Douglas, the First Amendment, and the Protection of Rights*   69

NADINE STROSSEN *The Religion Clause Writings of Justice William O. Douglas*   91

Drew S. Days III   *Justice William O. Douglas and Civil
Rights*   109

William Cohen   *Commentary: Douglas as Civil
Libertarian*   121

III.   DOUGLAS AND CIVIL LIBERTIES: CRIMINAL LAW AND PRIVACY

Samuel Walker   *Introduction: Douglas as Civil
Libertarian: Criminal Law and Privacy*   129

Steven B. Duke   *Justice Douglas and the Criminal Law*   133

Sanford H. Kadish   *Commentary: Justice Douglas and
the Criminal Law: Another View*   149

Dorothy J. Glancy   *Douglas's Right of Privacy:
A Response to His Critics*   155

Elizabeth M. Schneider   *Commentary: The Affirmative
Dimensions of Douglas's Privacy*   179

IV.   DOUGLAS AS ENVIRONMENTALIST

Ralph W. Johnson   *Introduction: Douglas as
Environmentalist*   189

Ralph W. Johnson   *"In Simple Justice to a Downtrodden People": Justice Douglas and the American
Indian Cases*   191

William H. Rodgers, Jr.   *The Fox and the Chickens:
Mr. Justice Douglas and Environmental Law*   215

Christopher D. Stone   *Commentary: William O.
Douglas and the Environment*   227

Charles F. Wilkinson   *Justice Douglas and the
Public Lands*   233

T. H. Watkins   *Commentary: Justice Douglas Takes
a Hike*   249

V. DOUGLAS AS INTERNATIONALIST

THOMAS M. FRANCK *Introduction: Douglas as Internationalist* 257

MICHAEL J. GLENNON *Douglas the Internationalist: Separation of Powers and the Conduct of Foreign Relations* 261

JULES LOBEL *Justice Douglas the Internationalist: The Connection Between Domestic Liberty and Foreign Policy* 279

HAROLD HONGJU KOH *Commentary: The Liberal Constitutional Internationalism of Justice Douglas* 297

HANS A. LINDE *Commentary: Douglas as Internationalist* 305

Selected Bibliography 315

Notes on Contributors 319

Table of Cases 323

Index 333

Foreword
"He Shall Not Pass This Way Again"

Charles A. Reich

JUSTICE WILLIAM O. DOUGLAS was a philosopher of liberty. His special focus was the threat to liberty from highly organized modern society. His critics denied that he had any consistent philosophy. They portrayed him as one who never took the time to work out his ideas in a reasoned and orderly fashion. I found the contrary. In many conversations — walking along the C&O Canal towpath, sitting in his spectacularly situated summer home at Goose Prairie — I learned that his ideas about liberty were the product of a lifetime of observation and thought.

Justice Douglas's philosophy of liberty was closely akin to his philosophy about the natural environment. The environment nurtures and preserves all natural life. Human beings, however, also live in an artificially constructed social environment. This social environment may nurture and preserve us, or, on the other hand, it may produce warped and stunted people who lack the kind of character that a democratic society needs. Douglas, in his talk and his writings, often compared the healthy effects of wilderness on people with the harmful impact of the civilized environment. Wilderness teaches equality, self-sufficiency, respect for others, a sense of community. Wilderness summons the best in people, commands them to excel, brings them to their true selves. But Douglas spoke with distress and concern about the effects of the social environment created by large organizations and by government. All too often, he believed, this artificial world debased human character, denied our spiritual life, made people afraid of freedom.

The mark of Justice Douglas's work on the Court is the great sophistication he showed about abuses of power by organized society and their threat to freedom. In contrast, most members of the Court were naively and uncritically deferential to government and large organizations, as if these giant agglomerations of power could do no wrong. All too often, a majority of the Court could not see the threats to freedom that Douglas correctly perceived. The Court was willing to squander liberty in the same way that many people were ready to squander air and water — as if there were an unlimited supply of it. Liberty, the Court seemed to think, was like the ocean. There is always more of it; it cannot be polluted or destroyed. And so we can take away a little liberty here, and a little liberty there, without endangering the supply. Liberty, like the air or the forests, can never be exhausted.

Just as he was among the first to recognize growing threats to the natural environment, so Justice Douglas was among the earliest to see that liberty is tremendously endangered by many features of the modern industrial state. He began his legal career as a student of the modern corporation, and later he became a student of that super-corporation, the managerial government. He saw that management is authoritarian and secretive rather than democratic and open, that it creates dependency rather than independence, that it coerces and controls individuals instead of nurturing their growth. Therefore one cannot take a passive view about threats to liberty. Today liberty, like nature, requires active protection.

One of Justice Douglas's greatest dissenting opinions involved a federal law that took away the privilege against self-incrimination—the constitutional right to be silent—and substituted a grant of immunity from prosecution. The Court majority held that there was no loss of liberty in this substitution; the right to silence protected only the threat of criminal prosecution for what a witness might be compelled to say. For Douglas, this was like the contention that clear-cutting an ancient cathedral forest poses no loss of environmental values so long as the area is reseeded for "managed growth." For the person who loses the right of silence may also lose his or her job, reputation, ability to earn a living, place in society. Immunity from criminal prosecution does not prevent the individual from being destroyed in other ways.

For Douglas, the guardian of liberty must always be ready to meet new threats. Accordingly, liberty cannot be a static concept, any more than the threats are static. There are many so-called judicial conservatives who are willing to allow the powers of government to grow and evolve with the times, while restricting liberty to the meaning it had when the nation was born. Thus the word "commerce" in the constitutional grant of power to the national government to regulate commerce has not been limited to its eighteenth-century meaning. Instead the Court has allowed Congress to regulate air travel and television. Likewise the presidency has not been kept to the limited office envisioned by the Framers, but has grown to permit the president to meet the needs of a world-wide system of international security. Douglas insisted that liberty must also be allowed to evolve.

One of the opinions for which Douglas will always be remembered is *Griswold v. Connecticut,* the first time the Court recognized that every individual has a right to privacy. Ever since he formulated this right, it has been under attack by those who would keep the Bill of Rights limited to its eighteenth-century meaning. Douglas argued that the rights explicitly enumerated have broader meanings today; in his memorable phrase, they have penumbras. They mark an area larger than themselves. They are like street lights illuminating a darkened street, the whole of the street representing liberty, the lights being only those aspects of liberty marked out by the Framers.

Privacy is a living, functional idea of liberty. It can advance as governmental intrusions advance—and they do advance all the time. New forms of technology, new kinds of regulation, all permit new intrusions. A static concept of liberty would be a sterile one. Justice Douglas tried to make liberty dynamic, because society itself is dynamic.

Beyond this, Justice Douglas warned us that we face a liberty crisis today, as profound and widespread as the environmental crisis. He thought that liberty was far more endangered than most people realize. And the liberty crisis is harder to notice, to observe, to measure, than the environmental crisis. So much of our liberty is given up incrementally, in bits and pieces, in response to pleas of necessity, that we don't realize what is happening. In fact, the only way we can recognize even an extreme liberty deficiency may be the evidence of its symptoms. Douglas saw such evidence in the loss of independent thinking, loss of courage, the inability of people to stand alone. He saw it in the advance of dependency and passivity.

Justice Douglas was extraordinarily creative in seeing the new dimensions that protection of the individual must assume in an ever more regulated world. He was the first to recognize a right to travel, between states and to foreign countries. He saw the need to expand the protection of family beyond the traditional limits of that concept. He spoke of the right to work, recognizing that freedom to work, which traditionally has been taken for granted, is more and more regulated by occupational and professional licensing, controlled by the concerted action of large employers, and thus in jeopardy unless afforded judicial protection. He was a student of every threat to liberty, every new form of power and its potential for abuse.

When Justice Douglas talked or wrote about wilderness, he described it not merely as a place away from civilization and therefore free of restraint, but as a positive, nurturing environment, a teacher, a friend, a source of support and strength. In the same way, he saw liberty not as the mere absence of restraint, but as a positive, helpful, nurturing social environment that *empowers* us. Thus, he lent his fullest support to the efforts of his lifelong friend, Robert M. Hutchins, to establish a center where scholars would be able to devote themselves to the study of freedom under ideal conditions. Liberty, in the Douglas sense, is the environment that makes it possible for people to think and act fully, that stimulates experimentation and creativity and challenges us to new thought.

Bill Douglas made himself a part of America's nurturing environment. He took on a role as a public philosopher, much like Ralph Waldo Emerson. Like Emerson, he traveled the country, speaking about liberty to audiences of citizens young and old, not just in the legal world, not just in the academic world. He even found time to write an Almanac of Liberty with a thought about liberty for each day in the year. Wherever he went, his message was the same: the answer to society's problems is more freedom, not less. The greater the problems, the greater amount of freedom we need to find solutions. By word and by example, he was America's teacher of liberty.

Introduction

Stephen L. Wasby

THE BASIC facts about William O. Douglas's life are clear:
- born in Minnesota;
- moved to the Pacific Northwest, where he grew up;
- struck by infantile paralysis — from which he recovered to the extent that we think of him as the quintessential outdoor hiker;
- raised in poverty;
- graduated from Whitman College and Columbia Law School, where he served on the law review;
- member of the Columbia Law School and Yale Law School faculties;
- member and chair of the Securities and Exchange Commission;
- and, finally, Associate Justice of the United States Supreme Court, from April 17, 1939, when he succeeded to the seat of Louis D. Brandeis, until 1975 — longer service than any other justice. During that service, he was a prolific and facile writer of off-the-bench statements, was a possible candidate for national political office, and was the object of impeachment attempts.

How much that says, but also how little!

When Justice Harry A. Blackmun, helping celebrate the fiftieth anniversary of Justice Douglas's appointment to the Supreme Court, said that Douglas was a "very *remarkable* man" with "tremendous talent," he got it right.

But what does "remarkable" mean for this man of many facets?

For one thing, the many facets meant, in the words of U.S. Court of Appeals for the Ninth Circuit Judge Betty Fletcher, "There are many Justice Douglases," so that "we each have our own Justice Douglas."

Justice Douglas had, said Justice Blackmun, "a lively, darting mind," a "love of the environment," an "abhorrence of pomposity," and a "reach for the jugular." He was "controversial," something Justice Blackmun says he thrived on and certainly made the most of. In terms of his ideology, he had what was almost a "veneration" of the First Amendment — "all of it."

Yet in view of the number of judicial opinions Justice Douglas wrote, he left us less doctrine than one might have expected. Perhaps this should not surprise us, because he was not a doctrinal analyst of the old school but a Legal Realist, seriously incorporating social concerns in his work, both on the Court and off. Whatever the doctrinal legacy, Douglas left us much in ideas and ideals. He was an exemplar — as someone holding convictions and holding them firmly, as a justice taking a firm stand in the anti-Communist cases and questioning executive authority in foreign policy, as an environmentalist.

This "astonishing person," whom his friend and walking companion Charles Reich has called impatient, "driven by demons," an insecure person calm only when walking at a very rapid pace and perhaps relaxed only around those concerned with the environment, was, Reich observed, a philosopher of liberty, someone who made for himself "a role as a public philosopher."

Fifty years after William O. Douglas's arrival at the Supreme Court, it seems fitting to direct our attention to this remarkable man and to review his views of and contributions to the law, the environment, and the international arena — a range of contributions that demands such attention.

Over the years, some of Justice Douglas's judicial opinions have been analyzed by writers, often critically, and his life has also been the subject of attention. More, however, is required. On April 15–17, 1989, a group of distinguished scholars came to Seattle, Washington, under the auspices of the William O. Douglas Institute, to bring their collective attention to bear in order to provide the first systematic inquiry into Justice Douglas's views on the wide range of subjects about which he spoke and wrote. Their analysis of Douglas's work that follows in these pages illuminates his many facets and helps explain why we can say that someone like him "will not pass this way again."

In this volume, those scholars examine four major aspects of Justice Douglas's work: his relations with his colleagues; his views on civil liberties, which primarily produced his reputation as a liberal; his stance as an environmentalist; and his views as an internationalist. Douglas's tenure at Yale Law School and on the Securities and Exchange Commission was important, but our focus is on his time on the Supreme Court. The civil liberties issues of freedom of expression, the relations between church and state, race relations, criminal law and procedure, and privacy have been with us for many years, but what Justice Douglas said on those subjects has not lost its importance. Indeed, he taught us "by precept and example." The emphasis Douglas placed on the environment and on the rights of native Americans anticipated the greater concern people were to give to those issues. The issue of the relative power of the branches of government in foreign affairs, at the heart of the Vietnam conflict, is of utmost contemporary importance, as are issues of world peace, to which Douglas also spoke eloquently.

In their examination of those topics, the writers both praise and criticize. Justice Douglas's deficiencies, for example, as an opinion writer, or as a person dealing with his law clerks, are not ignored. At the same time, the authors point not only to Douglas's doctrinal contributions but, more important, to his positions and to the example he provided of commitment to civil liberties, protection of the environment, and international peace. They also note that Douglas's views were not static—that, for example, he moved to a more absolutist position of separation of church and state, and that, after joining in support of the executive's actions in wartime, he moved to skepticism about and opposition to the executive's actions.

The contributors do not limit themselves to Justice Douglas's judicial opinions for their source material. They also use his autobiography, travel expositions, and public policy essays. Some draw on his private papers, including his letters and memoranda to colleagues, and on interviews with colleagues and clerks.

The chapters are contributed by a historian, a political scientist, and law professors. All have written previously either about Justice Douglas or about the substantive area they examine here. Among them and also among the commentators are some of Justice Douglas's former law clerks. The commentators on the principal chapters include a historian, an environmental editor, political scientists, a judge, and law professors. The chapters are grouped in five sets, including two on civil liberties. Each set begins with an introductory comment and includes commentaries on the chapters. The volume also provides a bibliography of Justice Douglas's writings and of writings about him, a table of cases, and an index.

I wish to acknowledge the assistance of those without whom this volume would not have been possible:

Hubert Locke, Director, William O. Douglas Institute, for arranging the conference at which the writings in this volume were first presented;

Norman Dorsen, New York University School of Law, and Samuel Walker, University of Nebraska at Omaha, who along with Hubert Locke and myself served as the planning committee for the conference;

Cathleen Douglas Stone, for the estate of William O. Douglas, for permission to use material from his autobiographical volumes, *Go East, Young Man* and *The Court Years;*

and to the contributors, for responding promptly and in general good grace to requests for editorial changes and all the other "necessaries" connected with publishing a book.

I consider it a signal honor to have been able to participate with all the distinguished members of the scholarly legal community who joined to explore the work of a most special jurist, whose striking impact on America can truly lead us to say, with both admiration and wistfulness, "He shall not pass this way again."

PART ONE

Douglas as Justice

INTRODUCTION:
DOUGLAS AS JUSTICE:
THE VIEW FROM POLITICAL SCIENCE

Stephen L. Wasby

IN OTHER CHAPTERS in this volume, the principal focus is on Justice Douglas's substantive views. In this section, however, authors and commentators take a different approach. They refer to Douglas's judicial opinions, but their primary concern is his relations with others at the Supreme Court — his colleagues and his clerks. They make major use of his private papers and of interviews with other justices and with some of his former law clerks.

Before we turn to the views of Douglas as justice provided by Howard Ball and Melvin Urofsky, some words are in order about political scientists' work on the behavior of Supreme Court justices. In examining judges' relations with their colleagues, political scientists have used a number of methods. For some, the focus has been on ideology, just as it is for many who comb a justice's opinions for their meaning. The methods, however, are different, and the *vote,* not the *opinion,* is the basis for learning about interaction among the justices — for learning how often Justice *A* votes with Justice *B* compared to how often Justice *A* votes with Justice *C* in cases where the Court is not unanimous. The result of this examination is the specification of the frequency with which pairs of justices, or blocs of more than two justices, occur over time rather than in individual cases. In a related method, the ideology of a justice in relation to the others sitting on the Court at the same time is determined by a method known as Guttmann scaling, in which the votes of a court's members on a common subject matter, like church-state relations or freedom of association, are arranged to allow a determination of whether a common dimension (an attitude or ideology) explains the pattern of votes. When a pattern appears, we can learn who is most liberal or most conservative among those justices, or who is at the center of the Court during the period under consideration.[1]

Findings from such studies serve to complement examination of the content of a justice's written opinions. At times the studies simply reinforce conclusions reached through examination of those opinions. However, at other times they can provide a view at variance with the results of doctrinal analysis or at least a more rigorous foundation for the results derived from opinion content.

Studies of justices based on bloc analysis and scaling have produced a number of findings about Justice Douglas. We learn, for example, that in the 1962–1964 Terms—the mid-Warren Court—Douglas was the Supreme Court's most liberal member as part of a bloc that also included Chief Justice Earl Warren and Justices Hugo Black, William Brennan, and Arthur Goldberg. When Justice Goldberg left the Court and was replaced by Abe Fortas, bloc alignments in the Court became more fluid, and the Chief Justice voted less frequently with Douglas (and with Black) than he had earlier. Throughout this period, Douglas was a reliable liberal vote but was not a cohesive member of a liberal bloc.[2]

When Warren Burger replaced Earl Warren as Chief Justice, the interaction between Justices Black and Douglas changed. Black now voted more often with the new Chief Justice than with Douglas.[3] Once Lewis Powell and William Rehnquist joined the Court in 1972, Douglas voted with Chief Justice Burger only 4.2 percent of the time, part of a polarization extreme for the modern Supreme Court. Moreover, Douglas and Rehnquist disagreed in two-thirds of the Court's cases, "a modern Supreme Court record."[4]

Studies based on scaling also provide interesting findings with respect to Justice Douglas. They show, for example, that in the Warren Court, Douglas was among six justices considered liberal because of a tendency to support two dimensions of civil liberties and another dimension (New Dealism) based on regulation of economic activity.[5] Such studies also show that Justice Douglas was most liberal in midcareer. His support for civil liberties traced a parabola, increasing from his early Supreme Court career to the midpoint of his Court service and then decreasing somewhat.[6] Whether this was the result of aging and the cognitive changes it produces, judicial experience, a change in attitudinal position, or a shift in the content of the cases coming to the Court and which it accepted for review, is not clear. However, the parabolic pattern should make us aware of the risks of thinking of Justice Douglas as uniformly "liberal" throughout his judicial career. Indeed, as Howard Ball shows, Douglas did not publicly adopt an antigovernment position in the Japanese-American relocation cases, which came relatively early in his Court career—perhaps a result of his relative judicial inexperience. As Michael Glennon demonstrates, a similar pattern can be found in his changing deference to the executive in the area of national security policy.

In addition to studies based on bloc analysis and Guttmann scaling, other vote-based studies also tell us about Justice Douglas's positions in particular issue areas. For example, in cases involving taxpayers, Bernard Wolfman and his colleagues have demonstrated that, although Douglas supported the taxpayer less than did the Court as a whole prior to 1942, his support of the taxpayer then became very much higher than the Court's average. In 1943–1959, when the taxpayer won one-fourth of the time, Douglas voted for the taxpayer in 47 percent of the cases; his support increased to 73 percent in the next five years, although the Court supported the taxpayer in only 17 percent of the cases in that period. For the 1964–1973 period, toward the end of Douglas's tenure on the Court, he supported the taxpayer in 59 percent of the cases, more than twice the taxpayer's overall 26 percent success rate.[7] Elsewhere in this volume, Ralph Johnson calls attention to Keller's study of Douglas's votes in Indian cases. Keller showed that Douglas voted with the majority in every instance when the Court favored Indian claims but dissented 11 of 19 times when the Court ruled against those claims.[8]

Studies of the types discussed here have advantages and disadvantages. Among the advantages are that they rely on votes rather than written opinions. Although not without their own ambiguity, votes are relatively easier to interpret than the written word, particularly when that written word was often hastily produced, as numerous authors note about Douglas. However, we must remember that dissents, at the core of these studies, which are based on nonunanimous decisions, may be written for varying reasons and for audiences outside as well as within the Court. Also important is that the votes on which these studies are based are drawn from *sets* of cases. This prevents us from misrepresenting a justice's position on the basis of one or two, perhaps idiosyncratic, opinions; an example would be characterizing Justice Douglas's position on church-state relations solely on the basis of *Zorach v. Clauson,*[9] before he had developed his more strongly separationist views, as Nadine Strossen explains. Another example would be basing Douglas's position on racial discrimination solely on his separate opinion in *DeFunis v. Odegaard,*[10] rather than including the sit-in cases examined by Drew Days. Using votes also allows us to see whether the *outcomes* the justice produces over time point in the same direction as the rhetoric in the justice's opinions. As we have learned from studies of Justice Felix Frankfurter, which demonstrated that the rhetoric of "judicial self-restraint" masked conservative outcomes, that is not always so.[11]

A chief disadvantage of relying on votes rather than on judicial opinions is that one loses much of the richness available from the written word set forth in a justice's opinions for the Court, concurring opinions, and dissents, or in the justice's other writings. In the chapters that follow, Howard Ball and Melvin Urofsky make this "other writing" a major source in their examination of interaction among members of the Supreme Court and between Justice Douglas and his clerks; in so doing, they provide a further dimension to those derived from opinions or from votes. The advantage of access to such sources, particularly where (as here) they are supplemented by interviews, is that one is able to interpret more directly the reasons for a justice's actions instead of having to infer those reasons from isolated written opinions or sets of votes.

In the chapters and commentary that follow, we see several dimensions of "Douglas as Justice." One, the focus of Ball's chapter, is how he dealt with his colleagues over some of the most controversial cases in which he was to participate—the Japanese relocation cases and flag salute cases of World War II and the Rosenberg espionage case. These cases, which caused

Douglas much anguish, illustrate his position as a lonely individual on the Court. Urofsky provides further attention to Douglas's interactions with his colleagues and adds to this the perspective of the justice's relations with his clerks. The latter do not place Justice Douglas, as an individual, in the most pleasing light. Robert Glennon then offers alternative hypotheses or perspectives for some positions taken by Ball and/or Urofsky. Then, using the theme of "getting the work out," present in Urofsky's discussion of Douglas's interactions with colleagues and clerks, Donald Jackson combines a look at Douglas as Legal Realist with an examination of types of political personality.

Notes

1. See Stephen L. Wasby, *The Supreme Court in the Federal Judicial System,* 3d ed. (Chicago: Nelson-Hall, 1988), pp. 248–49, for discussion of these methods.

2. Glendon Schubert, *The Constitutional Polity* (Boston: Boston University Press, 1970), pp. 124–25; Edward V. Heck, "Changing Voting Patterns in the Warren and Burger Courts," in Sheldon Goldman and Charles Lamb, eds., *Judicial Conflict and Consensus: Behavioral Studies of American Appellate Courts* (Lexington: University Press of Kentucky, 1986), pp. 77–78.

3. Heck, "Changing Vote Patterns," p. 86.

4. Russell W. Galloway, Jr., "The First Decade of the Burger Court: Conservative Dominance (1969–1979)," *Santa Clara Law Review* 21 (1981): 908.

5. Glendon Schubert, *The Judicial Mind* (Evanston: Northwestern University Press, 1965), passim.

6. S. Sidney Ulmer, "Parabolic Support of Civil Liberty Claims: The Case of William O. Douglas," *Journal of Politics* 41 (May 1979): 634–39. See also H. Frank Way, "The Study of Judicial Attitudes: The Case of Mr. Justice Douglas," *Western Political Quarterly* 24 (Mar. 1971): 12–23.

7. Bernard Wolfman, Jonathan L. F. Silver, and Marjorie A. Silver, *Dissent Without Opinions: The Behavior of Justice William O. Douglas in Tax Cases* (Philadelphia: University of Pennsylvania Press, 1975).

8. Robert H. Keller, Jr., "William O. Douglas, The Supreme Court, and American Indians," *American Indian Law Review* 3 (1975): 333–60.

9. 343 U.S. 306 (1952).

10. 416 U.S. 312, 320 (1974) (Douglas, J.) (seriously questioning the University of Washington's affirmative action plan unless it could be shown to operate in a racially neutral way, but also questioning the use of the Law School Admission Test [LSAT] for minorities).

11. See Joel B. Grossman, "Role-Playing and the Analysis of Judicial Behavior: The Case of Mr. Justice Frankfurter," *Journal of Public Law* 11 (1962): 285–309; Harold J. Spaeth, "The Judicial Restraint of Mr. Justice Frankfurter — Myth or Reality," *Midwest Journal of Political Science* 8 (Feb. 1964): 22–38.

Loyalty, Treason, and the State: An Examination of Justice William O. Douglas's Style, Substance, and Anguish

Howard Ball

ASSOCIATE JUSTICE Felix Frankfurter, during the Supreme Court's internal debates surrounding the first of the Japanese Exclusion Cases, *Hirabayashi v. United States,*[1] wrote a memo to Chief Justice Harlan Fiske Stone. It was written after Justice William O. Douglas had circulated a draft concurring opinion that addressed questions of loyalty and of due process even for the Japanese-Americans targeted by the military for curfew, exclusion, and finally, incarceration.

Douglas's opinion greatly angered Frankfurter, and his memo to the Chief reflected this attitude. He asked Stone, who had been one of Douglas's law professors at Columbia University, to "send for Brother Douglas and talk him out of his opinion by making him see the dangers he is inviting." Frankfurter, even in 1943, suspected that trying to change Douglas's mind in cases involving individual rights might prove to be a difficult task, for Frankfurter's memo ended with the observation that Douglas was "obdurate, largely because he will want to make the spread-eagle speech."[2] However, a review of some of Douglas's actions in time of national crisis suggests that Douglas was not as obstinate as Frankfurter had said. He was a vacillating justice in a number of these cases. The question, as yet unanswered, is simply: Why the vacillation?

I. William O. Douglas: Lonely Colleague

William O. Douglas, throughout his tenure on the Court, marched to the beat of his own drum. He rarely engaged in the practice of judicial majority coalition-building on the Court because he was not interested in converting his colleagues to his views. Explained Douglas to his wife: the "only soul I have to save is my own."[3] This attitude motivated him throughout his years on the Court. Douglas was certainly not a "consensus builder" on the high bench.[4] Far from that role he was, rather, the "quintessential loner" who, according to one justice, "never had a close friend."[5] One of his law clerks said that "Douglas was just as happy signing a one-man dissent as picking up four more votes."[6] Douglas would "rarely stoop to lobbying for his own position and seemed more interested in making his own stand public rather than in working to get it accepted."[7] And after making his stand known, Douglas, toward the end of many a Court term, often left his brethren in sweltering Washington, D.C., to take off for one of his summer adventures at home or abroad.

William O. Douglas was also an extremely shy person.[8] Because of his illness (polio) when he was quite young and the social isolation from other children that his sickness and his poverty led to when he was growing up in Yakima, Washington, Douglas turned inward at an early age.[9] Douglas himself wrote of this shyness when he described his law school teaching experiences: "I was terribly nervous as I entered each classroom to give a course. . . . I got no calmer as the year progressed."[10]

These twin characteristics of Douglas — that is, an inherent shyness and, perhaps because of that trait, by marching to his own beat, an unwillingness to become an active proselytizer in the Court's decision-making activities — have produced a not too flattering portrait of the man as justice of the United States Supreme Court. Justice Douglas's judicial style or behavior, described variously as impatient, cool, and remote,[11] shy,[12] accommodating,[13] or, to his critics, cynical,[14] warlike,[15] or "grandstanding,"[16] was a reflection of these characteristics. They were clearly evident in the Court's deliberations involving cases and controversies that came to the brethren during time of national emergency, especially those cases that came during and after World War II.

What was also present in these cases, surfacing from the memos, letters, and written opinions, was a strange dichotomy: William O. Douglas's intense verbal and written commitment to principles of justice and fairness in these cases, on the one hand, but, on the other, the obligation to support actions of the national leaders that restricted fundamental liberties. Unlike his close friend Hugo Black, who never modified his wartime observations about the military's forced exclusion of Japanese-Americans from the West Coast, Douglas did come to publicly express his regrets for some of his actions taken during times of national danger.

As a New Deal insider and someone who had spent time working for the executive branch, Douglas knew how easily presidential power could be abused in the name of national security and how hard it was to check executive power that abused the rights of individuals. He cared deeply for the principles of liberty and justice that were rooted in the dynamics of our changing constitutional law. If it was necessary, Douglas sincerely believed, he was prepared to be a loner in defense of these constitutional principles of liberty and justice. However, in these early national security cases (1942–1953), most of the time his commitment to these principles gave way to support for the national government.

An examination of the files reveals that Douglas's commitment to the defense of individual liberty frequently wilted. In the national emergency cases involving security and loyalty in wartime and in time of Cold War (*Rosenberg* case), Douglas and his brethren debated long and, on occasion, bitterly over questions that went to the very essence of loyalty and patriotism. For William O. Douglas, in the final analysis, these cases became a personal crucible for him as much as they were a time of testing of the general society's commitment to equal justice under law in time of national emergency.

II. Loyalty in Wartime: The Exclusion of Japanese-Americans

The tragedy that hit American citizens of Japanese ancestry during World War II is, by now, a familiar one to most Americans.[17] On February 19, 1942, 74 days after the Japanese attack on Pearl Harbor, President Roosevelt signed Executive Order 9066. The Order, ostensibly written to prevent espionage and sabotage, authorized Secretary of War Henry L. Stimson to establish military zones from which certain persons (Japanese-Americans and Japanese aliens living in America) would be excluded.

The constitutional controversy was clear: the war powers of the president and the Congress versus the due process requirement in the Fifth Amendment. Over 120,000 men, women, and children were forcibly removed from homes, businesses, and schools, and placed in barren, out-of-the-way, relocation centers — without benefit of any criminal charges or trials.[18] This lack of due process anguished Douglas as he struggled with the exclusion cases. A Douglas letter to Stone raised the fundamental normative issue clearly: "[Isn't it necessary that members of the group have the] opportunity . . . to prove that they are as loyal to the United States as the members of this Court."[19]

Hirabayashi v. United States, challenging the constitutionality of the curfew established by General DeWitt,[20] came to the Court's conference in early May 1943.[21] The defendant, then a senior at the University of Washington, had been convicted in federal court of "knowingly disregarding the curfew restrictions" and of failing to comply with the military orders that required all persons of Japanese ancestry to report to the assembly centers. Hirabayashi's appeal argued that the restriction on his freedom "unconstitutionally discriminated between citizens of Japanese ancestry and those of other ancestries in violation of the Fifth Amendment."[22] In the conference session, there was a clear desire on the part of the brethren to defer to military authorities.

The leading advocates of judicial deference were Justices Black and Frankfurter. While they had fundamental and life-long disagreements on other legal issues associated with judicial role, on the question of the scope of war powers, Black and Frankfurter agreed. In the Japanese Exclusion Cases, they worked hard to persuade two wavering colleagues, Douglas and Murphy, to join the majority.

William O. Douglas and Frank Murphy had prepared opinions (Douglas's was a concurring opinion, while Murphy's was a dissent) and had circulated them among their colleagues. Douglas was deeply concerned about the issue of loyalty in the Japanese Exclusion Cases. Loyalty was completely ignored by the military's view that the Japanese were an unassimilated race and not to be trusted. Loyalty, he wrote, is "a matter of mind and of heart, not of race." Due process had to be provided to these persons; the vast majority of them were as loyal as members of the Court.[23] In a letter to Stone arguing this point, Douglas pleaded with the Chief: "Is it not necessary to provide an opportunity at some stage . . . for an individual member of the group to show that he has been improperly classified?"[24]

For Douglas, the military orders were "justified only as a temporary expedient. And I would like to have it stated in substantially that way."[25] He had written to Stone in an effort to get the Chief Justice to craft the majority opinion from that perspective and with the following caveat: "That the [Japanese] individual must have an opportunity to be reclassified as a loyal citizen." If that modification were added to the Stone opinion, Douglas would not write. But Douglas realized "that [the issues he was pushing on the Chief] may be too great a gap for us to bridge."[26] He was correct in his assessment. Stone, two days later, rejected Douglas's suggestions. "It seems to me that if I accepted your suggestion, very little of the structure of my opinion would be left, and that I should lose most of my adherents."[27]

Douglas's concurring opinion concerned his friend Black and angered Frankfurter. In a strongly worded memo to the Chief, Frankfurter argued that Douglas's tack, quoting Black, was "an invitation to bring 'a thousand habeas corpus suits in Federal District Courts.'" Douglas's opinion clearly raised the possibility of encouraging "the institution of many such law suits. . . . It would be for me deplorable beyond words to hold out hopes [for those Japanese who were incarcerated] by any language that we use. [We ought not] encourage hopes, which, to put it very mildly, are not likely to be fulfilled." Douglas "ought to act like a collaborator" in this business but was, instead, behaving as though he was engaged "in a rival grocery business." But Frankfurter knew that trying to get Douglas to change his view was hopeless: Douglas would be "obdurate, largely because he will want to make the spread-eagle speech."[28]

Justice Murphy, confronting the issues in *Hirabayashi,* was another anguished justice.[29] He wrote a draft dissent based on what he saw as undisguised racial discrimination in violation of the Fifth Amendment. In it he said:

The discrimination is so utterly inconsistent with our ideals and traditions, and in my judgment so contrary to constitutional requirements, that I cannot lend my assent. It is at variance with the principles for which we are fighting and may well have unfortunate repercussions among peoples of Asia and other parts of the East whose friendship and good will we seek. It [the relocation program] bears a melancholy resemblance to the treatment accorded to members of the Jewish race in Germany and other parts of Europe.[30]

Justice Stanley Reed pointed out, in rebuttal, that "you cannot wait for an invasion to see if loyalty triumphs."[31] Frankfurter was Murphy's major challenger. "Please, Frank," he wrote to Murphy on June 5, 1943, "with your eagerness for the austere functions of the Court and your desire to do all that is humanly possible to maintain and enhance the *corporate* reputation of the Court, why don't you take the initiative with the Chief in getting him to take out everything that offends you."[32] Murphy rejected these appeals, but he was nevertheless "filled with nagging insecurities about a lone dissent in the middle of a war."[33]

Frankfurter did not relax the pressure on Murphy; as opinion day approached, he wrote Murphy another note about the dissent. In part, he said:

Do you think it is conducive to the things you care about, including the great reputation of this Court, to suggest that everybody is out of step except Johnny, and more particularly that the Chief Justice and seven other Justices of this Court are behaving like the enemy and thereby playing into the hands of the enemy. Compassion is, I believe, a virtue enjoined by Christ. Well, tolerance is a long, long way from compassion—and can't you write your views with such expressed tolerance that you won't make people think that when eight others disagree with you, you think their view means that they want to destroy the liberties of the United States and "lose the war" at home?[34]

Frankfurter's remarks, according to Murphy's biographer, "had the desired effect."[35] After a week of reflection, Murphy decided to concur on the "narrow holding that there was a rational basis for a discriminatory curfew during the critical period of early 1942."[36] Frankfurter, his task accomplished, congratulated Murphy "on the wisdom of having been able to reach a concurrence."[37] In the concurring opinion, Murphy reflected on the racially discriminatory policy that was clearly present in the military order: "Today is the first time, so far as I am aware, that we have sustained a substantial restriction of the personal liberty of citizens of the United States based upon the accident of race or ancestry. . . . In my opinion this goes to the very brink of constitutional power."[38]

On June 21, 1943, the *Hirabayashi* opinion was announced. Six justices reaffirmed the power and authority of the president, Congress, and the military authorities to take whatever action was necessary to maintain national security in time of war. "The war power of the national government is 'the power to wage war successfully.' . . . It extends to every matter and activity so related to war as substantially to affect its conduct and progress. The power is not restricted to the winning of victories in the field and the repulse of enemy forces. It embraces every phase of the national defense."[39] In such an environment, the Japanese who were affected by the military orders had not been treated in an unconstitutional manner. "In time of war, residents having ethnic affiliations with an invading army may be a greater source of danger than those of a different ancestry."[40]

Three anguished justices concurred. In addition to Douglas and Murphy, Rutledge wrote a short concurring opinion. Taking exception to judicial abstention in this area of constitutional law, he wrote a short statement indicating that, while he accepted the curfew ruling, the military did not have unlimited power to act and that "the courts . . . have power to protect the civilian citizen."[41]

The Court in *Hirabayashi* focused on the narrow issue of the curfew order. In *Korematsu v. United States*,[42] the issue was the constitutionality of the assembly and relocation centers located across the western United States. Fred Korematsu had been charged with failure to report to a civil control station (an assembly center) for evacuation from the Western Military Zone to a relocation camp. Korematsu claimed that the military's civilian exclusion order was unconstitutional because it violated the Fifth Amendment: the order was racially discriminatory, and citizens were being incarcerated without benefit of trial or other due process guarantees. In addition, he argued that the mass exodus of a racial class of citizens constituted cruel and unusual punishment, in violation of the Eighth Amendment.

In the October 16, 1944, Conference session, there was an initial sharp 5–4 split on the fundamental issue of whether the military could forcibly detain, exclude, and then relocate a racial class of citizens who had not been formally charged with any crime. Stone, Frankfurter, Black, Rutledge, and Reed continued to defer to the judgments of the military leaders. Four of the brethren, Roberts, Murphy, Jackson, and Douglas, maintained that the actions of the military went beyond the bounds of constitutionality and that the Court had to respond to that reality.

William O. Douglas once again struggled with the constitutional issue. He was concerned with the denial of due process. He was also disturbed because of the significance of racial discrimination claims in these cases. After the *Korematsu* conference, Douglas circulated a four-page dissenting opinion. For him, Korematsu's case was inextricably tied to the relocation orders. If you develop that linkage, noted Douglas, then "you come to the larger question," which was the legitimacy of the military plans that uprooted 120,000 persons, over 70,000 of them citizens of the United States, without trials or hearings. Douglas jotted down in his Conference notes the important question: "Was confinement included in the authorization — [there is] no suggestion of enforcement in [the] materials before Congress."[43] Douglas could not separate the exclusion and detention features of the military order that led to Korematsu's conviction. "By May, 1942," wrote Douglas in his draft dissent, "evacuation, detention in an Assembly Center and detention in a Relocation Center, were but steps in a program which had acquired a unitary character. . . . Korematsu's choice was to go to jail or to submit to an indefinite detention in a Relocation Center. That detention was plainly more than temporary detention as an incident to exclusion. I therefore find no authority for it."[44] His dissent met with a fire storm of criticism from Frankfurter, Black, and Stone, because he had offered loyal Japanese citizens a choice: "Stand on their own" or transfer to the relocation center "havens."[45] On December 6, with personal pain, Douglas changed his mind. He wrote to his friend Black, informing him that,

to lessen the confusion now existing from a multiplicity of opinions, [I would be] willing to waive my difficulties and join in the opinion of the Court provided one addition was made. As you know, I think evacuation and detention in an Assembly Center were inseparable. You do not think so. Therefore, I thought an accommodation could be made by adding a new paragraph to your opinion as follows: "A minority are of the view that evacuation and detention in an Assembly Center were inseparable."[46]

Black incorporated this language into the final version of the majority opinion. Douglas, seemingly motivated by loyalty to the Court majority, filed his dissent away. Understandably, Douglas, unlike his colleague Black, found that "the evacuation case . . . was ever on my conscience."[47]

Frank Murphy had no reservations about dissenting from the *Korematsu* majority. Justice Robert Jackson was a second dissenter. Like Murphy, he had been the U.S. Attorney General prior to coming on the Court. To the former attorney general, what was clear in the case was a fundamental principle: "Guilt is personal and not inheritable."[48] For the Court to validate the contested wartime military orders is to validate "for all time the principle of racial discrimination in criminal procedure and of transplanting American citizens."[49]

Owen Roberts was the third dissenter. He was of the opinion that the military action was a "clear violation of constitutional rights."[50] Korematsu was convicted "as a punishment for not submitting to punishment in a concentration camp, based on his ancestry, and solely because of his ancestry, without evidence or inquiry concerning his loyalty and good disposition towards the United States."[51]

Ex Parte Endo,[52] heard at the same time the Court was deciding *Korematsu,* involved a woman who attempted to leave her relocation center in Topaz, Utah, "by suing out a writ of habeas corpus."[53] Endo had received a permit to leave the camp but was not released due to "resettlement problems."[54] She then unsuccessfully petitioned the federal district court for a writ of habeas corpus. The court of appeals certified the case to the Supreme Court. Endo, like Hirabayashi and Korematsu, argued that she had been denied due process. She asked for summary judgment that would allow her to leave Topaz without any kind of "conditional, revokable, indefinite leave."[55]

The Court heard *Endo* immediately after oral arguments and discussions in *Korematsu.* From Douglas's notes, it is clear that there was instant unanimity by the brethren in the *Endo* case. The justices were of the opinion that she was being illegally detained in the relocation center in Topaz after her loyalty had been ascertained by the administrator. "Once loyalty is shown," wrote Douglas, "the basis for the military decision disappears—this woman is entitled to a summary release."[56] The justices agreed that the federal court had jurisdiction, and they had Douglas draft the opinion for the Court.

Douglas's opinion, typically, was written quickly. Consistent with some of his earlier views on this issue, he concluded that Congress did not envision a civilian authority, the War Relocation Authority, developing and implementing relocation policies and processes for loyal citizens. Justice Reed, a day after he received the Douglas draft, reflected the Court view when he replied: "I am quite satisfied with the opinion as a whole. [Since sabotage and espionage] are not done by a loyal citizen, it is not possible to restrain the loyal citizen for the purpose of avoiding espionage and sabotage for a longer time than is necessary to determine loyalty."[57]

Although the opinion was ready in early November 1944, Chief Justice Stone did not announce *Endo* until December 18. Douglas complained bitterly about the delay in a letter to Stone on November 28, 1944:

The matter is at a standstill because officers of the government have indicated that some changes in detention plans are under consideration. Their motives are beyond criticism and their request is doubtless based on important administrative considerations. Mitsuye Endo, however, has not asked that action of this Court be stayed. She is a citizen, insisting on her right to be released—a right which we all agree she has. I feel strongly that we should act promptly and not lend our aid in compounding the wrong by keeping her in unlawful detention any longer than is necessary to reach a decision.[58]

The reason for the delay was that Stone was working with War Department and Justice Department contacts to coordinate the Court's announcement in *Endo* with a major Roosevelt policy change regarding the Japanese in the camps. After the presidential election of 1944, the president decided to rescind the Exclusion Order. On Sunday, December 17, 1944, the War Department issued statements that announced the change in governmental policy. *Endo* came down the following day. "What Douglas never learned was that Stone had enlisted in the high-level campaign, directed by John McCloy, to protect President Roosevelt from the political consequences of the decision to end the internment program."[59]

Years after these cases were decided, Douglas wrote that "preventive detention . . . is inconsistent with the Fourth and Fifth Amendments of our Constitution."[60] But in 1943 and 1944, the majority of the justices, including a reluctant and saddened Douglas, supported a form of preventive detention.

III. Loyalty in Wartime:
Jehovah's Witnesses and the Flag Salute Cases

As Jehovah's Witnesses, who believe the literal command of the Bible that they should not worship graven images, the Gobitis children refused to participate in the pledge of allegiance and salute to the flag as required by the school board of Minersville, Pennsylvania. They were expelled and, under the state's compulsory attendance law, the family then had to shoulder the financial burden of sending them to private school. Mr. Gobitis sued to gain his children's readmission to the public school.

Justice Frankfurter wrote for the Court upholding the compulsory flag salute against the Jehovah's Witness challenge.[61] He wrote in part: "The mere possession of religious convictions which contradict the relevant concerns of a political society does not relieve the citizen from the discharge of political responsibilities." Only Stone dissented.

Several members of the Court had no desire to take the case in the first place. Chief Justice Charles Evans Hughes began the conference on the matter by saying: "I come up to this case like a skittish horse to a brass band."[62] For him, there was no issue of religious freedom presented in the case. It was a simple matter of the unquestioned power of the state to inculcate loyalty. The Court had already disposed of three cases of this type by *per curiam* opinions, denying that a substantial federal question had been raised. Frankfurter, like Hughes, was dismayed when he learned that some of his colleagues insisted upon taking *Gobitis*.[63] (When Stone indicated his intention to dissent, Frankfurter sent him a five-page letter in an unsuccessful effort to dissuade him.)[64]

Douglas and Black joined with the Frankfurter majority in *Gobitis*. Prior to the public announcement, Douglas wrote to Frankfurter, on the back of his *Gobitis* slip opinion, that "it is a powerful moving document of incalculable contemporary and historic value. I congratulate you on a truly statesmanlike job."[65] Hugo Black wrote to Frankfurter: "Like you, I don't like this kind of law and wish we could stop it, but I just don't see that there is anything in the [Gobitis] family claim that possibly can enable us to hold this unconstitutional."[66] Frank Murphy also joined his brethren in *Gobitis*. For Murphy, the value of local autonomy was important, more important than the religious freedom argument of the Witnesses.[67] Douglas, however, harbored, for a brief moment, the thought of joining Stone in dissent — but he did not act on that idea. Once again he backed off, taking a stand that differed from Black and Frankfurter. "It was difficult for a newcomer," wrote Douglas much later, "to withdraw his agreement to one opinion at the last moment and cast his vote for the opposed view."[68]

A year later, Black, Douglas, and Murphy changed their minds on this issue and, in Douglas's words, "deserted Frankfurter."[69] Evidently the first to fall away from Frankfurter's leadership was Hugo Black. Prior to the start of the October 1940 Term, after the *Gobitis* decision came down, Douglas told Frankfurter that Black would no longer support a *Gobitis*-type decision. Frankfurter asked: "Has Hugo been re-reading the Constitution during the summer?" "No," answered Douglas, "he's been reading the papers."[70] It was in the 1942 *Jones v. Opelika* case that Justices Black, Murphy, and Douglas filed their now famous dissent admitting their mistake in *Gobitis* and reversing their position in the Flag Salute Cases. Justice James Byrnes left the Court to be replaced by Wiley Rutledge. Those changes plus Justice Stone's vote meant a new majority on the Jehovah's Witnesses' cases and the free exercise issues they highlighted.

Douglas was often asked what caused him to join Frankfurter's first flag salute opinion but then to make such a dramatic switch in so short a time. Douglas proposed several explanations, but there probably was no single reason. Said Douglas of *Gobitis:* "In those days, Felix Frankfurter was our hero. He was indeed learned in constitutional law and we were inclined to take him at face value." Douglas believed that Black and he "were probably naive in not catching the nuances of his position from the opinion he had been circulating for some time."[71] Douglas also claimed that things might have been different had Stone's powerful dissent been presented earlier than the day before the last conference before the *Gobitis* opinion was released; Stone had made no effort to "campaign for it." At that late date, junior justices like Black and Douglas felt constrained to maintain the position they had taken in support of Frankfurter's opinion, though in later years neither would have hesitated to change his vote even at the last minute. However, Douglas said, "as the months passed and new cases were filed involving the same or a related problem, Black and I began to realize that we had erred."[72] In truth, Douglas later admitted, "Hugo and I could never understand why we agreed to [Frankfurter's *Gobitis* opinion] to begin with."[73] For his part, Frankfurter never could accept his colleagues' defection. The last straw came when his new brother, Robert Jackson, who was so often his ally, wrote the opinion that reversed *Minersville.*

IV. Loyalty in Wartime: Conscientious Objectors

Another controversy involving the values of religious freedom and national security that the Court had to face in wartime involved the proper interpretation of the 1940 Selective Service Act. Although these cases involved jurisdictional issues, they also touched upon some basic constitutional values. Important in the deliberations of the brethren was the fact that the Act did not specifically provide for judicial review. In the Court's first case involving the Act, a person (a Jehovah's Witness) was convicted of willfully failing to obey an order of a local draft board to report for assignment (as a Conscientious Objector) to work of national importance. The conviction was upheld in the court of appeals, and he appealed to the Supreme Court.

Black wrote for the majority.[74] Murphy dissented. For Black and the brethren in the majority, the basic question was: At what point in the draft process was a person's administrative remedies exhausted and judicial review applicable? The answer: only after the person has been inducted into the armed services in some capacity—either to report for active duty or to report for national duty as a Conscientious Objector. The Act did not have any provision for judicial review prior to the time a draftee had gone through all the administrative stages in the draft process and had been finally inducted. The majority took that position because they were concerned about the breakdown of manpower flow into the army if men were able to seek judicial recourse at any point prior to the final induction notification by the local draft board.[75] "Congress apparently regarded 'a prompt and unhesitating obedience to orders' issued in the process [as] 'indispensable to the complete attainment of the object' of national defense," concluded Black for the Court.[76]

For Murphy, however, the case presented yet another aspect "of the perplexing problem of reconciling basic principles of justice with military needs in wartime."[77] For Falbo, the Jehovah's Witness petitioner (sentenced to five years imprisonment), there was the governmental obligation to provide him—and others like him—with "the fullest hearing possible."[78] Mobilization of the armed services, concluded Murphy, was not "impeded nor augmented by the availability of judicial review of local board orders in criminal proceedings."[79] The fact that Falbo was going to remain in prison for five years "without being provided the opportunity of proving that the prosecution was based upon arbitrary and illegal administrative action is not in keeping with the high standards of our judicial system."[80] For the majority, the channeling of manpower into the war effort was critical. Douglas, unlike Murphy, was unwilling to risk the slowdown of the flow of personnel into the armed forces and into other national operations needed by the nation in order to win the war.

During the 1945 term of the Court, the Court had occasion to reexamine *Falbo*. The majority opinion was written by Justice Douglas. In the *Estep* litigation, the question for the justices was "whether there may be judicial review of his classification in a prosecution . . . where he reported for induction, was finally accepted but refused to submit to induction."[81] Estep and Smith (the companion petitioner) were Jehovah's Witnesses who had claimed exemption due to their ministerial responsibilities in the Witnesses. Both were indicted for willful failure to submit to induction. At their trials, they offered as defense the fact that they had been denied due process by the local board's irregular and unlawful proceeding. The federal courts refused to allow this defense.[82]

The Court heard oral arguments on November 7, 1945, and discussed the case in its November 10, 1945, Conference session. Chief Justice Stone believed that a draftee could challenge a classification "after induction."

According to Douglas's notes, "Black [is] doubtful—thinks Congress could draft all in army—can exempt same by act or by selective [service] administrative procedure—can make the action of that board final—if they can get habeas corpus it does not mean necessarily that they can get a review of the decision of the local boards." Reed, like Black and Stone, believed the "U.S. argument powerful." And Frankfurter believed that "habeas corpus is only remedy—question of constitutionality is question of law [and Court should not, cannot, hear that type of argument]." For their cases to be "tried in criminal case," concluded Frankfurter, "is to disrupt the Act's administration."[83]

Douglas was assigned to write for the Court. Chief Justice Stone, on November 24, 1945, wrote Douglas to assist him.

We have here no case of suspension of the writ, and so it seems to me that one who is restrained of his liberty may resort to habeas corpus to test the question whether his detention is lawful. . . . Due process is satisfied so long as the draftee can secure prompt review before he suffers the loss of substantial rights. . . . In view of the clear constitutional provision preserving the writ [of habeas corpus] for its appropriate traditional use, I think you might well walk up to that question, decide it and make it the peg on which you really hang the rest of your opinion.[84]

Douglas, a few weeks later, in a memo that shocked and angered some of his brethren, announced that he had rethought the idea of habeas corpus and had come up with a different jurisprudential basis for the opinion. "Since the [last circulation], I have been considering further the availability of the remedy of habeas corpus. The previous draft assumed that [it] was available only after induction. . . . I have become convinced, however, on further study, that habeas corpus would be available after conviction in these cases. If I am correct, the cases are put in quite a different posture, at least for me. For that reason I am circulating a [new opinion]."[85] Frankfurter's response, penciled in on the bottom of Douglas's memorandum and returned to the justice, was caustic: "The argument is: (1) *habeas corpus* lies after conviction, ergo (2) the same defense is open in the trial—(2) is an egregious *non sequitur*. FF."[86]

The Douglas opinion, as revised, indicated that congressional silence about judicial review was not necessarily a bar to federal judicial review. "The silence of Congress as to judicial review is not necessarily to be construed as a denial of the power of the Federal Courts to grant relief in the exercise of the general jurisdiction which Congress has conferred upon them."[87] Congressional silence enables the federal court to decide to review by looking at the context of the litigation, noted Douglas. If a local draft board "acts so contrary to its granted authority as to exceed its jurisdiction," the Court may grant a petition for habeas corpus.[88] Interpreting the intent of the Congress, Douglas concluded: "We cannot believe that Congress intended that criminal sanctions were to be applied to orders issued by local boards no matter how flagrantly they violated the rules and regulations which define their jurisdiction."[89] As a consequence, the majority reversed the convictions and ordered new trials for the two petitioners. "Since the petitioners were denied the opportunity to show that their local boards exceeded their jurisdiction, a new trial must be had in each case."[90]

There were other draft cases that came to the Supreme Court, for over 6,000 men were convicted of violating the 1940 Selective Service Act — essentially for willfully failing to be inducted into the armed forces. Douglas was given the task of expressing the views of the Court majorities in those cases that came to the Court after *Estep*.[91] During the tenure of Chief Justices Earl Warren and Warren Burger, the justices of the Court affirmed *Falbo*.

For the most part, Justice Douglas accepted the validity of this view. Certainly during World War II, he, along with his colleagues, deferred to actions of the local draft boards and, except for the most egregious violations of due process, believed that there should be minimal involvement by the federal courts with the executive's efforts to get the men in uniform. More recently, while the Warren and Burger Courts expanded the scope of the "Conscientious Objector" exemption,[92] the Warren Court also validated, with Douglas dissenting, the conviction of a petitioner who burned his draft card (as an action of "symbolic speech" to protest the Vietnam War), because the act blunted the government's interest in assuring the continuing availability of such draft cards.[93]

The cases presenting challenges to the validity of the war in Vietnam came in many forms, often in litigation concerning the draft. These 1960s-era draft cases ranged from classification questions, to preinduction resistance, to refusal to accept induction, to postinduction application for conscientious objector status, and to refusal to accept shipment to Southeast Asia. They presented First Amendment issues of free exercise of religion, Thirteenth Amendment claims of illegal involuntary servitude, and Fifth Amendment allegations of due process violations, but most also contained a foundation assertion that the legitimacy of the war itself was in question. Recalling this period, Douglas remembered: "I wrote numerous opinions stating why we should take these cases and decide them. Once or twice Potter Stewart and Bill Brennan joined me. But there was never a fourth vote. I thought then — and still do think — that treating the question as a 'political' one was an abdication of duty and a self-inflicted wound on the Court."[94]

During Vietnam, Douglas argued in vain for broad interpretation of conscientious objector status, in favor of checks on arbitrary behavior by draft boards, and in favor of protections against abuses by both military and civilian authorities.[95]

In the final analysis, as Douglas knew so well, World War II was much different from subsequent military engagements in which American men fought and died. Douglas saw that war as a war of good versus evil. The

Vietnam War was, given that frame of reference, an illegitimate war, and the justices of the Court, Douglas believed, should review the important question of executive power to wage war without constitutional authorization — and rule against the president.

V. Treason and Due Process in a Time of Cold War: The *Rosenberg* Case

By 1950, America and Russia had begun a protracted hot and cold war. A national anti-Communist hysteria had emerged in America. Fueling the fear was the Berlin airlift in 1948–1949 to counter Soviet efforts to isolate West Berlin from the Western allies. There was, in June 1950, the beginning of the "police action" in Korea. And, in the summer of 1950, there was the arrest of Julius and Ethel Rosenberg, American citizens who were avowed Communists. They were charged with violation of the 1917 Espionage Act in that they were allegedly involved in the transportation of the secrets of the atom bomb to the Russians between 1944 and 1950.[96] It was claimed that, because of their "treason,"[97] the Russians developed their atom bomb twenty years earlier than our military leaders believed they could. In a torrid trial, with worldwide publicity, the Rosenbergs were found guilty and sentenced to death under Section 34 of the Espionage Act. The Rosenbergs appealed their convictions to the Supreme Court in 1952 and 1953.

Between June 7, 1952, and June 18, 1953, the justices of the Supreme Court had an opportunity to review, on at least six occasions, on the merits, the convictions of Julius and Ethel Rosenberg for conspiring to pass atomic secrets to the Russians in violation of the 1917 Espionage Act.[98] The Supreme Court rejected every opportunity to review. The Court sitting in 1952, however, was the "Truman" Court. Wiley Rutledge and Frank Murphy, two liberal members of the Court who had developed a good rapport with Black and Douglas after *Gobitis,* were no longer on the bench. The political climate was red-hot regarding relations with the Soviet Union. By 1952 there were four conservative men appointed by Harry Truman sitting on the Court: Harold Burton, Sherman Minton, Tom Clark, and Chief Justice Fred Vinson. These were cautious men in an era historians soon began calling the Cold War or the McCarthy period. The Roosevelt liberals had been reduced in number, and the Warren Court revolution was still years away.

The attorneys for the Rosenbergs, beginning with their June 7, 1952, petition to the Court, argued that their clients had been deprived of due process: the trial judge's actions were prejudicial and the death penalty contravened the Eighth Amendment, the "treason" question, and the general lack of due process for the alleged Russian conspirators. Black and Frankfurter voted to grant certiorari in this petition (denied, 3–6), one in November 1952 (denied, 3–6), and in April 1953 (denied, 2–7). In late May 1953, after the Court had again voted 2–7 to deny cert. in another petition from the Rosenbergs, and after voting with the majority to deny cert. five times, Douglas then had a change of heart. Until then, Douglas explained, the questions presented to the Court were not "cert worthy."[99]

He changed his view, not because of any change in his views of the guilt of the Rosenbergs — he wrote that they "were probably very guilty" — but because the questions presented to the Court in May 1953 were related "to the indictment, statutes, and so called trial errors, and even though an accused is clearly guilty, he deserves, under our regime, a fair trial. By the time No. 687 [the May 1953 petition] reached us I was doubtful if the Rosenbergs had had one."[100] To the surprise of his brethren and the anger of some, on May 22, 1953, Douglas sent a memorandum to the Conference. It indicated that he would join Black and Frankfurter in voting for certiorari. This changed the vote to 3-6, still one vote shy for the granting of certiorari. However, Douglas was prepared to publish a brief statement explaining his cert. vote — and that concerned members of the Court. The language of the memorandum was harsh. After indicating that he had "done further work" and "given the problems more study," Douglas wrote:

I do not believe the conduct of the prosecutor can be easily disposed of as the Court of Appeals thinks. I therefore have reluctantly concluded that certiorari should be granted. Accordingly, I will ask that the order of denial carry the following notation: "Mr. Justice Douglas, agreeing with the Court of Appeals that some of the conduct of the United States Attorney was 'wholly reprehensible' but believing, in disagreement with the Court of Appeals, that it probably prejudiced the defendants seriously, votes to grant certiorari."[101]

Frankfurter immediately asked Vinson to reopen discussion on the certiorari petition, given the Douglas bombshell. Frankfurter's concern, and frustration, was that Douglas's statement would be published — if certiorari was not granted — and the world would be treated to the spectacle of a justice of the Supreme Court reaching substantive judgment on the behavior of the government in the *Rosenberg* case. Jackson was also angry. He had received a note from his law clerk, William Rehnquist, in which the future Chief Justice had written: "[To grant cert. now] would be allowing one justice — WOD — to force the hand of the Court and get the result which he now so belatedly wants."[102] Jackson had told Frankfurter that the Douglas memo "is the dirtiest, most shameful, most cynical performance that I have ever heard of in matters pertaining to law."[103]

Jackson, however, to avoid the embarrassment of the very substantive Douglas dissent from the denial of certiorari, announced that he was reluctantly prepared to grant certiorari in the *Rosenberg* case because of Douglas's threatened dissent. That gave the Rosenbergs the necessary "vote of four" to hear the case on the merits. Douglas, then, inexplicably, did a turnabout. He told his surprised brethren that he was withdrawing his memorandum —

specifically, the language referring to the behavior of the U.S. Attorney. Jackson, with this information, then changed his cert. vote—and Douglas did nothing. As a consequence, the vote to grant certiorari failed to garner the necessary four votes and Douglas had pulled his public statement. As Jackson told Frankfurter on May 25: "The SOB's bluff was called."[104] The Court again, on May 25, 1953, denied certiorari, but this time Douglas joined Black and Frankfurter in voting to grant cert.

On June 13, 1953, the last conference session of the 1952 Term of the Court, a deeply divided Court rejected another request from the Rosenbergs' attorneys. It was a request for a stay of execution, and it needed a majority vote (of five) of the justices in order to be granted. They had asked for oral argument before the Court on the question of a stay for the Rosenbergs (denied, 4–5) and had asked for a stay of the execution, scheduled for June 18, 1953 (denied, 4–5). Again, according to Frankfurter's notes, Douglas's actions were puzzling; they were also critically important.[105] He did not vote to hear oral argument on the defense lawyers' motions to stay the executions— and the defense lawyers lost that critical vote. Douglas then voted to stay the executions (without oral argument). Justice Burton, "who had been willing to hear oral argument, was unwilling to grant a stay without it. . . . Again the Rosenbergs lost."[106] On June 15, 1953, the last day of the 1952 Term, the Court rejected the Rosenbergs' motion for a stay of execution.

The *Rosenberg* litigation drama then took another unusual twist because of Douglas's unilateral actions. After the Court adjourned for the summer, two attorneys—not the Rosenbergs' attorneys of record—late on June 15, 1953, approached Douglas with a petition requesting a stay of execution and the granting of a writ of habeas corpus. He took the papers with him and saw them the following day to hear their legal arguments. After listening to them for two hours, Douglas spoke with Frankfurter, Black, and Vinson and then took a move that shocked the nation. Douglas issued an order that stayed the execution "on the penalty issue,"[107] pending further proceedings in the U.S. district court to determine the question of the applicability of the penal provisions of Section 10 of the Atomic Energy Act,[108] and pending a timely appeal to the court of appeals from the ruling of the district court.[109] Douglas then immediately left Washington, D.C., for a western vacation trip—not thinking that the Chief would do anything after the order was issued.

However, contrary to precedent, Vinson secretly talked with Attorney General Herbert Brownell and Justice Jackson—a day before Douglas granted the stay. In response to an appeal by Brownell, Vinson immediately called the Court into special session in order to examine the Douglas stay. Black complained bitterly to the Chief about the illegality of the call for a special session and about the unwarranted judicial examination of an order issued by a justice of the Supreme Court. It had never been done, pointed out Black, futilely.

On June 18, 1953, the day before the scheduled execution, the Court met in open court to hear arguments on two questions: (1) Could the Court vacate the Douglas stay? (2) Was the conflict between the Espionage Act and the Atomic Energy Act a "substantial" federal question? Douglas, in a letter to Fred Rodell some time later, pointed out that it was a closed issue by the time the brethren met in Court to hear arguments. "When the Court was convened, it was after the CJ had talked with six and got assurances from five to overrule me—in advance in argument—in advance of any exposure or explanation of the point."[110]

Vinson's opinion summarized the process that led to the Special Session of the Court and the unusual decision to set aside the Douglas stay order. "This Court has the responsibility to supervise the administration of criminal justice by the federal judiciary."[111] For Vinson, this supervision reached to punishments, that is, punishments were to be enforced in a timely manner. The Douglas stay would have delayed the punishment by many months. "We decided that a proper administration of the laws required the Court to consider that question forthwith."[112]

After poor oral arguments (no one had time to prepare meaningful presentations), the justices had two stormy conference sessions on June 18 and 19, 1953. Four justices (Frankfurter, Black, Douglas, and Burton) attacked the convening of the special session. These four voted to keep the Douglas stay in force; however, Vinson, Jackson, Clark, Reed, and Minton voted to vacate the stay. Clark said, starkly: "It was wrong to hold up the case any longer."[113] On June 19, 1953, the brethren met briefly in open court to announce its judgment: The stay was vacated and the legal question did not rise to the level of a substantial federal question. The Rosenbergs were executed later that afternoon. Much later, Douglas commented on the environment of the conference sessions. "Probably a fifth vote could have been summoned. Vinson was in a towering rage at the suggestion and finally no one pressed the point."[114]

Grimly, the justices filed their full opinions after the Rosenbergs had been put to death in the electric chair. For Frankfurter, the exercise "had the appearance of pathetic futility."[115] But, he said, "history also has its claims."[116] Five opinions were published on July 16, 1953. The Chief Justice delivered the opinion of the Court. Jackson wrote an opinion in which Vinson, Reed, Clark, and Burton joined. Clark also wrote an opinion, in which the other five joined. Black, Frankfurter, and Douglas issued dissents.

Jackson's concurring opinion criticized the irregularity of the attorneys' actions in bringing the appeal to Douglas after adjournment. "Edelman is a stranger to the Rosenbergs and to their case. His intervention was unauthorized by them. . . . We discountenance this practice [of] disorderly intervention."[117] Clark's opinion argued that the 1946 Atomic Energy Act did not apply in the Rosenbergs' case, because they were charged with a wartime (i.e., 1944), violation of the Espionage Act of 1917—before the Atomic

Energy Act was passed. To apply the 1946 Act would raise questions of "ex post facto criminality."[118]

The three dissenters sharply criticized their five brethren for the actions they took on June 18, 1953. Black's dissent maintained that the Court did not have the power to set aside the stay order issued by Douglas. He also reiterated the point he made earlier to Douglas, that the Rosenbergs' death sentences were imposed "in violation of law."[119] Frankfurter's dissent focused on whether Douglas's order was frivolous or serious. But even the Court majority, pointed out Frankfurter, concluded that Douglas's question was not a frivolous one, and the judicial process should have run its course. "The claim had substance and . . . the opportunity for adequate exercise of the judicial judgment was wanting."[120] Douglas's dissent was an opportunity for Douglas to state that he knew "deep in my heart that I am right on the law."[121] A death penalty, he wrote, cannot be imposed without the recommendation of a jury. The Congress, in 1946, adopted new penalties for crimes the Rosenbergs were charged with committing. There should have been an honoring of the stay and further proceedings in the federal courts, concluded Douglas.

To some scholars, the Douglas switches in *Rosenberg* were "grandstanding"[122] actions by a justice who did not want the Court to hear the case because of his hatred of Communists yet who wanted to retain his "libertarian credentials."[123] Michael Parrish maintains that Douglas withdrew his sharply worded dissent from the Court's denial of certiorari in late May 1953 "in order to kill the grant of certiorari." That paradox, for Parrish, is easy to explain: Even with his May 23, 1953, dissent, Douglas had no desire to grant certiorari for the Rosenbergs. When Jackson changed his vote—voting for certiorari in order to kill the Douglas dissent—Douglas was trapped. If Jackson's vote remained, then there would be four votes to hear the *Rosenberg* arguments on the merits in the Court. Douglas did not want that, so he withdrew his critical memo, thereby allowing Jackson to withdraw his vote for certiorari. Hence there was no Court review of the *Rosenberg* case on the merits, nor was there a sharply worded explanation by Douglas of why he had voted to grant certiorari. Under these circumstances, Jackson's comment to Frankfurter, that "the SOB's bluff was called," is understandable.

Disagreeing with Parrish on this account of Douglas's behavior is a law professor and former law clerk of Justice Douglas. William Cohen's explanation for Douglas's switch in *Rosenberg* is that the justice believed that there was no point in reviewing a case on the merits "unless [it] presented some legal issue that could arguably provide a basis for action by the Court."[124] According to Cohen, the reason Douglas changed his mind in *Rosenberg* was not the "grandstanding" one; rather, Douglas "took a fresh look at the briefs . . . and came to a different conclusion about the substantiality of the issue."[125] While acknowledging that Justice Douglas did make mistakes in the *Rosenberg* case,[126] Cohen has argued that he acted only when the data presented to him convinced him that substantial legal issues should be addressed by the Supreme Court. Interestingly, another law clerk (of Hugo Black's), Charles Reich, recently commented that years later Douglas would spend many long hiking miles along the C & O Canal with Reich talking about the *Rosenberg* case. In the late 1950s, Douglas was still saddened and obsessed with the case, because the Rosenbergs did not have a fair trial.[127]

The Court never did hear any of the substantive issues raised by the Rosenbergs. The case was one of the opening salvos in a new war—the Cold War—between the United States and its World War II ally, the Soviet Union. And the majority of the justices, like the brethren in World War II, were not very committed to hearing abstract legal issues raised by these new enemies of the American political system. The judicial process and the federal judges were again—as it always is in time of war and national emergency— "subjected to stress and strain."[128] Certainly, Justice Douglas was torn. He was, according to one scholar, "emotionally divided between his own self-image as judicial champion of the underdog and his equally powerful loathing for Communists—and those who betray their country."[129]

VI. Conclusion

It is very clear that Douglas's judicial style frequently reminded some of his brethren of someone who was "in a rival grocery business." He was viewed as reluctant to participate in the give-and-take of collective judicial negotiation and judicial creationism. Douglas would write his opinions very quickly, often in a "slapdash manner,"[130] drop them on his colleagues— even when he was writing for the majority—and take off on other pursuits.

The majority of cases examined in this chapter—*Korematsu, Gobitis, Estep,* and *Rosenberg*—clearly evidences manifestations of Douglas's penchant for backing off or changing positions originally taken by him in important cases and controversies. (This unsettling characteristic of Douglas's was not limited to the national security cases; he changed his mind, occasionally at the last minute, on other occasions during his long tenure on the Court.) "On further study" (*Estep*) or "having done further work [and] more study" (*Rosenberg*) were the kinds of explanations he gave to justify his judicial switches in important cases. Needless to say, this seemingly incautious, careless style angered friends, such as Frank Murphy,[131] as much as foes, such as Felix Frankfurter and Robert H. Jackson.

Some scholars maintain that Douglas "could never focus his energies . . . and became intellectually lazy in his Court work."[132] A review of his voluminous files in the Library of Congress, especially his exhaustive, comprehensive conference session minutes, however, suggests that Douglas was taking copious notes on every case argued in Conference from 1939 through the very end of his service on the high bench in 1975. Further, the opinion changes described in this chapter came during his early years on the Court, years when Douglas was clearly and vigorously into the work of the Court. These were years, also, when Douglas's strong civil libertarian views had not jelled.

Perhaps the reason for his judicial style was that he was very bright,[133] wrote very quickly (perhaps too quickly), and was very hesitant about participating in any extensive intellectual give-and-take except that which he engaged in with himself as he read and reread the materials associated with the litigation before him and his colleagues on the bench. Rewrites and changes in direction were therefore not unusual for such an unusual jurist: These back-offs and changes were, in his view, part of the dynamic of the law.

These judicial changes, a clear manifestation of Justice Douglas's style, may reflect the loneliness of the man and the secret desire he had to "act like a collaborator," that is, to be one of the boys. In the final analysis, after all, William Douglas, the champion of the underdog, set aside his personal judicial views and went along with his colleagues in *Korematsu* and in *Gobitis*. And these were two cases where an individual's civil liberties were dramatically curtailed for the sake of national order and in order to instill national loyalty in individuals!

Without a doubt, these national security cases seemed to be anguishing ones for Douglas. He was, in later years, to become recognized in the press and law journals as the staunch defender of the rights and liberties of individuals. These cases, coming to the Court in time of national danger, saw Douglas seesaw on the merits and then finally, in most of the cases, join with his colleagues. While some of these final decisions were, as he wrote, forever on his conscience, he did succeed, as best he could, in acting very much like a judicial collaborator. In that regard, he was certainly not the "obdurate" jurist on the Supreme Court as depicted by his critic and arch-rival, Felix Frankfurter.

Notes

1. 320 U.S. 81 (1943).

2. Memorandum, Felix Frankfurter to Harlan F. Stone, June 4, 1943, Harlan Fiske Stone Papers (hereafter, HFSP), Box 68, Library of Congress (hereafter LC), Washington, D.C.

3. Interview, Catherine Douglas Stone, Nov. 14, 1986, Boston.

4. Interview, William J. Brennan, Jr., Oct. 29, 1986, Washington, D.C.

5. Interview, Harry A. Blackmun, Nov. 19, 1986, Washington, D.C.

6. Quoted in Bernard Schwartz, ed., *The Unpublished Opinions of the Warren Court* (New York: Oxford University Press, 1985), p. 10.

7. Bernard Schwartz, *Super Chief: Earl Warren and His Supreme Court—A Biography* (New York: New York University Press, 1983), p. 51.

8. He was, however, a person with a ribald sense of humor and enjoyed sharing off-color stories and jokes with some of his colleagues, especially Byron R. White. Interview, Byron R. White, Nov. 18, 1986, Washington, D.C.

9. William O. Douglas, *Go East, Young Man: The Autobiography of William O. Douglas* (New York: Random House, 1974), p. 34.

10. Ibid., p. 150.

11. Interview, Byron R. White.

12. Interview, Catherine Douglas Stone.

13. Justice Brennan recalled that Douglas would say to him: "'You don't like it? What do you want?' Then, he'd change it." Interview, William J. Brennan, Jr.

14. Frankfurter told one of his law clerks, Philip Elman, that Douglas was an "absolute cynic." Quoted in Bruce Murphy, *The Brandeis/Frankfurter Connection* (New York: Oxford University Press, 1982), p. 266.

15. Felix Frankfurter told his law clerk, Elliot Richardson, that preparing for a conference session with Douglas present was much like going to war: "This is a war we're fighting! Don't you understand? A war!" Quoted in Leonard Baker, *Brandeis and Frankfurter* (New York: New York University Press, 1984), p. 418.

16. Michael E. Parrish, "Justice Douglas and the Rosenberg Case: A Rejoinder," *Cornell Law Review* 70 (1985): 1048, 1056.

17. For an interesting collection of essays on the issue, see Roger Daniels, Sandra Taylor, and Henry Kitano, eds., *Japanese Americans: From Relocation to Redress* (Salt Lake: University of Utah Press, 1986). During the final year of the Reagan administration (1988), Congress passed and the president signed a compensation bill that would provide $20,000 for each survivor of the camps. Unfortunately, to date no funds have been appropriated by the Congress.

18. The relocation centers, or "concentration camps," as Justice Owen Roberts and others referred to them, were technically known as War Relocation Authority (WRA) camps and were located in California, Arizona, Wyoming, Utah, Idaho, Colorado, and Arkansas. There were ten WRA camps and, between the years 1942 and 1946, these facilities housed a total population of 120,313 internees (including 5,918 children born in the camps).

19. Letter, William O. Douglas to Harlan F. Stone, May 31, 1943, William O. Douglas Papers (hereafter WODP), Box 91, LC, Washington, D.C.

20. In an interesting footnote to this litigation, I uncovered a letter from Douglas to his friend Hugo Black, written before the war began, while Douglas was traveling in the West. Douglas wrote, on June 21, 1941, that "we had dinner with some admirers of yours — General and Mrs. DeWitt. They really are grand people. We enjoyed them immensely." Letter, William O. Douglas to Hugo L. Black, Hugo L. Black Papers (hereafter, HLBP), Box 29, LC, Washington, D.C.

21. By the spring of 1943, military action in the Pacific theater of war had seen American victories in the battles of the Coral Sea, Midway, Guadalcanal, New Guinea, and the Solomon Islands. In 1943, American forces destroyed twenty-two Japanese vessels in the battle of the Bismarck Sea and in the battle at Rabaul, recaptured the Aleutian Islands and began the successful island-hopping operations in the Pacific, ultimately leading to victory in 1945.

22. *Hirabayashi v. United States,* 320 U.S., at 82.

23. Ibid., at 107 (Douglas, J., concurring).

24. Letter, William O. Douglas to Harlan F. Stone, May 31, 1943, HFSP, Box 68, LC, Washington, D.C.

25. Letter, William O. Douglas to Harlan F. Stone, June 7, 1943, HFSP, Box 68, LC, Washington, D.C.

26. Ibid.

27. Letter, Harlan F. Stone to William O. Douglas, June 9, 1943, HFSP, Box 68, LC, Washington, D.C.

28. Letter, Felix Frankfurter to Harlan F. Stone, June 4, 1943, HFSP, Box 68, LC, Washington, D.C.

29. Wiley Rutledge also felt this way. He wrote to Stone that "I have had more anguish over this case than any I have decided, save possibly one death case in the Ct of Appeals." June 8, 1943, HFSP, Box 68, LC, Washington, D.C.

30. Murphy draft dissent, *Hirabayashi,* WODP, Box 92, LC, Washington, D.C.

31. Memorandum, Reed to Frank Murphy, WODP, Box 92, LC, Washington, D.C.

32. Memorandum, Felix Frankfurter to Frank Murphy, June 5, 1943, Felix Frankfurter Papers (hereafter FFP), LC, Washington, D.C.

33. J. Woodford Howard, Jr., *Mr. Justice Murphy: A Political Biography* (Princeton: Princeton University Press, 1968), p. 307.

34. Letter, Felix Frankfurter to Frank Murphy, June 10, 1943, FFP, LC, Washington, D.C.

35. Howard, *Mr. Justice Murphy,* p. 308.

36. Ibid.

37. Quoted in Peter Irons, *Justice at War* (New York: Oxford University Press, 1983), p. 247.

38. *Hirabayashi v. United States,* 320 U.S., at 111 (Murphy, J., concurring).

39. Ibid., at 93.

40. Ibid., at 101.

41. Ibid., at 114.

42. 323 U.S. 214 (1944).

43. Conference notes, William O. Douglas, Oct. 16, 1944, WODP, Box 112, LC, Washington, D.C.

44. Draft dissenting opinion, William O. Douglas, Dec. 1, 1944, WODP, Box 112, LC, Washington, D.C.

45. Ibid.

46. Letter, Douglas to Hugo L. Black, Dec. 6, 1944, HLBP, Box 59, LC, Washington, D.C.

47. William O. Douglas, *The Court Years, 1939–1975: The Autobiography of William O. Douglas* (New York: Random House, 1974), p. 281.

48. *Korematsu v. United States,* 323 U.S., at 243 (Jackson, J., dissenting).

49. Ibid., at 246.

50. Ibid., at 225 (Roberts, J., dissenting).

51. Ibid., at 226.

52. 323 U.S. 283 (1944).

53. *Korematsu v. United States,* 323 U.S., at 233 (Roberts, J., dissenting).

54. *Ex Parte Endo,* 323 U.S., at 297.

55. Memo, Eugene A. Beyer, Jr. (law clerk) to William O. Douglas, n.d., *Endo,* WODP, Box 115, LC, Washington, D.C.

56. Conference notes, Oct. 16, 1944, *Endo,* WODP, Box 115, LC, Washington, D.C.

57. Letter, Stanley Reed to William O. Douglas, Nov. 9, 1944, WODP, Box 115, LC, Washington, D.C.

58. Letter, William O. Douglas to Harlan F. Stone, Nov. 29, 1944, WODP, Box 115, LC, Washington, D.C.

59. Irons, *Justice At War,* p. 344.

60. William O. Douglas, *The Anatomy of Liberty* (New York: Trident, 1963), p. 69. On April 19, 1984, U.S. Federal District Court Judge Marilyn Hall Patel granted a writ of *coram nobis* (a writ used to correct errors that result in a miscarriage of justice) in the case of *Fred Korematsu v. United States,* 584 F. Supp. 1406 (N.D.Cal. 1984). Korematsu brought the petition in an effort to vacate his 1942 conviction on grounds of government misconduct. The government, concluded the judge, acknowledged prosecutorial impropriety in the original litigation. While it still was precedent, "it is now recognized as having very limited application. . . . It stands as a caution that in times of distress the shield of military necessity and national security must not be used to protect governmental actions from close scrutiny and accountability." For basic materials concerning the efforts to vacate Korematsu's conviction and those in related cases, see Peter Irons, ed., *Justice Delayed: The Record of the Japanese American Internment Cases* (Middletown, Conn.: Wesleyan University Press, 1989).

61. *Minersville v. Gobitis,* 310 U.S. 586 (1940).

62. Cited in Howard, *Mr. Justice Murphy,* p. 287.

63. Alpheus T. Mason, *Harlan Fiske Stone* (New York: Viking, 1956), p. 526.

64. Letter, Felix Frankfurter to Harlan Fiske Stone, May 27, 1940, HFSP, LC, Washington, D.C.

65. Douglas to Felix Frankfurter, *Gobitis* slip opinion, n.d., FFP, Box 10, Harvard Law School (hereafter HLS), Cambridge.

66. Hugo L. Black to Felix Frankfurter, *Gobitis* file, FFP, Box 10, HLS, Cambridge.

67. Howard, *Mr. Justice Murphy,* p. 287.

68. Douglas, *The Court Years,* p. 45. In an interview shortly before his death, Douglas recalled that "part of the problem was that Stone didn't circulate his dissent until the last minute. I didn't have a chance to fully consider it." Quoted in James F. Simon, *Independent Journey: The Life of William O. Douglas* (New York: Harper and Row, 1980), pp. 11–12.

69. Douglas, *The Court Years,* p. 45.

70. Quoted in Baker, *Brandeis and Frankfurter,* p. 402.

71. Douglas, *The Court Years,* p. 44.

72. Ibid.

73. Interview, William O. Douglas by Elizabeth Black, quoted in Hugo Black and Elizabeth Black, *Mr. Justice and Mrs. Black* (New York: Random House, 1986), p. 72.

74. *Falbo v. United States,* 320 U.S. 549 (1943).

75. "The Act was passed to mobilize national manpower with the speed which that necessity and understanding, . . . integrating all the nation's people and forces for national defense, . . . required." Ibid., at 551–52.

76. Ibid., at 554.

77. Ibid., at 555–56 (Murphy, J., dissenting).

78. Ibid., at 556.

79. Ibid., at 560.

80. Ibid., at 560–61.

81. *Estep v. United States,* 327 U.S. 114, 116 (1945).

82. Cert. notes, *Estep,* WODP, Box 129, LC, Washington, D.C.

83. Conference notes, *Estep,* Nov. 10, 1945, WODP, Box 129, LC, Washington, D.C.

84. Letter, Harlan F. Stone to Douglas, Nov. 24, 1945, WODP, Box 129, LC, Washington, D.C.

85. Memorandum to the Conference, Dec. 14, 1945, *Estep,* WODP, Box 129, LC, Washington, D.C.

86. Ibid.

87. *Estep v. United States,* 327 U.S., at 120.

88. Ibid.

89. Ibid., at 121.

90. Ibid., at 125.

91. See, for example, his opinions for the majority, upholding convictions of petitioners who had claimed religious reasons for disagreeing with the local board's classification judgments, in *Eagles v. United States ex rel. Samuels,* 329 U.S. 304 (1946); *Sunal v. Large, Alexander v. United States ex rel. Kulick,* 332 U.S. 174 (1947).

92. See, for example, *Sicurella v. United States,* 348 U.S. 385 (1954); *United States v. Seeger,* 380 U.S. 163 (1964); *Welsh v. United States,* 398 U.S. 333 (1970).

93. *United States v. O'Brien,* 391 U.S. 367 (1967). Writing the opinion for the majority, Chief Justice Warren wrote: "Pursuant to this power [to conscript manpower for the military], Congress may establish a system of registration for individuals liable for training and service and may require such individuals within reason to cooperate in the registration system. . . .

"The issuance of certificates . . . is a legitimate and substantial administrative aid in the functioning of this system. And legislation to insure the continuing availability of issued certificates serves a legitimate and substantial purpose in the system's administration." Ibid., at 377–78.

94. Douglas, *The Court Years,* p. 55. See Douglas's dissent from the Court's refusal to hear *Massachusetts v. Laird,* 400 U.S. 886 (1970), for an example of his views in this period.

95. See, for example, *Gillette v. United States,* 401 U.S. 437 (1974) (Douglas, J., dissenting); *Oestereich v. Selective Service Board No. 11,* 393 U.S. 233 (1968); *Gutknecht v. United States,* 396 U.S. 295 (1970).

96. *Rosenberg et ux v. United States,* 346 U.S. 271 (1953).

97. The Rosenbergs were never charged with treason, although many persons, including the federal trial judge, accused them of committing treason against America. Naturally, if they had been charged with acts of treason, the provisions of Article III, Section 3, would have applied.

98. Section 32(a) of that Act provides that when a person or persons, for either the purpose of injuring the United States or giving a foreign country an advantage, transmits documents, etc., that person shall be punished by imprisonment for not more than twenty years, except that, in time of war, the penalty is either thirty years or death. When two or more so act, it is a conspiracy.

99. Letter, Douglas to Michael E. Parrish, Dec. 13, 1974, WODP, LC, Washington, D.C.

100. Ibid., p. 2.

101. Memorandum to the Conference, May 22, 1953, WODP, Box 233, LC, Washington, D.C.

102. Note, William Rehnquist to Robert H. Jackson, n.d., Robert H. Jackson Papers, LC, Washington, D.C.

103. Quoted in Simon, *Independent Journey,* p. 303. Also, FFP, Box 65, HLS, Cambridge.

104. Quoted in Simon, *Independent Journey,* p. 302.

105. In a memo to the Conference, Douglas wrote that since the Court decided not to take the case, "there would be no end served by hearing oral argument on the motion for a stay." WODP, Box 233, LC, Washington, D.C.

106. Simon, *Independent Journey,* p. 305.

107. Letter, Douglas to Michael Parrish, Dec. 13, 1974, p. 2, WODP, LC, Washington, D.C.

108. The lawyers argued that the Rosenbergs were convicted under the wrong statute, the Espionage Act of 1917; they should have been tried under the provisions of the Atomic Energy Act of 1946 — which had the death penalty for the transmittal of atomic secrets if done to injure the United States and if the death penalty had been determined by a jury.

109. Order, *Rosenberg v. United States,* June 17, 1953, WODP, Box 233, LC, Washington, D.C.

110. Quoted in Simon, *Independent Journey,* p. 307.

111. Ibid., p. 287.

112. Ibid.

113. Ibid., p. 310.

114. Douglas, *The Court Years,* p. 237.

115. *Rosenberg v. United States,* 346 U.S., at 310.

116. Ibid.

117. Ibid., at 292.

118. Ibid., at 296.

119. Ibid., at 298.

120. Ibid., at 310.

121. Ibid., at 313, 311.

122. Parrish, "Justice Douglas," p. 1054; see also Simon, *Independent Journey,* pp. 302 ff.

123. Parrish, "Justice Douglas," p. 1054.

124. William Cohen, "Justice Douglas and the Rosenberg Case: Setting the Record Straight," *Cornell Law Review* 70 (1985): 211, 217.

125. Ibid., pp. 234, 238.

126. Ibid., p. 236.

127. Conversation, Charles Reich, Apr. 16, 1989, Seattle.

128. *Rosenberg v. United States,* 346 U.S., at 310 (Frankfurter, J., dissenting).

129. Parrish, "Justice Douglas," p. 1056.

130. Melvin I. Urofsky and Philip E. Urofsky, eds., *The Douglas Papers* (Bethesda: Adler and Adler, 1988), p. x.

131. In another controversial World War II case, *Schneiderman v. United States,* 320 U.S. 118 (1942), Justice Murphy was assigned the task of writing the opinion for a very fragile majority. At the very last moment, Douglas, one of the majority

brethren, announced that he was publishing a concurring opinion. Murphy was incensed and told Frankfurter that Douglas's action was "skullduggery." Quoted in Joseph P. Lash, ed., *From the Diaries of Felix Frankfurter* (New York: W. W. Norton, 1975), pp. 257-58.

132. Urofsky and Urofsky, *The Douglas Papers,* p. x.

133. Many of his colleagues thought that Douglas was as close to a genius as anyone who had ever sat on the Supreme Court. All interviewed also said that he was not an endearing man. 1986 interviews with Arthur Goldberg, William J. Brennan, Harry Blackmun, Lewis Powell, Warren Burger, and Byron White, Washington, D.C., and Virginia.

Getting the Job Done: William O. Douglas and Collegiality in the Supreme Court

Melvin I. Urofsky

WHEN WILLIAM O. DOUGLAS retired as Associate Justice of the United States Supreme Court on November 12, 1975, he had served on that bench over thirty-six years, longer than any other member in the Court's history. During those years Douglas was often described as a loner who supposedly refused to play according to the rules of the game, and there is some truth in that allegation. James Simon, however, probably captured it best when he depicted Douglas's life as an "independent journey."[1]

Some recent writings on Douglas have taken him to task for the apparent contradictions in his views and his at times quite offensive behavior.[2] It is not my purpose here to defend Douglas against these charges, but rather to explore certain aspects of his judicial career, namely relations with his fellow justices and clerks. I will suggest that Douglas's commitment to a work ethic on the Court explains some — but not all — of his behavior, and also allows us to understand a little better this most complex of men.[3]

I. Douglas and the Brethren

In his thirty-six-year career on the bench, Douglas served with twenty-nine other men, nearly a third of the total justices appointed between 1789 and 1975. Some of these men, like Stanley Reed, James Byrnes, and Sherman Minton, left little impression on the Court and its work; others, like Harlan Fiske Stone, Felix Frankfurter, Hugo Black, and Earl Warren, reshaped the contours of our constitutional geography. Douglas enjoyed good relations with nearly all of them, including men whom he ideologically opposed, but conversely, again with few exceptions, he had no close friendships on the Court. The chief exceptions to this generalization are, of course, Felix Frankfurter, whom he despised and who in turn despised him, and Hugo Black, whom he adored.[4]

Douglas discussed nearly all of these men in the last volume of his memoirs, but the characterizations there are often unreliable, as, in fact, is much of the book, written in his last years when he suffered nearly constant physical and mental anguish.[5] Interviews with recent members of the Court, as well as examination of Douglas's correspondence with his colleagues, indicate a relaxed, comfortable attitude in the early years, but one which tended to become more aloof later on, especially in the late sixties and seventies. At all times, as Professor Robert Glennon has suggested, Douglas related well to men of high intelligence who could handle their share of the Court's work; long before he came on the Court he had ceased to suffer fools, gladly or otherwise.[6]

Douglas arrived at the Court in April 1939, and immediately established the work pattern that he more or less followed for the next third of a century. Although he had been a rather gregarious and easygoing member of the Yale law faculty, he had found the work of the Securities and Exchange Commission far more demanding of his time and energy. During his years at the SEC, Douglas had disciplined himself to work intensely for long hours at a stretch, and he continued that habit when he joined the Court. Douglas would arrive in the morning and, without any chitchat, go to his desk and start working. His first clerk and long-time friend, C. David Ginsburg, recalled:

I see him as a man focussed on his work, absolutely determined to get through and get through fast. The books would be brought down. . . . He would close the door [and work]. If you went in, you felt you were interrupting him. He would look up and seem to say, "Why did you come in?" It wasn't put that way, but that was the feeling that was conveyed. There he was, working with the yellow sheets of paper and with the books spread out in front of him, writing everything in longhand and then he would call in the secretary, Edith Waters, and he would dictate, piece by piece. But he was hard at work every moment of the time. This was not a man who took lightly the burden he had assumed getting on the Court.[7]

This work pattern, which he followed up until the time of his stroke, did not encourage socializing from either his clerks or his colleagues, and in fact there appears to have been little visiting back and forth between Douglas and the other justices, as there often was with Frankfurter, Black, and Brennan. Occasionally a justice would stop by to see Douglas, and they would talk for a few minutes, but it became clear early on that, while Douglas may have tolerated these visits out of courtesy, he did not welcome the interruptions.

If we look at Douglas's work pattern, as seen in his relations with his colleagues and clerks, we can begin to understand one aspect of his personality. Douglas had almost a puritanical attitude toward getting the work done, by which I mean processing the various petitions that came to his office and getting out his opinions and dissents in as short a time as possible. Although in his earlier years he seemed more willing to fine-tune his opinions in order to secure or keep a majority, by the 1950s the notion of building a consensus around his ideas did not seem to matter as much. Douglas wanted to get the opinion out, and if it won over converts, well and good; if not, as he often said, he had "only one soul to save"—his own.[8] This is not to imply that Douglas would tolerate sloppy or inaccurate work to go out of his chambers; all the clerks I interviewed agreed on the high standards he expected. Rather, he worked at his pace and on his agenda, which required that he do his work as expeditiously as possible, and not allow "distractions" to get in the way.

A good example of Douglas's work attitude can be found in Harry Blackmun's recollection of a conversation with Douglas. Blackmun was somewhat in awe of Douglas, and found it difficult to approach him. One day he screwed up his courage and asked Douglas, "Who was the greatest justice you ever served with?" Without any hesitation, Douglas answered: "Charles Evans Hughes." This surprised Blackmun, but Douglas went on to describe Hughes as a person of complete fairness in administering the Court, and one who recognized other points of view. Douglas drew a highly flattering portrait of Hughes in his memoirs, and declared that "as a living, active Chief, as an administrator, as the head of the federal system of law and justice, he had few peers."[9]

Blackmun then asked him about Harlan Fiske Stone, who had been Douglas's teacher at Columbia. Douglas said that both Stone and Felix Frankfurter bothered him a lot. They were always proselytizing, coming down after Conference to try to persuade him to change his mind, *wasting his time.*[10]

In his last few years, when he was senior justice, Douglas occasionally presided over the Conference when Warren Burger was absent. According to one of his colleagues, "Bill was impatient at Conference. . . . He would run the Conference with great expedition. So instead of really encouraging people to discuss a case, all he was interested in was how they were going to vote."[11] Getting the work out won Douglas's respect, whether he agreed with the person or not. One of his former clerks once asked him what he thought of William Rehnquist, who stood ideologically at the other end of the judicial spectrum. "He's an OK guy," Douglas answered. "He gets his work out on time."[12]

Douglas had little patience for those who could not or would not get their work done. Among the many things that Felix Frankfurter did that irritated Douglas, none seemed to bother him so much as Frankfurter's failure to do his Court work. He charged that Frankfurter deliberately delayed getting out the opinions assigned to him in the fall in order to avoid getting new cases assigned in the spring. "That gives him time to dabble in State Dept. affairs, Army affairs, Dept. of Justice affairs, etc. He actually does very little [Court] work."[13] One can also sense the scorn that Douglas had for someone like Charles Whittaker, who at times seemed totally overwhelmed by the Court's work.[14]

Because Douglas worked so fast, he assumed that others could work as rapidly, an assumption that rarely proved true, and in part it led to one of the few idiosyncrasies which really upset the brethren. At the end of the Term, as soon as Douglas had finished his own work, he left. He would announce, "My work is done, and I'm leaving for Goose Prairie tomorrow." It did not matter that the Court had not completed its work and still had opinions to hand down; Douglas left. Sometimes he would not even bother to inform the Court; he would just go. The summers were *his* time, and as Justice Marshall recalled, Douglas "resented anybody interfering with it. That's where you could get hurt. . . . He was about as independent a cuss as I knew."[15]

Despite his concentration on the work, and his aggravating habit of disappearing before the end of the Term, there was considerable interaction between Douglas and the brethren, primarily through notes and memoranda. Most of these dealt, of course, with cases under consideration, but one finds all sorts of personal notes in the files. Running throughout these messages is a chummy, unbuttoned, relaxed persona, somewhat at odds with the conventional portrait of Douglas as a loner or recluse. According to several sources, Douglas was a "man's man," one to whom people such as Earl Warren and Hugo Black—but not Felix Frankfurter—could easily warm.[16] Charles Reich provides a good example of this in a story about Douglas and Robert Jackson. Jackson, a close ally of Frankfurter and reputedly angry at Douglas for his alleged duplicity in the Rosenberg case,[17] had had a heart attack in the summer of 1953. When he returned to the Court that fall he gave a cocktail party in his chambers for the justices and their staff. No one had seen Douglas, or knew if he would come to the party, when

All of a sudden the door opened and there was Douglas, and everybody's heart stopped, waiting to see what would happen. And he said, "The name's Douglas," to the assembled group, sort of John Wayne coming in. He had a skill of this type of man-to-man friendliness . . . that he was able to use very effectively with most of the justices. Sort of "You know, we may be shooting at each other most of the time, but here, let's have a drink at the saloon." A lot of people liked that.[18]

Douglas also had a sense of humor which, except when dealing with Frankfurter, could be quite dry. Douglas teased Lewis Powell once after Powell had suggested moving the Friday conference to Wednesday during Thanksgiving week. "Lewis, these holidays are meaningless," Douglas boomed. As the color drained from Powell's face Douglas went on, "I hate Christmas. You should be in here as I am on Christmas day at 10 A.M. to work in your chambers."[19] It took Powell a moment to realize that Douglas was kidding.

Douglas could, however, also be kind. Shortly after Powell had joined the Court, Jack Anderson wrote a column criticizing the new justice for failing to disclose, at his confirmation hearings, a memorandum he had written to a Virginia associate about some things business might do to improve its public image. Anderson implied that this represented a probusiness orientation that would influence Powell's decisions. Douglas, who had often been the victim of gossip columnists, made a point of seeing Powell and reassuring him that this sort of thing "happened in Washington all the time," and that he should just ignore Anderson. Powell, still unsure of the proprieties associated with the Court, felt relieved, and more than fifteen years later recalled Douglas's "thoughtful" gesture.[20] Douglas and his wife also showed a great deal of kindness to Charles Whittaker when the latter found the pressure of the Court too much to handle; they convinced Whittaker that he should seek medical attention, and were involved in the deliberations that led to his resignation.[21]

Douglas was not an easy person to befriend; many people knew him, but only a few got close to him. Nearly every source describes him as a loner, a term he applied to himself.[22] On the Court, aside from Hugo Black, he had few if any close friendships, and Douglas could, without any explanation, freeze out a colleague who had displeased him for some reason. As Justice Brennan recalled, "None of us ever understood what happened; when Bill froze one out, he really froze them out. . . . We never discovered the reason, and then his attitude changed overnight just as quickly as it had come on."[23] Yet his colleagues seemed genuinely fond of him, and at the time of attempted impeachment, although he asked none of them for help, they would have been quite willing to testify for him or do anything he asked for in the way of assistance.[24] These are the relations, however, of one colleague to another, not of friend to friend. A far different relationship existed between Douglas and his clerks, one in which, even more than with the brethren, a work ethic prevailed.

II. Douglas and His Clerks

The work in the Court takes place not only among the justices, but between the justices and their clerks as well. In the four decades of his service as an active and then retired member of the Supreme Court, fifty-four men and women served as law clerk to William O. Douglas.[25] No two of them had exactly the same experience; for some it proved a time of anger and frustration, while others would remember it in a positive manner the rest of their lives. Douglas's relations with his clerks tell us a great deal about the man, about how he worked, and also about perceptions.

Clerks are an important part of the Court's work; indeed, it would probably be impossible for the Court to maintain its current work load and process several thousand petitions for certiorari each year without clerks. Over the years various justices have used them in different ways, and have given them a variety of tasks to do, ranging from cite-checking and basic research up to and including drafting opinions for the Court. In this regard, a justice's relations to his or her own clerks, and to those of others, is as much part of the Court's collegiality as relations among the justices.

During most of his tenure, Douglas, unlike the rest of the Court, had only one clerk at a time; two, he thought, would spend their time writing memos to each other.[26] He made it a practice, with only a few exceptions, to take his clerks from law schools in the Ninth Circuit. The first few years he accepted the person the dean of the University of Washington Law School named. Then in 1946 he asked his good friend Max Radin of the law school at Berkeley to take over the selection process and enlarge it to include all of the schools in the Ninth Circuit. "This is the big league," he told Radin:[27]

I think you know exactly the kind of man[28] I want. I need not only a bright chap, but also a hard-working fellow with a smell for facts as well as for law. I do not want a hide-bound, conservative fellow. What I want is a Max Radin—a fellow who can hold his own in these sophisticated circles and who is not going to end up as a stodgy hide-bound lawyer. I want the kind of fellow for whom this work would be an exhilaration, who will be going into teaching or into practice of law for the purpose of promoting the public good. I do not want to fill the big law offices of the country with my law clerks.[29]

None of the clerks met Douglas prior to showing up for work at the Court, and some of them did not see him then for a while. Douglas expected that the outgoing clerk(s)[30] would show the incoming clerk(s) the ropes in the month or so before the Court convened in October; if he had any additional or special instructions at this time, he would send them to the clerk in writing.[31] "My predecessor," one clerk said, "told me my responsibilities, not how to do them. Douglas never told me anything about my job."[32]

When Douglas did arrive, he might—or might not—introduce himself, and then it was right to business, and the first month or so could be quite rough until a clerk picked up the rhythm of what the justice wanted. Within a few weeks there would often be a big blowup, and at least one clerk believed this was a set pattern; he could not believe it a mere coincidence that every clerk would botch up an assignment within the third to eighth week, so that Douglas could raise questions about the clerk's fitness for the job and whether the chambers needed another clerk so the work could get done properly.[33] His clerk for the 1956 Term, William Cohen, claims that the justice put all his clerks through one month of sheer hell, which Cohen compared to boot camp; if you got through it in reasonably good shape, then the rest of the year was pretty pleasant.[34] Another believed that if Douglas liked his clerk at the beginning, things would go fine; if he took a dislike to the clerk, "you were probably finished."[35]

The one thing that all of his clerks to whom I spoke agreed upon was that he worked them hard, but that he himself worked just as hard if not harder. As one put it, "He worked the hell out of his clerks, but . . . he worked the hell out of himself, too, and if he could do it indefinitely, I could do it for a year."[36] Another called him "a very demanding man. If he thought he had a right to make a demand on you, he made it."[37] "He was all work, and expected that of the clerks," recalled another, "and to that extent it was pretty rough. . . . He worked pretty hard. He was in Court every day."[38] Douglas believed that in a twenty-four-hour period "you would get a certain amount of work done, whether it took 10 or 12 or 14 hours, you would do it." But "he himself was very intense, and he would work long hours himself."[39]

Yet not a single one of the clerks I spoke to complained that Douglas worked them unfairly. Part of it was the fact that he himself worked very hard. Another believed that the "overworked thing" is a bad rap. "You worked hard, you worked very hard, but it was not at all unbearable or undoable. You're young, you're full of energy. It was a great job."[40] One clerk discerned that the very heavy workload — especially when the other justices had three clerks — was not an impossible task. "What he was doing," Jerome Falk explained, "was exacting very high standards."[41]

Douglas could be a difficult taskmaster, and he often blew up at his clerks, firing them on the spot. When they staggered out of his office, the secretary would say, "Pay absolutely no attention to it. He'll never speak of it again." So they would be back on the job, although a few of them went through that experience more than once.[42]

The experience, however, just added to the general sense of terror that Douglas seemed to generate among his clerks. Lucas Powe, who clerked in the 1970 Term, recalled that he lived in constant fear that he might do something wrong. One night he dreamed that he heard the buzzer Douglas used to summon his clerks, and sat bolt upright, totally awake and ready to work.[43]

In terms of the work itself, all of his clerks worked on the certiorari petitions, and any particular research that the justice required for particular cases. In addition, Douglas was quite conscientious about the *in forma pauperis* petitions, and had them reviewed in his chambers, unlike some of the other justices who agreed to have the Chief Justice's clerks review them. Beyond that, the particulars appeared to have varied from term to term, and from clerk to clerk.

In the beginning, the clerks did no writing at all; a memo they might do on some point of law would occasionally appear in abbreviated form as a footnote. Later on, however, he began allowing his clerks to draft an occasional dissent or concurrence, although he himself always did at least the first draft of any majority opinion for the Court. All clerks did cite-checking and research, and were expected to review his drafts for factual accuracy and clarity, although how he received their comments depended on how much he trusted them. Some, like Vern Countryman and Jerome Falk, took a very active role in critiquing his opinions and arguing points of law with him; others did not. From the various interviews it does appear that Douglas did allow his clerks in later years somewhat more of an active role in the work than those who worked for him in the 1940s, although here again the experience varies considerably depending upon the relationship between the two.

Douglas obviously changed his work pattern over the years, and there are several possible reasons. Most likely, as he settled in to the work of the Court and mastered the law, he felt able to give up the tight control he exercised in the first years. His extrajudicial activities and writings also expanded after 1948, and some terms his clerks would do as much research for his popular writing as they did on his opinions.[44] Perhaps most important, if he felt comfortable with the clerks, and if they were not afraid of him, he would allow them into a limited intellectual partnership. This was the obvious case with Vern Countryman and Jerome Falk; other clerks had less pleasant experiences.

One time Stanley Sparrowe thought a Douglas opinion technically wrong, and he "got up the nerve" to ask if the justice would consider changing it. Douglas listened, but not very receptively, and then exclaimed "I don't know what the hell you're talking about."[45] Charles Ruckershauser recalled an incident involving an opinion in an antitrust case that Douglas had dashed off in a hurry. Douglas originally spoke for a 5–4 Court, but Justice Harlan prepared a very lawyerly dissent. Ruckershauser thought that Harlan's opinion was so good it had to be answered in more detail and with more analysis than Douglas had provided. He spent the entire weekend working on a draft, and left it on Douglas's desk with a note explaining why and what he had done. Soon after Douglas came into the office on Monday morning, Ruckershauser heard the clerk's buzzer. He went into Douglas's office and saw the justice hold up his draft and then drop it into the wastebasket. It was all right, Douglas said, but the issue was not that important. Douglas stuck to his original draft, and Tom Clark, who rarely voted against the government, changed his mind and joined Harlan, giving him a majority.[46]

Another story, ten years later, illustrates that time and the clerk did make a difference. Jerome Falk admitted starting the year "scared to death" of Douglas, but found that if he took the time to compose his suggestions and put them in writing, Douglas would listen, and he gradually began to give Falk's ideas serious consideration. Falk read a Douglas draft in a First Amendment case that just did not seem to work, because, he discovered after some research, Douglas had relied on the winning brief for information, and the lawyer had misquoted the statute. Based on a misprint in the brief, Douglas had described the statute as vague, and Falk believed it was not vague, at least not in the way Douglas had said. So Falk redrafted it as an overbreadth opinion, managing to retain much of what Douglas had written, but shifting the basis from one First Amendment doctrine to an entirely different one. After finishing the job on Friday evening, Falk left it on Douglas's desk with a memorandum of what he had done, and then "shook all weekend long, wondering what was going to happen. Nothing happened. He agreed it was fine, and the opinion was recirculated."[47] So Douglas would take substantive suggestions from his clerks, providing the ideas had been thought out and the quality of the product met his standards. But "you did have to hold your breath with this. You never knew how he would take it."[48]

Douglas would often impose the silent treatment on a clerk if he failed to produce. Charles Miller recalled a case involving city health inspectors, and whether they could enter premises without a search warrant.[49] Nearly everyone on the Court thought of it as a simple case, since the Fourth Amendment had previously been held to apply only in criminal situations. Frankfurter, who considered the Fourth Amendment as his private preserve, got the assignment. Douglas disagreed, and set Miller to work on a dissent:

I got a bunch of books down from the library, and I struggled for a week or so, and produced nothing of value. He got very frustrated, and in a pique of anger said, "Bring all the books you got, and let me see what I can do." So I wheeled in the cart, and for two or three days he never said anything to me. At the end of that time he had produced an opinion, working off the stuff I had scratched around, a ten-page opinion that bowled me over. It was the most persuasive thing I had ever seen in my life. He circulated it to the Court, and immediately three justices switched their votes. The minute he got a reaction like that, all ice melted away between us.[50]

Incidents like this may not have inspired love, but they often inspired awe.

At least with the clerks I spoke with, there was a great deal of respect for Douglas, and at least in a few instances, real liking as well. All agreed, however, that he was not a man one got close to, nor did he see himself as a father surrogate to the clerks; one just does not hear the type of warm, personal stories about Douglas akin to those told about Black, Frankfurter, and Brennan. But they all could recall instances when, if you could get Douglas out of the work relation — an admittedly rare occurrence — he could be friendly, charming, and even cordial.

Marshall Small recalled one evening after work when Douglas sat down his secretary, clerk, and messenger and made martinis for them, "just the way he'd made them for FDR in the old days," and regaled them with stories from the New Deal years.[51] David Ginsberg remembered a poker game; Stanley Sparrowe, a Christmas dinner with the Douglases and Blacks and all their children;[52] Charles Ruckershauser, a hike along the C & O Canal; and Harvey Grossman, a time Douglas had gotten a new camera, and the two of them ran around the Court grounds taking pictures. Away from the Court, Douglas would seem to unwind and open up, and seemed genuinely happy to see former clerks at various occasions.

III. Perceptions and Misperceptions

Douglas in general does not appear to have been a "warm" person, one to whom the social amenities or personal touches meant a great deal. Many people commented upon this nastiness, yet here one must be careful, for perceptions varied depending on from which chambers one looked at Douglas. Charles Reich chose William O. Douglas as a hero, recognizing that he had a flawed personality. "Most of his flaws were personal and forgivable," Reich explained. "He had egregious personal flaws, but so what — he was a great man."[53] Among these "egregious" flaws was his treatment of his staff, his demands that they lay themselves out for him. He often seemed totally divorced from any sense of basic social kindness, and perhaps this derived from his work orientation. A job had to be done, and all else took second place to the work; if he could work hard, why then, so could his staff, and why should it be necessary to be kind to them for doing what they were paid to do, and what they knew the job entailed.[54] Douglas had no desire to play teacher to the clerks, as Felix Frankfurter did, or establish the type of paternal relations that existed between Hugo Black and William Brennan and their clerks.

The result is that both colleagues and other law clerks saw him as mean and nasty. Justice Blackmun declared that Douglas treated his clerks "in ways I couldn't accept. He went too far with them. One time he said to me, 'Law clerks are the lowest form of animal life.'"[55] Douglas could be nice — very nice — Justice Marshall recalled, but most of the time "he was awful rough on his staff." One time the brethren got a memorandum that said, in effect, "I apologize for the mistake in not having done something on a motion. This was caused solely by the stupidity of my secretary." The memorandum had been typed by that same secretary, which seemed a terrible thing to Marshall. He went down the hall to Douglas's chambers to tell her how upset he was at this callousness on her boss's part. She responded: "It doesn't matter to me; I get worse than that. But I love the man. He is a great man."[56] Justice Brennan confirmed that Douglas's secretaries tolerated a great deal of bad behavior from him, including frequent bawling outs, firing them one minute and rehiring them the next.[57]

Chief Justice Rehnquist recalled that, as a clerk, he did not view Douglas as one of the more friendly justices to the anonymous law clerks walking through the hall. "I don't think he was standoffish," he said. "I think he was just probably thinking about something else."[58] Other clerks were less charitable. Several described him as a "surly recluse." Donald Trautman (Frankfurter, 1952 Term) described Douglas as "surly, arrogant, and having no interest in his law clerks or anybody else's law clerks."[59] Lewis Hankin, another Frankfurter clerk (1946 Term), considered him the most unpopular justice. "He was so unfriendly. He never talked to the other law clerks. He was sour and unfriendly."[60] Daniel Meador, who clerked for Black in the 1954 Term, recalled that no one saw very much of Douglas. "He was something of a loner, he wasn't very social or gregarious," a view echoed by Norman Dorsen, who clerked for Justice Harlan a few terms later.[61] Even Charles Reich admits that his hero treated his law clerks "very badly" and never allowed them to get close to him in any way.[62]

The clerks to the other justices believed that Douglas not only treated his clerks badly, but did not use them well in terms of the Court's work. During the year Gerald Gunther clerked for Chief Justice Warren (1954 Term),

Harvey Grossman worked for Douglas. Gunther claimed that Grossman "was very much of a fringe figure" among the clerks, overworked but "out of the loop."[63] Robert O'Neill believed Jared Carter, Douglas's clerk in the 1962 Term, "didn't do a hell of a lot."[64] Donald Trautman recalled that the clerks his year believed that Douglas treated Charles Ares "very badly," there was little personal contact between them, and Douglas would sometimes not even comment on the memoranda Ares submitted.[65]

One episode that seemed to stick in everyone's mind involved the brown-bag lunches held periodically by the clerks, to which the justices would be invited. Frankfurter loved these events, and turned them into seminars, often keeping the clerks far beyond their allotted lunch breaks, much to the annoyance of some of his colleagues. Douglas, for what seems to be primarily shyness, did not wax enthusiastic over the luncheons, and kept trying to get out of them. According to various recollections, he came and talked about his travels,[66] or he did not come at all.[67]

Yet when one asks Douglas's own clerks about their work, their treatment, and even the brown-bag lunches, one hears an entirely different side of the story. It is true that they had less interaction with the other clerks, because they worked so hard; after all, Douglas's chambers had as much work as those of the other justices, but only one clerk compared to their two or three. The Douglas clerk had no more time to "waste" socializing than did his boss. But none of the ones I spoke to saw this as a hardship or terrible experience; in fact, they all had a sort of perverse pride in the fact that they could and did work that hard. As Gary Torre said, he wanted you to go all out, "which I was perfectly willing to do; I think I did, and I think every clerk did."[68]

The picture of overworked clerks "would be fairly reasonable" as seen from the other chambers, Jerome Falk agreed, but it would not be accurate:

They would see only the worst of it. They could see that I could never have lunch with them when he was in town because he would work through the lunch hour. So I would get a sandwich sent in. . . . The law clerks did not like that. The other judges would let them go for lunch, and the law clerks were very loyal to each other. So their perception was that I was having some sort of a hard time. In fact, I felt pretty lucky to be there, and I was having a good time.[69]

"Poor" Harvey Grossman, the clerk for the 1954 Term, also seemed surprised that other clerks thought him ill-used. The year he served at the Court, Douglas was happy in his second marriage, and the addition of Earl Warren began to swing some decisions in the liberal direction. Grossman worked not only on Douglas's Court work, but also—and willingly—extended himself to work on some of the extrajudicial writings. Douglas had an "intensity" about him that rubbed off on his clerks as well.[70]

It is true that Douglas sometimes resisted the clerks' lunches. Small, Grossman, and Falk told essentially the same story — of Douglas breaking dates and of them practically dragging him to the dining room; Miller and Campbell, on the other hand, had no problem at all. He did come, however, and they all agreed that once there, he enjoyed himself. Part of his reluctance seems to have been shyness. Another reason may well be that he knew Frankfurter shone in this situation, and even after Frankfurter left the Court, all those clerks from Harvard and Yale allegedly had imbibed the Frankfurter dogma. This seems to have been the case in Falk's term:

Douglas saw my colleagues as cookie-cutters from [Harvard and Yale], and didn't want to come. On the day of the thing he was late, and didn't want to do it. I finally dragged him out of the chambers and walked him down the hall, and he's grumbling at me all the way. I was very embarrassed. So he walks in, he sits down, he's looking kinda grumpy, and we start to talk to him and we have lunch. People asked him questions, and they were good questions. These are bright people. They came in sort of skeptical too. Well, the long and short of it is he had a really good time. He became more and more expansive, more and more charming, as he could be. . . . On the way back I teased him that he had had a good time, and he mumbled "Oh, well."[71]

Some clerks from other chambers remember Douglas showing up at various social occasions, and even hosting a party for them from time to time. But, again, perceptions vary. Two clerks who served in the 1954 Term, Gerald Gunther (Warren) and Daniel Meador (Black), both recalled a cocktail party Douglas gave for the other justices and their staffs. Meador remembered him standing around somewhat stiffly, uncomfortable at his own party, and not a very good conversationalist. Gunther, on the other hand, said that Douglas "looked like a different person, talking to people," and apparently having a good time.[72]

And despite the fact that he could be cold, aloof, even nasty to his clerks during their tenure, some warmth, some affection developed.[73] For a few, he took an interest in their subsequent careers, and tried to help them from time to time, especially those who entered teaching.[74] Whenever his former clerks returned to Washington and came by to visit him at the Court, he seemed genuinely happy to see them. At the five-year reunions, "he would open up and have a hell of a time."[75] While some clerks developed close, ongoing relations, the dominant sentiment, however, remained respect rather than affection.

IV. Conclusion

Douglas's relations with his colleagues and his clerks cannot be characterized in any simple manner. An often shy man, people had trouble getting close to him, yet he seemed to inspire respect and even some affection from those with whom he worked so closely on the Court. If we look at Douglas's focus on the work, on getting the job done, some of the idiosyncrasies begin to make a little sense. With the exception of his relationship to Felix Frankfurter, he could be a pleasant colleague to those who, whatever their jurisprudential views, got on with the business of the Court; those who could not keep up, or dissipated their energies in other directions, earned his scorn.

As for his clerks, he could be nasty to them, and he surely worked them hard, almost as hard as he worked himself. For most of them, however, it became and remained a memorable experience. As several of them noted, that is what they were there for — to work — and while it might have been nice to have had the surrogate familial relationships that Hugo Black, Felix Frankfurter, and William Brennan extended to their clerks, they did not expect it from Douglas, and were therefore not disappointed at its absence.

I am not suggesting that this emphasis on work is the only criterion by which we can evaluate Douglas's relationships in the Court, but it does help to make some aspects of his collegiality or lack of it more understandable. Whether this concentration on work puts Douglas in James Barber's "active-negative" category, as Professor Jackson suggests, is debatable.[76] There is no question that Douglas worked very hard, but it is not clear that he derived little satisfaction from all his efforts. Certainly the fact that he was so often in the minority must have been at times depressing, but he won his share of victories. Moreover, there is little in common between Douglas and Barber's classic example of "active-negative" behavior, Richard Nixon. Douglas took great joy in life, and if he sometime seemed to enjoy his extrajudicial activities more than the Court work, that by itself does not mean that he derived no satisfaction on the bench.

Douglas embodied a nearly puritanical attitude toward work, which he seems to have inherited from his mother. He worked hard at everything he did — teaching, the SEC, the Court, writing, traveling, saving the environment — during years when, for the most part, his liberalism did not command widespread support either among his colleagues or the general population. Perhaps the victories that he did achieve in civil liberties or in saving some stretch of wilderness just did not compensate for all the defeats. And so he and his clerks worked, and worked hard, and while he may have claimed that he had only one soul to save, somehow one gets the impression that in the work he hoped to save others as well.

Notes

1. James F. Simon, *Independent Journey: The Life of William O. Douglas* (New York: Harper and Row, 1980).

2. See, for example, Michael E. Parrish, "Cold War Justice: The Supreme Court and the Rosenbergs," *American Historical Review* 82 (1977): 805; and especially G. Edward White, "The Anti-Judge: William O. Douglas and the Ambiguities of Individuality," *Virginia Law Review* 17 (1988): 74. Simon, *Independent Journey,* while

sympathetic, is not uncritical, and points up some of the less admirable of Douglas's personality traits.

3. This chapter is based primarily on interviews with current and former members of the U.S. Supreme Court, former clerks to Justice Douglas and other justices, and with three of his wives, as well as on the voluminous William O. Douglas Papers in the Manuscript Division of the Library of Congress (hereafter cited as Douglas MSS). For a more extended treatment of the material on clerks, see Melvin I. Urofsky, "William O. Douglas and His Clerks," *Western Legal History* 3 (1990): 1–20.

4. The often stormy relations between Douglas and Frankfurter are explored in Melvin I. Urofsky, "Conflict Among the Brethren: Felix Frankfurter, William O. Douglas and the Clash of Personalities and Philosophies on the United States Supreme Court," *Duke Law Journal* 71 (1988). The Douglas-Black relationship is the subject of Howard Ball and Phillip Cooper, *Of Power and Right: Justices Black and Douglas and America's Tumultuous Years, 1937–1975* (New York: Oxford University Press, 1991).

5. William O. Douglas, *The Court Years, 1939–1975: The Autobiography of William O. Douglas* (New York: Random House, 1980).

6. See Robert Jerome Glennon, "Commentary: Collegialism and Change over Time: William O. Douglas as Justice," which follows this chapter.

7. Interview with C. David Ginsburg, June 16, 1988. Ginsburg, a recent graduate of the Harvard Law School, had worked closely with Commissioner Douglas at the SEC, and when Douglas went to the Court in the middle of a term, he asked Ginsburg if he would come over and help out until he could get on a regular cycle of hiring clerks the following term.

8. Simon, *Independent Journey,* p. 250. Besides, during his entire career on the bench, Douglas could rely first on Hugo Black and later on William J. Brennan to do the proselytizing and consensus-building for the liberal bloc.

9. Douglas, *The Court Years,* p. 215.

10. Interview with Justice Harry Blackmun, May 17, 1988. William H. Rehnquist also said that Douglas admired Hughes and "was not particularly an admirer of Stone." Interview with Chief Justice William H. Rehnquist, May 17, 1988. Vern Countryman confirmed that during the 1942 Term, Stone used to stop by Douglas's chambers fairly frequently. Interview with Vern Countryman, Aug. 29, 1988.

11. Interview with Justice Lewis F. Powell, Jr., Apr. 5, 1988.

12. Interview, Vern Countryman.

13. Douglas to Fred Rodell, May 22, 1949, Fred Rodell Papers, Box 4, Haverford College Library, Haverford, Pennsylvania. The Douglas MSS are full of notes complaining that Frankfurter delayed or was very late in getting out opinions.

14. Douglas, *The Court Years,* pp. 173–74.

15. Interview with Justice Thurgood Marshall, May 17, 1988; interview, Blackmun; Simon, *Independent Journey,* p. 432. According to Albert J. Rosenthal, Frankfurter's clerk in the 1947 Term, Douglas was already infuriating the brethren with this habit in the midforties. Rosenthal to author, June 1, 1988.

16. Simon, *Independent Journey,* ch. 21.

17. Parrish, "Cold War Justice."

18. Interview with Charles Reich, Aug. 29, 1988.

19. Interview, Justice Blackmun.

20. Interview, Justice Powell.

21. Interview with Mercedes Eichholz, Aug. 22, 1988.

22. William O. Douglas, *Go East, Young Man: The Autobiography of William O. Douglas* (New York: Random House, 1974), p. 35.

23. Interview with Justice William J. Brennan, Jr., May 17, 1988.

24. Interview, Justice Marshall.

25. The full list of clerks is in Douglas, *The Court Years,* pp. 415–16.

26. Interviews with Marshall Small, Aug. 26, 1988, and with Joan Martin Brown, Mar. 2, 1989. In 1947 Douglas asked his clerk, Stanley Sparrowe, what he thought about having two clerks, since some of the other justices already had two, and Black was about to hire a second one. Sparrowe said that he would prefer to be in a one-clerk office where he would have a part in everything rather than only in some parts. Douglas agreed, and added: "Two clerks would just write memos to one another." Interview with Stanley Sparrowe (Douglas's clerk, 1947 Term), Aug. 30, 1988. Charles Miller, another clerk, also said that he preferred a one-clerk office, and despite the heavy work load, believed most of the other clerks from that time also would not have changed the arrangement; interview with Charles Miller, Mar. 2, 1989.

27. Douglas to Max Radin, May 27, 1946, Douglas MSS. Radin chose Douglas's clerks for several years, until he became ill. Then Stanley Sparrowe, who had clerked for Douglas in the 1947 Term and was practicing in Oakland, took over the task in 1950, and handled it until 1967, when Thomas Klitgard (1961 Term) assumed the responsibility. In 1970 a committee of three former clerks, Charles E. Ares (1952), William Cohen (1956), and Jerome Falk (1965), took on the assignment.

28. Douglas, in fact, hired the first woman clerk at the Court, Lucille Loman, during the war, when he could not get a man because of the draft. But he did not consider women as good as men (see letter to Stanley Sparrowe, June 13, 1950, in Melvin I. Urofsky and Philip E. Urofsky, eds., *The Douglas Letters: Selections from the Private Papers of Justice William O. Douglas* [Bethesda: Adler and Adler, 1987], p. 49), and he did not take another woman clerk until 1972, when he took two. It was not a happy experience; see Robert Woodward and Scott Armstrong, *The Brethren: Inside the Supreme Court* (New York: Simon and Schuster, 1979), pp. 285–89.

29. Brandeis had a similar philosophy, as did Frankfurter. Of Douglas's fifty-four clerks, at least a dozen went into academia, and a few others have taught in addition to their law practice.

30. Douglas experimented with two clerks occasionally, and finally went to two clerks in the 1970 Term, and three starting in 1972. After his retirement, he had one clerk again.

31. Interviews with Gary J. Torre (Douglas clerk, 1948 Term), Aug. 29, 1988; Marshall Small; Harvey Grossman (1954 Term), Aug. 18, 1988; and Charles E. Ruckershauser, Jr. (1957 Term), Aug. 18, 1988.

32. Interview, Charles Ruckershauser. According to Professor Harold Koh of Yale, a former clerk to Justice Blackmun, this pattern by itself is not that unusual. Most justices do not train their clerks personally, but rely upon one year's clerks breaking in their successors. However, most justices do see their clerks before the term begins, if for no other reason than to interview them.

33. Interview, Charles Ruckershauser.

34. Telephone interview with William Cohen, July 25, 1988; Jerome Falk compared it to "basic training." Douglas's blowups at his clerks were legendary. Robert O'Neill, former professor of law at the University of California at Berkeley, believes

that the interview committee would deliberately act in an offensive manner to see how the applicants could handle themselves, and also to alert them to the type of experience they might have with Douglas. O'Neill had himself been a clerk, to Justice Brennan in the October 1962 Term. Interview with O'Neill, Aug. 13, 1988.

35. Interview, Charles Miller. For an example of the Douglas temper when he disliked a clerk, see his letter to Peter K. Westen, Oct. 1, 1968, in Urofsky and Urofsky, *Douglas Letters,* p. 52.

36. Interview, Vern Countryman.

37. Interview, Gary Torre.

38. Interview with Walter B. Chaffee (Douglas clerk, 1941 Term) Aug. 19, 1988.

39. Interview, Harvey Grossman.

40. Interview with James Campbell, Mar. 2, 1989. Charles Miller expressed a similar sentiment: "I was single, I was young, I had worked hard in law school. I wasn't afraid to work hard. It was damned hard work, but it wasn't oppressive."

41. Interview with Jerome Falk (Douglas clerk, 1965 Term) Aug. 26, 1988.

42. Of the nineteen clerks I interviewed, not one had himself been fired, but they all assured me that Douglas had fired, and then rehired, clerks who displeased him.

43. Interview with Lucas Powe, Apr. 16, 1989. Powe also recalled that he worked so hard that his marriage and family suffered; his child was sick much of that term, and he was totally unable to help out because of the demands of the clerkship. With Powe, as with others, Douglas had little concern for their private lives.

44. The year Harvey Grossman clerked for him, he did a great deal of work on Douglas's Tagore Lectures, *We, the Judges* (Garden City: Doubleday, 1956). Douglas evidently did not force this type of work on his clerks, but if he found they were interested in the subject, he had no compunctions of piling such assignments on top of their regular work.

45. Interview, Stanley Sparrowe.

46. Interview, Charles Ruckershauser; the case is *Nashville Milk Co. v. Carnation Co.,* 355 U.S. 373 (1958). Douglas's statement for the four dissenters — originally the majority opinion — is at 383.

47. Interview, Jerome Falk; the case was *Elfbrandt v. Russell,* 384 U.S. 11 (1966), which struck down a state loyalty oath.

48. Interview, Jerome Falk. Falk also noted that "I have a sense my experience was not atypical of clerks immediately preceding me or following me."

49. *Frank v. Maryland,* 359 U.S. 360 (1959).

50. Interview, Charles Miller. Justice Whittaker almost joined Douglas, and finally, after intense lobbying from Frankfurter, stayed with the majority but wrote a separate one-paragraph concurrence. *Frank v. Maryland,* 359 U.S., at 374. The Douglas dissent, joined by Warren, Black, and Brennan, is also at 374. Eight years later, the Court overruled the Frankfurter opinion and adopted Douglas's view in the companion cases of *Camara v. Municipal Court of San Francisco,* 387 U.S. 523 (1967), and *See v. Seattle,* 387 U.S. 541 (1967).

51. Interview, Marshall Small.

52. Clerks were told by their predecessors that Douglas would invite them to his house or apartment for Thanksgiving and Christmas, but often Douglas would not extend that invitation until just a day or two before the holiday.

53. Interview, Charles Reich.

54. Stephen Duke (1959 Term) commented that not once in the year he worked for Douglas did the justice ever tell him that he had performed satisfactorily, a statement quickly endorsed by other former Douglas clerks present. Interview with Stephen Duke, Apr. 16, 1989.

55. Interview, Justice Blackmun. Douglas's third wife reported that she fought a great deal with him over his bad treatment of his clerks.

56. Interview, Justice Marshall.

57. Interview, Justice Brennan.

58. Interview, Chief Justice Rehnquist.

59. Interview with Donald Trautman (Frankfurter clerk, 1952 Term), June 29, 1988.

60. Interview with Lewis Hankin, June 30, 1988; Hankin added, however, that "my own views may have been colored by Frankfurter."

61. Interview with Daniel Meador, July 13, 1988; interview with Norman Dorsen, July 7, 1988.

62. Interview, Charles Reich.

63. Interview with Gerald Gunther, Aug. 26, 1988. Daniel Meador, who clerked for Black that same term, also saw Grossman as "quite reclusive," and out of the swing of things. Interview, Meador.

64. Interview, Robert O'Neill.

65. Interview, Donald Trautman.

66. Telephone interview with Murray L. Schwartz (clerk to Chief Justice Vinson, 1949 and 1950 Terms), July 15, 1988.

67. Interview, Gerald Gunther; interview with Harry Wellington (Frankfurter clerk, 1955 Term), June 28, 1988.

68. Interview, Gary Torre.

69. Interview, Jerome Falk. All of the other clerks I spoke to also said they considered themselves lucky to be there, and that they expected to work hard.

70. Interview, Harvey Grossman.

71. Interview, Jerome Falk; James Campbell reported that Douglas charmed everyone, and when they started asking him questions, he "hit 'em out of the park." Interview, James Campbell.

72. Interviews, Gerald Gunther and Daniel Meador.

73. George Rutherglen, who clerked for Douglas during the few months of the 1975 Term before he retired, reports that the justice was fairly kind to his clerks, chatted with them, and told stories about the Roosevelt days. This was, of course, after his stroke, when he could no longer sustain his former work pace. Interview with George Rutherglen, Aug. 13, 1988.

74. James Campbell said that when he first started in practice, he believes it was Douglas who arranged for him to be named counsel in one of the *in forma pauperis* cases the Court accepted, and he thought Douglas had done this for other of his former clerks as well. Interview, James Campbell.

75. Interview, Walter Chaffee.

76. See Donald W. Jackson, "Commentary: On the Correct Handling of Contradictions Within the Court" (concluding this section), utilizing the categories developed by James David Barber in *The Presidential Character: Predicting Performance in the White House* (Englewood Cliffs: Prentice-Hall, 1972).

COMMENTARY:
COLLEGIALISM AND CHANGE OVER TIME:
WILLIAM O. DOUGLAS AS JUSTICE

Robert Jerome Glennon

I

BALL AND UROFSKY examine Douglas as justice, one from the vantage of his personal relations with other justices and his law clerks, the other by examining Douglas's performance in several important issues that arose during the Second World War and shortly thereafter. Drawing on unpublished papers and memoranda, and from personal interviews with justices and law clerks, they make a valuable contribution to understanding a most complex man and offer numerous insights about Douglas's personal style.

Appellate courts range across a spectrum. At one end, the corporate model, typified by some European countries, particularly France, issues all opinions *per curiam*. The author of the opinion for the court remains anonymous, and public dissent is unknown. Collegialism is the most important value. In contrast, imagine a totally individualized court, whose members resolve every question according to his or her own conceptions of proper legal rules, never accommodating to or compromising on the varying opinions of his or her colleagues. Under such a system, the result is determined by what the majority votes, regardless of the rationale of each judge's opinion. Such results offer little in the way of principled guidance for future cases. Our Supreme Court has much of the individualized model within it, for we attribute publicly the authorship of the Court's opinion, and concurring and dissenting opinions are under the name of a particular justice.[1]

These two chapters present fresh evidence that Justice Douglas leaned toward the individualistic end of the spectrum. As a justice, he apparently felt little or no obligation to "get a court," an opinion whose rationale is agreed to by a majority. In large measure, Douglas did not conceive his role as one of attempting to persuade others to his point of view. As Ball quotes, "[The] only soul I have to save is my own." Douglas was prepared to write separately and even to dissent solely rather than to struggle to achieve a consensus on a particular position. In this regard, his philosophy as a justice is in marked contrast to that of Chief Justice Taft, Justice Brennan, and perhaps, on the basis of emerging evidence, even Chief Justice Rehnquist.

Rehnquist recently commented on the difference between serving as an Associate Justice and as Chief Justice. Since he speaks first at Conference (rather than ninth, eighth, or seventh), he feels an obligation to state fairly all questions posed, rather than comment only on issues that engage him, because he is setting the terms of debate. He also acknowledges a greater concern with "getting a Court" than he did previously.

At the same time, Ball and Urofsky somewhat surprisingly indicate that, on occasion, Douglas would attempt to persuade. Through memos and letters, even the "quintessential loner" embraced a measure of collegialism.

II

Urofsky helps us to understand that Douglas was so riveted by his concern with efficient work habits and productivity that it left little time for socializing and idle conversation. To outsiders, this frequently appeared asocial — arrogant and aloof. But to those who knew him well, it was an idiosyncratic habit which, though not warm and affable, they overlooked as they developed for him respect and even admiration. He could be friendly, personable, kind during crises, and concerned about a law clerk's future. This analysis helps round out a portrait of Douglas.

Yet there is also a limit to what "getting the job done" explains. Urofsky's title, "Getting the Job Done," means implicitly that the "job" of an Associate Justice is to vote on cert. petitions and to prepare opinions either for the Court or writing separately. Yet, Douglas's personal style may have impeded "getting the job done." His treatment of his law clerks, not simply brusque or curt but occasionally mean and cruel, may have impeded their efficiency. He apparently never gave a law clerk instructions on performing his tasks or stated his expectations. To have an employee begin a job without ever having met the boss and to work for a period of time without the boss ever having told him or her how to proceed is not a case study of efficient management that will soon be taught at the Harvard Business School.

One could also conceive "getting the job done" differently — as securing the most favorable results and the best rationale in cases. Douglas's intense individualism allowed for a quick work product, but slighting the collegial character of Supreme Court decision making may have relegated Douglas to a more marginal role in terms of immediate influence on the Court's decisions. Despite his record-length service on the Court, Douglas authored a relatively modest number of seminal opinions.

In the *Nashville Milk* case described by Urofsky, personal pique or desire to demean a law clerk with the temerity to raise questions about Douglas's opinion may have changed dramatically the result in the case. Douglas began writing an opinion for the Court and ended up in dissent. Douglas regularly left for Goose Prairie as soon as he had finished writing his opinions but long before the Term ended. During this interval, Douglas lost the opportunity to react to opinions of other justices and to influence the disposition in these cases. These examples make one wonder about how seriously

Douglas cared about the substantive results that the Court reached in individual decisions. This style perhaps interfered with getting the job done.

RELATIONS WITH COLLEAGUES

Urofsky makes the good point that Douglas's friendly relations with other justices were not a function of ideological approval or agreement. Let me suggest as a thesis that Justice Douglas related well to people of keen intelligence, so long as they were genuine. It is not surprising that he had good relations with Justices Harlan, Rehnquist, Powell, and Black. In contrast, as *The Brethren* has made plain, almost no one respected the abilities of Warren Burger and all found his self-aggrandizing style offensive. As recent commentators, including Urofsky, have demonstrated, Felix Frankfurter's pomposity interfered with his relations with practically all of his colleagues on the Court. Pomposity brought out Douglas's most nettling sense of humor. It was not all in good fun.

Justice Douglas was an elitist in his relations with colleagues. If a justice had a keen intelligence and abundant talent, he was within the pool of possible friends. Nina Totenberg has suggested that Douglas did not associate with justices who lacked a first-rate intellect. But even the smartest justice, if he were full of pretenses, would be dismissed by Douglas.

Hugo Black was not well schooled, but he was certainly well read and, until his philosophy verged on the simplistic in the late sixties, his jurisprudence certainly demanded that it be reckoned with. He had abundant practical wisdom. Good relations with William Brennan would be expected, as Brennan may very well be the most influential justice to have served on the Court in the last half century.

DOUGLAS AND HIS CLERKS

In his discussion of Douglas's relations with his clerks, Urofsky observes that one's perspective may very well inform what one thinks of Justice Douglas. Those outside his chambers thought poorly of him because he appeared cool, detached, and arrogant. But those in his chambers accepted the parameters of working long hours with few or no breaks and came to appreciate what a rare opportunity it was to work for a year with someone of Douglas's talents.

At the same time, no amount of explanation can escape the fact that Douglas could be cruel, nasty, aloof, and insensitive. Clerks began work without ever having met Douglas and, even after his return from Goose Prairie, he frequently did not even bother to introduce himself. A clerk's most diligent efforts went without praise or, often, even acknowledgment.

I remain a bit dubious about Urofsky's perspective thesis. The justice's own clerks naturally would attempt to make the best of a difficult situation and, after all, it remained a rare and privileged job to clerk for William O.

Douglas. Urofsky suggests that the work pattern of Douglas's clerks changed over the years as Douglas relaxed his tight control and accepted more comments from his clerks. Yet the two clerks whose comments apparently epitomize this view are Jerome Falk from the October Term 1965 and Vern Countryman from the October Term 1942. After quoting Falk, Urofsky concludes that Douglas would take substantive suggestions from his clerks so long as the ideas were well thought out and the work product of high quality. Yet Douglas perfunctorily rejected a memorandum, apparently of high quality, prepared by Ruckershauser. Consistency is not the hallmark of Douglas's personal or professional career.

III

A theme I extract from Ball's chapter is that despite the image of Douglas as the "quintessential loner" he operated in a collegial fashion in many instances and even subordinated his personal views on important issues when the country faced critical periods. Ball presents evidence that Douglas anguished over certain opinions and even tried to lobby Chief Justice Stone on how one opinion would be written. Through his chapter, one sees a portrait of Douglas as more of a collaborator than is generally understood. One also sees Douglas struggling with some wrenching issues raised during World War II.

It is not clear what binds together the Japanese Internment Cases, the Flag Salute Cases, and the Conscientious Objector Cases, which all arose during the Second World War, with the *Rosenberg* case, which arose thereafter. Nonetheless, Ball's discussion of Douglas's switch in the Flag Salute Cases is revealing in confirming that Douglas respected Frankfurter early on but that the relationship between Frankfurter and Douglas deteriorated after this incident.[2]

The Selective Service Cases had more to do with jurisdiction than with the merits. Thus one can interpret them not as revealing Douglas's support for the military's need for an unimpeded flow of personnel but rather as disclosing that Douglas accepted that Congress sets the parameters of federal jurisdiction. In particular, the *Estep* case merely allows conscientious objectors to raise, as a defense at a criminal trial for refusing induction, that the draft board acted beyond its jurisdiction. This defense was clearly available on habeas corpus review. *Estep* did not allow preinduction or preindictment judicial review.

Ball and Urofsky part company when Ball quotes Urofsky to the effect that Douglas could never focus his energies and became intellectually lazy in his Court work. Ball disputes this point and insists that Douglas maintained comprehensive Conference notes right up to the very end of his career. A middle ground may be that Douglas worked hard at his Court duties *when* he worked on them, but that Douglas refused to allow this work to consume him. His penchant for travel, hiking, and nonjudicial writing received the rest of his energy.

In the end, Ball suggests that Douglas changed his position on a number of important cases and hypothesizes that perhaps this is because he was so bright or perhaps because he sought to be more the collaborator than we normally credit Douglas with. He explains Douglas's Vietnam War decisions as a reflection of Douglas's views on the war itself. Douglas considered Vietnam an illegitimate war, quite different from the United States' noble efforts during the Second World War.

The historian in me wonders if a different hypothesis, one rooted in changes over time, might not account better for Douglas's performance in the cases Ball analyzes. If we contrast these cases with ones from the 1960s, one might fashion a thesis that has Douglas early in his tenure operating rather conventionally. He deferred to Congress on jurisdictional matters (Conscientious Objector Cases), to the military on the Japanese internment program, and to state legislative judgment on economic matters.[3] Fifty years ago, when Douglas ascended the Court, the conventional wisdom for liberals was judicial restraint. Any justice who joined the Court in *Gobitis* and *Korematsu* could hardly be described as a radical civil libertarian.[4]

Douglas sat on the Court for over one-third of a century. By the 1960s, Douglas's judicial philosophy and judicial style had evolved and matured. It is difficult to think that he would have joined *Gobitis* and *Korematsu* in the 1960s. Now, trees had standing;[5] conscientious objectors obtained immediate judicial review of a selective service reclassification, despite a congressional statute that required the person first to be inducted or indicted;[6] married persons had a right of personal privacy;[7] and the free speech rights of civil rights protestors included unconventional methods.[8] He spoke eloquently of the rights of school children[9] and of women.[10] His mistrust of the executive's handling of the Vietnam War prompted him to order the cessation of the bombing of Cambodia[11] and repeatedly to vote to grant review in cases challenging the constitutionality of the Vietnam War.[12] Frequently, he dissented from denials of certiorari, wanting the Court to take and decide more cases. He lowered justiciability hurdles that bar the Court deciding the merits: standing, ripeness, and the political question doctrine. He had become an activist civil libertarian. Practically every change and inconsistency finds Douglas moving toward greater judicial power and greater protection of civil rights and liberties.

Notes

1. See Maurice Kelman, "The Forked Path of Dissent," *Supreme Court Review* 1985:227.

2. Urofsky has recently shown that the relationship deteriorated earlier, at least so far as Frankfurter was concerned. See Melvin Urofsky, "Conflict Among the

Brethren: Felix Frankfurter, William O. Douglas and the Clash of Personalities and Philosophies on the United States Supreme Court," *Duke Law Journal* 1988:71.

    3. *Williamson v. Lee Optical of Oklahoma,* 348 U.S. 483 (1955).

    4. *Minersville School District v. Gobitis,* 310 U.S. 586 (1940); *Korematsu v. United States,* 323 U.S. 214 (1944).

    5. *Sierra Club v. Morton,* 405 U.S. 727 (1972).

    6. *Oestereich v. Selective Service System Local Board No. 11,* 393 U.S. 232 (1968).

    7. *Griswold v. Connecticut,* 381 U.S. 479 (1965).

    8. *Adderley v. Florida,* 385 U.S. 39 (1966).

    9. *Wisconsin v. Yoder,* 406 U.S. 205 (1972).

    10. *Alexander v. Louisiana,* 405 U.S. 625 (1972).

    11. *Holtzman v. Schlesinger,* 414 U.S. 1304 (1973).

    12. *Mora v. McNamara,* 389 U.S. 934, 935 (1967); *Holtzman v. Schlesinger,* 414 U.S. 1316 (1973); *United States v. O'Brien,* 391 U.S. 367 (1968).

COMMENTARY:
ON THE CORRECT HANDLING OF
CONTRADICTIONS WITHIN THE COURT

Donald W. Jackson

BOTH THE BALL and the Urofsky chapters focus on the personality of William O. Douglas rather than on the substance of the issues he was required to judge. Two sets of personal attributes emerge from the chapters. The first set involves Douglas's relations with his fellow workers, most prominently with his fellow justices and his clerks. The second set, barely separable from the first, involves Douglas's own decision-making style. The second set is separable only if we focus on the the personal attributes that Mr. Justice Douglas seemed to exhibit when working alone.

Professor Urofsky uses Justice Douglas's work patterns and decision-making style to explain, in part, the nature and quality of his relations with fellow workers. Urofsky's main point is that Douglas's commitment to a work ethic tended to exclude the "normal" range of human sociability. "Getting the work out" thus became the single-minded objective by which he judged himself and others — and by which he often found others to be wanting. As my title suggests, some of the "contradictions" between Douglas and his fellow justices, Frankfurter especially, seem to have been "antagonistic," though whether that antagonism resulted chiefly from ideological differences or from Douglas's perception of Frankfurter's "wasting time" is not easy to determine.

Ball examines Justice Douglas's personality in the context of several important wartime and postwar cases (1940–1953). His key point is that Douglas was sometimes uncertain and indecisive, rather than obdurate as Frankfurter charged. Ball suggests that, at least during these years, Justice Douglas was capable of seeking consensus, even on issues that required him to set aside or temper his personal views.

Urofsky reviews characterizations of Douglas that describe him as a loner, shy, hard to get close to, not a warm person, not big on social amenities, and hard but fair. In this company, Frankfurter's judgment of Douglas as being "completely evil, malignant, narrow-minded, cynical, shameless," and the like, stands pretty much alone.

Ball recalls Frankfurter's characterization of Douglas as "obdurate" but also reviews the evidence that Douglas was not a consensus builder; was the "quintessential loner who never had a close friend"; was extremely shy, impatient, cool, and remote; was one who would rarely stoop to lobbying; was a very bright man, was one who wrote very quickly — as sometimes suggested, perhaps too quickly — and who did not participate much in the intellectual give and take of the court.

Of course, it is impossible to reach definitive conclusions about a person from this sort of anecdotal evidence, but it is possible to suggest some interesting alternative interpretations. Urofsky has offered one through his explication of Douglas's work ethic. Ball has shown that Douglas's decisional behavior could, on occasion, contradict facile characterizations of the man. Other interpretations, however, should also be considered. Let me briefly propose two different ones.

I. Legal Realism

It is possible to interpret Justice Douglas's decision-making style, and particularly the nature of his written opinions, by taking him seriously as a prominent Legal Realist of his day. If we adopt that view, then Douglas's understanding of the nature of law and of judicial decision making would provide a partial interpretation of his own decision-making style. On the other hand, his relations with fellow justices seem to require some sort of psychological interpretation — and one not confined to his commitment to a strict work ethic. These two disparate interpretations probably cannot be completely reconciled, but a psychological interpretation may complement what can be said about Douglas as a Legal Realist.

Ball cites Urofsky as one who has concluded that Douglas became "intellectually lazy" on the Court. Urofsky has faulted Douglas for his failure to "forge a coherent *legal* as well as moral argument as to why a certain result is necessary."[1] If I understand G. Edward White correctly, his recent assessment of Justice Douglas is even more severe. His characterization of Douglas as the "Anti-Judge" rests on the assertion that Douglas "rejected both of the twentieth-century devices designed to constrain subjective judicial lawmaking: fidelity to constitutional text or doctrine, and institutional deference." His point is not necessarily that judges *are* constrained to base their judgments on sources other than their personal preferences, but that they are required "to act as if they are."[2]

Even Black or Warren, White argues, sought to create an impression of "jurisprudential orthodoxy." Douglas did not. White concludes that Douglas's opinions reflect the "Realists' characterization of doctrinal analysis as a sham," despite the fact that he clearly had the intellectual power and legal skills to harness doctrinal analysis to his own purposes. White's alternative conclusions about this are quite amazing.

Douglas is to be indicted *either* for being a whistle blower ("the judge who reveals what judges really are") *or,* at a less cynical level, for failing to play the game of doctrinal justification, since such justifications provide legitimacy, through the appearance of impartiality, to judges' decisions. White acknowledges, however, that Douglas's opinions are not lacking in "the passion of . . . language on behalf of values and goals in which he believed." And analysis is not lacking either — it is merely "doctrinal analysis of the unconventional sort."[3] So what is the problem? Perhaps Douglas wrote for a different audience. Exactly so!

Thurman Arnold, with Douglas a member of the Realist movement at Yale, has written candidly of "The New Constitution" that was the product, as he saw it, of "the first eight years of the administration of Franklin Roosevelt." The new Constitution, he wrote in 1965, "stands as a vision of racial equality, civil rights, and human freedom. It is no longer available as a weapon against social reform of any kind." He then asked who won the Court-packing battle of 1937, and his answer was, "The people of the United States won it."[4] His is a blatantly political assessment of the nature of constitutional change. Can the people stand that much realism?

Writing in 1939, Fred Rodell, another Yale Realist, asked an important question: "Why should not the ideas, vitally important to someone as they always are, which are said to lie behind any glob of legal language, be common property, freely available to anyone interested, instead of being the private and secret possession of the legal fraternity?"[5] He answered his own question with the following:

The principles of The Law are made of those outlandish words and phrases because they are not really reasons for decisions but obscure and thoroughly unconvincing rationalization of decisions — and if they were written in ordinary English, everybody could see how silly, how irrelevant and inconclusive they are. If everybody could see how silly legal principles are, The Law would lose its dignity and then its power — and so would the lawyers.[6]

Rodell concluded that, "What lawyers care about in a judge or a fellow lawyer is that he play the legal game with the rest of them — that he talk their talk and respect their rules and not go around sticking pins in their pretty principles."[7] Again, if I understand him correctly, that is exactly the basis of Edward White's criticism of Douglas as the "Anti-Judge."

It is not important whether you or I agree entirely, or in part, with Legal Realism. It is important to remember that such was the milieu which nurtured Douglas's intellectual development, along with that of Thurman Arnold, Jerome Frank, Abe Fortas, and Fred Rodell, among others.[8] It is not surprising that Rodell wrote that Douglas was often "get-it-over-and-done-with decisive" or that Rodell would quote Frank Murphy with approval for these words: "The law . . . knows no finer hour than when it cuts through formal concepts . . . to protect unpopular citizens against discrimination and persecution."[9] So rather than condemning Mr. Justice Douglas for not always playing a traditional judicial game, a game that Realists might have seen only as an exercise in obfuscation, we might try to understand that

Douglas's opinions do make sense as persuasive essays written in support of certain important social values. Constitutional adjudication inevitably requires judges to choose between competing values, often with little textual guidance, and with precedents often offering at best a weak and wavering compass. Who is to say that ordinary citizens are incapable of understanding that? Certainly not Justice Douglas.

II. Active-Negative "Character"

Psychological interpretations of the behavior of political actors are perilous at best. Harold Lasswell was perhaps the key innovator in this area almost sixty years ago,[10] yet anything that can be written on the subject today must still be prudently tentative. In many respects the most interesting and provocative recent work in this area has been James David Barber's attempt to explain American presidents' leadership styles. His use of two dimensions, one, activity/passivity, which involves an assessment of how much energy a president invests in his office, and the other, positive/negative affect, which asks whether a president experiences his office as "happy or sad, enjoyable or discouraging, positive or negative in its main effect," yields a fourfold table into which he is able to sort presidents. The leadership style that seems to include Justice Douglas if we review his published letters, autobiography and published biographies, and the Ball and Urofsky chapters, is the "active-negative," of which Barber writes:

The contradiction here is between relatively intense effort and relatively low emotional reward for that effort. The activity has a compulsive quality, as if the man were trying to make up for something or to escape from anxiety into hard work. He seems ambitious, striving upward, power-seeking. His stance toward the environment is aggressive and he has a persistent problem in managing his aggressive feelings. His self-image is vague and discontinuous. Life is a hard struggle to achieve and hold power, hampered by the condemnations of a perfectionistic conscience. Active-negative types pour energy into the political system, but it is an energy distorted from within.[11]

Certainly Urofsky's "work ethic" thesis can be subsumed under the active-negative type, but the active-negative explanation provides some additional insight. Barber's active-negative type is for most purposes a description of obsessive-compulsive traits. Obsessive-compulsive types are known for the quantity of their activity as well as for its intensity and concentration. Moreover, they exhibit a "special kind of self-awareness, an awareness of the overseer sitting behind and issuing commands, directives, and reminders. . . . It is the self-awareness of a person who is working under pressure with a stopwatch in hand." When not working, obsessive-compulsive people tend to be uncomfortable with activities that lack an aim or purpose; they seek a continuous sense of progress, advancement, or achievement. They have difficulty maintaining warm personal relationships. They are often viewed as cold and distant by others.[12]

Surely, any reader of the two chapters, of White's criticism of Douglas, or of James Simon's biography of Douglas,[13] will be struck by the aptness of these descriptions of obsessive-compulsive personality traits. To be sure, there is not a perfect fit, for there are complexities and contradictions in any human being that cannot be considered in a few pages here. The point is that there may be more involved than a simple commitment to a work ethic in an adequate explanation of Douglas.

According to Barber, active-negative presidents like Lyndon Johnson or Richard Nixon tend eventually to become inflexible in times of crisis; they become less effective at negotiation, less willing to compromise. They tend to fixate on a particular policy and to pursue it with dogged determination even against overwhelming odds. They are likely to go down to ignominious defeat. An active-negative president eventually lives in a world in which he sees himself as besieged by enemies — by antagonistic contradictions.

Barber argues that those are likely to be undesirable traits and disastrous outcomes for our chief executive. However, that may not be so for a Supreme Court justice. Clearly, an active-negative justice would get little psychic gratification from his work. No amount of praise and admiration would ever be sufficient compensation for the emotional energy he would expend. He would have difficulty pausing to enjoy his achievements, whether alone or with others. The work style of the justice would be intense and, while the work lasts, consuming, but when done, it would be something to escape from — even if only into some extrajudicial form of obsessive-compulsive activity like long strenuous hikes. Such a justice would probably have difficulty maintaining warm personal relations — except with a few trusted allies — because of his insecurity and because of the stern measures by which he would judge himself and others. He would accumulate enemies, perhaps even antagonistic ones. Yet such a justice would, in the end, continue to fight doggedly in defense of his principles and values — if need be, alone. All of these traits are described in published accounts of Douglas's life, particularly in Simon's biography. They are not all such bad qualities in a justice of the Supreme Court, depending, of course, on what principles and values the justice holds dear.

Notes

The title (intended somewhat whimsically) was suggested by Mao's 1957 essay "On the Correct Handling of Contradictions Among the People." Excerpts from that essay were prominent in the Little Red Book of Cultural Revolution fame. Note especially the following: "We are confronted by two types of social contradictions — those between ourselves and the enemy and those among the people themselves. The two are totally different in their nature. . . . The contradictions between ourselves and the enemy are antagonistic contradictions" (*Quotations from Chairman Mao*, pp. 45–47).

1. Melvin I. Urofsky and Philip E. Urofsky, eds., *The Douglas Letters: Selections from the Private Papers of Justice William O. Douglas* (Bethesda: Adler and Adler, 1987), p. xix.

2. G. Edward White, "The Anti-Judge: William O. Douglas and the Ambiguities of Individuality," *Virginia Law Review* 74 (1988): 78.

3. Ibid., p. 80.

4. Thurman Arnold, *Fair Fights and Foul: A Dissenting Lawyer's Life* (New York: Harcourt, Brace, and World, 1965), pp. 68–69.

5. Fred Rodell, *Woe Unto You, Lawyers* (New York: Reynal and Hitchcock, 1939), p. 187.

6. Ibid., p. 193.

7. Ibid., p. 196.

8. Laura Kalman, *Legal Realism at Yale, 1927–1960* (Chapel Hill: University of North Carolina Press, 1986).

9. Fred Rodell, *Nine Men: A Political History of the Supreme Court from 1790 to 1955* (New York: Random House, 1955), pp. 273, 279.

10. Harold D. Lasswell, *Psychopathology and Politics* (New York: Viking, 1960).

11. James David Barber, *The Presidential Character: Predicting Performance in the White House* (Englewood Cliffs: Prentice-Hall, 1972), p. 12.

12. David Shapiro, *Neurotic Styles* (New York: Basic Books, 1965), ch. 2.

13. James F. Simon, *Independent Journey: The Life of William O. Douglas* (New York: Harper and Row, 1980).

PART TWO

Douglas and Civil Liberties:
The First Amendment
and Civil Rights

INTRODUCTION:
DOUGLAS AND CIVIL LIBERTIES

Norman Dorsen

IN INTRODUCING the first section of this book that is devoted to civil liberties, I'd like to comment on some themes suggested in the chapters by Professors Days, Powe, and Strossen.

It is no secret that Douglas was a devoted civil libertarian. In every area touched by the Bill of Rights he made a special mark. Free expression, religious freedom, equality, criminal justice, and privacy were all enhanced by his judicial opinions. The volume and consistency of his efforts projected an ethos of liberty to lawyers and the public alike, an ethos that blended with the glamour and vigor of his nonjudicial activities.

Despite this deep commitment to civil liberties, the record suggests that it is the environment that held pride of place in Douglas's hierarchy of values. Professor Ralph Johnson describes how, in a fishing rights case, Douglas voted against strong claims of Native Americans in order "to save the fish." Douglas also wrote an opinion for the Court upholding on environmental grounds — some would say not very strong grounds — a town's zoning law that impaired freedom of association by preventing more than two unmarried people from living in the same household. These and other instances suggest that Charles Reich is correct when he says that the natural environment was at the apex of the Justice's concerns, because, as he saw it, it nurtures all of life and not just human life, the province of civil liberties.

Whether or not civil liberties ranked first among Douglas's concerns, they certainly ranked high. Was his contribution commensurate with his devotion? Scott Powe is dubious, at least in the First Amendment area. He writes that in only six free speech cases did Douglas leave a "substantial doctrinal residue." Accepting this conclusion *arguendo,* one must nevertheless conclude that Douglas's legacy was extremely important. In the first place, six major contributions to free speech doctrine do not seem a small number; few justices have been as fruitful.

Moving to other areas, Douglas's opinion for the Court in *Griswold* and his concurring opinion in *Roe v. Wade* broke much new ground, whatever the ultimate fate of the sexual privacy doctrine. Further, as Professor Strossen demonstrates, there are many seminal Douglas opinions concerning religious liberty. Similarly, Professor Days's chapter convincingly shows how, in the sphere of racial discrimination, Douglas contributed innovatively to the law of state action under the Fourteenth Amendment and to a broad reading of Reconstruction era civil rights statutes. For a final example, Professor Duke's chapter, in the following section, observes that criminal law casebooks have included more of Douglas's opinions on criminal justice than those of any other Supreme Court justice and concludes that he was "the pre-eminent justice in criminal matters." While comparative judgments are always debatable, in my view the record demonstrates that only William J. Brennan, Jr., is Douglas's lifetime competitor in the range and significance of civil liberties opinions.

If Douglas did not do even more, it is widely believed that a principal reason was his failure to attend properly to craft, to the quality of his judicial work. Since it is obvious from many of Douglas's opinions, as well as his earlier law review articles, that he was capable of writing highly professional opinions, one may speculate on why he did not do so consistently. Initially, there were other demands on his life that he was not prepared to sacrifice—books, travel, lectures; the time constraints these activities caused led to hurried, at times almost offhand, opinions. There is also the flattering suggestion that Douglas wrote for a wider world than the legal profession. This thought has a populist ring, because if social change must emanate from the people, it is important for them to understand the principles at the root of their fundamental law.

Another possible reason for apparent deficiencies in his opinions is that, for much of his judicial career, Douglas was trying to change constitutional law in a basic way, and it is not easy to do this while simultaneously linking one's argument to what has gone before. This is especially true for majority opinions, where it is necessary to garner five votes. Some justices may be willing to go along with a ground-breaking doctrine but are not prepared to overrule an earlier case. This means that the opinion for the Court must distinguish the earlier case, but it is not possible to do this if the earlier case is not in fact distinguishable. The attempt to do so will fall flat and leave the author open to criticism for writing an unpersuasive opinion. In addition, a justice such as Douglas who is breaking new ground will often write vague majority opinions either because five justices cannot be mustered to support a specific doctrinal innovation,[1] or it may be the better part of wisdom to be imprecise about the standard of review in a wholly new area.[2] Douglas is not the only example of the phenomenon; William Rehnquist also came to the Court with an agenda for basic change and he, too, has been subjected to the criticism that his opinions are unpersuasive or mask the extent of doctrinal change.

In assessing Douglas's influence, it should be recalled that a Democratic president has not appointed a Supreme Court justice since Lyndon Johnson nominated Thurgood Marshall in 1967. As new colleagues ascended the bench with philosophies largely antithetical to his, natural lines of growth in his opinions were truncated and promising doctrine was eroded. However rigorous his writing, there probably was no way for Douglas to avoid this in the face of an increasingly conservative Supreme Court. Despite the unfavorable political trends, which may have been the greatest impediment to his long-term impact, Douglas left behind a major body of constitutional law. We may hope that the future, perhaps not the immediate future, will witness a renaissance of his ideas for the benefit of generations yet unborn.

Notes

1. See, for example, Douglas's opinion in the poll tax case, *Harper v. Virginia Board of Elections,* 383 U.S. 663 (1966).

2. See, for example, Douglas's opinion in *Levy v. Louisiana,* 391 U.S. 68 (1968), the first case upholding constitutional rights of nonmarital children.

Justice Douglas,
The First Amendment,
and the Protection of Rights

L. A. Powe, Jr.

Reputations evolve. Sometimes the reasons are internal, sometimes external and, of course, often, at least while the subject is living, the two reinforce each other. Justice William O. Douglas fits this pattern. During the 1950s he was one of the few who consistently and publicly opposed all the manifestations of McCarthyism, part of the famous twosome, "Black and Douglas dissenting." During the 1960s, he was an important part of the Warren Court revolution as well as the individualist staking out new frontiers of individual liberties. His reputation as a champion of individual liberties accelerated in the 1970s, partially as a result of his own legend-making and partially because *Griswold* and his separate opinion in *Roe v. Wade* took on great significance in an overpowering social issue.[1]

Three aspects of his career have stood out regardless of specific issues nagging at the body politic. First, few have seen Douglas as a model judge, and almost no one can be found to defend seriously the written part of his judicial career.[2] He came to the bench a Legal Realist; he left it in the same school; and that had consequences. Second, he came to the bench to complete the New Deal revolution and did. He never looked back on the legal issues that had been dominant in the 1930s. Finally, he stood for the individual as no other justice ever has, and nowhere was this more heartfelt, thoroughly documented, and longer on display than in the area of freedom of expression. Anthony Lewis, writing in the *New York Times* on Douglas's retirement, easily observed: "Freedom of thought and expression was his best known theme as a judge."[3] It is thus hardly surprising that discussion of Douglas will revert to this topic.

Years ago, on the occasion of his thirty-fifth anniversary on the Court, I wrote an article, "Evolution to Absolutism: Justice Douglas and the First Amendment," in an attempt to correct the then-prevailing view (aided by Douglas himself) that Douglas had always been at the frontiers of First Amendment protection.[4] In fact, Douglas joined the Court as a mainstream New Deal liberal quite content to work within Holmes's clear and present danger test. But with the beginnings of McCarthyism, Douglas moved toward a more speech-protective stance; that turned into a progression that

eventually led him to the most speech-protective positions ever taken and
to his mislabeled liberal absolutism.

Because such progressions do not just happen, my other goal was to identify the factors that pushed Douglas into his leftward evolution. I suggested
one was the passing from the scene of his patron, Franklin Delano Roosevelt; another was his summer travels in the Third World; and a final one
was experience *simpliciter,* which by the mid-1950s caused him to believe
that restrictions on speech were invariably motivated by fear or worse and
were virtually, per se, unconstitutional. I omitted one other factor; understandably, if not entirely commendably, I pulled my punches and failed to
attribute part of the evolution to the waning of Douglas's presidential ambitions. With that omission corrected and possibly more emphasis on the ways
McCarthyism seared the conscience, I think the impetus for this shift is there.
But even if one disagrees on the reasons, that Douglas moved from mainstream liberalism to something radically different is not challengeable.

With the passage of time, possibly the easiest way to show how far Douglas moved is by comparison to other accepted liberals. In the 1970s when
Justices Brennan and Marshall were establishing their reputations as important members of the Court's long-standing tradition of liberal dissent, Douglas was dissenting from their positions. Thus while academic liberals embrace
Justice Marshall's opinion in *Grayned v. City of Rockford,*[5] using it instead
of Douglas's impassioned and eloquent dissent in *Adderly v. Florida,*[6] as a
cornerstone of how a well-functioning public forum doctrine should work,[7]
Grayned, in fact, was an 8-to-Douglas opinion. His solo dissent, like his
dissent in *Adderly,* raised serious questions about whether there was any
disruption shown, and if there were, whether it was caused by police action.
Brennan and Marshall were moving left, and at least in part like Douglas
in the early 1950s, they were able to establish clearly their liberalism because
of the movement of the Court the other way. Yet had Douglas remained
on the Court as a measuring stick, they would have been consistently flanked.

But there is vastly more to Douglas and the First Amendment than his
ability to significantly flank the two justices who currently pose as the principal champions of unrestricted freedom of expression. There is no easy way
to capture the totality of Douglas's positions on freedom of expression, because conventional standards of evaluation are not fully adequate to assess
his contributions. For example, I have already suggested that Douglas had
an insignificant doctrinal impact on any area of law (the fundamental rights
strand of equal protection possibly excepted), including the First Amendment. Yet to evaluate Douglas by doctrine alone would be not only to use
a standard he would be offended by, but to miss the significant aspects of
his contribution to our understanding of the First Amendment.

Also commenting on the occasion of Douglas's thirty-fifth Court anniversary, Thomas Emerson, the foremost academic writer on the First Amendment, singled out for special praise Douglas's "remarkable ability to grasp

the realities of the system of freedom of expression . . . understand[ing] the apparatus of repression."[8] Although Emerson also thought Douglas praiseworthy for his doctrinal efforts, his focus on Douglas's "grasp [of] the realities" is the key. It is Douglas's comprehension of how factual situations play out in the First Amendment context that sets him apart. But demonstrating that proper First Amendment adjudication requires eyes focused on underlying realities was not his signal contribution. No, that contribution, in which Black joined equally, was to demonstrate, contrary to the then-prevailing ideology, that judges could in fact vigorously enforce constitutional rights and need not defer to the institutions attacking these rights. It took time, but the courageous stands of Douglas and Black throughout the McCarthy era allowed a subsequent era of law professors and law students to understand that enforcement of constitutional guarantees was inconsistent with neither democratic governance nor judicial independence. That is quite a legacy, and in the final section of this paper I wish to discuss it more fully.

I. Doctrine

When Douglas came to the Court, he, like the others, adopted Holmes's clear and present danger test. For a decade the test provided a helpful and workable methodology for disposing of the expression cases coming to the Court. Then *Douds* foreshadowed the reluctance in *Dennis* to apply clear and present danger seriously to the Smith Act convictions of the Communist Party leadership.[9]

Douglas dissented in *Dennis* and made a heroic attempt to apply clear and present danger to the facts of the postwar reformation of the Communist party. Neither Court nor country seemed particularly interested. A year later, the majority sustained a group libel conviction based on words alone in *Beauharnais v. Illinois,*[10] and Douglas again applied the Holmes test in dissent. Douglas easily showed there was no clear and present danger, while Frankfurter, for the Court, simply announced that clear and present danger was irrelevant because the category of speech involved was wholly unprotected. For Douglas that was it; if no one else was going to use clear and present danger, neither would he.

Beauharnais was prologue for the obscenity discussion in *Roth v. United States.*[11] There being no clear and present danger and the majority not wishing to invalidate obscenity law, the majority again found clear and present danger irrelevant. Dissenting, Douglas announced the test that would be his trademark. Speech could not be suppressed until it became so brigaded with action that it was indistinguishable from action itself. This test, which because it did not as rigidly dichotomize, is a smoother formulation than either Emerson's expression/action[12] or Justice Black's speech/conduct[13] distinction, but it never took hold. There are several reasons for its lack of success, two of which merit notice. The first is that in all probability it would protect too much speech and therefore is useful only to those who wish to protect more speech than the Court was. Second, Justice Douglas could not apply his own test, and if he could not, the odds are favorable that others could not either.

As to the first, Douglas first enunciated his test in the obscenity context. If applied, all obscene materials would receive constitutional protection unless reading the materials operated as an instantaneous trigger to illegal sexual conduct. Given that there was no evidence that obscenity led to any illegal conduct, even a weak version of the clear and present danger test would have been sufficient to invalidate the laws; speech brigaded with action was overkill. The same holds true for the group libel treated in *Beauharnais*.

Where Douglas's test would work well was in the Smith Act context. Douglas's *Dennis* dissent emphasized from the beginning that the government failed to show *any* acts at all. The case was speech and speech alone. Douglas's new test would require that any future prosecution demonstrate not only the requisite speech but also some other actions—such as, for example, the illegal purchase of explosives.

Douglas's test, coming in the context of cases involving Communists, racists, and pornographers, could hardly have been expected to command a majority, when in fact a majority of the Court found the traditional clear and present danger test too speech protective. It is possible, of course, that Douglas was betting on the future and hoping that a newly constituted majority would adopt his very speech protective test.

Yet even assuming that was the case, Douglas's own inability to use the test properly in certain circumstances could not have enhanced its appeal to others. Consider first, *O'Brien v. United States*,[14] the draft card burning case. Initially, Douglas dissented, with the irrelevant argument that the case was about the legality of the Vietnam War. Then a year later, in his *Brandenburg* concurrence, he announced a right to burn the draft card.[15] That's fine, but on *O'Brien*'s facts why wasn't that either action *simpliciter* or "speech brigaded with action"? He never answered, although presumably O'Brien's pure heart would make his flame basically speech.

Much more troublesome than *O'Brien* is Douglas's opinion in the second *Communist Party v. Subversive Activities Control Board* case.[16] At issue was the requirement, after the findings of the SACB, that the party register with the government. As Douglas and everyone else knew, registration was a death sentence for a political group, because exposure as a member of a perceived fifth column would lead to unemployment and ostracism. Yet Douglas sustained the requirement against the party's First Amendment challenge by finding—for the first and only time—an example of speech brigaded with action.[17] What is so interesting about his 1961 opinion is that it tracks all too well Justice Jackson's explanation a decade earlier of why it was legitimate to single out Communist party members for special disabilities.[18] Nearing the end of the era of Communist party litigation, Douglas was, for the first time, buying into the rationale that the Court's majority had been using to justify its fairly consistent rejections of First Amendment claims. As a result, he split from Black for the only time subsequent to the initiation of the loyalty-security program, when Black, rather than Douglas, would adopt the more speech-protective position.

Maybe there is an explanation for Douglas's opinion. The one that jumps to mind is that every so often his mind was simply too quick and he got something completely wrong and never looked back. *Communist Party v. Subversive Activities Control Board* was hardly the most important of the Communist cases of 1961,[19] and Douglas's First Amendment statements came in the context where he was striking down the registration requirement on Fifth Amendment grounds, anyway. Nevertheless, his opinion there and in *O'Brien* suggest that his overall formulation, like those of Emerson or Black or anyone else, was no panacea — even for himself.

No overview could solve the myriad problems facing the Court. Speech brigaded with action was, in fact, vastly superior to the gutting of the First Amendment advocated and implemented by Vinson, Frankfurter, and Harlan, with their balancing tests spewing forth "government wins" automatically. And there is no need to fault Douglas doctrinally because his solution was no better than some others.

Were that all, Douglas would get off lightly. But despite thirty-five years on the Court, it is difficult to suggest a Douglas First Amendment opinion, whether written for the Court (which would have to come from two periods, the 1940s or the mid-1960s) or separately, that is of any doctrinal importance. My list of potential candidates consists of only six opinions. Four are majority — *Terminiello*[20] (1949) and three mid-1960s leftovers from the McCarthy era[21] — and two are separate opinions — *Adderly,* involving a jail demonstration, and *CBS v. Democratic National Committee,*[22] in which Douglas concluded that radio and television were entitled to the same full First Amendment protections as newspapers.

Terminiello, with its breathtaking language that speech may "best serve its high purpose" when it creates dissatisfaction or "even stirs people to anger,"[23] had a long season of importance during the heyday of overbreadth analysis.[24] Many statutes, even narrowed down a bit, would cut off speech well before Douglas's *Terminiello* language, when taken seriously, would allow. No Douglas opinion in the speech areas has ever matched the importance of this one.

Yet *Terminiello* was a missed doctrinal opportunity. The facts called out for some discussion of the circumstances under which police should arrest rather than protect the speaker.[25] Indeed, *Terminiello* was that rarest of hostile audience cases, for it appears the police might not have been able to engage in successful crowd control. Had Douglas written *Terminiello* to deal with its actual facts, it seems unlikely that we would have had the absurdity of the Court's authorizing the shutting down of Feiner's speech on the basis

of modest heckling two years later,[26] and we might still have that key opinion delineating appropriate police behavior in the hostile audience situation,
one that might last to this day.

The three mop-up Communist cases were decided years after the hysteria
ended; as such, they afforded an opportunity to clarify entire areas. But
Douglas wrote such short — and presumably quick — opinions that the full
opportunity to clarify may have been lost. Because hysteria-driven periods
occur only episodically, the fact that Douglas's opinions do not clarify will
make them decidedly easier to ignore.

Lamont v. Postmaster General[27] is important for two reasons. One hundred and seventy-four years after ratification of the Bill of Rights, the Court
finally held that a federal statute violated the First Amendment. *Lamont* also
has doctrinal significance. By invalidating the requirement that a person register in order to receive literature from certain Communist countries, *Lamont* implicitly recognizes that the First Amendment includes a right to receive information — "implicitly" because Douglas's majority opinion does not
say so explicitly. Brennan's concurring opinion does, however, and because
of that, when *Lamont* is mentioned for its notion of a right to receive, the
citation is to Brennan, not Douglas.[28] Brennan was able to make the obvious explicit in a little over a page; not only is it inexplicable, it is inexcus-
able, that Douglas did not do so too.

Neither *Elfbrandt,* a loyalty oath case, nor *DeGregory,* an investigating
committee case,[29] contains something equivalent of a right to receive, although
in the event of another hysteria their teachings could become important.
Elfbrandt applied the *Scales*[30] criminal standard — knowing membership with
specific intent — in the civil disabilities area. Although, as in *Lamont,* Douglas
did not explain that this was what he was doing and therefore did not explain
why the criminal standard was appropriate in these civil disability cases, the
fact is that *Elfbrandt* necessarily held their equivalence, and that could be
important in the future.

DeGregory seems to hold that when a person questioned says he is not
a Communist and has no current information about the party, he may not
be questioned about distant membership absent a compelling state interest.
This would mean a witness could demand that the bingo question — "are
you now or have you ever been" — be broken into two parts, and a negative
answer to the first might preclude the need to answer the second. Yet the
facts — New Hampshire's Attorney General acting as a one-man legislative
investigating committee to protect that state from its internal Communist
menace — could serve to limit the holding.

The *Adderly* dissent, involving the jailhouse civil rights demonstration,
may well be Douglas's finest single opinion. It blends the facts into a doctrinal view that makes sense, while reaching the correct result with an underlying passion and appeal to history. The Court could adopt the dissent in
Adderly today and markedly improve its public forum doctrine. But public

forum doctrine has gone a long way from *Adderly,* and it appears that time and events have passed it by. By contrast, Douglas's opinion in *CBS v. Democratic National Committee* has been ignored for its fifteen-year existence, although it remains the exclusive statement by a justice that broadcasting and print are entitled to identical First Amendment rights.

Although I can find only these few Douglas doctrinal contributions, Emerson believed that Douglas made a major theoretical contribution—indeed a "totally new dimension"[31]—to freedom of expression with his emphasis on individual fulfillment as one of the cornerstone values protected. In like vein, Vincent Blasi was able to find the single best example of his checking value theory in a Douglas opinion.[32] Neither view is surprising. Douglas wrote extensively in the First Amendment areas, he believed more strongly than any other justice in the individual, and his fear of governmental oppression, which grew steadily as he aged, may never be matched. But it was for others, the Emersons, the Blasis, the Meiklejohns, to piece together the theoretical structures of the First Amendment. Douglas opinions would naturally be helpful, but as William Cohen so accurately notes, Douglas was a pragmatist; he left theory-building to others.[33]

All in all, Douglas's doctrinal contributions are simply not impressive. Moreover, it is not a matter of passage of time, the normal fading of an ex-justice. The record shows that Douglas's many critics, both while he was sitting and afterward, were right. His opinions were not models; they appear too hastily written; and they are easy to ignore. For those of us who think Douglas was correct in his results and instincts, this is too bad.

The reasons for his doctrinal insignificance are not news to anyone: one was Legal Realism and the other, not unrelated by any means, was his contempt of what he perceived as the legal establishment—the Harvard Law School and its law review alumni association functioning as the American Law Institute. So long as he perceived that the criticisms of his opinions came from a conservative legal establishment, he did not care. His pejorative reference to doctrinal argument in Supreme Court opinions as "Harvard fly paper" fully states his position and the contempt he felt for his critics.[34]

Furthermore, Douglas simply drank at the well of Legal Realism too long and too thoroughly. With the other founders of the movement, he stripped away the silly doctrinal shrouds that marked legal activities. In the process, he concluded that doctrine was irrelevant, the explanatory cloak for decisions reached on more significant grounds, and thus he did not—indeed he could not—take doctrine seriously.

Douglas, the Legal Realist, turns out not to have been much of a judicial realist. He had to know that almost everyone else believed or wanted doctrine to have a part in the legal system. By wholly eschewing doctrine, he not only suffered a loss of professional esteem, he suffered a loss of influence. He erred in failing to realize that others, including those not wedded to the judicial conservatism of Harvard, did take doctrine seriously. With his acknowledged abilities he could have held to the view that doctrine was a joke and nevertheless explained well enough in traditional terms to bind others who believed in doctrine, whether by lack of insight or an acceptable alternative, to his own views. Unfortunately, the intense combination of Legal Realism and impatience prevented this.[35]

Douglas was a man of action, not reflection. He wrote his dissents before the author of the majority would put pen to paper; he chafed while waiting for the Chief Justices to assign majorities; he began writing his own instantly — I mean that literally, not figuratively — on receipt of assignment.[36] In a large, unfortunate sense, Douglas was miscast in the judiciary. Although elevation to the Supreme Court seems the appropriate reward for a president to bestow on an outstanding lawyer, in Douglas's case, high executive office would have better suited his abilities. He was the quintessential executive. He believed in and exemplified efficiency; he knew how to make decisions, even tough ones. With the sole exception (see Part III) of the willingness to stand up and be counted when doing so had obvious costs and seemingly few benefits, the executive strengths that propelled his meteoric rise were not judicial strengths. Because Douglas was a genius, there is a feeling of loss from so wonderful a mind's eschewing the minimum formalities of the job, even if Douglas was right that the formulation of doctrine was wholly irrelevant to the true operation of the legal system.

II. Facts

If Legal Realism was Douglas's undoing when it came to doctrine, it turned out to be his strength when analyzing how to proceed. The sine qua non of Legal Realism was the belief that doctrine obscured more than it explained about why a court decided as it did. Thereafter, Legal Realists split into a variety of approaches to the law.

Douglas was a functionalist. For him, nothing mattered more than the facts, and he saw no inherent limits on where he should look. In this regard, he stands in stark contrast to Holmes and the tradition he helped impart to libertarians. Holmes never cared much for facts: when he sent Eugene Debs to jail, his opinion did not bother to mention who Debs was.[37] Brandeis, by contrast, was known for his devotion to facts. Douglas would follow in Brandeis's steps, but when the key cases came up it was not only his opinion, but also his reading of the facts and vote, that protected freedom of speech; thus it is not conceivable that Douglas would have voted to sustain Anita Whitney's conviction, as Brandeis did.[38]

Any justice who successfully searches out the underlying facts of litigation will be rewarded. But as important as facts are generally, nowhere do they attain the significance they hold in the First Amendment area. Difficult cases often turn on determinations of dangerousness of a surrounding situation, and any mistake made by miscalculating or overemphasizing the danger turns what should be a constitutionally protected activity into criminal conduct instead. Furthermore, as Douglas recognized, speech is often fragile; self-censorship comes too easily. A mistaken conviction of a dissenter may not only silence him, but many others as well, who now have reason to fear similar police action against themselves.

Douglas found facts for his opinions in two places. First came the record—what happened and why. Vastly more important in the First Amendment area were Douglas's sensitive antennae for the necessary preconditions for freedom of speech. Emerson aptly noted that Douglas "understood the apparatus of repression and sought to attack it at every point."[39] Whether by action or inaction, governments would attempt to ignore the command of the First Amendment to tolerate even caustic attacks on the established order, and Douglas, more than any other justice, was sensitive to the realities surrounding political dissenters.

Nowhere was Douglas's ability to work with facts better displayed than the case that could have been (but was not) the most important First Amendment case ever decided: the Communist conspiracy in *Dennis*. Ironically, the grant of certiorari in *Dennis* was limited specifically to exclude the facts.[40] Nevertheless, the opinions of Vinson as well as Jackson and Douglas looked to both the record and contemporary America for factual predicates. Black and Frankfurter did not, as each presented a theory for decision that was not fact-specific.

Unlike the other opinions, Douglas's was fact-specific, albeit by beginning with what was *not* in the record. Douglas was taking the government argument head on, by pointing out that there was no conspiracy to attempt an overthrow. Indeed, there was no "teaching the techniques of sabotage, the assassination of the President, the filching of documents from public files, the planting of bombs, the art of street warfare, and the like."[41] Thus the case was about speech. Douglas, alone among the justices, tells what was introduced at trial: principally the teachings of four books about Marxist-Leninist doctrine.[42] The books were not banned—just teaching them with the appropriate belief in their contents, the evidence on which a jury convicted and the Second Circuit Court affirmed.

Frankfurter sharply rejected any notion of "preferred freedoms"; for Frankfurter there were no exceptions to the rule of the presumption of constitutionality.[43] Douglas took the contrary position, that "freedom of speech is the rule, not the exception."[44] He saw the case as appropriate for application of clear and present danger. And unlike anyone else, he made a serious effort to apply the test beginning with the essential, yet overlooked, point that the issue was whether the Communist party in the United States presented a clear and present danger, not whether "Soviet Russia and her Red Army are a threat to world peace."[45]

With the focus on the Communists in America, Douglas noted that free speech had destroyed the party as a political force, and economic recovery had ended the chance for revolutionaries to gain adherents: "the doctrine of Soviet revolution is exposed in all of its ugliness and the American people want none of it."[46] But he also could note that the fact Communists were not a political force was not dispositive. To find a clear and present danger, the Court would need to know the extent of successful infiltration into the military, transportation, and other critical industries—and the record was silent on this. Furthermore, the Court was being asked to assume that all the efforts of Congress, the states, labor unions, and various loyalty boards "were so futile as to leave the country on the edge of grave peril."[47] Instead, Douglas concluded that "the invisible army of petitioners is the best known, the most beset and the least thriving of any fifth column in history."[48]

Douglas summed up the majority vote acidly. "Only those held by fear and panic could think" that the Communist party was an internal menace.[49] As he and Black would note with unfortunate regularity, the methods of a Communist state were used to fight internal Communism.[50] Thus Douglas quoted Vishinsky's *The Law of the Soviet State* for the proposition that there could be no freedom of speech for foes of socialism and stated that "our concern should be that we accept no such standard for the United States."[51]

Douglas's opinion presented facts based on what was not charged, what was introduced into the record, and what the best available extrajudicial evidence of the party position was. It marks the first and last time a justice attempted seriously to use the clear and present danger test in circumstances when the outcome might have been in doubt. Almost forty years later, his analysis still holds. It would be hard to do much better today.

A similar claim can be made for his early perception of the undercurrent of repression that was building in the late 1960s. To be sure, Douglas was sensitive to the problems of antiwar dissent, and it would have been preferable had he not taken *O'Brien* so casually. Yet it was not just his lone vote to allow draft card burning that set him apart again; a new brand of dissent was in the air, Douglas felt, along with a new willingness to use the power of government to repress. His willingness to identify himself extrajudicially with youth questioning authority all over the nation led him to write *Points of Rebellion*[52] and Representative Gerald Ford to attempt to gain Douglas's seat for another safe establishment vote on the Court.

It also was the impetus for his intemperate separate opinions in the *Younger v. Harris* sextet[53] and the *Keith*[54] litigation. However spineless and establishment-oriented federal judges might seem, in many communities they provided the only hope, "the thin black line between order and chaos."[55] In various places—from Mayor Daley's Chicago to the Deep South—the only chance for recognition of constitutional rights, especially that of political dissent, came in getting protection at the federal courthouse.

These cases marked another split, and an exceptionally important one, between Black and Douglas. Just as Black had left the facts for others in *Dennis,* so too, here, he ignored the underlying possibilities of repression, this time to author the majority opinions barring federal judicial intervention on behalf of political dissent, leaving the would-be federal claimant at the mercy of the very government he wished to protest. For Douglas, this was an abdication of the judiciary's "special responsibility to prevent an erosion of the individual's constitutional rights."[56]

Douglas really let his views come out in the *Keith* litigation. At issue was the constitutionality of the Nixon administration's domestic national security wiretapping. While the Court agreed with Douglas, he went far beyond his brethren in describing the domestic climate as he saw it:

We are currently in the throes of another national seizure of paranoia resembling the hysteria which surrounded the Alien and Sedition Acts, the Palmer Raids, and the McCarthy era. Those who register dissent or who petition their governments for redress are subjected to scrutiny by grand juries, by the FBI, and even by the military. Their associates are interrogated. Their homes are bugged and their telephones are wiretapped. They are befriended by secret government informers. Their patriotism and loyalty are questioned.[57]

What is striking, even at this distance, is that this wholly unjudicial and seemingly injudicious blast is so accurate in describing the Nixon repression in action. Yet Douglas's opinion was delivered a month *before* the Watergate break-in and therefore before a single revelation of the Nixon encroachment on civil liberties had been made public. Douglas's *Keith* opinion, like his *Dennis* dissent, demonstrated his comprehension of what was really happening in America and a call to be willing to enforce the Constitution in the face of adversity.

While it is easy to say there is a model there, in fact I doubt it. G. Edward White's portrayal of Douglas as a cosmic anti-judge, even if overstated, captures an essential point: Douglas was unique.[58] He was part of the governing establishment of the nation for forty years. Yet the intensity of his fear of government, with its ability to oppress individuals in body and spirit, was genuine and unmatched.

Douglas may have been a one-shot error of the appointing process, yet his sensitive treatment of facts in the First Amendment area provides a yardstick for criticism of others. In our own era of the anesthetizing "formulaic Constitution,"[59] more factual inquiry into social conditions offers a way to comprehend the workings of the system of freedom of expression as well as a way of enriching the judicial dialogue. We could use a little of both right now.

III. By Example

With his emphasis on individual actions and responsibilities, I do not think it would bother Douglas at all to hear that, when it was all said and done, his major First Amendment contribution was having been on the Court during the 1950s and demonstrating for all to see—and for many to condemn—that a justice could defend civil liberties during crisis times. Furthermore, the prevailing legal theory was that it could not and should not be done—that judges should recognize limits on judicial competence and recognize and validate the actions of democratic institutions, unless those actions were manifestly unreasonable. The Japanese Exclusion Cases demonstrate how circumscribed a class "unreasonable" can be, especially in times of great national stress.[60] By going against the grain during the McCarthy era, Douglas suffered a professional loss of reputation but also assisted in the discrediting of the prevailing ideology, which in the First Amendment area self-destructed in a series of cases beginning in 1959.

Dennis decapitated the Communist party leadership and finished justifying the constitutionality of the essentials of the government program.[61] The issues that remained to be decided were (1) Did the First Amendment place any limits on the new type of legislative investigation the House Un-American Activities Committee (HUAC) was pioneering? (2) Was it relevant that a person joined the Communist party for political rather than revolutionary reasons? and (3) Would the parallel state loyalty-security program receive a like imprimatur to that given the federal program? The first would wait until the end of the decade and the settling of the constitutionality of southern segregation. The latter two were ready for resolution almost immediately, the membership problem being presented in the context of exiling long-term resident aliens.

Part of the 1950 McCarran Act implemented Congress's awesome power over resident aliens. At issue in *Galvan v. Press*[62] was a statutory deportation of an alien who had lived and worked here for thirty years, marrying while here. But he had the misfortune of joining the party during World War II, when to do so was perfectly legal. Although Galvan ceased membership in 1946 (some four years before the Act was passed), the statute retroactively reached him, and the majority sustained its application. Douglas and Black were able to use the retroactive harshness of the statute as well as the appealing (and therefore appalling) facts to dissent effectively, even in the face of a long-standing rule of complete congressional power. Exiling people, especially those with American spouses and children and no real connection with their original homeland, leaves all the rhetorical cards in the hands of those who oppose it. But Douglas and Black were alone; aliens remained an easy target for majoritarian wrath and xenophobia.

Deportation as punishment for innocent membership was harsher, but the outcome was no different than occurred in almost all the Red cases prior to McCarthy's fall. The two cases sustaining facets of New York's loyalty-security program showed that nuanced distinctions were not of great interest to the majority of the Court. *Adler*[63] sustained (in the preenforcement stage) the Feinberg Law, with its prima facie presumption that membership in a listed organization was grounds for taking a teacher out of a classroom. Only Black and Douglas thought that important First Amendment rights — not to mention careers — would be sacrificed by the law's operation.

More than a hint of how it would operate came when New York's governing board of the medical profession stripped Dr. Edward Barsky of his right to practice medicine for six months because he had been convicted of failing to turn over to HUAC the subpoenaed papers of the Joint Anti-Fascist Refugee Committee, an organization he had joined after he returned from treating Loyalists wounded during the Spanish Civil War.[64] Douglas closed with another plea: "When a doctor cannot save lives in America because he is opposed to Franco in Spain, it is time to call a halt and look critically at the neurosis that has possessed us."[65] And in fact, largely on technical, nonconstitutional grounds, the Court began to do so for several years beginning in 1955, thereby alleviating, in individual cases, the hardships inflicted.[66] Not until the end of the decade would major constitutional issues return.

During the 1950s, a generation of scholars firmly committed to the legitimacy of both the New Deal and the Rule of Law made Harvard the "place to be," by grappling with nothing less than creating a new jurisprudence recognizing and building on Realist insights but nevertheless striving to cabin judicial discretion in ways consistent with democratic governance.[67] Process jurisprudence[68] first and foremost stressed the reasoning process used by judges to reach and explain results. Adherents saw the Supreme Court as engaged in a collective reasoning process, achieving the correct result by a mature judgment, which would then be explained in an opinion written so that all readers could see that the relevant considerations had been vented fully.[69] Because judges were necessarily *not* the predominant lawgivers when significant, rather than interstitial, choices were to be made, it was essential to the cabining process that they give due deference to prior doctrinal development.

Beyond, but a necessary part of, its doctrinal emphasis, the process jurisprudence would further limit discretion by institutional allocation. That is, on issues where other institutions have superior knowledge or fact-finding abilities, judges should defer. The judiciary did not have to roll over and die, but simply recognize, as Stone had said in 1936, that judges are not the only actors who have the capacity to govern.[70] Much of the judicial function would be process-oriented: demanding that institutions maintain procedural regularity and choosing the institution best suited for deciding the question at hand. The central allocational fact in constitutional adjudication was that the judiciary was the inappropriate institution when the issues were political — that is, when the outcome depended on a choice to interpret the social world in one way rather than another.[71] Thus a deference to the outcomes of the democratic process was an inherent facet of process jurisprudence.

Because the new jurisprudence was the creation of New Dealers, there was no necessary reason why Black and Douglas should have fallen outside its pale. But its demands pushed in directions Black and Douglas could not go — even if they had wished. First, a demand for deference to various decision makers, be they the president, Congress, state legislators, HUAC, or the Board of Regents in New York, could not be squared with what Black and Douglas in a post-Roosevelt America felt was their duty to defer to the Constitution. The superior competence of HUAC to ascertain the needs to invade political associations did not seem to them to be particularly apt. And, one might add, given Douglas's incredible mind, he was not the deferring type.

Second, in the various civil liberties areas there either were no well-developed sets of precedents or those that existed were, from Black's and Douglas's perspectives, simply wrong. Accordingly, following precedent would produce unacceptable results. The two justices simply did not believe there was a necessity of lengthy explanation of why (or why not) civil liberties were to be protected in either good times or bad. Furthermore, Douglas, as explained in Part I, flatly rejected the craft demands of process jurisprudence.

Surprisingly, Harvard scholarship of the 1950s did not touch the Communist cases.[72] The scholarly focus was on other areas where, in fact, Black and Douglas were not as far apart from their brethren. But that did not help the reputations of either Douglas or Black, for a number of reasons.[73] One was Frankfurter, who helped create process jurisprudence and, in turn, for whom process jurisprudence was made. A belief flourished that Frankfurter — "Our Felix" as he was known at Harvard Law School — was, at that time, a shining light of Western jurisprudence. It did not take a Harvard education to see he was voting differently in the First Amendment McCarthy era cases than Black and Douglas.[74]

A basic point was that Black and especially Douglas were not of the caliber to be taken seriously as judges. One law professor who was a Harvard Law School 1950s LL.B. and an early 1960s teaching fellow described it as an overwhelming ambiance of real hostility to Douglas and Black; in the converse, it was described by a president of the *Review* as a generally accepted dogma that Frankfurter was right on issues of constitutional law. Well-trained Harvard lawyers in the prestigious positions of American law praised Frankfurter while they treated Black and Douglas with scorn and contempt. Their votes, their analyses, were simply not the workings of "first-rate lawyers."[75]

Law professor Jack Getman (Harvard Law School class of 1958) writes of going to Harvard after City College of New York and a two-year military enlistment, with Douglas and Black as his legal heroes. But he soon discovered that they "turned out to be woefully deficient in all . . . technical professional ways." He has wryly summed it up: "One of the things that makes you proudest of a Harvard legal education is that you can explain why Douglas is wrong."[76]

When the Supreme Court returned to the Communist cases as the 1960s were about to begin, the major opinions were written by Harlan (who was perceived to be a weaker, junior version of Frankfurter), joined by Frankfurter, since they were following in the footsteps of his *Dennis* opinion, with Black and Douglas (and now Warren and Brennan) dissenting.[77] Once again, the adherents of process jurisprudence concluded that Black and Douglas had been bested. In dissent, Black and Douglas argued that the First Amendment was an absolute.[78] The majority, by contrast, viewed that claim as preposterous and held that balancing all the various interests at stake was the appropriate way of solving the issue. The academic debate accepted the debate on the terms set by the justices. On those terms, Black and Douglas "had" to be wrong. It was simply inconceivable that "all" speech was "absolutely" protected under the Constitution. Numerous counterexamples were possible — and Harlan supplied them in a single devastating and unanswered footnote[79] — and if Black and Douglas believed, for example, that perjury was the exercise of First Amendment rights, then they were not merely wrong; their position was not worthy of discussion. Harvard's dean, Erwin Griswold, made the point wonderfully when he recalled a large illuminated sign outside a New Orleans church which read: "God said it. We believe it. That's all there is to it."[80] The absolutism of Black and Douglas "seems a similar approach."[81] What was not considered was that Black and Douglas were using absolutism as a summation of how the "balance" worked out after a decade of deciding cases growing out of the hysteria.[82]

It was unacceptable under process jurisprudence to use absolutism as a rhetorical device to express an attitude about how First Amendment adjudication should be approached,[83] because if absolutism was rhetorical, it would "gravely . . . deprecate and damage the process" of decision making which must be "as deliberate and conscious as men can make it."[84] Both possibilities, rhetorical or *sub silentio* summation of experience, were incompatible with the premises of process jurisprudence; furthermore, Black and Douglas by their willingness to reassess the need for action were invading the legislative province of value choice. Thus they were taken literally, which, not surprisingly, confirmed existing prejudices.

Nor did process jurisprudence adherents ask whether, in operation, balancing was also a rhetorical cover. One facet of the cases was the fact that the majority seemed at least as absolutist as Black and Douglas. The majority was absolutely convinced that no matter what was in the scales to be balanced, when the government was on the prowl for Communists, the balance was always to favor the government. *Barenblatt,*[85] *Wilkinson,*[86] *Konigsberg,*[87] and *Anastaplo*[88] make clear for any who would read that Black and Douglas were right not only in their criticisms of the balancers' technique, but in the process were validating their positions taken in the earlier cases.

Lloyd Barenblatt had been called before HUAC in 1954 and was asked questions pertaining to whether he had been a party member as a graduate student at Michigan after World War II. Barenblatt eschewed the Fifth and instead took the First. Harlan's majority embraced the competency point of process neutrality by stating that the Court would not pass judgment on either the wisdom or efficacy of the activities of HUAC. Without even considering First Amendment interests, the majority bluntly announced in the penultimate paragraph: "We conclude that the balance between the individual and the government interests here at stake must be struck in favor of the latter, and that therefore the provisions of the First Amendment have not been offended."[89]

Black and Douglas demolished the majority, first by demonstrating that balancing was inappropriate and then by showing that, if the Court really believed balancing was valid, a proper balance would have resulted in reversal of Barenblatt's conviction. Had the balancing debate ended here, *Barenblatt* might have passed as a somewhat belated validation of HUAC, years after the issue was relevant. But in several 1961 cases the same majority made clear that when it said "balance" in the context of any mention of the 'c'-word, it meant that the government was to win no matter what the facts.

The Court adopted the same stance when Wilkinson "took the First" on being haled before HUAC in 1958(!) and when Konigsburg and Anastaplo refused to answer bar committees' questions about party membership and were refused admission to legal practice. Black and Douglas powerfully demonstrated that balancing "proves pitifully and pathetically inadequate to cope with an invasion of individual liberty so plainly unjustified that even the majority apparently feels compelled expressly to disclaim 'any view upon the wisdom of the State's action.'"[90]

If Black and Douglas were right in 1961, saying the same things that they had always said, maybe they were right earlier. Maybe protecting First Amendment rights against government would not have brought either the nation or the judiciary to its knees. Maybe it makes sense to stand up for constitutional rights and stand against injustice even when democratic institutions and the legal establishment argue to the contrary. A generation of law students coming into law schools in the 1960s would find those "maybes" unnecessary. When southern governments attempted to wrap themselves in the cloak of the Court's Red-hunting doctrines to fight civil rights groups, it was impossible to argue plausibly—although Harlan for one tried[91]—that neutrality required blacks to lose because Reds had lost earlier. The civil rights litigation provided timely and powerful reinforcement for the positions of Black and Douglas. Moreover, Black's aging separated the two, to Douglas's overwhelming advantage.

Although the results of Black and Douglas were accepted and validated, their styles, especially Douglas's, were not. As G. Edward White demonstrates, there are incredible institutional pressures for judges to eschew Douglas's Realist stance, and subsequent justices have had little trouble there.[92] Furthermore, process jurisprudence in operation, although not in intent, had turned out to be a conservative doctrine in the sense that its application tended to reinforce the status quo.[93] As the status quo became a liberal one, liberals could more easily embrace its tenets, while conservatives would wonder why liberal doctrine was entitled to respect simply because it was there. In the years following their respective departures from the Court it was not necessary to embrace either Douglas's style or Black's attempt to create a jurisprudence to justify liberalism. Douglas and Black were right, and they showed that by being willing to stand for what was right: men, lawyers, judges — yes, maybe even the law — can do what is right.

IV. Conclusion

With Frankfurter off the Court, a firm majority existed to implement most positions that Black and Douglas voted for. No longer was it an open question of whether the Constitution would be actively enforced to protect individual liberties but rather only to what lengths the Warren Court majority was willing to go. Although both Black and Douglas lived to see majorities holding to their views, Douglas again moved to dissenter and began to stake out positions for the next generation, one that never came because the era of liberal dominance of the presidency had ended.

   Unlike Black in his twilight, Douglas found a new constituency, the nation's youth. At a time when many under twenty-five years of age believed it was impossible to trust anyone over thirty, Douglas achieved the status of a folk hero. His positions on the environment and civil liberties resonated with the views of youth, and in *Points of Rebellion* he explicitly embraced their antiestablishment views and tweaked his contemporaries by referring to the Establishment as the new George III, implicitly suggesting a revolutionary change would be a good idea.[94]

   There would be interstitial debate on how much judicial protection of which rights, but the battles that Douglas and Black fought in the McCarthy era were formally "won": a new consensus emerged recognizing the importance of an independent judiciary willing to sustain political dissent and essential personal liberties. Yet even as the new consensus that Black and Douglas helped pioneer has achieved an amazing breadth, it splintered and has been attacked. Both to the left in Critical Legal Studies and to the right in The Federalist Society, younger scholars reject the rights-based liberalism that Douglas championed. Both groups put in debate the legacy of the Warren Court.

   Douglas's choices during the McCarthy era were fundamentally different in kind from the Warren Court's dismantling of segregation, rural domination of legislatures, and an antiquated criminal justice system. In those areas, where the modern debate about judicial activism began, there was always a powerful constituency on the sidelines applauding the Court and encouraging it to do more to create a better society. That was not the case when the issue was protecting Reds and pinks in the early 1950s. Those who saw the necessity of protecting civil liberties of the despised were, sadly, few and far between. Had other members of the Warren Court majority been on the Court during the early 1950s they might have performed as Black and Douglas did. Alternatively, however, they might not. Warren, for instance, had the opportunity to show how he would vote as late as 1954, and he voted with the majority, not with Black and Douglas, in both *Barsky* and *Galvan v. Press*.

What I have suggested provides some basis for a reevaluation of Douglas's legacy and his importance. No one can erase his cavalier attitude toward doctrine. But, as time passes, any given justice's contribution to doctrine and illustration of craft demands recedes. To use the most obvious example, John Marshall has been acclaimed constantly as the greatest justice of all time, but his greatness is entirely divorced from the reasoning of his opinions and rests instead on the fact that he turned the Court into a major and unique institution of American government and, from a retrospective view, we approve of the way he voted.

Douglas, too, was a "founder" albeit a different one — a founder of a school that holds that even in the worst of times judges can actually stand up and demand we adhere to our ideals. If that got Douglas little credit at the time from the elites of the profession, it and his subsequent actions gave him a unique credibility with American youth at a time when almost no other politically prominent Americans had any. There indeed, his eschewing legalisms and resting on a blunt moral basis may have proven no small part of his charm.

Douglas's importance stems from the stands he was willing to take and the ways those stands helped transform subsequent beliefs about the appropriate functions — beliefs that hold it proper to do what Douglas did so long as the justices heed, as Douglas did not, the craft demands of the profession. Those beliefs operate to this day, as Robert Bork learned at his confirmation hearings.

We cannot freeze the law or any given perception of it. It may well be that a new conception of the function of courts will form and replace the liberal consensus that finds individual rights and liberties worthy of judicial protection in the worst of times no less than in the best of times. Attitudes, like reputations, are not static. But for over a quarter of a century, thanks in no small part to the courageous stands of Black and Douglas, an ideology of judicial protection of individual liberties has dominated our legal culture. Each generation must decide how it wishes to choose, and Douglas would have been the last to suggest the dead should govern the living.[95] Yet by one precept, being right on the major issue of his times when the ideology and other major actors held he was wrong, he may have assisted future generations in choosing wisely.

Notes

1. *Griswold v. Connecticut,* 381 U.S. 479 (1965); *Roe v. Wade,* 410 U.S. 113 (1973).

2. G. Edward White, "The Anti-Judge: William O. Douglas and the Ambiguities of Individuality," *Virginia Law Review* 74 (1988): 17.

3. Anthony Lewis, "Mr. Douglas: 36 Years Out on the Frontier," *New York Times,* Week in Review, Nov. 16, 1975.

4. L. A. Powe, Jr., "Evolution to Absolutism: Justice Douglas and the First Amendment," *Columbia Law Review* 74 (1974): 371.

5. 408 U.S. 104 (1972).

6. 385 U.S. 39, 48 (1966).

7. For example, Geoffrey R. Stone, "Fora Americana: Speech in Public Places," *Supreme Court Review* 1974: "The right to a public forum came of age" (p. 251).

8. Thomas Emerson, "Mr. Justice Douglas' Contribution to the Law: The First Amendment," *Columbia Law Review* 74 (1974): 354.

9. *American Communication Workers v. Douds,* 339 U.S. 382 (1950); *Dennis v. United States,* 341 U.S. 494 (1951).

10. 343 U.S. 250 (1952).

11. 354 U.S. 476 (1957).

12. Thomas Emerson, "Toward A General Theory of the First Amendment," *Yale Law Journal* 72 (1963): 877; Emerson, *The System of Freedom of Expression* (New York: Random House, 1970).

13. *Cox v. Louisiana,* 379 U.S. 559, 577 (1965).

14. 391 U.S. 367 (1968).

15. *Brandenburg v. Ohio,* 395 U.S. 444, 455 (1969) (Douglas, J., concurring).

16. 367 U.S. 1 (1961).

17. Ibid., at 172–73 (Douglas, J., dissenting).

18. *American Communication Workers v. Douds,* 339 U.S., at 424–33 (Jackson, J., concurring).

19. For example, *Scales v. United States,* 367 U.S. 203 (1961); *Noto v. United States,* 367 U.S. 290 (1961); *Wilkinson v. United States,* 365 U.S. 399 (1961); *Konigsberg v. State Bar of California,* 366 U.S. 36 (1961); *In re Anastaplo,* 366 U.S. 82 (1961).

20. *Terminiello v. Chicago,* 337 U.S. 1 (1949).

21. *Lamont v. Postmaster General,* 381 U.S. 310 (1965); *DeGregory v. New Hampshire,* 383 U.S. 825 (1966); *Elfbrandt v. Russell,* 384 U.S. 11 (1966).

22. 412 U.S. 94, 148 (1973) (Douglas, J., concurring).

23. *Terminiello v. Chicago,* 337 U.S., at 3–4.

24. See Harry Kalven, *A Worthy Tradition* (New York: Harper and Row, 1988).

25. Powe, "Evolution to Absolutism," p. 386.

26. *Feiner v. New York,* 340 U.S. 315 (1951).

27. 381 U.S. 310 (1965).

28. For example, *Stanley v. Georgia,* 394 U.S. 557, 564 (1969).

29. *Elfbrandt v. Russell,* 384 U.S. 11 (1966); *DeGregory v. New Hampshire,* 383 U.S. 825 (1966).

30. *Scales v. United States,* 367 U.S. 203 (1961).

31. Emerson, "Mr. Justice Douglas' Contribution," p. 354.

32. Vincent Blasi, "The Checking Value in First Amendment Theory," *American Bar Foundation Research Journal* 1977: 621.

33. William Cohen, "William O. Douglas," in Leonard Levy, ed., *Encyclopedia of the American Constitution,* 2d ed. (New York: Macmillan, 1986), pp. 579, 580.

34. Ibid.

35. I disagree with Justice Hans Linde, cited in White, "Anti-Judge," p. 47, n. 159, that the members of the Court changing to justices whose intellect Douglas could not respect had an effect on him.

36. L. A. Powe, Jr., "Mr. Justice Douglas," *Washington Law Review* 55 (1980); 285, 286.

37. *Debs v. United States,* 249 U.S. 211 (1919).

38. *Whitney v. California,* 274 U.S. 357, 372 (1927).

39. Emerson, "Mr. Justice Douglas," p. 354.

40. 340 U.S. 863 (1950) (grant of certiorari); *Dennis v. United States,* 341 U.S., at 495–96.

41. *Dennis v. United States,* 341 U.S., at 581.

42. Ibid., at 582: Joseph Stalin, *The Foundations of Leninism* (1924); Marx and Engels, *Manifesto of the Communist Party* (1848); Lenin, *The State and Revolution* (1917); *History of the Communist Party of the Soviet Union (B)* (1939).

43. *Dennis v. United States,* 341 U.S., at 525.

44. Ibid., at 585.

45. Ibid., at 588.

46. Ibid.

47. Ibid., at 589.

48. Ibid.

49. Ibid.

50. For example, *Yates v. United States,* 354 U.S. 298, 343 (1957) (Black, J., concurring, joined by Douglas, J.).

51. *Dennis v. United States,* 341 U.S., at 591.

52. William O. Douglas, *Points of Rebellion* (New York: Random House, 1969).

53. *Younger v. Harris,* 401 U.S. 37 (1971); *Samuels v. Mackell,* 401 U.S. 66 (1971); *Boyle v. Landry,* 401 U.S. 77 (1971); *Perez v. Ledesma,* 401 U.S. 82 (1971); *Dyson v. Stein,* 401 U.S. 200 (1971); *Byrne v. Karalexis,* 401 U.S. 216 (1971).

54. *United States v. United States District Court,* 407 U.S. 297 (1972).

55. Charles Alan Wright, "The Wit and Wisdom of Bernie Ward," *Texas Law Review* 61 (1982): 13, 19.

56. *Younger v. Harris,* 401 U.S., at 58.

57. *United States v. United States District Court,* 407 U.S., at 329–31.

58. White, "Anti-Judge," pp. 77–86.

59. Robert Nagel, "The Formulaic Constitution," 84 *Michigan Law Review* (1985): 165.

60. *Korematsu v. United States,* 323 U.S. 214 (1944); *Hirabayashi v. United States,* 320 U.S. 81 (1943).

61. *Bailey v. Richardson,* 341 U.S. 918 (1951); *Joint Anti-Fascist Refugee Committee v. McGrath,* 339 U.S. 123 (1950).

62. 347 U.S. 522 (1954). See also *Harisiades v. Shaughnessy,* 342 U.S. 480 (1952).

63. *Adler v. Board of Education,* 342 U.S. 485 (1952).

64. *Barsky v. Board of Regents,* 347 U.S. 442 (1952).

65. Ibid., at 474.

66. For example, *Peters v. Hobby,* 349 U.S. 331 (1955); *Cole v. Young,* 351 U.S. 536 (1956); and for a two-time winner, Steve Nelson/Mesarosh for *Pennsylvania v. Nelson,* 350 U.S. 497 (1956) (state sedition statute preempted) and *Mesarosh v. United States,* 352 U.S. 1 (1956) (Smith Act conviction overturned on Solicitor General's statements to Court that at least some parts of testimony against Nelson/Mesarosh were untrue).

67. G. Edward White, "The Evolution of Reasoned Elaboration," *Virginia Law Review* 59 (1973): 279; Gary Peller, "Neutral Principles in the 1950s," *Michigan Journal of Law Reform* 21 (1988): 561. See also Edward Purcell, *Crisis in Democratic Theory: Scientific Naturalism and the Problem of Value* (Lexington: University of Kentucky Press, 1973).

68. I have taken the term from G. Edward White, *The American Judicial Tradition* (New York: Oxford University Press, 1976).

69. Henry Hart, "Foreword: The Time Chart of the Justices," *Harvard Law Review* 73 (1958): 84; Herbert Wechsler, "Toward Neutral Principles of Constitutional Law," *Harvard Law Review* 73 (1958): 1.

70. *United States v. Butler,* 297 U.S. 1, 87 (1936) (Stone, J., dissenting).

71. Peller, "Neutral Principles," pp. 594–605.

72. An exception was Harvard Dean Erwin Griswold's timely publication of three speeches defending the right to claim the privilege against self-incrimination before legislative committees. Erwin Griswold, *The Fifth Amendment Today* (Cambridge: Harvard University Press, 1955).

73. Obviously, I was not at Harvard during the period under discussion. In putting this together I have relied on what was written and on oral tradition. As to the latter, during my early years in teaching I, as a former Douglas clerk, was regaled by stories of the way Harvard professors would take potshots at Douglas. I could remember the attitude, if not the story or the storyteller. In preparation for writing this I talked to a number of law professors who were at Harvard during the period and then gave each of them my draft with the express injunction to correct me in any ways necessary. Those I consulted include Vern Countryman, Norman Dorsen, Jack Getman, George Schatzki, Ernest Smith, and Russell Weintraub. What appears in text is the outgrowth of this process, although the final choice of language and emphasis is, of course, mine. See also Norman Dorsen, "Book Review," *Harvard Law Review* 95 (1981): 367, 385, n. 101.

74. It was well known, of course, what Frankfurter thought of Black and Douglas. See, e.g., Melvin I. Urofsky, "Conflict Among the Brethren: Felix Frankfurter, William O. Douglas and the Clash of Personalities and Philosophies on the United States Supreme Court," *Duke Law Journal* 71 (1988).

75. The phrase is Henry Hart's. See Phillip Bobbitt, *Constitutional Fate* (New York: Oxford University Press, 1982), p. 53.

76. Julius Getman, *Notes of an Academic Dissident* (forthcoming).

77. For example, *Barenblatt v. United States,* 360 U.S. 109 (1959); *Konigsberg v. State Bar of California,* 366 U.S. 36 (1961); *In re Anastaplo,* 366 U.S. 82 (1961).

78. *Barenblatt v. United States,* 360 U.S., at 134; *In re Anastaplo,* 366 U.S., at 97.

79. *Konigsberg v. State Bar of California,* 366 U.S., at 49, n. 10: "That view, which of course cannot be reconciled with the law relating to libel, slander, misrepresentation, obscenity, perjury, false advertising, solicitation of crime, complicity by

encouragement, conspiracy, and the like, is said to be compelled by the fact that the commands of the First Amendment are stated in unqualified terms."

80. Erwin Griswold, "Absolutes in the Dark," *Utah Law Review* 8 (1963): 172.

81. Ibid.

82. Powe, "Evolution to Absolutism," p. 408.

83. Charles L. Black, "Mr. Justice Black, the Supreme Court and the Bill of Rights," *Harper's,* Feb. 1961, p. 63.

84. Alexander Bickel, *The Least Dangerous Branch* (Indianapolis: Bobbs-Merrill, 1962).

85. *Barenblatt v. United States,* 360 U.S. 109 (1959).

86. *Wilkinson v. United States,* 365 U.S. 399 (1961); the opinion of the Court was written by Justice Stewart.

87. *Konigsberg v. State Bar of California,* 366 U.S. 36 (1961).

88. *In re Anastaplo,* 366 U.S., at 134.

89. Ibid., at 97.

90. Ibid., at 111.

91. *Gibson v. Florida Legislative Investigating Committee,* 372 U.S. 539 (1963); *Dombrowski v. Pfister,* 380 U.S. 479 (1965).

92. White, "Anti-Judge," pp. 77–86.

93. Bobbitt, *Constitutional Fate,* pp. 52–53; White, "Reasoned Elaboration," p. 290.

94. Douglas, *Points of Rebellion,* pp. 95–97.

95. The issue of Douglas, courts, and rights is treated more fully in L. A. Powe, Jr., "Justice Douglas After Fifty Years: The First Amendment, McCarthyism and Rights," *Constitutional Commentary* 6 (1989): 267–87.

THE RELIGION CLAUSE WRITINGS
OF JUSTICE WILLIAM O. DOUGLAS

Nadine Strossen

AFTER PROVIDING brief overviews of Justice Douglas's opinions under the Establishment[1] and Free-Exercise Clauses,[2] this chapter explores some themes contained in those opinions that characterize Douglas's individual rights jurisprudence more generally. For example, Douglas's general tendency to construe constitutional provisions as absolutely protecting individual rights is well illustrated by his literal application of the prohibitions in the two religion clauses.

Next, the chapter focuses on an important facet of Douglas's unique perspective on the proper relationship between government and religion. Consistent with his absolutist bent, Douglas believed that the religion clauses apply broadly to all conscientious beliefs, no matter how different from—or even hostile to—traditional religious beliefs they might be.

Finally, the chapter discusses some issues and problems raised by Douglas's religion clause opinions. In this context, the theme of absolutism is explored in terms of the potential conflict between the two religion clauses. Although this potential is heightened the more absolutely each clause is interpreted, and although Douglas was inclined toward an absolutist construction of both clauses, he nevertheless did not even confront the resulting tension, let alone resolve it.

I. Overview of Douglas's Religion Clause Opinions

ESTABLISHMENT CLAUSE OPINIONS

Douglas authored ten separate opinions on the merits of cases directly presenting Establishment Clause issues.[3] Only one of these was an opinion for the Court. Three were concurrences, one was a partial dissent, and the remaining five were all dissents.

The sole majority opinion that Douglas authored under the Establishment Clause was his controversial paean to the role of religion in our national life in *Zorach v. Clauson*,[4] upholding a "released-time" program under which public school children whose parents consented were released from school to attend religious classes at other facilities. He wrote:

We are a religious people whose institutions presuppose a Supreme Being. . . . When the state encourages religious instruction or cooperates with religious authority by adjusting the schedule of public events to sectarian needs, it follows the best of our traditions. For it then respects the religious nature of our people and accommodates the public service to their spiritual needs.[5]

Zorach was also Douglas's only opinion rejecting an Establishment Clause challenge. With the exception of this uncharacteristic opinion, Douglas consistently maintained that the Establishment Clause erected a complete "wall of separation" between church and state.

The fact that the anomalous *Zorach* opinion was written at the beginning of Douglas's judicial exploration of the Establishment Clause — it was his first separate opinion construing that provision — is consistent with the general trend of his Establishment Clause jurisprudence. Over time, Douglas interpreted the clause as demanding ever more complete separation between government and religion, leading to an increasing divergence from the majority's construction. The growing gap between Douglas and the rest of the Court on this issue is reflected in the fact that, during his last five years on the Court, Douglas was the sole dissenter in the *Wheeler* and *Walz* decisions, which rejected Establishment Clause challenges; not a single one of his brethren read the clause so strictly as he did.

FREE EXERCISE CLAUSE OPINIONS

Douglas also authored ten separate opinions directly addressing Free Exercise Clause claims.[6] The general tenor and trend of Douglas's free exercise opinions parallels those of their Establishment Clause counterparts.

Every Douglas opinion in cases that expressly asserted free exercise claims invalidated the challenged government actions. Nevertheless, in one case with clear free exercise implications, notwithstanding the parties' failure explicitly to raise a free exercise claim, Douglas's majority opinion revealed an unusual insensitivity to free exercise values. This opinion, in *Cleveland v. United States,* affirmed Mormons' convictions under the Mann Act for interstate transportation of women to maintain polygamous marriages, rejecting the argument that the defendants lacked the requisite criminal intent because they were motivated by religious beliefs. It is as uncharacteristic of Douglas's writings in the free exercise area as *Zorach* was of his writings in the establishment area.

Douglas's atypical opinion in *Cleveland,* parallel to that in *Zorach,* was authored early in his judicial consideration of the religion clause at issue. Over time, Douglas's free exercise opinions, like his establishment opinions, expressed increasingly absolutist views, leading to growing divergences from the majority's positions. Accordingly, the three majority opinions that Douglas himself wrote in free exercise cases — in *Follett, Ballard,* and *Murdock* — were among his earliest opinions in this field.

After 1944, Douglas never authored a majority opinion in a free exercise case, and after 1965, he did not author a concurring opinion in such a case. Douglas's last three separate opinions in free exercise cases, written during his last five years on the bench — in *Johnson, Yoder,* and *Gillette* — were all dissents. Moreover, in all three cases, Douglas was the sole dissenter.

II. Themes Common to Douglas's Religion Clause and Other Decisions

Douglas's religion clause opinions provide significant insights into, and examples of, certain pervasive aspects of his judicial approach that characterize his opinions concerning other individual liberties as well. Among these are his reliance upon wide-ranging materials, including materials from nonlegal disciplines, and pertaining to non-American cultures; his view of individual privacy or autonomy as an overarching general right from which all other, more specific freedoms are derived; and his tendency to view constitutional guarantees as protecting individual rights from any government encroachments whatsoever.

RELIANCE UPON WIDE-RANGING MATERIALS

One distinctive pattern common to Douglas's constitutional opinions in general, which is illuminated by his religion clause opinions, is his reference to a wealth of information from wide-ranging sources, including much empirical data, material from social sciences, and cross-cultural information.

The myriad types of materials upon which Douglas drew, and the various uses to which he put them, are illustrated by the following examples from his religion clause opinions: in *Murdock,* Douglas cited authorities regarding the beliefs, training, and compensation of Jehovah's Witness *colporteurs* to justify his conclusion that their evangelical activities — selling books and playing records in public places — should be given Free Exercise Clause protection coextensive with that granted to more conventional religious activities, such as preaching from church pulpits;[7] in *Walz v. Tax Commission,* he recited statistics regarding church-owned assets and income to vindicate his conclusion that tax benefits to religious institutions violated the Establishment Clause;[8] in *Tilton v. Richardson,* he linked statistics about churches' growing wealth to historical information about revolutionary expropriations of church property in various other countries, to explain his concern that government aid to religion could lead to divisiveness along sectarian lines;[9] in *Lemon v. Kurtzman,* he outlined the historical conflict between Protestants and Catholics concerning the public school curriculum in the United States to bolster his conclusion that sectarian schools are inherently and pervasively religious in nature;[10] and in *Wisconsin v. Yoder,* he cited psychologists and sociologists concerning the moral and intellectual maturity of children and adolescents to legitimate his conclusion that Amish youth should make their own choices about whether to attend public school, notwithstanding their parents' religious objections.[11]

As these examples indicate, Douglas used many different types of information to support multiple points relevant to his religion clause opinions. However, the predominant type of nonlegal source material that pervaded his opinions in this area, and which was most directly linked to his increasingly absolutist views, was material concerning non-Christian religions. For example, concurring in *Sherbert v. Verner,* Douglas described certain religiously mandated practices of Moslems, Sikhs, Jehovah's Witnesses, Quakers, and Buddhists that could easily be violated by government regulations otherwise justifiable in terms of public health, safety, or welfare. Accordingly, Douglas concluded that generally applicable and justifiable government regulations should be subject to exceptions for religious dissenters. As Professor Powe has observed, Douglas's exposure to a multitude of religions—through both his reading and his worldwide travels—provides a key to his free exercise opinions, since it accounts for his heightened sensitivity to the importance of protecting even religious beliefs that differed markedly from more conventional ones.[12]

Douglas's cross-cultural reading and travels also made an important contribution to the increasing liberality of his religion clause jurisprudence in another respect. These experiences nurtured Douglas's awareness of the threat posed to civil liberties by communism and other authoritarian forms of government. In response, Douglas increasingly emphasized that the U.S. government had a responsibility to serve as a meaningful alternative model for developing nations, by allowing individual freedoms to flourish.[13] Douglas voiced this attitude in some of his religion clause opinions. For example, in his *Sherbert* concurrence, Douglas observed that the "interference with the individual's scruples or conscience" that resulted from such laws "here is as plain as it is in Soviet Russia, where a churchgoer is given a second-class citizenship."[14]

VIEW OF INDIVIDUAL PRIVACY OR AUTONOMY AS FUNDAMENTAL RIGHT FROM WHICH ALL OTHERS ARE DERIVED

A second theme pervading Douglas's constitutional rights opinions, forcefully expounded in his religion clause writings, is his conception that every specific liberty is founded upon an all-encompassing general right of individual privacy or autonomy from governmental control. In his view, "The right to be let alone is indeed the beginning of all freedom."[15] In Douglas's special conception, privacy constitutes individuals' overarching freedom from government intrusion of any sort—not just the physical intrusion associated with more traditional privacy notions, but also the intrusion upon thought processes or decision making generally associated with concepts of individual liberty or autonomy.[16]

Douglas's general outlook on privacy is important in the specific context of the religion clauses. Douglas maintained that the right of privacy entails the freedom to choose one's own religious beliefs.[17] Thus, he viewed religious freedom as an "aspect of the right of privacy."[18]

Just as Douglas's notion of privacy embraced elements traditionally associated with liberties, including religious freedom, so too his concept of First Amendment liberties encompassed elements often associated with privacy. As Professor Thomas Emerson has noted, Douglas saw the First Amendment as helping individuals to realize their full potential by ensuring "freedom of lifestyle, and freedom to expand, grow, and be oneself."[19]

Thus, for Douglas, the conventionally separate concepts of privacy and liberty coalesced. He had an integrative vision of the two sets of rights as interrelated parts of the realm in which the individual reigned supreme, free from government interference. Some of Douglas's religion clause opinions expressly advert to his ideas concerning the interrelationship between privacy and liberty, including religious liberty.[20]

ABSOLUTIST VIEW OF INDIVIDUAL RIGHTS

As Professor Powe has thoroughly documented, Douglas displayed a general "evolution to absolutism" in interpreting all the First Amendment guarantees.[21] Douglas's movement toward absolutism in the Establishment Clause sphere is most forcefully demonstrated by contrasting his early establishment opinion in *Zorach v. Clauson* with subsequent rulings. In *Zorach,* Douglas listed types of government assistance to religion that he assumed would be held clearly constitutional, consistent with his then-expressed idea that government should accommodate religion.[22] Yet, in stark contrast, Douglas's concurring opinion in *Engel v. Vitale,* written ten years later, used a similar argumentative technique—listing numerous examples of government aid to religion, which he assumed should be viewed as clearly unconstitutional—to justify his then-asserted notion that the Establishment Clause proscribes any such aid.[23] The contrast between these inconsistent rationales in support of opposing Establishment Clause interpretations is heightened yet further when one considers that two specific types of government-religion interaction which Douglas's *Zorach* opinion presumed to be *permissible*—legislative prayers and presidential religious proclamations—were presumed in his *Engel* opinion to be *impermissible*.

Douglas's uniquely strict view of the Establishment Clause is demonstrated even more forcefully by a relatively early case in which he was the sole dissenter. In *Arlan's Department Store v. Kentucky,* Douglas alone dissented from the Court's dismissal of an appeal from convictions under Kentucky's Sunday closing law. Unlike the laws upheld in the previous Sunday closing law cases, the Kentucky statute exempted "members of a religious society which observes as a Sabbath any other day . . . than Sunday."[24] Nevertheless, Douglas condemned the Kentucky statute as violating the Establishment Clause. He reasoned that "the law is . . . plainly an aid to all organized religions, bringing to heel anyone who violates the religious scruples of the majority by seeking his salvation not through organized religion but on his own."[25]

In its fully developed form, Douglas's literal reading of the Establishment Clause as proscribing *all* laws regarding an establishment of religion[26] led him to find the clause violated by *any* government assistance to religion, no matter how minuscule, how indirect, or how long-standing and widely accepted. Accordingly, he joined in every decision that invalidated government aid to religious schools and dissented from every decision that upheld any such aid.

Douglas asserted three principal rationales in support of his strict reading of the Establishment Clause, aside from his reliance on its plain, unqualified text. First, in his opinions and extrajudicial writings, he repeatedly cited the passage in James Madison's famous *Memorial and Remonstrance Against Religious Assessments,* which warned against even a "three pence" tax in support of religion because of the adverse aggregate effect to which such a seemingly trivial tax could ultimately lead, by serving as a precedent for ever-increasing government involvement with religion.[27]

Second, Douglas asserted that total government-religion separation was necessary to preserve equality among religions. Because giving some aid to one or more religions would inevitably result in unequal treatment, even as among the aided religions, let alone as between the aided and the unaided ones, the only option consistent with equality would be to give no aid to any religions.[28] A third rationale was Douglas's firm belief that any government aid to religion would have adverse effects both upon the civilian polity, by engendering divisiveness along religious lines,[29] and upon the ostensibly aided religious institutions, by making them dependent on government, by subjecting them to government surveillance and control, and by making them prey to secular influence.[30]

Douglas's movement toward absolutism in interpreting the Free Exercise Clause can also be charted by contrasting an early opinion—his majority opinion in *Cleveland*—with his subsequent free exercise rulings. *Cleveland* did not expressly raise a free exercise issue. However, from the perspective of Douglas's significantly broadened vision of the Free Exercise Clause that developed within the following decade, the free exercise problems with the Court's ruling should have been apparent.

Douglas dismissed the Mormons' religious claims almost cavalierly, simply reciting approvingly the Court's earlier decisions that had rejected Mormons' Free Exercise Clause challenges to bigamy convictions. This curt dismissal was uncharacteristic of Douglas's subsequent Free Exercise Clause writings in two significant, interrelated respects. First, asserting conclusorily that "Congress has provided the standard,"[31] he denied the Mormons the right to formulate and abide by their own concept of morality, rather than defending the right of the individual or minority religious group member to defy majoritarian moral precepts. Second, his opinion uncritically accepted standards of Christianity and western civilization as the sole touchstone for permissible conduct, even when inconsistent conduct reflected religious beliefs. This approach contrasts starkly with Douglas's subsequent invocation of other religious traditions and cultures to support a broad view that the religion clauses protect all conscientious beliefs, no matter how unorthodox or even abhorrent they might appear from the perspective of Christian or western standards.

Perhaps Douglas's judicial views on polygamy were influenced by his personal views regarding marriage, much as his personal religious tenets influenced his religion clause decisions generally, as will be discussed later. The fact that Douglas himself was married four times may suggest that he held traditional views about the importance of monogamous marriage. He forcefully expressed such views in *Griswold v. Connecticut:*

We deal with a right of privacy older than the Bill of Rights. . . . Marriage is a coming together for better or worse, hopefully enduring, and intimate to the degree of being sacred. It is an association that promotes a way of life, not causes; a harmony in living, not political faiths; a bilateral loyalty, not commercial or social projects. Yet it is an association for as noble a purpose as any involved in our prior decisions.[32]

Douglas never expressly retracted his holding or rationale in *Cleveland,* but his subsequent writings demonstrated a growing willingness to include religiously motivated polygamy within the ambit of the Free Exercise Clause. Although his 1958 book *The Right of the People* still concluded that it was acceptable to place polygamy outside Free Exercise Clause protection, because it was "alien to Western moral codes,"[33] Douglas displayed some movement toward a more generous view of free exercise by acknowledging that the proposition was "debatable." Douglas's rationale for holding polygamy unprotected at this early stage of his Establishment Clause jurisprudence apparently depended on the dichotomy between beliefs and practices that underlay the Court's rulings in the Mormon bigamy cases, as well as other early free exercise decisions; practices were deemed unprotected either completely or at least whenever they were offensive to the majority's beliefs or values, even if they caused no tangible harm.[34]

By the early 1960s, however, Douglas had developed a more limited view of acceptable rationales for government regulation of religiously based conduct. He indicated some discomfort with the notion that harm to society's sense of decency or morality alone—unaccompanied by some more concrete harm—could justify limitations on religiously motivated action.[35] Douglas applied this developing perception specifically to polygamy in 1963, commenting in *The Anatomy of Liberty* that it was "dangerous" to outlaw polygamy on the ground that it was offensive to the American community. Here he also repudiated the bright-line distinction between beliefs and conduct, stressing that "freedom to practice a religion is as much a part of religious freedom as freedom to believe," and articulating a strictly limited description of the religiously based conduct that would be subject to government regulation: only conduct constituting a clear and present danger.[36]

Douglas's first judicial opinion to express this mature view was his partial dissent in *Wisconsin v. Yoder*. There, completely reversing his initial views concerning Mormon polygamy, he applauded the Court for "rightly reject[ing] the notion that actions, even though religiously grounded, are always outside" Free Exercise Clause protection.[37] Douglas's mature view of the Free Exercise Clause still drew some distinction between beliefs and conduct, holding only the former to be absolutely protected, but for two reasons this distinction may be more theoretical than real. First, Douglas apparently categorized many undertakings that plausibly could be considered actions—for example, delivering sermons and holding meetings—as absolutely protected beliefs.[38] Second, few regulations indeed could satisfy Douglas's stringent version of the clear and present danger test, although neither in judicial opinion nor in his extrajudicial writings did he give an example of religiously-based conduct that would satisfy that standard.

III. Douglas's Conception of the Scope of Religion Clauses

Unlike the themes previously discussed, Douglas's theory that the religion clauses protect a broadly conceived freedom of conscience—encompassing not only unorthodox religious beliefs, but also irreligion—pertains only to this area of the law. This position first surfaced near the beginning of Douglas's judicial career, in his earliest religion clause opinions in *Murdock* and *Follett*. These majority opinions emphasized that the relatively unconventional evangelical activities of Jehovah's Witnesses, including door-to-door distribution of religious literature in exchange for money, should be protected under the Free Exercise Clause as fully as the more conventional religious activities of ministers delivering sermons from church pulpits.

Douglas's opinion that the Free Exercise Clause prohibited discrimination against beliefs alien to conventional religions was powerfully stated in his *Ballard* majority opinion, where he held that the trial court correctly prohibited the jury from making any determination as to the truth or falsity of defendant "I Am" movement's asserted religious beliefs. He ruled that the jury should instead be confined to assessing whether the defendants actually held such beliefs in good faith, else the jurors would in effect be empowered to express their disapproval of or disagreement with defendants' unconventional religious beliefs.

Douglas's expansive interpretation that the beliefs protected by the religion clauses included nontheistic beliefs and even nonreligious philosophical, moral, or ethical beliefs was exemplified by his position in the Conscientious Objector (c.o.) Cases. In *Seeger,* the majority construed the draft law's Conscientious Objector provision, which applied to beliefs "in relation to a Supreme Being," as including any belief that occupies a place in the life of its possessor parallel to that filled for others by an orthodox belief in God. In contrast with the majority's failure to address any constitutional issue, Douglas, concurring, stressed that any other construction of this provision would violate both religion clauses by preferring some religions over others.[39]

The extent to which Douglas's unusually broad view of the beliefs protected by the religion clauses separated him from the Court's majority became even clearer in *Gillette,* where the majority rejected a religion clause challenge to the draft law provision granting c.o. status only to those who oppose participation in all war, not to those who object solely to particular wars. Dissenting eloquently, Douglas articulated a sweeping vision of the religion clauses as protecting all conscientiously held beliefs, regardless of whether they are grounded on traditional religious tenets: "Conscience is often the echo of religious faith. But . . . it may also be the product of travail, meditation, or sudden revelation related to a moral comprehension of the dimensions of a problem, not to a religion in the ordinary sense."[40]

Douglas recognized that the Free Exercise Clause expressly refers only to religion specifically and not more generally to conscience or belief. However, he justified constitutional protection for beliefs beyond the traditionally religious by relying on the entire First Amendment's overall thrust and asserting that an implicit right to freedom of conscience, broadly understood, underlay the amendment's particular guarantees. Douglas consistently expounded a concept of undifferentiated freedom of conscience, which would be violated if any conscientiously held beliefs were treated with less respect than any others.[41]

The most extreme manifestation of this stance was Douglas's view that the Free Exercise Clause protects freedom of antireligious, as well as religious, views. Even Douglas himself did not initially conceive of the religion clauses as extending to irreligion. His early opinion in *Zorach,* extolling as it did the special role of theistic religion in American life, seems inconsistent with the idea that the religion clauses protect irreligion. By 1958, in *The Right of the People,* Douglas did suggest that the religion clauses could be viewed as protecting atheism, but he also acknowledged that this issue "has not been authoritatively decided."[42] By 1961, Douglas seemed to have resolved the matter conclusively to his own satisfaction. In his *McGowan* dissent, Douglas asserted conclusorily that religious freedom includes "the freedom of atheists or agnostics."[43] Similarly, in his *Walz* and *Gillette* dissents, he expressed the view that the First Amendment was intended to maintain government neutrality between believers and nonbelievers.[44]

IV. Problems Presented by Douglas's
Religion Clause Jurisprudence

Douglas's religion clause opinions on the whole constitute a coherent doctrinal body, reflecting an absolutist and broad interpretation of the protections guaranteed to all individuals and all beliefs under these constitutional provisions. However, the foregoing discussion also indicates some problematic aspects of Douglas's religion clause writings. Two are addressed here.

INCONSISTENCY BETWEEN ZORACH
AND OTHER RELIGION CLAUSE WRITINGS

Despite its discordance with his subsequent writings, Douglas never expressly even questioned, let alone recanted, his *Zorach* opinion. Douglas did explicitly disavow certain other opinions that he later viewed as wrong.[45] In contrast, even in his *Engel* concurrence, where he took a dramatically different view of the Establishment Clause, Douglas quoted *Zorach*'s pronouncement that "We are a religious people whose institutions presuppose a Supreme Being."[46] Perhaps Douglas himself, in contrast with his critics, did not view *Zorach* as being irreconcilable with his subsequently espoused views.[47]

Douglas never directly acknowledged the apparent discrepancy between *Zorach*'s expansive view of acceptable interaction between religion and government and his subsequent insistence upon absolute separation. Some of his post-*Zorach* writings do suggest possible theories for harmonizing these seemingly inconsistent views, although there is no principled explanation for Douglas's particular holdings that the released-time program in *Zorach* did not violate the Establishment Clause, and that this program could be distinguished from the released-time program that the Court had struck down on Establishment Clause grounds in *McCollum*.

First, Douglas's dissenting opinion in *McGowan,* containing an initial formulation of his absolutist approach to the religion clauses, could be seen as attempting to bridge *Zorach*'s encomium to the important role of religion in our national life with his subsequent declarations that government should play no part in fostering this role. In *McGowan,* Douglas wrote: "those who fashioned the First Amendment decided that if and when God is to be served, His service will not be motivated by coercive measures of government. . . . The . . . religion clauses mean . . . that if a religious leaven is to be worked into the affairs of our people, it is to be done by individuals and groups, not by the Government."[48]

As Douglas himself acknowledged, it is hard to draw the line he posits between permissible state "encouragement" of private religious activity and impermissible state "promotion" of such activity. Moreover, it remains inexplicable why he classified the released-time program in *McCollum,* but not the one in *Zorach,* as being on the impermissible side of that line.

A second possible means for reconciling Douglas's tribute to religion in *Zorach* with his subsequent absolutist Establishment Clause interpretation lies in his view that vigorous enforcement of the Establishment Clause would *protect* religion. Religion might seem to be benefited, at least in the short run, by government assistance, but Douglas consistently maintained that, in the long run, religion would actually be undermined by such "aid." For example, Douglas's *Engel* concurrence described state "sustenance" of religion as a form of "interference."[49] As a result of the separation that has been maintained between church and state in this country, Douglas opined, churches have prospered in the United States more than anywhere else.

Another perspective from which Douglas's subsequent absolutist Establishment Clause opinions might be harmonized with *Zorach* is afforded by his own religious beliefs, as well as his understanding of the nation's spiritual heritage. Douglas's father was a Presbyterian minister. Although the Reverend Douglas died when Douglas was only five years old, Douglas's mother — who had met her husband while serving as the organist at his church — was a devout Presbyterian, who gave her children a strictly religious upbringing. Throughout his childhood, Douglas attended three church services a week. While a college student, he was also very active in the Presbyterian church. Although he later questioned some specific elements of the Presbyterian creed, on his death, at his request, Douglas was given a Presbyterian memorial service.[50]

For Douglas, religious beliefs and individual freedoms were closely intertwined and, to some extent, overlapping or even identical. He directly expressed this conception of religion in his *Walz* dissent in quoting Madison's declaration that "violation of religious freedom is an abuse against God, not man."[51] To the extent that religious values are coextensive with those protected in the Bill of Rights, it would not violate religious freedom for the government to promote religious values. In Douglas's view, belief in the freedoms guaranteed in the Bill of Rights was tantamount to belief in a Supreme Being, and vice versa; both were sources and guarantors of individual freedom. He expressed this idea in his *McGowan* dissent:

The institutions of our society are founded on the belief that there is an authority higher than the authority of the State; that there is a moral law which the State is powerless to alter; that the individual possesses rights, conferred by the Creator, which government must respect. The Declaration of Independence stated the now familiar theme: "We hold these Truths to be self-evident, that all Men are created equal, that they are endowed by their Creator with certain unalienable Rights.[52]

Douglas's extrajudicial writings similarly develop this theme.[53]

In *McGowan,* Douglas also referred to the Puritan heritage that has influenced both our legal and our religious institutions, and said that the Puritans had "put individual conscience and individual judgment in the first place."[54] In other words, according to Douglas, our nation's religious heritage, no less than the First Amendment itself, enshrines individual conscience. That Douglas intended to invoke this understanding of our religious heritage in *Zorach* — or at least as he subsequently construed his *Zorach* opinion — is underscored by his quotation of *Zorach* in *McGowan.*

In this same vein, Douglas wrote that our nation's religious traditions include specifically principles of toleration of diverse beliefs and separation between church and state — the same principles embodied in the religion clauses. As he noted in *The Right of the People,* although there was religious discrimination in American colonies, a number of sects flourished, which led to toleration; also, because many colonists did not belong to churches, they opposed tax support of churches.[55] Given this perspective on our religious traditions, Douglas's deference to them, as expressed in *Zorach,* is not inconsistent with his strong protection of religious liberty, as expressed in subsequent opinions.

In addition to believing that individual rights flowed from some general notions of religion and a Supreme Being, Douglas also saw them as flowing specifically from the Christian concepts of God and Jesus. He wrote: "Though our concepts of equity and justice come from numerous sources, they have been more greatly influenced by Jesus than anyone else. The Sermon on the Mount is a charter of political freedom."[56] Moreover, Douglas saw Jesus's teachings as embodying not only many principles of freedom in general but also the specific principles of religious freedom enunciated in the Free Exercise and Establishment Clauses. He interpreted Jesus's statement about rendering unto Caesar what is Caesar's and unto God what is God's as encapsulating the values reflected in both First Amendment guarantees.

In light of his belief that religious tenets and constitutional guarantees are significantly coterminous, it is not surprising that Douglas frequently referred to precepts of freedom in reverential terms. For example, he described the individual mind as a "sacred precinct," which government may not enter, and wrote that protecting liberty will give the United States "spiritual strength."[57]

POTENTIAL CONFLICTS BETWEEN ESTABLISHMENT AND FREE EXERCISE CLAUSES

Douglas's tendency toward absolutist interpretations of both religion clauses gives rise to potential conflicts because, as Justice Burger noted in his majority opinion in *Walz,* if either clause is interpreted strictly, it will necessarily clash with the other. Yet Douglas's judicial opinions never explicitly acknowledged this potential conflict, let alone explained how he would resolve it.

Never discussing such a conflict in general terms, Douglas only adverted to it with respect to one particular situation, and then just indirectly. In his *Sherbert v. Verner* concurrence, he acknowledged that a conflict between the two religion clauses might be posed by the Court's holding that a state must make an exception to its general eligibility requirement for unemployment compensation, availability for Saturday work, for an employee with religious objections to such work. However, the potential conflict he recognized — that a sabbatarian employee might donate to her church some of the unemployment benefits she received from the state — was not the significant one the case raised. Rather, it was Justice Stewart, concurring, who noted the major Establishment Clause problem resulting from upholding Ms. Sherbert's free-exercise rights: the Establishment Clause, as the Court had construed it in cases such as *Abington* and *Engel,* would be violated by the state's mandating an exemption from the Saturday work requirement only for employees who had religious objections to such work and not for employees with any other objections.[58] In effect, the Court required the state to grant a benefit solely to unemployed members of a particular religion, but not to any other unemployed individuals. Under Douglas's absolutist view that the Establishment Clause prohibits any and all government assistance to religion, this benefit raises serious problems.

In approving an exemption from generally enforced obligations for adherents of only particular religious beliefs, Douglas's *Sherbert* opinion also appears to be in tension with some of his other religion clause writings. In his separate opinions in cases concerning Conscientious Objector exemptions from the military draft, Douglas adamantly opposed limiting the exemption to adherents of particular religious beliefs. He believed that the First Amendment would be violated by any exemption that did not broadly encompass all conscientious objections, whether based on philosophical or on religious grounds.

Douglas's *Sherbert* opinion is arguably consistent with his c.o. opinions, insofar as *Sherbert* did not squarely present the issue of how the state should extend the exemption from the Saturday work requirement. Nevertheless, it is noteworthy that Douglas did not take the opportunity that *Sherbert* presented to stress that, for purposes of any state benefit, including the exemption at issue, religious beliefs could be treated no differently from any other conscientious beliefs. Such an observation would have been particularly appropriate in response to Justice Stewart's concurring opinion. The unarticulated balance that Douglas's *Sherbert* opinion struck in favor of free exercise, versus establishment, values distinguishes that opinion from others in which Douglas struck the opposite balance, again without explaining his analysis. For example, although Douglas had joined the majority's opinion in *Everson v. Board of Education,* he subsequently repudiated that ruling and opined that the Establishment Clause prohibits state financing of parochial school students' bus transportation.[59] The apparent inconsistency between that position and Douglas's absolutist opinions upholding free exercise claims, including in *Sherbert* and *Barnette,* has been noted by some commentators.[60]

Douglas's failure to grapple with principled resolutions to conflicts between two constitutional values, each of which he viewed as affording absolute or near-absolute protection, is not peculiar to his religion clause jurisprudence. When faced with competing values of privacy or individuality, Douglas wrote near-absolutist opinions favoring one or the other. Although Douglas was apparently engaging in an unarticulated balancing process, he refused to say so expressly, leading an observer to conclude: "The cases of conflicting values reveal an unresolved tension in Douglas's opinions."[61]

V. Conclusion

William O. Douglas's interpretations of the First Amendment religion clauses not only reveal his uniquely protective approach to those provisions but also illustrate many significant aspects of his individual rights jurisprudence more generally. For example, Douglas viewed religious liberties — along with other individual rights — as being based upon, and in turn serving as a foundation for, the fundamental right of individual privacy or autonomy. This strong vision of religious freedom as an integral aspect of the core privacy right helps to explain Douglas's broad and absolutist construction of the religion clauses.

Douglas's absolutist view also drew force from his personal religious tenets and his understanding of this nation's religious heritage. In Douglas's view, individual freedoms, including religious liberties — which he defined broadly to include rights of conscience — were divine gifts. Thus in zealously defending the rights protected by the religion clauses, Douglas was acting upon his religious, as well as his constitutional, ideals. In so doing, he made an invaluable contribution to maintaining the "sacred precincts" of the human mind and its beliefs inviolate from governmental intrusion.

Notes

The author gratefully acknowledges the research assistance of Bernard Lee.

1. This clause provides: "Congress shall make no law respecting an establishment of religion." U.S. Constitution, First Amendment. It is binding on the states. *Everson v. Board of Education,* 330 U.S. 1, 15 (1947).

2. This clause provides: "Congress shall make no law . . . prohibiting the free exercise [of religion]." U.S. Constitution, First Amendment. It is binding on the states. *Cantwell v. Connecticut,* 310 U.S. 296 (1940).

3. Douglas's views can also be inferred from the opinions he joined, but because his separate opinions afford the most direct insights into his personal views concerning the religion clauses, the chapter focuses on these. See *Wheeler v. Barrera,* 417 U.S. 402, 429 (1974) (dissenting); *Lemon v. Kurtzman (Lemon II),* 411 U.S. 192, 209 (1973) (dissenting); *Tilton v. Richardson,* 403 U.S. 672, 689 (1971) (dissenting in part); *Lemon v. Kurtzman (Lemon I),* 403 U.S. 602, 625 (1971) (concurring); *Walz v. Tax Commission of City of New York,* 397 U.S. 664, 700 (1970) (dissenting); *Board of Education v. Allen,* 392 U.S. 236, 254 (1968) (dissenting); *School District of Ab-*

ington Township v. Schempp, 374 U.S. 203, 227 (1963) (concurring); *Engel v. Vitale,* 370 U.S. 421, 437 (1962) (concurring); *McGowan v. Maryland,* 366 U.S. 420, 561 (1961) (dissenting); *Zorach v. Clauson,* 343 U.S. 306 (1952) (majority). See also *United States v. Seeger,* 380 U.S. 163, 188 (1965) (concurring); *Arlan's Department Store of Louisville v. Kentucky,* 371 U.S. 218 (1962) (dissenting).

   4. 343 U.S. 306 (1952).

   5. Ibid., at 313–14.

   6. *Johnson v. Robison,* 415 U.S. 361, 386 (1974) (dissenting); *Wisconsin v. Yoder,* 406 U.S. 205, 241 (1972) (dissenting in part); *Gillette v. United States,* 401 U.S. 437, 463 (1971) (dissenting); *United States v. Seeger,* 380 U.S. 163, 188 (1965) (concurring); *Sherbert v. Verner,* 374 U.S. 398, 410 (1963) (concurring); *Poulos v. New Hampshire,* 345 U.S. 395, 422 (1953) (dissenting); *United States v. Ballard,* 322 U.S. 78 (1944) (majority); *Follett v. McCormick,* 321 U.S. 573 (1944) (majority); *West Virginia Board of Education v. Barnette,* 319 U.S. 624, 643 (1943) (concurring; coauthored with Black); *Murdock v. Pennsylvania,* 319 U.S. 105 (1943) (majority). See also *McGowan v. Maryland,* 366 U.S. 420, 576–77 (1961) (dissenting); *Fowler v. Rhode Island,* 345 U.S. 67 (1953) (majority); *Cleveland v. United States,* 329 U.S. 14 (1946) (majority); *Girouard v. United States,* 328 U.S. 61 (1946) (majority).

   7. *Murdock v. Pennsylvania,* 319 U.S., at 108–09 and n. 6.

   8. *Walz v. Tax Commission,* 397 U.S., at 714.

   9. *Tilton v. Richardson,* 403 U.S., at 695–96.

   10. *Lemon v. Kurtzman,* 403 U.S., at 628–29.

   11. *Wisconsin v. Yoder,* 406 U.S., at 245 and n. 3.

   12. L. A. Powe, Jr., "Evolution to Absolutism: Justice Douglas and the First Amendment," *Columbia Law Review* 74 (1974): 371, 409. See also William O. Douglas, *An Almanac of Liberty* (New York: Doubleday, 1984), p. 172.

   13. See, e.g., William O. Douglas, "The Bill of Rights is Not Enough," *New York University Law Review* 38 (1963): 207, 242.

   14. *Sherbert v. Verner,* 374 U.S., at 412.

   15. *Public Utilities Commission v. Pollak,* 343 U.S. 451, 467 (1952) (Douglas, J., dissenting).

   16. See Note, "Toward a Constitutional Theory of Individuality: The Privacy Opinions of Justice Douglas," *Yale Law Journal* 87 (1978): 1579.

   17. See William O. Douglas, *Freedom of the Mind* (New York: American Library Association, 1962), p. 11.

   18. *Doe v. Bolton,* 410 U.S. 179, 211 (1973) (Douglas, J., concurring). See also *Public Utilities Commission v. Pollak,* 343 U.S., at 467–68.

   19. Thomas Emerson, "Justice Douglas's Contribution to the Law," *Columbia Law Review* 74 (1974): 353, 356.

   20. See, e.g., *Sherbert v. Verner,* 374 U.S., at 412 (Douglas described individual conscience as "an important area of privacy which the first amendment fences off from government").

   21. Regarding Douglas's religion clause opinions, see Powe, "Evolution to Absolutism," p. 402.

   22. *Zorach v. Clauson,* 343 U.S., at 312–13.

   23. *Engel v. Vitale,* 370 U.S., at 437 and n. 1, quoting David Fellman, *The Limits of Freedom* (New Brunswick, N.J.: Rutgers University Press, 1959), pp. 40–41.

   24. *Arlan's Department Store of Louisville v. Kentucky,* 371 U.S., at 219, n. 1.

25. Ibid., at 220. See David Louisell, "The Man and the Mountain: Douglas on Religious Freedom," *Yale Law Journal* 73 (1964): 975, 986 (referring to "extremism of this notion of establishment").

26. See *McGowan v. Maryland*, 366 U.S., at 561.

27. Douglas attached Madison's essay as an appendix to his dissent in *Walz v. Tax Commission*, 397 U.S., at 719, and cited it in *Wheeler v. Barrera*, 417 U.S., at 180; *Lemon II*, 411 U.S., at 166; *Tilton v. Richardson*, 403 U.S., at 809; *Lemon I*, 403 U.S., at 767–68; *Board of Education v. Allen*, 392 U.S., at 1078; *Engel v. Vitale*, 370 U.S., at 444; and *McGowan*, 366 U.S., at 533. See also Douglas, *An Almanac of Liberty*, p. 183.

28. See *Walz v. Tax Commission*, 397 U.S., at 711, citing Edmond Cahn, *Confronting Injustice: The Edmund Cahn Reader*, ed. L. Cahn (Boston: Little, Brown, 1966), pp. 180–87.

29. See *Tilton v. Richardson*, 403 U.S., at 695–96.

30. See *Walz v. Tax Commission*, 397 U.S., at 712; *Tilton v. Richardson*, 403 U.S., at 693–94.

31. *Cleveland v. United States*, 329 U.S., at 20.

32. *Griswold v. Connecticut*, 381 U.S. 479, 486 (1965).

33. Douglas, *The Right of the People* (Westport, Conn.: Greenwood, 1958), p. 140.

34. See, e.g., *Reynolds v. United States*, 98 U.S. 145, 166 (1878) (affirming bigamy conviction of a Mormon whose religious beliefs required him to practice polygamy).

35. See William O. Douglas, *A Living Bill of Rights* (New York: Doubleday, 1961), p. 30 (beliefs should be completely free from government regulation because they cannot possibly harm society); *McGowan v. Maryland*, 366 U.S., at 565 (Free Exercise Clause should protect religiously based acts which are not antisocial).

36. William O. Douglas, *The Anatomy of Liberty* (New York: Trident, 1963), pp. 26–27.

37. *Wisconsin v. Yoder*, 406 U.S., at 247. Douglas voiced the hope that the Court would some day overrule *Reynolds v. United States*, 98 U.S. 145 (1878), upholding Mormon bigamy convictions on the ground that actions are per se unprotected.

38. See *Poulos v. New Hampshire*, 345 U.S., at 422 (Douglas, J., dissenting from Court's upholding of conviction for conducting unlicensed public religious meeting).

39. *United States v. Seeger*, 380 U.S., at 188.

40. *Gillette v. United States*, 401 U.S., at 466.

41. See, e.g., Douglas, *An Almanac of Liberty*, p. 135; Douglas, *The Right of the People*, p. 144; *Wisconsin v. Yoder*, 406 U.S., at 43; *Gillette*, 401 U.S., at 845.

42. Douglas, *The Right of the People*, p. 139.

43. *McGowan v. Maryland*, 366 U.S., at 564. Accord, William O. Douglas, *The Bible and the Schools* (Boston: Little, Brown, 1966), p. 9.

44. See *Gillette*, 401 U.S., at 468; *Walz*, 397 U.S., at 700.

45. See Vern Countryman, "The Contribution of the Douglas Dissents," *Georgia Law Review* 10 (1976): 349–50.

46. *Zorach v. Clauson*, 370 U.S., at 442.

47. Professor Louisell analyzed several possible bases for distinguishing Douglas's position in *Zorach* from that in *Engel* and other subsequent opinions, but concluded

that, "however much one juggles the contingencies, it is impossible honestly to acquit Justice Douglas of gross inconsistency." Louisell, "The Man and the Mountain," p. 993. Noting that the case "was decided before the Democratic National Convention of 1952 had foreclosed the last reasonable hope of the Presidency" (p. 995), Louisell suggested that the *Zorach* opinion may be made explicable by Douglas's presidential ambitions.

48. *McGowan v. Maryland,* 366 U.S., at 563.

49. *Engel v. Vitale,* 370 U.S., at 615.

50. See James S. Simon, *Independent Journey: The Life of William O. Douglas* (London: Penguin Books, 1980), pp. 1, 19, 23, 24, 28, 44–45, 48–49.

51. *Walz v. Tax Commission,* 397 U.S., at 705.

52. *McGowan v. Maryland,* 366 U.S., at 562–63. Accord, *Girouard v. United States,* 328 U.S., at 68.

53. See, e.g., Douglas, *An Almanac of Liberty,* p. 184; Douglas, *The Right of the People,* pp. 89–90.

54. *McGowan v. Maryland,* 366 U.S., at 525, quoting Roscoe Pound, *The Spirit of the Common Law* (Boston: Marshall Jones, 1921), p. 42.

55. Douglas, *The Right of the People,* p. 137.

56. Douglas, *An Almanac of Liberty,* p. 184.

57. Douglas, *Freedom of the Mind,* p. 11; Douglas, "The Bill of Rights is Not Enough," p. 242.

58. *Sherbert v. Verner,* 374 U.S., at 414–15 (Stewart, J., concurring in result).

59. See *Walz v. Tax Commission,* 397 U.S., at 703.

60. See Louisell, "Man and the Mountain," p. 995 and n. 92; Leonard F. Manning, "The Douglas Concept of God in Government," *Washington Law Review* 39 (1964): 67–69. In Professor Louisell's view, Douglas overemphasized Establishment Clause values at the expense of competing free exercise values. Regardless of whether one shares the opinion that the Free Exercise Clause should prevail over the Establishment Clause when the two conflict, Louisell is correct that Douglas did not suggest any approach for resolving such conflicts. "Man and the Mountain," p. 993.

61. See Note, "Toward a Constitutional Theory of Individuality," pp. 1595–96.

Justice William O. Douglas and Civil Rights

Drew S. Days III

I. Reading the Constitution Broadly

O N DECEMBER 14, 1964, the United States Supreme Court unanimously upheld in *Heart of Atlanta Motel v. United States*[1] the constitutionality of Title II of the Civil Rights Act of 1964, which prohibited racial discrimination in places of public accommodation. The decision represented, in one sense, a vindication of Congress's power to address such discrimination, a power that had been placed in substantial doubt by the Supreme Court's 1883 *Civil Rights Cases*[2] decision declaring the Civil Rights Act of 1875 unconstitutional. In another sense, however, *Heart of Atlanta,* by relying only upon Congress's powers under the Commerce Clause, brought to a rather inauspicious conclusion a campaign initiated by the first Justice Harlan in his *Civil Rights Cases* dissent and carried on by Justice William O. Douglas. Both had sought to establish that the Thirteenth and Fourteenth Amendments to the Constitution also authorized Congress to reach such discrimination.

The majority opinion in the *Civil Rights Cases* held that the 1875 Act was unconstitutional on two basic grounds. First, it concluded that the Thirteenth Amendment was designed to emancipate blacks from slavery to ensure that they were not subjected to conditions bordering on slavery and to free them from any "badges or incidents" of slavery, disabilities growing out of their prior state of bondage. Racial discrimination in places of public accommodation could not be viewed, it held, as slavery or involuntary servitude or properly characterized as a "badge or incident of slavery."[3] Second, the Fourteenth Amendment could not be relied upon to support the Act's constitutionality, since the discrimination at issue was the result of private action. The Fourteenth Amendment, said the majority, could authorize federal legislation directed only against "state action."[4]

In dissent, Justice Harlan contended, first, that places of public accommodation, although technically private, were sufficiently "clothed with a public interest"[5] to make the denial of access to such facilities on the basis of race "a badge of servitude," which Congress could forbid pursuant to the Thirteenth Amendment.[6] Second, he read the "privileges and immunities" clause of the Fourteenth Amendment as a positive grant of authority, which Congress could exercise pursuant to Section 5 of that amendment, to ensure that black citizens were not discriminated against on the basis of race or color.

This power was available even in the absence of evidence that the state had any role in the discriminatory practices.[7]

Third, to the extent that the Fourteenth Amendment's reach had to be limited to addressing discriminatory state action, "railroad corporations, keepers of inns and managers of places of public amusement [were] agents or instrumentalities of the State,"[8] given the pervasive nature of government regulation. Consequently, the 1875 Act was, according to Harlan, amply supported by the Thirteenth and Fourteenth Amendments to the Constitution. Harlan emphasized that what was at issue before the Court was the vindication of civil, not social, rights.[9] Harlan employed much of this same analysis in arguing in dissent in *Plessy v. Ferguson*[10] that a Louisiana law requiring separate railroad compartments for white and black passengers violated the Fourteenth Amendment.

Justice Harlan's dissent in *Plessy* became, of course, the bedrock for the Court's 1954 decision in *Brown v. Board of Education,*[11] declaring unconstitutional the "separate-but-equal" doctrine with respect to public education. His dissent in the *Civil Rights Cases* appeared to have been lost to history, however, until Justice Douglas assumed responsibility for its revival in the early 1960s. The occasion was not the Court's consideration of another civil rights act addressing discrimination in places of public accommodation. Rather, it was the Court's growing docket of appeals from state convictions of civil rights demonstrators who had engaged in sit-ins to protest racial segregation in restaurants, cafeterias, and lunch counters throughout the South.

In *Garner v. Louisiana,*[12] the Court concluded that the constitutionality of the state convictions of the sit-in demonstrators for disturbing the peace did not have to be reached because the convictions were "so totally devoid of evidentiary support as to declare them unconstitutional under the Due Process Clause of the Fourteenth Amendment."[13] However, Justice Douglas went on in his concurrence to address the merits, holding that restaurants, although private enterprises, were "public facilities in which the States may not enforce a policy of racial segregation."[14]

Striking a theme that appeared often in his subsequent opinions, Douglas concluded that, even though the Louisiana law in question did not explicitly require racial segregation, the proprietors "were segregating blacks from whites pursuant to Louisiana custom." This custom, "basic to the structure of Louisiana as a community," according to Justice Douglas, was "at least as powerful as any law"[15] and equally violative of the Fourteenth Amendment. Moreover, Douglas was able to rely upon a recent Court decision to reinforce Harlan's point about the degree to which government regulation of places of public accommodation, especially licensing, implicated the Fourteenth Amendment.[16] There, the Court held that a state's leasing space in a government-owned parking facility to a private restaurant that refused to serve blacks violated the Equal Protection Clause.

Justice Douglas's determination to put the constitutional issue with respect to criminal sanctions against sit-in demonstrators on the table was most likely an outgrowth of his growing concern over race relations generally. In the introduction to his only book that addresses the issue of race discrimination in any detail, Douglas explained his motivation for writing the volume by describing an incident that occurred in 1961 a few days after he had joined the Kenyan leader, Tom Mboya, on a program where Douglas read briefly from the Declaration of Independence and commented on Lincoln's view of it.[17] Subsequently, he encountered a high State Department official who told him that he had misread the Declaration of Independence. According to the official, it dealt only with equality between Americans and British subjects and had nothing to do with race problems. Justice Douglas responded that he "thought Lincoln had won that argument a century ago." He went on to say in the introduction that "since the ideas of white supremacy seem to linger on even in high places, I concluded that all of us should know more about the Great Debates of the 1850's and 1860's."[18]

In subsequent sit-in cases, Douglas assumed the responsibility for acquainting the American people and reminding his colleagues on the Court of the Great Debates of the 1850s and 1860s, even where matters could be resolved on more limited grounds. For example, in *Lombard v. Louisiana,*[19] the majority found that a lunch counter proprietor's decision to refuse service to an integrated group of students and to call the police to have them arrested was in response to prior public warnings by the police chief and mayor that desegregation of such facilities would not be tolerated. Applying fairly straightforward Fourteenth Amendment doctrine, the Court held that the refusal to serve and the subsequent arrests were discriminatory state actions that violated the Constitution.

However, Justice Douglas felt the need to demonstrate in his concurrence, "why Louisiana had become involved to a significant extent in denying equal protection of the laws to petitioner."[20] In addition to making explicit for the first time his reliance upon the arguments in Justice Harlan's *Civil Rights Cases* dissent,[21] Douglas also wove into his opinion the principle established by the Court in *Shelley v. Kraemer,*[22] a 1948 decision that held that a state court's enforcement of a racially restrictive covenant constituted an equal protection violation. According to Douglas, the state court's conviction of the sit-in demonstrators established similarly unconstitutional state action.

Lombard also reveals another dimension of the sit-in cases that must have been especially fascinating to Justice Douglas. Douglas is justifiably recognized for the development of the privacy doctrine in such cases as *Skinner v. Oklahoma*[23] and *Griswold v. Connecticut.*[24] There appears to be substantially less awareness, however, that well before his opinion in *Griswold* Douglas was working out in the sit-in cases questions relating to what activities were public and, thereby, subject to state regulation and which were properly private and, consequently, secure against both public and private intrusions. Note the echoes of *Griswold* in this passage from *Lombard:*

The court below based its affirmance of these convictions on the ground that the decision to segregate this restaurant was a private choice, uninfluenced by the officers of the State. . . . If this were an intrusion of a man's home or yard or farm or garden, the property owner could seek and obtain the aid of the State against the intruder. For the Bill of Rights, as applied to the States through the Due Process Clause of the Fourteenth Amendment, casts its weight on the side of the privacy of homes. The Third Amendment with its ban on the quartering of soldiers in private homes radiates that philosophy. The Fourth Amendment, while concerned with official invasions of privacy through searches and seizures, is eloquent testimony of the sanctity of private premises. . . . But a restaurant, like other departments of this retail store where Negroes are served, though private property within the protection of the Fifth Amendment, has no aura of constitutionally protected privacy about it.[25]

Justice Douglas gave fullest expression to his views on state action in the sit-in context in his 1964 opinion in *Bell v. Maryland*.[26] Black sit-in demonstrators had been convicted under Maryland's criminal trespass law for refusing to leave a Baltimore restaurant when asked to do so. Their convictions were affirmed on appeal to the state's highest court. United States Supreme Court review was being sought when the Maryland legislature enacted a public accommodations law that made it unlawful for restaurants to deny their service to any person because of his race.

The Court granted review and, in an opinion by Justice Brennan, vacated and reversed the convictions, remanding the case to the Maryland Court of Appeals for reconsideration in light of the supervening change in state law. In so doing, the Court once again avoided confronting the constitutional principle for which Justice Douglas had argued in his *Lombard* concurrence— namely that *Shelley v. Kraemer* must be read to condemn as unconstitutional state action any judicial enforcement of private discriminatory conduct. Justice Brennan's resolution, however, did not deter Justice Douglas from addressing himself to the merits and concluding that the convictions should be reversed and the indictment dismissed outright.

Douglas reached this result from essentially three lines of argument, two of which are clearly reminiscent of Justice Harlan's *Civil Rights Cases* dissent. First, the denial to blacks of service in places of public accommodation was a deprivation of one of the incidents of national citizenship. According to Douglas, the Civil War amendments' "dominant purpose was to guarantee the freedom of the slave race and establish a regime where national citizenship has only one class."[27] Second, Douglas argued that the "duty of common carriers to carry all, regardless of race, creed or color" should become the "common law of the Thirteenth and Fourteenth Amendments so to speak" and made applicable to places of public accommodation.[28] Third, he contended that *Shelley* controlled, since Maryland had put its "full force" behind a policy of segregation in places of public accommodation and "enforced that policy with her police, her prosecutors, and her courts."[29]

Justice Douglas's opinion is notable not so much because of its discussion of legal doctrine but rather because of its extensive consideration of the realities of segregation in places of public accommodation and its plain talk about who practiced that form of segregation and for what reasons. Defenders of the state enforcement of trespass laws against sit-in demonstrators often argued, as Justice Black did in voting to affirm the convictions in *Bell,* that the Fourteenth "Amendment does not forbid a State to prosecute for crimes committed against a person or his property, however prejudiced or narrow the victim's view may be."[30] Put this way, the state's action becomes an understandable effort to protect the "personal prejudices" of one person (the restaurant owner) with respect to the use of his private property from unwanted invasion by another. Justice Douglas's opinion, however, bolstered by four factual appendixes, established that segregation in places of public accommodation had very little to do with the "personal prejudices" of the restaurant employees and largely to do with a calculated decision by corporate owners that they "could make more money by running a segregated restaurant."[31]

Justice Douglas's analysis of the underlying economic causes of segregation in places of public accommodation did not persuade the Court to address the merits or Justice Black to withdraw his vote for affirmance. But history has proven that he was right. In his opinion, Douglas made the following prediction: "Were we today to hold that segregated restaurants, whose racial policies were enforced by a State, violated the Equal Protection Clause, all restaurants would be on an equal footing and the reasons given in this and most of the companion cases for refusing service to Negroes would evaporate."[32] It was Congress, in the Civil Rights Act of 1964, not the Court, that outlawed segregation in most places of public accommodation. But the Act's passage largely destroyed any economic incentive to segregate and brought about in a relatively short time the result that Justice Douglas anticipated.[33]

Justice Douglas's opinion in *Bell* also provided him with an opportunity to express his frustration over what he saw as the Court's reluctance to address difficult civil rights issues head-on, deferring instead to the state courts for initial decision: "The people should know that when filibusters occupy other forums, when oppressions are great, when the clash of authority between the individual and the State is severe, they can still get justice in the courts. When we default, as we do today, the prestige of the law in the life of the Nation is weakened."[34]

Given this campaign by Justice Douglas to establish Congress's power under the Fourteenth Amendment to reach discrimination in places of public accommodation, the Court's decision in *Heart of Atlanta* came as an understandable disappointment for him. In his concurrence, Douglas made clear that he did not dispute the Court's conclusion that the Commerce Clause gave Congress ample power to enact Title II. It was simply his "belief that the right of people to be free of state action that discriminates against them because of race, like the 'right of persons to move freely from State to State . . . occupies a more protected position in our constitutional system than does the movement of cattle, fruit, steel and coal across state lines.'"[35]

Of course, the Court's strategic reliance upon the Commerce Clause, a power suggested by the *Civil Rights Cases* majority, ensured that the constitutionality of Title II would be upheld and, consequently, that millions of racial minorities would gain access over the years to places of public accommodation on a nondiscriminatory basis. Yet the views of neither Justice Harlan nor Justice Douglas found vindication in the decision. And American constitutional law is still unclear as to how far Congress can go under the Fourteenth Amendment in regulating behavior that would under most circumstances be viewed as private, not governmental. The *Civil Rights Cases* majority appears to have had the last word for the time being. Yet it should be noted that *Heart of Atlanta* did not discourage Justice Douglas from pressing his view that many activities customarily regarded as private were instead sufficiently public to constitute state action in cases involving a state anti-fair-housing initiative and referendum,[36] reversion of a segregated park to the testator's heirs,[37] a privately owned utility corporation,[38] and a fraternal organization,[39] as well as in school desegregation cases.[40]

Reading the Reconstruction Era Civil Rights Statutes Broadly

As the foregoing should suggest, Justice Douglas's efforts to persuade his fellow justices that the Thirteenth, Fourteenth, and Fifteenth Amendments should be broadly construed to reach arguably private conduct were largely unsuccessful. In contrast, his readings of both the criminal and civil Reconstruction era civil rights statutes have been adopted by the Court in several instances and remain the prevailing interpretations up to the present.

CRIMINAL

In *Screws v. United States,*[41] the Court confronted a constitutional challenge to a federal statute that made punishable "willful" deprivations of civil rights "under color of" state law. Douglas, writing for a plurality,[42] had to address two issues raised by the statute. First, how should "under color of" state law be defined? The defendants, law enforcement officers, argued that they were not acting pursuant to any state law when they caused the beating death of a black youth. Citing the Court's earlier decision in *United States v. Classic,*[43] Douglas responded to this claim by holding that "misuse of power, possessed by virtue of state law and made possible only because the wrongdoer is clothed with the authority of state law, is action taken 'under color of state law.'" Since they were "clothed" with that authority, the statute properly reached them.[44]

Second, how could the term "willfully" in the statute be construed to comport with due process requirements that a criminal statute be specific enough so that a person of ordinary intelligence will know in advance what conduct is prohibited and what is not? Douglas solved this second problem by engrafting onto the statute an interpretation of "willfully" that has survived the test of time for the most part: what is required is "an intent to deprive a person of a right which has been made specific either by the express terms of the Constitution or laws of the United States or by decisions interpreting them."[45] Prior to 1945, one authoritative commentator reports, "federal criminal sanctions had not been applied against conduct — private or official — in derogation of Fourteenth Amendment rights." *Screws* began the "process of transforming §§241 and 242 into effective sanctions" against such interference.[46]

In *United States v. Williams,*[47] the Court reviewed convictions that had been overturned by the court of appeals on the grounds that the civil rights criminal statute, 18 U.S.C. 241, reached only conspiracies by private parties to violate civil rights. Conspiracies involving state officials allegedly designed to violate rights protected by the Fourteenth Amendment were not covered. Justice Douglas dissented, and his dissent was subsequently adopted by the Court in the cases stemming from the murders of three civil rights workers in Mississippi.[48]

Douglas was unable, however, to persuade the Court to read the civil rights removal statute broadly. He argued in *Greenwood v. Peacock*[49] that the Court should adopt a construction that would allow a federal court to accept removal of a state court criminal case where it is "persuaded that the state court . . . will not make a good-faith effort to apply the paramount federal law pertaining to 'equal rights.'"[50] Instead, the Court held that removal would be allowed "only in the rare situation where it can be clearly predicted . . . that federal rights will inevitably be denied by the very act of bringing the defendant to trial in the state court."[51] The decision in *Peacock* has meant, for all practical purposes, that removal under the criminal civil rights provision is nonexistent.

CIVIL

In *Monroe v. Pape,*[52] Justice Douglas wrote for the Court in a case presenting questions about 42 U.S.C. 1983, the major statute authorizing civil suits in federal courts for civil rights violations. The plaintiff in *Monroe* alleged that Chicago police officers had violated his and his family's civil rights by conducting a search of his home and arresting him without a warrant for either action. The city of Chicago was also a defendant. The lower courts rejected the claims on grounds that the officers were not acting "under color of state law," as required by the statute, and that the city of Chicago was immune. Justice Douglas was able to dismiss the first defense by relying once again on *Classic,* and the later case, *Screws.* He held, further, that Section 1983 authorized a plaintiff to file an action directly in federal court without having first to exhaust state remedies. On the second defense, Douglas concluded, based upon his reading of the legislative history of Section 1983, that municipalities were immune to damage actions. Justice Douglas's opinion in *Monroe* has withstood the test of time on the "under color of law" and "no exhaustion of state remedies" points. As a result, a statute that had been all but forgotten until *Monroe* became the major vehicle by which victims obtained redress for abuse at the hands of state and local officials.

Douglas's reading of the legislative history of Section 1983 on the issue of municipal immunity was subsequently relied upon by the Court to impose even greater restrictions upon civil rights actions. In *Kenosha v. Bruno,*[53] the Court held that towns and cities were immune to Section 1983 suits even for injunctive relief. Douglas filed only a short dissent. However, in *Monell v. Department of Social Services,*[54] decided shortly after Douglas left the bench, the Court overruled the holding in *Monroe* with respect to absolute municipal immunity. Based upon a closer reading of Section 1983's legislative history, the Court concluded that municipalities could be sued where the violation was alleged to have been the result of an official "policy or custom."[55]

Section 1982 (42 U.S.C. 1982) guarantees equal rights with respect to real and personal property. Like Section 1983, this provision had been largely overlooked as a basis for redress. Justice Douglas played an important role in resurrecting it. In *Jones v. Mayer Co.,*[56] the Court held that Section 1982 was enacted by Congress pursuant to its powers under Section 2 of the Thirteenth Amendment and, consequently, could reach racial discrimination in housing by private parties. The opinion for the Court, written by Justice Stewart, essentially gave Justice Douglas in this statutory context what he had sought in vain in constitutional cases, namely, that certain modern forms of racial discrimination constituted "badges and incidents" of slavery. In his concurring opinion, Justice Douglas took the occasion to challenge "ideas of white supremacy in high places" by recounting the myriad ways in which blacks faced discriminatory barriers to advancement in modern-day America.[57] In this regard, he played a role like that often assumed now by Justice Thurgood Marshall in cases like the affirmative action rulings of *Regents of University of California v. Bakke*[58] and *City of Richmond v. Croson*[59] or by Justice William Brennan in the race discrimination death penalty case, *McClesky v. Kemp.*[60]

In a second case involving Section 1982, *Sullivan v. Little Hunting Park,*[61] Justice Douglas held that a remedy for its violation could be obtained in state courts and that both federal and state rules on damages, whichever served the federal interest better, might be utilized. In much the same way as he had done with Section 242 in *Screws,* Douglas gave life to Section 1982 as to both forum and remedy. Justice Harlan, in dissent, warned that Douglas's approach was bound to create a "common law of forbidden racial discriminations," when it would have been preferable to leave Section 1982 alone and urge complainants to rely instead upon the Fair Housing Act of 1968, in which Congress had addressed explicitly questions of forum and remedy.[62] Section 1981, the companion statute to Section 1982, affords the right to "make and enforce contracts" on a nondiscriminatory basis. Relying on its decisions in *Jones* and *Sullivan,* the Court ruled in 1976 that Section 1981 also reached private conduct.[63]

One final decision deserves mention in connection with Justice Douglas's inclination to read the Reconstruction era statutes broadly. In *Adickes v. Kress,*[64] the Court addressed the question of whether the trial court properly granted summary judgment for defendants in a Section 1983 action brought by a white school teacher who was arrested for seeking service, as part of an integrated group, at a Mississippi lunch counter. The Court also considered at some length how one would go about proving a violation "under color of any . . . custom or usage," in the words of one provision of Section 1983, as Ms. Adickes had alleged.

Justice Harlan's opinion for the Court adopted the formulation that Justice Douglas himself had developed in the early sit-in cases, which required a showing that the discriminatory custom, although not embodied in law, was in some way backed up by the coercive power of the state.[65] Justice Douglas, however, took a much more expansive view, seeming to hold that, even in the absence of coercive state power in the background, a Section 1983 violation based upon "custom" might be established. According to Douglas, "the 'custom' to be actionable must obviously reflect more than the prejudices of a few; it must reflect the dominant communal sentiment."[66] At root, Douglas seemed to be saying again what he always believed, namely, that the Fourteenth Amendment, and statutes like Section 1983 that are derived from it, can reach what is conventionally viewed as purely private discrimination.

III. Conclusion

Justice Douglas was fully committed to giving both the Constitution and federal civil rights statutes broad readings in order to reach continuing public and private discrimination against blacks. In this regard, although he was rarely successful in constitutional cases and largely successful in statutory cases, the following critical words directed by Justice Douglas at his fellow justices perhaps capture best his overall attitude toward the enterprise: "It is time we stopped being niggardly in construing civil rights legislation. It is time we kept up with Congress and construed its laws in the full amplitude needed to rid their enforcement of the lingering tolerance for racial discrimination that we sanction today."[67]

Notes

1. 379 U.S. 241 (1964).
2. 109 U.S. 3 (1883).
3. Ibid., at 24–25.

4. Ibid., at 17–18.

5. Ibid., at 42.

6. Ibid., at 43 (Harlan, J., dissenting).

7. Ibid., at 34–36.

8. Ibid., at 58.

9. Ibid., at 59 ("the rights which Congress, by the act of 1875, endeavored to secure and protect are legal, not social rights").

10. 163 U.S. 537, 552 (1896) (Harlan, J., dissenting).

11. 347 U.S. 483 (1954).

12. 368 U.S. 157 (1961).

13. Ibid., at 163.

14. Ibid., at 177 (Douglas, J., concurring).

15. Ibid., at 181.

16. Ibid., at 178, citing *Burton v. Wilmington Parking Authority,* 365 U.S. 715 (1961).

17. W. O. Douglas, *Mr. Lincoln and the Negroes* (New York: Atheneum, 1963).

18. Ibid., p. v.

19. 373 U.S. 267 (1963).

20. Ibid., at 274 (Douglas, J., concurring), citing *Burton.*

21. 109 U.S., at 26 (Harlan, J., dissenting).

22. 334 U.S. 1 (1948).

23. 316 U.S. 535 (1942).

24. 381 U.S. 479 (1965).

25. *Lombard v. Louisiana,* 373 U.S., at 274–75.

26. 378 U.S. 226 (1964).

27. Ibid., at 250.

28. Ibid., at 255.

29. Ibid., at 257.

30. Ibid., at 327.

31. Ibid., at 245.

32. Ibid., at 246.

33. *Federal Civil Rights Enforcement Effort,* A Report of the United States Commission on Civil Rights (Washington, D.C.: GPO, 1971), p. 10.

34. *Bell v. Maryland,* 378 U.S., at 245. This theme appears in a number of other Douglas opinions having to do with federal court vindication of federal rights, such as *England v. Louisiana State Board of Medical Examiners,* 375 U.S. 411 (1964) (concurrence); *Georgia v. Rachel,* 384 U.S. 780 (1966) (dissent); and *Younger v. Harris,* 401 U.S. 37 (1971) (dissent). Justice Douglas's views on this issue are dealt with comprehensively in Richards, "Justice Douglas and the Availability of the Federal Forum to Civil Rights Litigants," *Baylor Law Review* 28 (1976): 221.

35. *Heart of Atlanta Motel v. United States,* 379 U.S., at 279. (Douglas, J., concurring).

36. *Reitman v. Mulkey,* 387 U.S. 369 (1969) (concurrence).

37. *Evans v. Abney,* 396 U.S. 435 (1970) (dissent).

38. *Jackson v. Metropolitan Edison,* 419 U.S. 345 (1974) (dissent).

39. *Moose Lodge v. Irvis,* 407 U.S. 163 (1972) (dissent).

40. *Keyes v. School District No. 1,* 413 U.S. 189 (1973) (concurrence); and *Milli-*

ken v. Bradley, 418 U.S. 717 (1974) (dissent). However, Justice Douglas's opinion was joined by another justice in only one, *Moose Lodge,* of the foregoing cases.

41. 325 U.S. 91 (1945).

42. Douglas's opinion was for himself, Chief Justice Stone, and Justices Black and Reed. Justice Rutledge concurred in the result.

43. 313 U.S. 299 (1941).

44. *Screws v. United States,* 325 U.S., at 107–13.

45. Ibid., at 104.

46. T. Emerson, D. Haber, and N. Dorsen, *Political and Civil Rights in the United States,* vol. 2 (Boston: Little, Brown, 1979), p. 511. See also R. Carr, *Federal Protection of Civil Rights: Quest for A Sword* (Ithaca: Cornell University Press, 1947), pp. 106–15.

47. 341 U.S. 70 (1951).

48. See *United States v. Price,* 383 U.S. 787, 796–807 (1966).

49. 384 U.S. 808 (1966).

50. Ibid., at 851 (Douglas, J., dissenting).

51. Ibid., at 828.

52. 365 U.S. 167 (1961).

53. 412 U.S. 507 (1973).

54. 436 U.S. 658 (1978).

55. Ibid., at 690–91.

56. 392 U.S. 409 (1968).

57. Ibid., at 445–46.

58. 438 U.S. 265 (1978).

59. 109 S.Ct. 706 (1989).

60. 107 S.Ct. 1756 (1987).

61. 396 U.S. 229 (1969).

62. Ibid., at 247.

63. *Runyon v. McCrary,* 427 U.S. 160 (1976). The Court recently reaffirmed this holding in *Patterson v. McLean Credit Union,* 109 S.Ct. 2363 (1989).

64. 398 U.S. 144 (1970).

65. Ibid., at 152.

66. Ibid., at 179 (Douglas, J., dissenting in part).

67. Ibid., at 198.

COMMENTARY:
DOUGLAS AS CIVIL LIBERTARIAN
William Cohen

IT HAS NEVER been possible to put the Douglas judicial record on civil liberties in a nutshell. If there were nothing else, there is the length of that record, spanning more than a third of a century — decades in which the issues changed and in which, in a number of areas, Douglas's basic approach to the problems changed. It is inevitable that, with hundreds of relevant opinions, there would be puzzles, inconsistencies, and lapses. With all those difficulties, the three sections of Professor Powe's chapter do the best job to date of summarizing the major themes.

Most important, he says, is the Douglas-Black legacy of the 1950s, in which the two dissented in a series of cases curbing civil liberties during the Cold War hysteria. In civil liberty cases during the late 1940s, Black, Douglas, Murphy, and Rutledge were a consistent voting coalition.[1] In the summer of 1949, Justices Murphy and Rutledge died, to be replaced by Tom Clark and Sherman Minton. Douglas was seriously injured and incapacitated by a freak accident that summer. At the same time, the Court began its recurring capitulation to claims of internal security in the Cold War. When Douglas returned to the Court after his recuperation, there were two consistent votes to strike down legislation spawned by the nation's Cold War hysteria — Black and Douglas, dissenting. In the later 1950s the Cold War waned, and the dissenting bloc grew to four with the added votes of Warren and Brennan.[2] In 1962, with the replacement of Justice Frankfurter by Justice Goldberg, a solid majority entrenched the substance, if not the rhetoric, of the Douglas and Black positions,[3] and Black and Douglas have been vindicated by current free-speech doctrine that codifies most of the results they argued for.[4] This was, however, a joint venture. Although the other two themes identified by Professor Powe — an indifference to doctrine and mastery of the facts — are more the essence of Douglas, as opposed to Hugo Black, Black deserves at least equal credit for keeping the flame of freedom alive during a very dark period for the Court's jurisprudence on civil liberties.[5]

Everyone knows that Douglas was impatient with and careless in his use of conventional legal doctrine. Moreover, he did not seem to care whether other justices accepted or rejected his doctrinal formulations. Professor Powe concludes that Douglas's doctrinal contributions to freedom of speech law

121

are "all in all . . . not impressive"; Professor Days says that Douglas "was rarely successful" in arguing for constitutional control of private discrimination; and Professor Strossen discusses the unresolved conflicts in the doctrine announced in Douglas's free exercise and establishment opinions.

Douglas firmly believed in the Realist tenet that doctrine obscures, rather than explains, the reasons for rules. Moreover, at least in the First Amendment area, Douglas evolved his eventual positions as a dissenter. Some of the Court's more memorable dissents have counted most for memorable prose demonstrating the flaws in the majority's position. Dissenters — even great dissenters — are not required to build the doctrinal bridges that will hold a current coalition of judges together.

As Professor Powe points out, Douglas's indifference to doctrine was not without cost — particularly in the few cases where he wrote for a majority and forfeited the chance to announce a doctrine that could have controlled later cases. There were, moreover, occasional situations where Douglas found his own stands in irreconcilable conflict and was uninterested in extricating himself from the contradiction. As Professor Strossen points out, Douglas's opinions often failed to grapple with resolution of conflicts between competing absolutes.

An example beyond the religion clause cases discussed by Professor Strossen is *Lehman v. City of Shaker Heights.*[6] At issue was the refusal of a city's public transit system to accept paid political advertisements for inclusion with the commercial advertisements inside its vehicles. In a dissenting opinion in *Public Utilities Commission v. Pollak,*[7] more than twenty years earlier, Douglas had championed the privacy rights of a captive audience subjected to programs broadcast on transit vehicles. Even earlier, however, he had written for the Court in sustaining the First Amendment rights of those who wished to use sound trucks to broadcast their messages.[8] *Lehman* provided a perfect opportunity for reconciling rights of privacy and speech, since the eight other members of the Court divided 4–4.

Douglas's opinion, citing only the *Pollak* decision, voted for commuters' rights to be free from offensive political messages. His argument that streetcars were not newspapers or parks never satisfactorily explained why people in their homes were not equally captive auditors of sound trucks. The case, moreover, involved a transit company policy that subjected commuters to unlimited "commercial" advertising. Douglas insisted that the principle would be the same if a commuter challenged the policy of accepting commercial advertising,[9] but Lehman was not a commuter. Lehman was a political candidate who had been denied the right to advertise only because his message was political. Douglas validated the transit company rule that drew a distinction between political and commercial advertising. He voted to dismiss a challenge to it, because he concluded that no one had a right to subject commuters to unwanted messages of any kind. His vote insured, too, that Justice Brennan's powerful argument for a public forum theory — a theory that Douglas would accept in other contexts — would be a dissent. Brennan's position that distinctions between categories of speech were as impermissible as distinctions between points of view was one with which Douglas agreed.[10]

If Douglas was indifferent to doctrine, the usual label applied to him — "result-oriented" — is partially inaccurate. In cases involving speech, religion, and racial civil rights, Douglas often refused to join opinions that reached his results for other reasons. A great many of the Douglas positions discussed by Powe, Strossen, and Days were marked out in concurrences. Where freedom of expression, religious conscience, and racial justice were concerned, Douglas cared a great deal what the law should be. Yet he was indifferent to the layers of supporting doctrinal arguments that a conventional common law opinion used to support announcement of a legal principle, to concerns about exceptions or qualifications to a large principle, and to logical reconciliation of all the contradictions.

As Powe points out, if Douglas's doctrinal contributions have not been impressive, his strength was in the appreciation of the importance of facts — including facts that had not been brought to the Court by the parties and their lawyers. In addition to the dissent in *Dennis v. United States,*[11] discussed by Professor Powe, *Lehman* is also typical, with Douglas being the only judge to champion fully the rights of the third, and absent, party in a dispute between an advertiser and the transit company. There are hundreds of other examples of opinions that are vintage Douglas. A particularly interesting one is *Papachristou v. Jacksonville,*[12] where Douglas wrote for the Court, striking down a municipal vagrancy ordinance under the Due Process Clause. His recitation of the facts of the case takes up three pages in the official reports.[13] (Unfortunately, like much of Douglas's potential doctrinal contributions, *Papachristou* has not been a source for constitutional doctrine in the Supreme Court.)

There has always been one Douglas opinion that doesn't fit — the opinion for the Court in *Zorach v. Clauson.*[14] Professor Strossen makes a valiant attempt to reconcile *Zorach* with Douglas's later absolutist Establishment Clause opinions. At most, however, Douglas's religiosity would explain why he began with the oft-quoted dictum, "We are a religious people whose institutions presuppose a Supreme Being."[15] If Douglas always believed that the religion clauses forbid government to work "a religious leaven . . . into the affairs of our people,"[16] the result in *Zorach* is hard to understand.

Douglas's *Zorach* opinion portrayed the issue as identical to that posed by excusing a Jewish student from compulsory school attendance on Yom Kippur, a Catholic student on a holy day to attend mass, or a Protestant student to attend a family baptism.[17] The problem, however, was not that a truant officer might check up on the excused students, any more than the problem in *Zorach* was that excused students were required to attend the religious classes for which they were excused. The problem was the likely coercive impact of the program on those who were left behind. Douglas left it to the dissenters to explain, with considerable force, the way New York's released time would operate in practice. For example, Justice Jackson explained that, with school activities effectively suspended during released time, school "serves as a temporary jail for a pupil who will not go to church."[18]

Douglas never explained to us the doctrinal and verbal inconsistencies between his *Zorach* opinion and his later establishment opinions. In his concurrence in *Engel v. Vitale*,[19] Douglas's list of permissible accommodations in *Zorach* becomes a list of forbidden violations of the establishment clause. Douglas's footnote admits there is inconsistency with his past positions, but the inconsistency he points out is with *Everson v. Board of Education*,[20] where he joined the Court's opinion permitting public funding of transportation to religious schools. Aside from quoting the famous dictum that "we are a religious people," there is no analysis of *Zorach*.[21] Yet it was characteristic of Douglas not to be particularly attentive to straightening out the inevitable inconsistencies in thirty-five years of decisions.[22]

What is puzzling is not the failure to recant *Zorach* in the later opinions. What is puzzling is *Zorach* itself. In a case where facts were crucial, it was Douglas who ignored the facts. His description of the released-time program is extremely summary, containing only the information that (1) pupils are released during the school day to attend religious exercises on written request; (2) pupils not released stay in classrooms; (3) churches report to the school the names of pupils who did not report for religious instruction.[23] He left the lame conclusion that coercion of the students who remained behind was irrelevant, because there was no "evidence" of coercion in the record; in a footnote, Douglas stated that plaintiffs had not been permitted to prove coercion in the state courts because the issue had not been raised in the manner required by state practice.[24]

All the explanations in the world have not convinced me that this is not a case where Homer nodded. In saying that "today's judgment will be more interesting to students of psychology and of the judicial process than to students of constitutional law," Justice Jackson may have been saying that Douglas's position was only explicable because he still had political ambitions for the 1952 Democratic nomination.[25] However, Douglas has denied that he ever had political ambitions,[26] and Professor Powe concludes that there were presidential ambitions, but that they had waned by the 1950s.[27] Despite this possibility, the explanation for the lapse still remains to be given.

Notes

1. For example, in *Adamson v. California,* 332 U.S. 46 (1947), in which the majority held the Bill of Rights inapplicable to the states, Black, Douglas, Murphy, and Rutledge dissented. In *Terminiello v. Chicago,* 337 U.S. 1 (1949), discussed by Professor Powe, the majority consisted of these four justices plus Justice Reed.

2. All four dissented in cases involving legislative and state bar investigations

for communism. *Barenblatt v. United States,* 360 U.S. 109 (1959); *Wilkinson v. United States,* 365 U.S. 399 (1961); *Konigsberg v. State Bar of California,* 366 U.S. 36 (1961); *In re Anastaplo,* 366 U.S. 82 (1961).

3. *Gibson v. Florida Legislative Investigation Committee,* 372 U.S. 539 (1963) had first been argued in the 1962 Term. Arthur Goldberg took his seat on Oct. 1, 1962. *Gibson* was reargued on Oct. 10 and 11. When it was decided nearly six months later, Goldberg wrote the Court's opinion for himself, Black, Douglas, Warren, and Brennan.

4. For example, *Brandenburg v. Ohio,* 395 U.S. 444 (1969). See also *Elfbrandt v. Russell,* 384 U.S. 11, 15–16 (1967); *Keyishian v. Board of Regents,* 385 U.S. 589, 606 (1967); *Law Students Research Council v. Wadmond,* 401 U.S. 154, 165 (1971); *Landmark Communications, Inc. v. Virginia,* 435 U.S. 829 (1978).

5. Even the doctrinal formulation that Professor Powe gives Douglas credit for may have been the product of Justice Black. In the 1950s, the Black-Douglas dissents were often joint products, with particular phrases suggested by the justice who was not the nominal author of the dissenting opinion. Powe identifies the "speech brigaded with action" formula as having been formulated in the Douglas-Black dissent in *Roth v. United States,* 354 U.S. 476 (1957), an obscenity case. That case was decided June 24, 1957. The formula also appears in a Douglas-Black dissent that came down a week earlier in *International Brotherhood of Teamsters v. Vogt,* 354 U.S. 264 (1957), a labor picketing case. The dissent argued that picketing could be regulated "only to the extent that it forms an essential part of the course of conduct which the State can regulate or prohibit." Ibid., at 297. I was the Douglas law clerk in 1957, and I recall that the quoted language was inserted at the request of Justice Black, who thought it was the principle announced in his opinion for the Court in *Giboney v. Empire Storage & Ice Co.,* 336 U.S. 490 (1949).

6. 418 U.S. 298 (1974).

7. 343 U.S. 451 (1951).

8. *Saia v. New York,* 334 U.S. 558 (1948). Only a year later, the Court upheld a different ordinance regulating sound trucks. *Kovacs v. Cooper,* 336 U.S. 77 (1949). Black, Douglas, Rutledge, and Murphy dissented.

9. Douglas stated that the content of the message was relevant neither to the petitioner's right to express it nor to the commuter's right to be free from it. Since the commuter had a right to be free from it, however, it followed that the petitioner had no right to express it.

10. See *United States v. New Jersey Lottery Commission,* 420 U.S. 371, 374 (1975); *Erznoznik v. City of Jacksonville,* 422 U.S. 205, 218 (1975).

11. 341 U.S. 494 (1951).

12. 405 U.S. 156 (1972).

13. Ibid., at 158–61.

14. 343 U.S. 306 (1952).

15. Ibid., at 313.

16. *McGowan v. Maryland,* 366 U.S. 420, 561 (1961).

17. Ibid.

18. Ibid., at 324.

19. 370 U.S. 421, 427, 437, n. 1.

20. 350 U.S. 1 (1947).

21. *Engel v. Vitale,* 370 U.S., at 442. Moreover, the rationale of his concurrence

in *Engel* — that there is impermissible financial support of a religious activity because a public employee, paid by public funds, leads the prayer — should also apply to the larger teacher involvement in implementing the released-time program in *Zorach*.

22. That does not mean that Douglas was reluctant to recant an early position or concede a major shift in his approach over time. See Vern Countryman, "The Contribution of the Douglas Dissents," *Georgia Law Review* 10 (1976): 349-50.

23. *Zorach v. Clauson,* 343 U.S., at 308.

24. Ibid., at 311, n. 7. See also the opinion for the Court in *Terminiello v. Chicago,* 337 U.S. 1 (1949). Here, too, the opinion is short on facts, while Justice Jackson spends nearly 10 pages of the U.S. Reports spelling out the details. Ibid., at 14–22. But Douglas's opinion ended up sustaining a First Amendment claim by reaching out to decide that the statute involved was unconstitutional on its face, as construed in the charge to the jury. He argued that it would "strain at technicalities" not to reach this question, just because it had not been posed in this precise form either in the Illinois courts or the Supreme Court. Ibid., at 6.

25. David Louisell, "The Man and the Mountain: Douglas in Religious Freedom," *Yale Law Journal* 73 (1964): 995.

26. William O. Douglas, *The Court Years, 1939-1975* (New York: Random House, 1980), pp. 281, 290.

27. One strong Douglas critic points out that Douglas made no effort to secure the 1952 nomination and had no "coherent political organization." Michael E. Parrish, "Cold War Justice: The Supreme Court and the Rosenbergs," *American History Review* 82 (1977): 805, 801, quoted in William Cohen, "Justice Douglas and the Rosenberg Case: Setting the Record Straight," *Cornell Law Review* 70 (1985): 211, 215, n. 25.

PART THREE

Douglas and Civil Liberties:
Criminal Law and Privacy

Introduction:
Douglas as Civil Libertarian:
Criminal Law and Privacy

Samuel Walker

THE TWO CHAPTERS in this section seem appropriately paired. While all civil liberties issues involve controversy and a continual evolution of the law, the two issues under discussion here—criminal procedure and privacy— seem far more unsettled today than free speech, church-state relations, and race relations.

The common element shared by the criminal procedure and privacy issues is the extent to which both touch particularly sensitive nerves in the general public and the extent to which the political passions they have aroused have affected the course of Supreme Court decisions.

One might say that the public controversies over these two issues are, literally, "in the streets." Public fear of crime in the streets has been one of the dominant political themes of the past twenty-five years. Ever since the Supreme Court's 1961 decision in *Mapp v. Ohio,*[1] the issue has been framed politically in terms of a conservative attack on court decisions favoring "the criminal" at the expense of the law-abiding public. Despite a large body of scholarship indicating that the various Warren Court decisions have in no way impeded the local police or allowed criminals to "beat the system,"[2] this argument has had enormous appeal. Public concern about crime has contributed to the conservative tenor of presidential politics since the mid-1960s, with the result that the composition of the Supreme Court has shifted in a conservative direction.

Many Court observers argue that the greatest erosions of Warren Court precedents by the Burger and Rehnquist Courts have come in the area of criminal procedure. Indeed, the Burger Court proved to be surprisingly activist and civil libertarian in the areas of women's rights and abortion and did not dismantle the wall of separation between church and state as much as the Reagan administration had hoped.[3] The substantial erosion of Warren Court precedents in the area of criminal procedure can be explained, I would argue, by the Court's responsiveness to the widespread public fears of crime in the streets.

It is in this context that we should read Steven Duke's chapter on Douglas's contributions in the area of criminal procedure. Duke offers a provocative thesis: that despite the fact that Douglas had no reputation for great contributions in this area, in fact he appears to have been particularly influential. Duke finds Douglas the most oft-cited justice in criminal procedure case books. The source of this influence seems to have been Douglas's capacity to frame issues in broad humanitarian terms, terms that later acquired greater specificity in the hands of other justices. The capacity of the Court to respond to broad appeals to justice for the underdog is precisely what separates the Warren Court from its successors. That mood has passed, replaced by solicitude for the "haves," seen as the victims of rampant crime. In his commentary, Sanford Kadish argues, with considerable insight, that the questions of criminal procedure under discussion here ultimately turn not on narrow issues of constitutional doctrine but rather on broader questions of judging and the role of the Court. It would seem that those questions are, in turn, highly responsive to public passions about crime in the street.

The issue of privacy is also very much "in the streets." In the week before the fiftieth anniversary of Justice Douglas's joining the Court, between 300,000 and 600,000 people marched in Washington, D.C., in support of abortion rights. Political commentators called it the largest political demonstration in the nation's capitol ever, on any issue. Over the past fifteen years, meanwhile, antiabortion activists have also been in the streets, in their own marches on Washington and in constant and often disruptive demonstrations in front of abortion clinics. In many respects, abortion has been the most volatile domestic political issue of the past fifteen years. The Supreme Court's decision in *Webster*,[4] on July 3, 1989, only served to inflame political passions even further. Crime, of course, is a potent issue, but only one side seems to have any effective political organization.

The right to an abortion, of course, rests on the constitutional right to privacy that the Court enunciated in *Griswold v. Connecticut*.[5] In *Griswold*, Justice Douglas may well have made his greatest contribution to American law. Greatness in this sense is measured in terms of the enormous political controversies it has aroused and the many important and still unresolved questions about the scope of privacy rights. As both the chapter by Dorothy Glancy and the commentary by Elizabeth Schneider suggest, Douglas framed his *Griswold* opinion in broad humanitarian terms. This is precisely what discomfits critics of the opinion—the inattention to careful constitutional reasoning—and stirs its defenders—its protean capacity to sustain individual rights in a wide variety of contexts, with abortion being only one.

Both issues under discussion in this section have aroused public passions and seem more unsettled than those other civil liberties issues with which we associate Douglas's name. The source of both of these factors would seem to be Douglas's capacity to frame his opinions in broad humanitarian terms— terms that simultaneously expand the horizons of individual liberty and raise the most controversial political questions about judging, the role of the Court, and the meaning of the Constitution.

Notes

1. 367 U.S. 643 (1961).
2. Samuel Walker, *Sense and Nonsense About Crime,* 2d ed. rev. (Pacific Grove, Calif.: Brooks/Cole, 1989), pp. 116–43.
3. Vincent Blasi, ed., *The Burger Court: The Counter-Revolution That Wasn't* (New Haven: Yale University Press, 1983); Herman Schwartz, ed., *The Burger Years: Rights and Wrongs in the Supreme Court, 1969–1986* (New York: Viking, 1987).
4. *Webster v. Reproductive Health Services,* 109 S.Ct. 3040 (1989).
5. 381 U.S. 479 (1965).

Justice Douglas and the Criminal Law

Steven B. Duke

Few LAW PROFESSORS are unabashed admirers of the work of Justice Douglas. His opinions were terse and lacked the footnotes and other clutter that most opinions of the Court now contain. No one would liken an opinion by Justice Douglas to a law review article. As Vern Countryman noted, Douglas did not write for law professors and "seldom employed the forms of argument they use to persuade each other: the elaborate paraphernalia of analysis, distinction, reconciliation, extension of precedent, and the . . . elusive search for the 'original intent' underlying constitutional provisions."[1] Though a venerator of Douglas, I think there was even more to it than that. Douglas's opinions were often obscure in their reasoning and even their holdings. Many were drafted in twenty minutes. Some were written on the bench during oral argument. Editing was minimal.[2] His published opinions often read like rough drafts.

Despite these faults in his opinions — doubtless there are more — Douglas was one of our great justices. That he could easily have been greater is a disappointment that should not obscure his achievements. He surely deserves a presence on the "all-time nine."

Opinions on such large questions are easy to assert and impossible to refute or to verify. A judicial career that lasted more than thirty-six years and included 1,200 opinions is difficult to describe, much less to analyze or to compare with others. Though my task is more modest, it is subject to the same difficulties. I proffer a tentative evaluation of Douglas's judicial career in a single field, a field in which he had no professional or academic experience, one in which he claimed no special expertise or interest: criminal law. I rely solely on eight majority or plurality opinions and ignore entirely his numerous dissents that were later vindicated.[3] On that evidence, I cannot hope to establish more than the plausibility of my thesis, which many will find startling: I think that Douglas was the Court's most important jurist in criminal matters and may have been the most creative and influential criminal law jurist in this century.[4]

Whatever our political persuasions or predilections, those of us who teach criminal law still do it, to an amazing extent, with opinions written by Justice Douglas. The law professors who edit criminal law casebooks put Douglas opinions in their teaching materials more often than the opinions of any other justice. Other justices commonly regarded as among the great and whose opinions are widely reproduced in casebooks, that is, Holmes, Cardozo, Brandeis, Black, Stone, or all of them combined, do not make the cut as often as Justice Douglas.[5] For a justice who didn't write for the professors, that result is remarkable. What would our casebooks look like if Douglas *had* tried to please the professors?

There are myriad factors that go into a decision to include a court opinion in a casebook, but surely the most common ones relate to the creativity, novelty, and importance of the opinion. "Landmark" or "bellwether" opinions are almost always included, along with more recent pronouncements for which there is a strong bias, especially in criminal procedure. Douglas's opinions are twenty, even forty, years old. It seems to me, therefore, that those who put together criminal law casebooks have, perhaps reluctantly or even unwittingly, cast their votes for Douglas. A perusal of their casebooks is tantamount to an informal poll, producing extrinsic evidence that attests to Douglas's impact on the field.

I have no wish, however, to rest on the implicit opinions of casebook editors. Let's consider the opinions themselves.

I. Substantive Criminal Law

In a 1945 decision, *Screws v. United States,*[6] the Court was confronted with a constitutional challenge to Section 20 of the United States Criminal Code, which had been enacted in 1870 as an accretion to the post-Civil War civil rights statutes.[7] Long dormant, Section 20 was dusted off and employed against a Georgia sheriff and his deputies who beat to death a black man they had arrested on a theft charge. A homicide prosecution in the state courts was apparently impossible because of the positions of the killers in the state criminal justice system.[8] A federal prosecution was brought under the statute, which made it a crime, under color of law, "willfully" to deprive anyone of "rights, privileges, or immunities secured or protected by the Constitution and laws of the United States."[9] Screws said that the statute was unconstitutional because it made any act criminal that was a violation of the Due Process Clause, and that was far too vague to pass muster.

Writing for the plurality, Douglas authored what appears to have been a dissent, hastily converted. He sympathetically expounded on Screws's claim that Section 20 incorporated a comprehensive law library; that determining what was a deprivation of constitutional rights required reference to a "large body of changing and uncertain" case law.[10] Douglas noted that much of what constitutes due process is fundamental fairness, an inherently uncertain and context-bound concept. Thus, police, prosecutors, judges, schoolteachers, and other public servants can violate the Due Process Clause without knowing or even having good reason to know that they have done so.

Every policeman who obtains an "involuntary" confession or who engages in an "unreasonable" search deprives someone of due process, as does any judge who erroneously admits the fruits of such violations into evidence. Similarly, a public schoolteacher who causes her students to salute the flag,[11] pray,[12] or perhaps, observe a moment of silence[13] violates the Constitution and thus, arguably, the civil rights statute.

Having made a seemingly devastating attack on Section 20, Douglas then proceeded to uphold it. He did so by manipulating the statute's requirement that the violator act "willfully." Among the possible meanings of "willfully," as they applied to the *Screws* facts, were: (1) Screws knew he was beating his prisoner, Hall; he did it intentionally; (2) in beating Hall, Screws consciously sought to punish Hall without a trial; (3) Screws believed that Hall had constitutional rights that Screws was violating; (4) Screws had a bad purpose in beating Hall; (5) Screws was motivated in his beating of Hall by his official duties or position; he was acting at least in part as a law enforcer rather than solely to achieve personal aims; (6) all or some combination of the above.

Douglas mentioned most of these possible meanings of "willfulness" and related them to the vagueness that Screws complained of. He then included in his definition of "willfully" those meanings that he thought were responsive to the vagueness complaint and to the need for "fair notice." Oddly, however, it is not clear which those meanings were. If Douglas intended to include in "willfully" a belief that the act was in violation of another's rights under the Constitution or federal law, he had authorities ready at hand to support that construction.[14] He cited them, but it is not clear to what purpose.[15] The *mens rea* of a violation of the criminal provisions of the civil rights statutes is still unsettled.[16] Reminiscent of Hemingway, who left much to the fiction reader's imagination, Douglas left plenty of room for creative interpretation of his opinions by later courts.

The *Screws* decision provoked powerful opposition. Justices Roberts, Frankfurter, and Jackson dissented, arguing that Section 20, if it authorized the indictment, was clearly invalid.[17] The significance of the holding, in allocating criminal jurisdiction between the state and federal courts and in protecting civil rights, cannot easily be gauged. Neither Section 20, now 18 U.S.C. §242, nor its companion, Section 19, now 18 U.S.C. §241, have been used often.[18] Section 242 mostly has been employed, as in *Screws,* to punish police brutality and murder. Section 241, which reaches conspiracies of private citizens (as well as officials) to deprive citizens of their rights, has been used very little.

Still, until Douglas's opinion in *Monroe v. Pape*[19] made recovery of damages against policemen possible, Sections 241 and 242 were virtually the only sanctions against police brutality.[20] In recent years, about fifty law enforcement officers annually are prosecuted under one or both of these provisions.[21] Sometimes these provisions have been employed in ways that Douglas would have found objectionable, as when one who is acquitted of a crime in state court is then prosecuted in federal court for the same crime characterized as a civil rights offense.[22] But they have apparently not been used against schoolteachers who encourage their students to pray, nor in any of the other inappropriate ways Douglas had listed in *Screws*.[23] Prosecutors have shown considerable restraint. Moreover, federal criminal jurisdiction over civil rights offenses was important in the desegregation movement of the 1950s and 1960s, even if few prosecutions resulted. The symbolic value of these provisions may also have been invaluable.

In any event, what makes *Screws* a "Bellwether"[24] decision is not merely, or even mainly, that it upheld the criminal provisions of the civil rights statutes, but that it contains influential ideas about the legitimacy of vague statutes. *Screws* was decided nearly half a century ago, on the heels of an era in which the Court had invalidated many new crimes on grounds of vagueness and in which the Court said that any criminal statute is void if "men of common intelligence must necessarily guess at its meaning and differ as to its application."[25] Another formulation, only six years before *Screws,* was that "no one may be required at peril of life, liberty, or property to speculate as to the meaning of penal statutes."[26] Slavish application of those dicta would invalidate *any* criminal statute. No statute, criminal or otherwise, lacks uncertainty and ambiguity at its margins. A doubtful hypothetical case can be conjured up for any statute.

In his *Screws* opinion, Douglas aired ideas that courts across the country later used to uphold statutes against vagueness attacks. Here are a couple of those ideas:

1. Douglas suggested that if the civil rights statute were construed so that it did not punish anyone unless he deprived his victim of specific rights previously and clearly established in the text of the Constitution or decisions construing it, legitimate vagueness concerns would be minimal.[27] In today's jargon, if the penal statute is applied only to conduct that is clearly within the core meaning of the statute, uncertainties around the edges of the statute will not support a vagueness objection.[28]

2. Douglas also implied that if a person believes that his conduct is illegal when he engages in it, he ordinarily has no ground to assert the vagueness or uncertainty of the statute he violated.[29] "Standing" to complain of such vagueness should be limited to persons who were in fact uncertain (or mistaken) about the legality of their conduct.

Where no First Amendment interests are at stake, the first proposition is current law.[30] The second has a following, and seems correct, but remains controversial.[31]

Although Douglas upheld Section 20 in *Screws,* it obviously bothered him that Congress had not actually specified the conduct it was criminalizing but instead incorporated an amorphous body of case law that no one could hope to know. He had found similar arguments persuasive only a few years before, in *United States v. Classic,*[32] when he dissented from the Court's approval of criminal prosecution under Sections 19 and 20 for infringing the right to vote in a primary election.

Douglas returned to this problem twelve years later, in *Lambert v. California.*[33] There, the Court voided a conviction because there was no showing that the accused had probably known of the law before she violated it. Ms. Lambert had been convicted of violating a Los Angeles ordinance that required persons with previous convictions to register as such with the chief of police. Failure to register was a misdemeanor. An exconvict, Ms. Lambert failed to register as required. At trial, she tried to testify that she had not known of the duty to register, but the trial judge excluded the testimony. Writing for a five-member majority, Douglas declared, with no support in precedent, that the rule that "ignorance of the law will not excuse" is constrained by the Due Process Clause.[34] Where the conduct criminalized is not traditionally regulated or otherwise a likely subject of legal requirements, to punish one who was ignorant of the law may deny due process. The Court held that due process had been denied to Ms. Lambert.

As with *Screws,* the rationale and holding of *Lambert* is less than clear. With some justification, Professor Herbert Packer attacked Douglas's opinion as "unilluminating," "confused," "elliptical," and "flabby."[35] Justice Frankfurter, in dissent, predicted that the case would prove to be "a derelict on the waters of the law."[36]

Frankfurter was partly right. *Lambert* is rarely cited or relied upon in later opinions, but it is still included in most criminal law casebooks. The core idea of the opinion has also become commonplace and is often used to interpret criminal statutes. *Lambert* underlies a host of Supreme Court decisions dealing with *mens rea* requirements. Since *Lambert,* serious regulatory offenses, that is, *malum prohibitum* felonies, are construed as requiring knowledge of illegality unless the accused had reason to know that his conduct (or omission) was subject to regulation.[37] Thus, the Court held, and Douglas wrote, in *United States v. Freed,*[38] that ignorance of a duty to register hand grenades is no defense to a charge of possessing unregistered hand grenades. Unlike a convicted felon living in a town requiring her registration, one who deals with hand grenades has good reason to believe that they are subject to regulation.

Douglas's opinion in *Lambert* is also the unacknowledged intellectual ancestor of an important line of cases that shortly followed *Lambert* and applied its basic principle. In *Raley v. Ohio,*[39] an Ohio "Un-American Activities Commission" informed witnesses before it that they could assert their Ohio privilege against self-incrimination. Although they asserted the privilege, they were later convicted of contempt of the commission for refusing to answer. The Ohio courts held that, since the witnesses had received immunity, they were not privileged. Moreover, they should have known the law. In an opinion by Justice Brennan, the Court reversed, holding that the

Due Process Clause forbids conviction for conduct which state agents had led the defendants to believe was lawful. The Court didn't cite *Lambert,* but should have. It was more to the point than anything the Court did cite.

The Court later relied on *Raley v. Ohio* to reverse a conviction for demonstrating "near" a courthouse when city officials had given permission to demonstrate a hundred feet from the courthouse. Treating the grant of permission as the equivalent of an advisory opinion about what was "near" the courthouse, the Court in *Cox v. Louisiana*[40] unanimously reversed the convictions.

Finally, the Court in *Bouie v. City of Columbia*[41] voided a conviction for trespassing (in the white section of a South Carolina restaurant) where the defendants entered the premises lawfully but then refused to leave when requested to do so. To treat a refusal to leave as a "trespass *ab initio,*" as the state court had, was to render an "unforeseeable" interpretation of the law and thus to deny due process to the defendants whose conduct preceded that interpretation.

Raley, Cox, and *Bouie* may have been decided the same way had Douglas's opinion in *Lambert* never been written, but they could not have been so decided without relying on *Lambert's* seminal idea that due process sometimes requires us to hold that ignorance of the law does excuse. Moreover, as *malum prohibitum* criminal proscriptions proliferate, courts will likely extend and refine *Lambert's* basic principle. The common law presumption that everyone knows the law is ludicrously at odds with reality. Douglas was prescient in acknowledging that.

In the same genre as *Screws* and *Lambert* is *Papachristou v. City of Jacksonville.*[42] There, the Court unanimously struck down a city ordinance that had at least three vices: (1) it punished persons for their status, for example, "common gamblers," "common drunkards," "lascivious persons"; (2) it was intolerably vague; and (3) it criminalized "innocent" conduct, that is, conduct that was commonly engaged in by the pillars of the community, such as "nightwalking" and "habitually . . . frequenting . . . places where alcoholic beverages are sold or served."[43] Douglas implied that each of these vices made the ordinance unconstitutional. What is unique about Douglas's opinion is the latter position: that an ordinance or statute can be constitutionally defective merely because it overcriminalizes — defines as criminal conduct which is "normally innocent" and which one who had not read the ordinance would never suspect was a crime.

The criminalizing of commonly engaged in, "innocent" conduct has invaded our legislatures like a virulent disease. It seems to be ineradicable.[44] In *Papachristou,* Douglas recognized, as few legislators, judges, or academics do, that such overcriminalizing is at least as dangerous as vagueness in criminal statutes, since it even more effectively arms the police with boundless discretion and "encourages arbitrary and erratic arrests and convictions."[45] An ordinance like the one in Jacksonville, that literally makes criminals of everyone, does more violence to the concept of legality than one which punishes vaguely defined behavior. An ordinance that defines everything, or everyone, as criminal defines nothing, and no one, as criminal, for the essence of criminality is deviance. The inevitable highly selective enforcement of such ordinances is tantamount to the official "entrapment" that invalidated the convictions in *Raley v. Ohio* and *Cox v. Louisiana.*[46]

Unfortunately, no one has yet determined just how to tell when legislatures are insincere. Legislatures give few clues when they do not mean to condemn the conduct they define as criminal, but instead use an overly broad definition in order to grant the police unlimited discretion. Hence, overcriminalization has not yet been generally accepted as a ground for invalidating a conviction. *Papachristou* stands virtually alone on the point. Douglas was ahead of his time. But if there are to be serious constitutional limitations on police discretion, Douglas's approach in *Papachristou* will eventually have to be accepted.

I rest my case that Douglas was preeminent in substantive criminal law on one more Douglas landmark, a decision that gave rise to a doctrine that every criminal lawyer knows by name: the *Pinkerton* doctrine. Its genesis was a mundane case involving two moonshining brothers, Walter and Daniel Pinkerton. Daniel went to prison and left Walter in charge of the still. Both were convicted of conspiring to violate the Internal Revenue Code and of several substantive offenses of that kind. Daniel complained that he was convicted of substantive crimes he could not possibly have committed since they took place when he was in prison. The Court, in an opinion by Douglas, affirmed.[47] He said that there was a continuing conspiracy that was not ended when Daniel went to prison and that the crimes committed by Walter were in furtherance of that conspiracy. Indeed, the conspiracy "contemplated precisely what was done" by Walter.[48] Hence, Walter was acting as Daniel's agent or partner, and his criminal acts were attributable to Daniel.

In the final paragraph of his opinion, Douglas opined that it would be a "different case" if the substantive offense committed by one of the conspirators was "not in fact in furtherance of the conspiracy . . . or . . . could not be reasonably foreseen as a necessary or natural consequence of the unlawful agreement."[49] Enterprising prosecutors sought to convert this negative, limiting language into positive doctrine: if *Pinkerton* does *not* apply when the co-conspirator does *not* act in furtherance of the conspiracy or, if he does so act, his act is *not* foreseeable, then it *does* apply when his acts *are* in furtherance and *are* foreseeable. Federal and some state courts acquiesced, and thus created the doctrine. It means that if you conspire to commit trespass, you may end up convicted of murder; if you conspire to commit theft, you may be convicted of kidnapping. Both results are possible under the *Pinkerton* doctrine if the murder or kidnapping is committed by a co-conspirator, is in furtherance, and is foreseeable. The latter tests are easily met.[50]

The Model Penal Code has rejected the doctrine,[51] as has virtually everyone else in recent years.[52] Even federal courts are retreating from it.[53] This move toward rejection is not a repudiation of Douglas's opinion but rather a return to "original intent." The *Pinkerton* doctrine shares little more than a name with the opinion Douglas wrote. On its own terms, the opinion is unassailable.

II. Criminal Procedure

During the first half of Douglas's tenure, the Court paid little attention to criminal procedure. Moreover, except for the brief flurry during the 1960s, when the Warren Court drastically enlarged the rights of criminal suspects and defendants, Douglas rarely agreed with the majority in cases involving criminal procedure. Thus, he did not have many opportunities to write majority opinions on this subject. Yet, he wrote at least four that are still reproduced in the casebooks and are still influential.

A landmark by anybody's measure is *Griffin v. California,*[54] which held that adverse prosecutorial or judicial comment on the failure of the accused to testify is a violation of the privilege against self-incrimination. The reason, according to Douglas, is obvious: such comment is "a penalty imposed by courts for exercising a constitutional privilege. It cuts down on the privilege by making its assertion costly."[55] Justice Stewart argued in dissent, however, that the matter had not been obvious to the California courts, to the drafters of either the Model Code of Evidence or the Uniform Rules of Evidence, to the American Bar Association, to the American Law Institute, or to the "weight of scholarly opinion."[56] Nonetheless, Douglas's opinion in *Griffin made* it obvious. Stewart later relied on *Griffin* in striking down the federal death penalty.[57]

A decade after *Griffin,* when it adopted Proposed Federal Rules of Evidence, the Court applied *Griffin*'s rationale to *all* privileges, constitutional and otherwise, providing in Proposed Rule 513, that "the claim of a privilege . . . is not a proper subject of comment by judge or counsel. No inference may be drawn therefrom."[58] The Uniform Rules of Evidence were also changed in 1974, Rule 512(a) thereof being identical to Proposed Federal Rule 513. While there are many disputes concerning the scope of *Griffin,* there is today virtually no scholarly opinion that challenges the basic holding of the case.[59] Finally, while it was not the first Supreme Court opinion suggesting that constitutional rights may not be burdened, *Griffin* has supported challenges to such burdens on a wide variety of constitutional rights.[60]

In *Douglas v. California,*[61] the Court struck down a California rule that provided a lawyer to an indigent who appealed a criminal conviction only if the court first determined that a lawyer would be "of advantage to the defendant or helpful to the court." Justice Douglas declared for the Court that "where the merits of the one and only appeal an indigent has as of right are decided without benefit of counsel, we think an unconstitutional line has been drawn between rich and poor."[62] *Douglas* has been followed and even extended. In *Anders v. California,*[63] the Court held that the right to counsel in *Douglas* required more than a warm body with an LL.B. Counsel on appeal is required to file a brief. In *Evitts v. Lucey,*[64] during the 1984 Term, the Court extended *Douglas* to criminal appeals by nonindigents. There, a defendant who appealed his conviction had the appeal dismissed because his *retained* lawyer failed to file a required statement of appeal. The Court held this to have been an unconstitutional denial of the right to "effective assistance of counsel" on appeal, relying almost entirely on *Douglas.*

In typical fashion, the *Douglas* opinion spawned controversy that persists a quarter century later. In 1974, in *Ross v. Moffitt,*[65] the Court was asked to extend *Douglas* to discretionary appeals that follow an appeal as of right, an issue that had been left open in *Douglas.* In the course of deciding that *Douglas* did not require counsel for a discretionary appeal, Justice Rehnquist wrote for the Court that "the precise rationale" for *Douglas* "has never been explicitly stated, some support being derived from the Equal Protection Clause of the Fourteenth Amendment, and some from the Due Process Clause of that Amendment."[66] He then analyzed discretionary appeals on the theory that *Douglas* had been based on *both* theories. A decade later, however, in *Evitts v. Lucey,* where the Court extended *Douglas* to appeals involving retained counsel, Justice Rehnquist claimed in dissent that *Douglas* had been based solely on the Equal Protection Clause and thus provided no support for any complaints about counsel from the appellant who was *not* indigent.[67]

In *Boykin v. Alabama,*[68] a black defendant was charged with five robberies. He was found indigent and counsel was appointed. Three days later, he pleaded guilty. The "judge asked no questions of [him] and he did not address the court."[69] A jury was convened to determine the penalty, and the jury adjudged that the defendant should die, five times. The Court, through Douglas, reversed, holding that there could be no valid waiver of the constitutional rights involved in a trial, including the privilege against self-incrimination, the right to trial by jury, and the right of confrontation, unless a colloquy on the record prior to the plea establishes such waiver. Acceptance of *Boykin* as a matter of constitutional law is still not complete, but its holding is now contained in Rule 11 of the Federal Rules of Criminal Procedure.

The Court has not treated Douglas's 1972 opinion in *Argersinger v. Hamlin*[70] so kindly. *Argersinger* involved the right of an indigent accused of a misdemeanor to have appointed counsel. Argersinger had been convicted of an offense for which the maximum sentence was up to six months in jail. He was sent to jail for ninety days. He had claimed, however, that he was entitled to a lawyer to assist him in preparing and presenting his defense. The Florida courts disagreed. The Supreme Court reversed. The state's main argument was that Argersinger had no right to a jury trial, since the Court had held that that right attached only for misdemeanors in which there was an authorized jail sentence of *more* than six months.[71] Therefore, no right to a court-appointed counsel existed, either. If a misdemeanor prosecution is not a "criminal prosecution" within the Sixth Amendment for purposes of determining the right to a jury trial, how can it be a criminal prosecution for determining the right to appointed counsel?[72]

Douglas had little difficulty with the argument, pointing out both historical and practical differences between the jury trial right and the right to counsel. A fair trial is possible without a jury, Douglas observed, but often impossible without counsel.[73] Douglas therefore added a special criterion for the right to counsel in misdemeanor cases: even if there otherwise would be no right to counsel, there is such a right if the state wishes to send the misdemeanant to jail. What he did was to create a two-tiered inquiry: first, is the misdemeanor a "serious" one for purposes of the right to a jury trial? If so, there is a right to counsel; second, if not, is the offense still a significant one, requiring counsel although not a jury?[74]

The Court has recently rewritten *Argersinger,* treating it as if it held that the Constitution requires "*only* that no indigent criminal defendant be sentenced to a term of imprisonment unless the State has afforded him the right to assistance of appointed counsel in his defense."[75] That ludicrous distortion of *Argersinger* cannot stand. It means that you can have a constitutional right to a jury trial but be compelled to defend yourself in that jury trial without counsel. It literally means that you can be convicted of murder without counsel, provided you are not sentenced to prison. Thus Douglas's opinion in *Argersinger* has been turned upside down. Its correctness, however, is clear, and its return to a proper place in the constitutional constellation is certain.

III. Conclusion

Why have Douglas's opinions in criminal law and criminal procedure been so influential? Why are they still so relevant although twenty, even forty, years old? The reasons range from the mundane to the mystical. As for the mundane, Douglas's opinions were concise and their ideas densely packed. They are easy to read and easy to edit for casebooks. They also expressly rely on policy and principle, rather than precedent, for their results. His opinions, moreover, are virtually the only Supreme Court opinions in recent generations that we can be sure were written by the justice whose name they bear. Most other Court opinions during Douglas's tenure, as now, are substantially written by fledgling law clerks. It is hard to understand why anyone pays much attention to the lucubrations of anonymous youngsters.

Other reasons are more elusive. The elliptical, sometimes cryptic, quality of many of the opinions invites speculation and provokes thought. Like many provisions of the Constitution, such opinions are easily adapted to the future because of their open texture.

If there is a single, substantial explanation, however, it inheres in Douglas's wisdom and vision. The decisions discussed in this chapter were not only right the day they were decided, they are equally right for today and for tomorrow. Douglas's prescience, at least in criminal matters, was astonishing. While certainly not causal, or even explanatory, Douglas's deep understanding of the world and its people was essential to his vision, and that understanding could neither have been acquired nor maintained had he closeted himself in the Court and become, as he often put it, a "dry husk." Instead, he lived a life so full, active, intense, and varied as almost to defy description. Nor would his vision have been possible without his acute sensitivity to the burdens of minorities. He believed that the Court had no higher role than to protect minority rights. He also knew, as many of us are prone to forget, that those accused of crime are the most vilified and vulnerable minority in any society.

Notes

I am indebted to Tahirih Lee, Yale Law School class of 1989, for invaluable research and editorial assistance.

1. Vern Countryman, "Scholarship and Common Sense," *Harvard Law Review* 93 (1980): 1408.

2. See William Cohen, "Justice Douglas: A Law Clerk's View," *University of Chicago Law Review* 26 (1958): 7. "My own suggestions would be considered and, more often than not, rejected. . . . Normally, the initial circulation of a Douglas opinion to the chambers of other Justices would, save for few formal modifications, be identical to the first handwritten draft." See also James F. Simon, *Independent Journey: The Life of William O. Douglas* (New York: Harper and Row, 1980), pp. 225–26, 353–54. For an extreme attack on Douglas's writing, see Yosal Rogat, "Book Review," *New York Review of Books,* Oct. 22, 1964, p. 5. See also Bernard Wolfman, Jonathan L.F. Silver, and Marjorie A. Silver, *Dissent Without Opinion* (Philadelphia: University of Pennsylvania Press, 1975).

3. On that subject, see Vern Countryman, "The Contribution of the Douglas Dissents," *Georgia Law Review* 10 (1976): 331; Charles Ares, "Constitutional Criminal Law," *Columbia Law Review* 74 (1974): 362; and Steven Duke, "A Tribute to Mr. Justice Douglas," *Akron Law Review* 9 (1976): 399. There are, of course, many other important opinions by Douglas that involve criminal law or procedure. I exclude those like *Craig v. Harney,* 331 U.S. 367 (1947), and *Terminiello v. Chicago,* 337 U.S. 1 (1949), however, because they involve the First Amendment.

4. There are other jurists who could claim greater creativity than Douglas, e.g., Roger Traynor of the California Supreme Court and David Bazelon of the U.S. Court of Appeals for the District of Columbia. Since they never sat on the Supreme Court, however, they clearly did not have Douglas's influence. It can be argued, of course, that eight opinions, even Supreme Court opinions, do not add up to a very large jurisprudential body. Judge Bazelon, however, developed a reputation as one of our greatest thinkers in criminal law largely on the basis of a single opinion in *Durham v. United States,* 214 F.2d 862 (D.C. Cir. 1954). His major writings on criminal law are collected in David Bazelon, *Questioning Authority: Justice and the Criminal Law* (New York: Knopf, 1988).

5. In Sanford Kadish, Stephen Schulhofer, and Monrad Paulsen, *Criminal Law and Its Processes,* 4th ed. (Boston: Little, Brown, 1983), substantial portions of 154 court opinions are reproduced. Five of those are by Justice Douglas. Black has three, Stone two, Cardozo one. Excluding justices now sitting, there are a total of eighteen opinions by all other justices combined. In Phillip E. Johnson, *Criminal Law,* 3rd ed. (St. Paul: West, 1985), there are 141 opinions reprinted, of which seven are by Douglas. Excluding sitting justices, there are only twelve by all other justices combined. Of the justices named in the text, Black has three opinions, Stone one, and Holmes one (when on the Massachusetts court). In Peter W. Low, John C. Jeffries, Jr., and Richard J. Bonnie, *Criminal Law,* 2d ed. (Westbury, N.Y.: Foundation Press, 1986), there are seventy-six opinions, three of which are by Douglas. Former justices combined have eleven opinions. Stone has two. None of the other justices named have any. In none of the casebooks surveyed does any justice, including any sitting justice, have as many opinions included as Douglas.

6. 325 U.S. 91 (1945).

7. The term "willfully" was added in 1909. Ibid., at 101.

8. See ibid., at 160 (dissenting opinion).

9. See 18 U.S.C. §242, in which the language remains the same but "or" has been substituted for "and" between "constitution" and "laws." This change was made in 1948. See *United States v. Williams,* 341 U.S. 58, 83 (1951) (appendix to opinion of Frankfurter, J.).

10. *Screws v. United States,* 325 U.S., at 96.

11. See *West Virginia Board of Education v. Barnette,* 319 U.S. 624 (1943).

12. *Engel v. Vitale,* 370 U.S. 421 (1962).

13. *Wallace v. Jaffree,* 472 U.S. 38 (1985).

14. *United States v. Murdock,* 290 U.S. 389, 396 (1933); *United States v. Ragen,* 314 U.S. 513, 524 (1942).

15. Here is a small sampling of what he said: "If we construe 'willfully' in §20 as connoting a purpose to deprive a person of a specific constitutional right, we would introduce no innovation." *Screws v. United States,* 325 U.S., at 101. "The fact that the defendants may not have been thinking in constitutional terms is not material where their aim was . . . to deprive a citizen of a right and that right was protected by the Constitution. When they so act they at least act in reckless disregard of constitutional prohibitions or guarantees." Ibid., at 106. "The punishment imposed is only for an act knowingly done with the purpose of doing that which the statute prohibits." Ibid., at 102. Section 20 is "applicable only where the requisite bad purpose was present." Ibid., at 103. "One who does act with such specific intent is aware that what he does is precisely that which the statute forbids. He is under no necessity of guessing whether the statute applies to him . . . for he either knows or acts in reckless disregard of its prohibition of the deprivation of a defined constitutional or other federal right." Ibid., at 104. "He who defies a decision interpreting the Constitution knows precisely what he is doing." Ibid., at 104–05.

16. In one of the Watergate prosecutions, *United States v. Ehrlichman,* 546 F.2d 910 (D.C. Cir. 1976), Ehrlichman claimed to have believed that the warrantless entry and search of a psychiatrist's office was not a violation of the Fourth Amendment because of a "national security" exception. He thus claimed that he did not intend to violate anyone's constitutional rights because he didn't think he was doing so. The trial judge rejected the defense and the appellate court affirmed: "Specific intent under

Section 241 does not require an actual awareness . . . that they are violating constitutional rights. It is enough that they engage in activity which interferes with rights which as a matter of law are clearly and specifically protected by the constitution." Ibid., at 928. The same court, hearing an appeal from different defendants convicted of conspiring with Ehrlichman to conduct the same search and seizure, reversed their conviction, holding that the belief of the burglars in the legality of their search *was* a defense under §241. *United States v. Barker,* 546 F.2d 940 (D.C. Cir. 1976). For further obfuscation, see *United States v. Guest,* 383 U.S. 745 (1966); *Anderson v. United States,* 417 U.S. 211, 226 (1974).

    17. *Screws v. United States,* 325 U.S., at 138. The dissenters also argued that the defendant's crime was not "under color of any law" and therefore not covered by Section 20. Ibid., at 148. Justice Murphy also dissented, but for entirely different reasons.

    18. As of 1985, fewer than 450 federal prosecutions had invoked §§241 and 242. Harry A. Blackmun, "Section 1983 and Federal Protection of Individual Rights— Will the Statute Remain Alive or Fade Away?," *New York University Law Review* 60 (1985): 23.

    19. 365 U.S. 167 (1961).

    20. See U.S. Department of Justice, Office of Attorney General, *1961 Annual Report* (Washington, D.C.: GPO, 1961), pp. 179–81: the Constitutional Rights Unit was the sole unit responsible for prosecuting police brutality cases, as well as the sole unit responsible for prosecuting cases under Sections 241 and 242; of its twenty-six federal cases, at least five involved instances of police brutality or deadly force tried under Section 242; *1960 Annual Report,* pp. 184–86: the Constitutional Rights Unit brought thirty-eight federal prosecutions, at least nineteen of which involved police brutality or deadly force tried under Section 242; *1959 Annual Report,* pp. 186–89: the Civil Rights Division handled all Section 241 and 242 prosecutions, with the Due Process unit of the General Litigation Section of the Division prosecuting twenty-two federal cases, at least six involving police brutality or deadly force tried under Section 242; *1958 Annual Report,* pp. 176–78: "By far the most frequent type of complaint of violation of [Sections 241 and 242] is the . . . claim of an arbitrary victimization of some individual by local officials . . . [e.g.] a police officer acting in his official capacity has beaten a person in his custody without justification"; *1957 Annual Report,* pp. 109–10: "A considerable volume of the work of the Civil Rights Section is devoted to deprivation of constitutional rights of citizens by law enforcement officers or jail personnel"; *1955 Annual Report,* p. 134: there was at least one prosecution of a police brutality case under Section 242.

    21. See U.S. Department of Justice, Office of the Attorney General, *1985 Annual Report* (Washington, D.C.: GPO, 1985), p. 147.

    22. See *United States v. Hayes,* 589 F.2d 811 (5th Cir. 1979). Douglas rejected the dual-sovereignty doctrine, which permitted such prosecutions. *Abbate v. United States,* 359 U.S. 187 (1959) (dissenting opinion); *Bartkus v. Illinois,* 359 U.S. 121 (1959) (dissenting opinion).

    23. Douglas later approved the use of Section 20 against a policeman who obtained a confession by force. The gravamen of the offense, however, was the force rather than obtaining the confession. The crime would have been committed even if no confession had resulted. *Williams v. United States,* 341 U.S. 97, 102 (1951).

    24. Herbert Packer, "Mens Rea and the Supreme Court," *Supreme Court Review* 1962: 122.

25. *Connolly v. General Construction Co.,* 169 U.S. 385 (1926).

26. *Lanzetta v. New Jersey,* 306 U.S. 451 (1939).

27. *Screws v. United States,* 325 U.S., at 103–04.

28. *Parker v. Levy,* 417 U.S. 733, 755 (1974); *United States v. National Dairy Products Corp.,* 372 U.S. 29 (1963); *United States v. Harriss,* 347 U.S. 612 (1954).

29. *Screws v. United States,* 325 U.S., at 104.

30. See n. 28. On First Amendment issues, see Henry Monaghan, "Overbreadth," *Supreme Court Review* 1981:1.

31. See Wayne LaFave and Austin W. Scott, *Criminal Law,* 2d ed. (St. Paul: West, 1986), p. 94; Duke, "Legality in the Second Circuit," *Brooklyn Law Review* 49 (1983): 911, 928. Actually, that may have been the rationale of *United States v. Ragen,* 314 U.S. 513 (1942).

32. 313 U.S. 199 (1941).

33. 355 U.S. 225 (1957).

34. Ibid., at 229–30.

35. Packer, "Mens Rea," pp. 132–33.

36. *Lambert v. California,* 355 U.S., at 232 (dissenting opinion).

37. See generally, *Encyclopedia of Crime and Justice,* vol. 3 (1983), pp. 1067–78. In *United States v. International Minerals Corp.,* 402 U.S. 558 (1971), Douglas also applied this principle — or perhaps misapplied it — in construing a federal statute. This opinion is also often included in the casebooks. I'm not sure why. The opinion is fascinating, however, because Douglas holds that, although the ICC had been rebuffed when it went to Congress to try to get a change in the statute (no legislation resulted), the change that it sought was somehow accomplished by the trip. Douglas succeeds in making this ludicrous proposition sound plausible.

38. 401 U.S. 601 (1971).

39. 360 U.S. 423 (1959).

40. 379 U.S. 559 (1965). That the Court did invalidate the statute under the void-for-vagueness doctrine suggests how dead that doctrine is. Indeed, the Court described the statute as "precise, narrowly drawn." Ibid., at 562.

41. 378 U.S. 347 (1964).

42. 405 U.S. 156 (1972).

43. Ibid., at 156 n. 1.

44. See generally, Sanford Kadish, "The Crises of Overcriminalization," *Annals of the American Academy of Political and Social Sciences* 157 (1967), reprinted in Kadish, *Blame and Punishment* (New York: Macmillan, 1987), p. 21.

45. *Papachristou v. City of Jacksonville,* 405 U.S., at 162.

46. Compare discussion of desuetude in Alexander Bickel, *The Least Dangerous Branch,* 2d ed. (New Haven: Yale University Press, 1986), pp. 148–56; Arthur Bonfield, "The Abrogation of Penal Statutes by Nonenforcement," *Iowa Law Review* 49 (1964): 389.

47. *Pinkerton v. United States,* 328 U.S. 640 (1946).

48. Ibid., at 647.

49. Ibid., at 647–48.

50. See *State v. Stein,* 70 N.J. 369, 360 A.2d 347 (1976).

51. Model Penal Code, Section 2.04, comment at 21 (Tent. Dr. No. 1, 1953).

52. See collection of authorities in House Report No. 96-1396, Criminal Code Revision Act of 1980, p. 40., 96th Cong. 2d Sess., Sept. 25, 1980.

53. See *United States v. Sperling,* 506 F.2d 1323 (2d Cir. 1974).

54. 380 U.S. 609 (1965).

55. Ibid., at 614.

56. Ibid., at 617, 622 (dissenting opinion).

57. *United States v. Jackson,* 390 U.S. 570, 583 (1968).

58. Congress deleted the proposed rules dealing with privileges, so they never became effective. The proposed rules remain influential, however.

59. See generally, Charles T. McCormick, *McCormick on Evidence,* 3rd ed. (St. Paul: West, 1984), §131.

60. See, e.g., *United States v. Jackson,* 390 U.S. 570 (1968); *Wisconsin v. Yoder,* 406 U.S. 205 (1972).

61. 372 U.S. 353 (1963).

62. Ibid., at 357.

63. 386 U.S. 738 (1967).

64. 469 U.S. 387 (1985).

65. 417 U.S. 600 (1974).

66. Ibid., at 608–09. Justice Douglas dissented. He thought, as had the court of appeals, that the *Douglas* rationale applied to discretionary appeals. Ibid., at 619.

67. *Evitts v. Lucey,* 469 U.S. 387, 406 (1984) (dissenting opinion).

68. 395 U.S. 238 (1969).

69. Ibid., at 239.

70. 407 U.S. 25 (1971).

71. *Baldwin v. New York,* 399 U.S. 66 (1970).

72. The Sixth Amendment provides as follows: "In *all criminal prosecutions,* the accused shall enjoy the right to a speedy and public *trial, by an impartial jury* of the State and district wherein the crime shall have been committed, which district shall have been previously ascertained by law, and to be informed of the nature and cause of the accusation; to be confronted with the witnesses against him; to have compulsory process for obtaining witnesses in his favor, *and to have the Assistance of Counsel for his defense.*" (emphasis supplied)

73. *Argersinger v. Hamlin,* 407 U.S., at 30–31.

74. I have elsewhere elaborated on the acuteness of Douglas's analysis. Steven B. Duke, "The Right to Appointed Counsel: Argersinger and Beyond," *American Criminal Law Review* 12 (1975): 601. Justice Brennan agreed with my interpretation in *Scott v. Illinois,* 400 U.S. 367, 380 (1979) (dissenting opinion).

75. *Scott v. Illinois,* 440 U.S., at 374 (1979) (emphasis supplied). Justice Rehnquist, for the Court, expressed doubt that the Sixth Amendment contemplated *any* right to appointed counsel. Ibid., at 370.

COMMENTARY:
JUSTICE DOUGLAS AND THE CRIMINAL LAW: ANOTHER VIEW

Sanford H. Kadish

I HOPE THAT it will not be thought graceless if, in a volume designed (in part, at least) to pay homage to a famous man, I take a more guarded view than does Professor Duke of Justice Douglas's opinions in the field of criminal law.

Duke makes an interesting point when he observes that Douglas's opinions appear more than those of any other justice in the several criminal law casebooks he mentions. Of course it's not clear what that signifies, since we are dealing with such small numbers—for example, in my book, Douglas's five opinions to three for Black and two for Stone. On the other hand, Douglas did write the opinion in some notable cases, as Duke demonstrates; that the casebooks continue to reproduce them is surely evidence of their importance in the criminal law area.

Whether those opinions support Duke's daring conclusion that Douglas was the Court's "most important jurist in criminal matters and may have been the most creative and influential criminal law jurist in this century" is more problematical. That is a lot to rest on eight cases. Moreover, four of these were criminal procedure cases. And since the justice's contribution to the Warren Court's constitutional revolution in this area was very small—largely confined to these four cases—they couldn't support Duke's claim for the justice's preeminence. So let's look at the other cases.

In his *Screws* plurality opinion, Douglas rescued the Civil Rights Act as a federal weapon against violations of people's constitutional rights by state officials. At the time of the decision, there was considerable disagreement over the appropriateness in a federal system of supervening federal prosecutions against perpetrators of state crimes—the animating consideration in the dissent of Justices Roberts, Frankfurter, and Jackson. As they observed, "Of course the petitioners are punishable. The only issue is whether Georgia alone has the power and duty to punish, or whether this patently local crime can be made the basis of a federal prosecution."[1] On that issue, Douglas's view was vindicated by subsequent events: the moral imperative of the civil rights revolution turned out to dwarf in importance the traditional restraints of federalism. It is also an estimable feature of the Douglas opinion that it squarely confronted the vice of vagueness in a criminal statute that made

149

criminal whatever actions of state officials should turn out to be violations of the Constitution. However, I have more reservations than Duke as to how well Justice Douglas's opinion met the challenge of vagueness.

It is interesting that we should have this different view, because we apparently see the same things in the opinion. Douglas purports to save the statute by interpreting "willfully" to require that the defendant have been aware — or have acted in reckless disregard (he waffles on this) — that his action violated his victim's constitutional right. However, as Duke observes, Douglas never makes clear which of a variety of possible meanings of the term "willfully" he had in mind. Then Duke gives Douglas credit for having "aired ideas" that later proved helpful to courts in dealing with vagueness challenges. The point is well taken. However, it is also true that these ideas are tossed off as cryptic hints, with no attempt at anything approaching a rigorous analysis.

A perplexity about his opinion that has long bothered me is this: Douglas reasoned that the requirement that the defendant have acted willfully saves the statute against a vagueness challenge, on the ground that a person who knows his act violates a constitutional right can hardly complain that he was left at sea as to what rights the Constitution affords. To this, the dissent responded that it hardly could help to be told that you must not do something "willfully" if you are not told what that something is.[2] To this, Douglas replied that it does indeed help where there is no vagueness about the criminality of what you have done, notwithstanding the vagueness as to the criminality of other actions the statute arguably prohibits.[3] However, if this is the basis of the Douglas opinion, then it is hard to see what "willfully" has to do with the matter. Consider *Screws*. So long as the constitutional right the defendant is charged with violating was clearly established before he acted, there is no ground for his complaint that the law failed to give him adequate notice, and this must be so whether or not he acted willfully, since there is no constitutional requirement that a defendant know the law.

Lambert is the next case Duke relies on to support his judgment. Now I thoroughly approve of the result in this case. It makes a desirable inroad into the conventional doctrine that ignorance of the law can never be a defense. But can the opinion withstand scrutiny? Here again, Duke and I appear to be in agreement in description but not in judgment. He appears to accept at least some of Herbert Packer's severe criticism of the opinion,[4] but nonetheless puts it in his Hall of Fame because of what the holding accomplished — imposing due process restraints on the doctrine that ignorance of law does not excuse. I applaud that result as well, but in judging the work of a jurist as significant as Justice Douglas one would have hoped for more.

As Duke stated, Justice Douglas held that due process prevented the conviction of Mrs. Lambert because she could not have been fairly expected to have known that, as an ex-felon, she was required to register with the police in order to live in Los Angeles. And this was so despite the generally prevailing rule that ignorance of the law is no defense. Well then, what does this mean for all those cases where the Court had upheld the imposition of strict liability against similar due process challenges?[5] These were also cases where the defendant could not have been fairly expected to know that what he was doing was criminal. To be sure, those cases differed in that the plight of the defendant arose from an innocent ignorance of some factual circumstance rather than ignorance of the law. However, if anything, that should make those cases *a fortiori* beneficiaries of the *Lambert* doctrine. Douglas's response was that in *Lambert* there was a failure to act — rather than a positive action — in circumstances that could not have alerted the actor to the consequences of her deed.[6]

But what about cases in which the defendant did a positive action in circumstances that could not have alerted him to the consequences of his deed? Shouldn't that person have the benefit of the *Lambert* doctrine as well? If so, strict liability becomes unconstitutional. However, this is a conclusion that Douglas explicitly resisted. On what grounds? No satisfactory answer was forthcoming, which is, I take it, what was behind Justice Frankfurter's retort in his dissent that "If the generalization that underlies, and alone can justify, this decision were to be given its relevant scope, a whole volume of the United States Reports would be required to document in detail the legislation in this country that would fall or be impaired."[7]

Duke believes that Frankfurter was partly right in predicting that *Lambert* would prove to be "a derelict on the waters of the law." I think Frankfurter was altogether right on the level of constitutional adjudication. Neither the Supreme Court nor, so far as I am aware, any other court has used *Lambert* to cast doubt on the constitutionality of strict criminal liability or to impose further due process restraints on the traditional mistake of law doctrine. The cases Duke offers in support of his view of the significance of *Lambert (Raley, Cox,* and *Bouie)* seem to me to cut the other way. All involved situations where there was some misleading of the defendant by officials as to what the law was. *Lambert* might have been cited, as Duke says, but the fact is that it was not — not in any of these cases. It is as if the Court went out of its way to keep the *Lambert* germ isolated. Even Justice Douglas, in his brief opinion in *Bouie,* chose to ignore *Lambert,* simply stating that he would reverse for the reasons he gave in his opinion in *Bell v. Maryland.* There, he preferred to rest reversal of defendant's conviction on the ground that the alleged offense occurred in the exercise of the defendant's constitutional rights.[8] All the earmarks of a derelict, it seems to me. On the other hand, *Lambert* has not been a derelict in another sense: it has served to give impetus to and an authority for efforts to change the law in the direction of easing the strict common law rule that legal mistake can never be a defense.[9]

Among the other major opinions Duke discussed, *Papachristou* was, I agree, a notable opinion. It went far to sealing the doom of vagrancy-like statutes in American jurisprudence and gave convincing constitutional form to a decade of increasingly powerful attack against the use of criminal statutes of this genre. *Pinkerton,* however, is a different matter. Duke makes an interesting and original defense of Douglas's opinion: it is the distortion of *Pinkerton*'s language by subsequent lower courts that is responsible for the *Pinkerton* doctrine, not Douglas's opinion itself. One might read Douglas's opinion differently, but even conceding Duke's point, it says nothing affirmatively about the opinion, which has in fact served as whipping boy of law reformers.

Let me close with a more general observation about the contrasting perspectives Duke and I have on Justice Douglas's opinions. Our main difference is not primarily over what each of us sees in those opinions, but over appraising what we see, and it is a difference that marks a great divide in theories of constitutional decision making. What is the appropriate role of the Supreme Court? What makes for greatness in a Supreme Court justice? No doubt one could formulate answers to these questions in numerous ways, but there are two formulations which provide an interesting contrast.

One formulation (let's call it the policy-oriented model) is roughly that the role of the Supreme Court, like that of other organs of government, is to make good decisions that produce good results in terms of the ends of the society and its principal values. By the same token, a justice succeeds to the extent that he or she reaches results in particular cases that are right and good in this sense. A contrasting formulation (the law-oriented perspective) would place less emphasis on furthering the right policy and reaching the right result and more on the process of reasoning, through which the result reached is justified. Good results are to be sought, of course, but only within the framework that a democratic government provides. The Court, unlike the Congress or the president, is not vested with powers of government. It is an elite institution with justices appointed for life, and it derives its power solely from its mission to interpret and apply the law. And the function of its opinions is to justify its assertion of power by demonstrating that the judgment reached rests squarely on the law. To the extent that the Court goes beyond the law to reach what it considers right results, it usurps power that was not given to it. And to the extent that it writes opinions that fail to justify the result in terms of the law, it fails in its responsibility to ground its decisions in the law.

I think it fair to say that Justice Douglas would not have been impressed by the law-oriented model of the function of the Court. He was not a justice who devoted a great deal of time and effort seeking to satisfy the professors that he had his law right, as he would have put it. Results and sound policy were what mattered to him. And so, if one prefers the policy-oriented model, Justice Douglas gets high marks, at least by people who find themselves often in agreement with the results he reached. If one favors the competing model, on the other hand, the justice receives very much lower grades.

Which model has it right? That involves a very long debate. I suspect that neither Duke nor I would want to embrace either model without qualification. However, I would guess that my more guarded judgment of the work of the justice stems from a greater sympathy for the law-oriented model than Duke has.

Notes

1. *Screws v. United States,* 225 U.S. 91, 139 (1945).

2. "'Willfully' doing something that is forbidden, when that something is not sufficiently defined according to the general conceptions of requisite certainty in our criminal law, is not rendered sufficiently definite by that unknowable having been done 'willfully.'" Ibid., at 154.

3. "Of course, willful conduct cannot make definite that which is undefined. But willful violators of constitutional requirements, which have been defined, certainly are in no position to say that they had no adequate advance notice that they would be visited with punishment." Ibid., at 105.

4. Herbert Packer, "Mens Rea and the Supreme Court," *Supreme Court Review* 1962:132–33.

5. For example, *United States v. Balint,* 258 U.S. 250 (1922); *United States v. Dotterweich,* 320 U.S. 277 (1943).

6. *Lambert v. California,* 355 U.S. 225, 228 (1957).

7. Ibid., at 232.

8. *Bell v. Maryland,* 378 U.S. 242 (1963).

9. See, e.g., California Joint Legislative Committee for Revision of the Penal Code, Penal Code Revision Project, Tentative Draft No. 2, Comments (1968), pp. 64–67.

Douglas's Right of Privacy: A Response to His Critics

Dorothy J. Glancy

Ir HAS BEEN almost a quarter of a century since Justice Douglas persuaded a majority of the United States Supreme Court to agree with his concept of a right of privacy in *Griswold v. Connecticut.*[1] Ever since Douglas launched it, his concept of the right of privacy has remained a lively topic of controversy.[2] Critics of Douglas's concept of the right of privacy have expressed views ranging from an ostrich-like position of "I cannot see it" to strident calls for the defense of morality against it. At the same time, Douglas's concept of the right of privacy has also affected the way they, and we, understand the Constitution. Five aspects of Douglas's provocative idea have provided major focal points for debate about the right of privacy: its penumbral character, its constitutional status, its natural law attributes, its individual nature, and its political quality. Before considering each of these five facets of Douglas's right of privacy, it is important to understand how his controversial idea of the right of privacy evolved.

I. Douglas's Evolving Idea of the Right of Privacy

Douglas's views about the right of privacy developed after his appointment to the Supreme Court. Professor Powe has remarked, "The measure of Justice Douglas has been change and growth. Thirty-five years after he ascended to the bench it is easy to believe he was always a great civil libertarian, and to forget that he was the nation's expert on issues of corporate finance."[3] In his biography of Douglas, *Independent Journey: The Life of William O. Douglas,* James Simon noted that, when Douglas was doing his early bankruptcy research, "it did not seem to occur to Douglas that there were values at stake that might have transcended the practical problems of a researcher. The privacy of the debtor, for instance."[4]

Douglas seemed well aware that his views on legal and constitutional matters, including the right of privacy, shifted over time.[5] During his first decade on the Court, Douglas's writings rarely mentioned privacy. For example, in 1942 Justice Douglas wrote the opinion for the Court in *Skinner v. Oklahoma,* a decision in which the Supreme Court struck down as a denial of equal protection a state statute providing for the sterilization of certain repeat offenders. That opinion did not even mention a right of privacy. Douglas focused, rather, upon the "basic liberty" involved in marriage and procreation.[6] Justice Douglas could have described that basic liberty as an aspect of the right of privacy. He later would do so. However, in 1942, Justice Douglas did not think about the *Skinner* case in right of privacy terms. Justice Douglas's attitude toward privacy during the 1940s is illustrated by his opinion for the Court in *Zap v. United States.* In *Zap* the Court upheld a warrantless seizure by FBI agents engaged in a lawful search with the consent of the employees of the defendant, a Navy contractor. Justice Douglas readily found a waiver of privacy rights: "The waiver of such rights to privacy and to immunity as petitioner had respecting this business undertaking for the Government made admissible in evidence all the incriminating facts."[7]

By the early 1950s Douglas began to be concerned about privacy, particularly in the context of electronic surveillance. In his *An Almanac of Liberty,* published in 1954, Douglas did not use "right of privacy" as the title of any of the 365 items on which he chose to present his views about liberty. These views were, he explained, wider "than civil liberties in the conventional sense." Douglas did include four entries decrying wiretapping as a violation of the Fourth Amendment. But the index yields nothing listed under "privacy." Nevertheless, in the Foreword, dated May 18, 1954, Douglas asserted that he ranked "the right to property with the right of privacy" and specifically associated himself with the views of Louis D. Brandeis. He also explained that the *Almanac* was a project he had started "many years ago." It is therefore likely that, between starting the *Almanac* and publishing it, Douglas began to turn his attention to the right of privacy. In the last of the three *Almanac* entries regarding "Wire Tapping," Douglas described his concerns about electronic surveillance: "The invasion of privacy is ominous. It is dragnet in character. . . . It is specially severe in labor espionage, in loyalty investigations, in probes to find out what people think."[8]

In the spring of 1952, Douglas published three dissenting opinions, in *On Lee v. United States,* in *Beauharnais v. Illinois,* and in *Public Utilities Commission v. Pollak,* which reveal his then-evolving views about the right of privacy. In the background were the earlier Communist party cases, especially *Dennis v. United States,* which involved the prosecution of Communist party recruiting. Douglas dissented in *Dennis* on the ground that the defendants had taken no action, but "were charged with a conspiracy to form a party." He did not argue for recognition of a general right of privacy. However, he expressed outrage: "We then start probing men's minds for motive and purpose; they become entangled in the law not for what they did but *for what they thought;* they get convicted not for what they said but for the purpose with which they said it."[9]

Writing about Douglas's right of privacy in 1965, Arthur Sutherland pointed out, "Between 1938 and 1948, a change of political theory developed in the intellectual life of the United States. . . . things done in Germany, Italy, and Russia as well as certain activity in the United States, had unsettled previous premises of democratic political thinking."[10] Douglas's increasing interest in the right of privacy was in part a reaction to the loyalty investigations of the 1950s, which greatly concerned him: "The extensive and intensive investigations of the loyalty of government employees, which we have experienced in recent years, have trenched heavily on the rights of citizens."[11]

Dissenting in *On Lee v. United States,* a case involving an undercover narcotics agent wired for sound with a hidden microphone, Douglas began to express his perception of the right of privacy under the Fourth and Fifth Amendments. Douglas confessed error in not having earlier insisted on protection of privacy from electronic surveillance:

I now feel that I was wrong in the *Goldman* case [in not voting to overrule *Olmstead*]. Mr. Justice Brandeis in his dissent in *Olmstead* espoused the cause of privacy—the right to be let alone. . . . The nature of the instrument that science or engineering develops is not important. The controlling, the decisive factor is the invasion of privacy against the command of the Fourth and Fifth Amendments.[12]

As of that point, Douglas publicly espoused Brandeis's cause of privacy.[13]

A curious quirk in Douglas's concept of right of privacy is that Douglas always wrote and spoke in terms of a right *of,* rather than *to,* privacy. Brandeis had consistently written in terms of a right *to* privacy. Douglas was perhaps seeking to distinguish his concept of a constitutional right of privacy from the tort right to privacy, about which Brandeis had first written in his famous 1890 law review article.[14] Douglas rejected the tort right to privacy as unconstitutional, because it would impose damage liability on the press. Use of "of" rather than "to" also made the right of privacy parallel with other constitutional rights, such as rights of free expression and of association. "Of" placed privacy along with other inherent rights of the people to be free from government interference.

However, even during his "privacy spring" of 1952, Douglas did not seem to think about the right of privacy in a comprehensive sense. In *Beauharnais v. Illinois,* the Court upheld a criminal conviction under a controversial "group libel" statute. In dissent, Douglas referred to the right of privacy by way of contrast to the preferred position of freedom of expression: "For example, privacy, equally sacred to some, is protected by the Fourth Amendment only against unreasonable searches and seizures. There is room for regulation of the ways and means of invading privacy."[15] He did not then connect the Fourth Amendment to the First, Third, and Fifth Amendments, as he would do later in fashioning a broader right of privacy.

In another 1952 dissent, announced after *Beauharnais* but before *On Lee,* Justice Douglas laid the foundation for a more expansive vision of the right of privacy. In *Public Utilities Commission v. Pollak,* the legality of broadcasting radio programs in the publicly licenced streetcars then serving the

District of Columbia was at issue. In his dissenting opinion, Douglas presented the outlines of the right of privacy he would later persuade the Court to adopt in *Griswold v. Connecticut.* He argued, "Liberty in the constitutional sense must mean more than freedom from unlawful governmental restraint; it must include privacy as well, if it is to be a repository of freedom. The right to be let alone is indeed the beginning of all freedom." He then went on to catalogue various "aspects of the constitutional right to be let alone." Douglas conceded that "one who enters any public place sacrifices some of his privacy. My protest is against the invasion of his privacy over and beyond the risks of travel."[16] Douglas insisted that the right of privacy requires government to let people alone to choose for themselves.

By the spring of 1957, Douglas devoted one of the three lectures later published as *The Right of the People* to "the Right to Be Let Alone." The lecture began with a section on "The Right of Privacy," in which Douglas argued, "There is, indeed, a congeries of these rights that may conveniently be called the right to be let alone. They concern the right of privacy— sometimes explicit and sometimes implicit in the Constitution. . . . The penumbra of the Bill of Rights reflects human rights which, though not explicit, are implied from the very nature of man as a child of God."[17] Justice Douglas's concept of the right of privacy was by then fairly complete.

Four years later, in his dissent in *Poe v. Ullman,* Justice Douglas returned to this implicit and explicit constitutional right of privacy. The issue in *Poe v. Ullman* was the constitutionality of a Connecticut statute criminalizing the use and distribution of contraceptives. Although the majority found that the issue was not justiciable, Justice Douglas disagreed. To Douglas, the statute was unconstitutional on both First Amendment and right of privacy grounds: "This Connecticut law as applied to this married couple deprives them of 'liberty' without due process of law, as that concept is used in the Fourteenth Amendment." He explained,

"Liberty" within the purview of the Fifth Amendment includes the right of "privacy," a right I thought infringed in that case [*Public Utilities Commission v. Pollak*] because a member of a "captive audience" was forced to listen to a government-sponsored radio program. "Liberty" is a conception that sometimes gains content from the emanations of other specific guarantees (*NAACP v. Alabama,* 357 U.S. 449, 460) or from experience with the requirements of a free society.

Douglas denounced the statute as "an invasion of the privacy that is implicit in a free society." He insisted that this implicit right of privacy "is not drawn from the blue. It emanates from the totality of the constitutional scheme under which we live."[18]

Four years later, Justice Douglas's earlier dissenting view became the Court's rationale for invalidating the same Connecticut statute on right of privacy grounds in *Griswold v. Connecticut.*[19] However, the right of privacy was not the original basis Douglas presented for striking down the statute. His first draft of the opinion of the Court relied on First Amendment guarantees of "freedom to associate and privacy in one's association." Douglas himself seemed somewhat unpersuaded by his own argument: "The foregoing [First Amendment freedom of association] cases do not decide this case." The first draft suggested that the freedom of association cases did, however, "place it in the proper frame of reference. Marriage does not fit precisely any of the categories of First Amendment rights. But it is a form of association as vital in the life of a man or woman as any other, and perhaps more so." By the end of the draft opinion, Justice Douglas seemed to throw up his hands in desperation over articulating a coherent freedom of association theory and ended the draft with a single citation: "Cf. *Rochin v. California,* 342 U.S. 165 (1951)."[20]

The concluding "Cf." citation to *Rochin* seems to indicate that Douglas thought his initial freedom of association rationale for the *Griswold* decision was weak. Douglas had earlier objected to the majority opinion in *Rochin,* where Justice Frankfurter endorsed a concept of fundamental freedoms against government action flouting "the decencies of civilized conduct." Justice Douglas had concurred in the result in *Rochin.* But he excoriated Justice Frankfurter's substantive due process theory as turning "not on the Constitution but on the idiosyncrasies of the judges who sit here. . . . It is part of the process of erosion of civil rights of the citizen in recent years."[21]

It is not clear in the first draft of his *Griswold* opinion why Douglas did not immediately reach back to the right of privacy theory for which he had argued so passionately in *The Right of the People,* and which he had urged the Supreme Court to accept in *Poe v. Ullman.* Douglas may have felt that the right of privacy rationale would not attract a majority of the justices, since the Court had not accepted it just a few years earlier. In any event, perhaps at the suggestion of Justice Brennan, Douglas abandoned his earlier draft and circulated a second version of the opinion, which, with minor revisions, became the opinion for the Court in *Griswold.*[22] Freedom of association and reference to *Rochin* remained, but they faded into the background of a different, strongly-stated, comprehensive right of privacy implied from various aspects of the Bill of Rights.

Five years after *Griswold,* Douglas returned to write again about the right of privacy in his concurring opinion to the abortion cases decided as *Roe v. Wade* and *Doe v. Bolton.*[23] As in *Griswold,* the decisional process developed rather differently from the way Douglas initially expected.[24] Indignant that he was not assigned the majority opinion, Douglas nevertheless quickly wrote a memorandum deciding *Doe v. Bolton* on privacy grounds.[25] Justice Blackmun's first drafts of the majority opinions invalidated the abortion statutes on overbreadth and vagueness grounds, rather than the right of privacy.[26] In the meantime, over Douglas's objections, the majority voted to have the abortion cases reargued. After reargument, Justice Blackmun's new draft of the opinion for the Court relied on Douglas's opinion in *Griswold* and the right of privacy as an aspect of liberty protected under the Fourteenth Amendment. Douglas concurred in that opinion and also published a concurring opinion, perhaps out of pride of authorship, but also to explain further his own particular views about the right of privacy.

II. Penumbral Right of Privacy

Most of the criticism of Douglas's concept of right of privacy has focused on its penumbral character. Critics of the penumbral right of privacy usually have two interrelated objections: that Douglas's concept is vague and imprecise and that the reasoning behind it is insufficiently analytical. These criticisms usually boil down to a complaint that the critics "just don't see it"— "it" being Douglas's notion of a penumbral constitutional right of privacy. These critics, in my view, suffer from self-inflicted myopia.[27]

Penumbral criticism usually begins by deriding the right of privacy as being unpredictable and vague, an ambiguous concept lacking coherence and craftsmanship as legal doctrine. "Douglas's imaginative phraseology has been the subject of much hilarity among conservative jurists," according to Harry Jaffa.[28] Such critics accuse Douglas of having created the right of privacy, almost by sleight of hand, as a shadowy concept without real substance and form; they describe it as politics masquerading as a constitutional right. Dinesh D'Souza, managing editor of *Policy Review,* has scoffed, "Look over the Constitution and you find no such right. Hold it up to the light, read it backwards in the mirror — still nothing."[29] Robert Bork has been the most prominent recent proponent of attacks on the penumbral right of privacy as "a concept without limits."[30] According to Bork, Douglas's penumbral "right of privacy strikes without warning. It has no intellectual structure to it so you don't know in advance to what it applies."[31]

Such views have been part of the critical reaction to Douglas's penumbral right of privacy at least since the *Griswold* decision.[32] Justice Black dissented in *Griswold* in part because "'privacy' is a broad, abstract and ambiguous concept which can easily be shrunken in meaning" or enlarged beyond the "simple language" used by the framers of the Constitution.[33] Constitutional scholars, such as Thomas Emerson, who had represented Griswold before the Supreme Court, reacted to Justice Douglas's majority opinion with concern about "the vagueness of the concept, and the general lack of precise standards."[34] On the other hand, the young men who served as editors of *The Harvard Law Review* praised Douglas's penumbral privacy "since it adopts the narrowest ground necessary" to reach the result in the case.[35]

The ambiguity of the penumbral right of privacy garnered renewed criticism after the decision in the abortion cases. For example, Professor Richard Epstein groused, "it does seem fruitless to look to *Griswold* for either guidance or authority. . . . It is nice to be able to make constitutional generalizations, which use isolated words as slogans to solve hard questions raised by the Bill of Rights."[36] Chief Justice Rehnquist has expressed similar concerns in his extrajudicial writing: "Widely divergent claims, which upon analysis have very little in common with one another, are lumped under the umbrella of 'privacy.' . . . This may be done in the belief that if they can remain under this umbrella their chances of being accepted *en masse* will be improved by the 'good' connotation the word privacy presently has."[37]

Coming from a quite different angle, favoring a right of privacy, Louis Lusky has criticized Douglas's penumbral right of privacy because it "gave privacy a new and indefinitely extensible dimension." Deploring Douglas's penumbral right of privacy as "shoddy doctrine," Lusky has denied that it is really privacy at all. Rather, Lusky has called it "neo-privacy," which mysteriously appears as "the efflorescence of constitutional protection for newly established personal liberties."[38] Some legal academics from the left of the political spectrum, such as Paul Brest, have dismissed Douglas's penumbral right of privacy as inconsequential: "The Court has not since recurred to penumbral analysis."[39]

It is true that Douglas's penumbral right of privacy and his rationale in *Griswold* are rather different from conventional legal concepts and analysis. According to Douglas's biographer, James Simon, "The Douglas opinion [in *Griswold*] outraged many legal scholars, who found his pinning of privacy labels to various constitutional amendments, without thoroughly documenting his conclusions, reckless to the point of being irresponsible." Simon has agreed with criticism that "Douglas did not provide a thorough analysis to support this new constitutional right to privacy."[40]

And yet it is important to remember that Douglas never pretended that his penumbral right of privacy was conventional or that his arguments for it were ordinary, deductive, legal analysis. Justice Douglas's mode of argument for the right of privacy is more inductive and impressionistic than deductive and categorical. He surveyed decisions involving a wide variety of constitutional rights to look for a common element or thread that tied them together and brought coherence to the constitutional right of privacy. In *Griswold* Douglas explained, "The foregoing cases suggest that specific guarantees in the Bill of Rights have penumbras, formed by emanations from those guarantees that help give them life and substance."[41] Later, in his concurring opinion to the abortion cases, Justice Douglas described his penumbral analysis as simply "a reasoning," which, except in areas absolutely protected from regulation by the First Amendment, must be balanced against arguments regarding the state's interests.[42]

Douglas's method of widely viewing all sorts of legal rules and decisions in order to find the principle underlying them is similar to the mode of Brandeis's argument for recognition of a common law right to privacy in his famous 1890 *Harvard Law Review* article.[43] Having found the penumbral right of privacy principle, Justice Douglas then projected it onto the specific facts involved in such cases as *Griswold* and the abortion cases to ascertain whether the particular state action at issue intruded into constitutionally protected areas. Douglas's argument was deliberately open-textured and suggestive, rather than closely argued and definitive. He would rather point to instances of the right of privacy than describe it abstractly. The fact that this type of impressionistic reasoning is unconventional does not necessarily mean that it is wrong. Vern Countryman has reminded us, "Scholarship is not a very precise term and, as currently practiced off and on the bench, is no sure guide to a sound and just decision. In any event, it is no substitute for common sense." According to Countryman, Douglas's reply to critics who charged that Douglas's opinions lacked craftsmanship and were result-oriented was, "For those who liked the result, it was scholarship."[44]

Many of Douglas's critics, such as Brest and Bork, seem to have misperceived what Douglas meant by a penumbral right of privacy. Douglas was making an important point in choosing the word "penumbra" to describe the constitutional right of privacy. His allusion was to an old and, to Douglas, familiar constitutional law concept of the implied powers of the federal government.[45] In writing about the right of privacy in penumbral terms, Justice Douglas was suggesting that there were also implied limitations on legitimate government action.[46] Douglas was probably most familiar with the word "penumbra" as a favorite of Justice Holmes, who used it in the opening lines of his dissent in *Olmstead v. United States*. Holmes began that dissent with a disclaimer that he was unwilling to agree with Brandeis's privacy theory because Holmes was "not prepared to say that the penumbra of the 4th and 5th amendments" prohibited the wiretapping involved in that case.[47] Justice Holmes occasionally used "penumbra" to contrast with the "sharp lines" that he felt the law should draw. Holmes urged avoiding "questions of penumbra, of shadowy marches where it is difficult to decide."[48]

Justice Douglas may have borrowed the word "penumbra" from Holmes, but Douglas gave it a different meaning in connection with the right of privacy. Justice Douglas was not alluding to shadows and obscurity. Rather, he invoked a meaning of penumbra that refers to the halo of light that surrounds an eclipsed sun.[49] This sense of halo or aura was also represented in Douglas's reference to emanations in *Poe v. Ullman*.[50] For Douglas, the Constitution was not a source of shadows, but rather of a grand aurora borealis, of which the right of privacy was a part. In contrast to Holmes's use of penumbra as half shadow, Douglas emphasized it as half light.[51] To the extent that we too can see the outlines of an implied right of privacy, Douglas's penumbral right of privacy has affected the way we see the world, and the Constitution.

III. Constitutional Right of Privacy

For Douglas, the penumbral right of privacy was emphatically a constitutional right.[52] Douglas's critics have objected to his notion of the right of privacy as a constitutional right for three reasons: first, because privacy is not mentioned in the text of the Constitution; second, because it seems to embody substantive due process; and, third, because it serves as a vehicle for activist judges to enforce their personal political views. The constitutional status of the right of privacy has been, from the beginning, perhaps its most controversial aspect for legal scholars. In his dissent in *Griswold v. Connecticut,* Justice Black complained, "I like my privacy as well as the next one, but I am nevertheless compelled to admit that the government has a right to invade it unless prohibited by some specific constitutional provision."[53]

Robert Bork has been Douglas's most prominent critic regarding the constitutional aspect of the right of privacy. Bork described Douglas's opinion in *Griswold* as "choosing . . . between competing gratifications without constitutional guidance."[54] Bork has also urged that

when a judge chooses a still higher level of generality, finding that the amendments create a general right of privacy (actually autonomy), he reaches a result far beyond anything the Framers intended (they could certainly have articulated a general right had they intended one) and creates a concept without limits, thus ensuring erratic judicial enforcement.[55]

When questioned about these views before the Senate Judiciary Committee in 1987, Judge Bork explained, "All I have done was point out that the right of privacy, as defined or undefined by Justice Douglas, was a free-floating right that was not derived in a principled fashion from constitutional materials."[56] Bork's views are sometimes associated with the interpretivist or intentionalist schools of constitutional theory, which urge basing interpretation of the Constitution solely on the text and the intent of the Framers of the Constitution.[57]

Douglas did not share this narrow intentionalist or interpretivist view of the Constitution. His views about the Constitution's embrace of the right of privacy began with the text, but did not stop there. Douglas considered himself a "strict constructionist," in the sense that he took the Constitution "to mean what it says." But Douglas also believed that his judicial role involved "the adjustment of the Constitution to the needs of the time."[58] In describing the constitutional right of privacy in his concurring opinion in *Roe v. Wade,* Douglas was careful to explain, "There is no mention of privacy in our Bill of Rights but our decisions have recognized it as one of the fundamental values those amendments were designed to protect."[59] In Douglas's view, the constitutional right of privacy was directly rooted in the Bill of Rights, which protects some rights explicitly (e.g., free speech), others implicitly (e.g., free association), and still others in both ways. The right of privacy was, for Douglas, in the latter compound category of constitutional rights and therefore had both absolute (freedom of communication) and non-absolute (freedom to choose an abortion) aspects.

Some constitutional scholars have asserted that the right of privacy is simply not translatable into any articulable principle of constitutional law.[60] Such criticism is, of course, similar in its basis to that underlying the penumbral criticism discussed earlier. Other constitutional scholars do not agree that this criticism should apply to Douglas's concept of the constitutional right of privacy. For example, John Hart Ely has criticized the majority opinion in *Roe v. Wade* in such terms, but not Douglas's constitutional right of privacy.[61] In *Democracy and Distrust,* Ely contrasted Douglas's theory in *Griswold* with that of the majority in *Roe v. Wade* and concluded that Douglas's right of privacy "reveals strong interpretivist urges, struggling to relate its holding to the First, Third, Fourth and Fifth Amendments."[62]

Critics who do not see Douglas's right of privacy as directly (or for some, even indirectly) derived from the text of the Constitution typically have concluded that the right of privacy is nothing more than an aspect of substantive due process.[63] Douglas's views of substantive due process, like his idea of the right of privacy, shifted somewhat over time. At the time he wrote the opinion for the Court in *Griswold,* the fundamental rights decisions in which Douglas and Black had consistently dissented were the controlling precedent. It was necessary to cite precedent to get a majority of the justices to join the opinion.[64] Therefore, in addition to relying on implications from various specific provisions in the Bill of Rights, Douglas cited *Rochin* and at least nodded to the fundamental rights notion associated with the views of Justice Frankfurter.

However, Douglas's own view of the constitutional basis for the right of privacy did not, in the end, consider the right of privacy to be an aspect of substantive due process. Rather, Douglas conceived of the right of privacy as an aspect of the Bill of Rights incorporated into the liberty which the Fifth and Fourteenth Amendments guarantee. Douglas's concurring opinion in the abortion cases returned to these incorporationist views of the Fourteenth Amendment. He described various zones of privacy to emphasize that his view that the right of privacy was defined by the implications of various parts of the Constitution. He even included a long footnote specifically disagreeing with Justice Stewart's view that the right of privacy reintroduces substantive due process.[65]

Douglas's constitutional critics were right about one aspect of the right of privacy. The right of privacy was clearly the fruit of judicial activism. Justice Douglas was unabashedly an activist judge. Responding to a question about the role of precedent, Douglas characteristically replied: "I once said, to the consternation of a group of lawyers, that I'd rather create a precedent than find one. Because the creation of a precedent in terms of the modern setting means the adjustment of the Constitution to the needs of the time."[66] Conservative critics of this activist stance abound. For example, Bruce Fein has urged rejection of "a constitutional right of privacy," because the main question "is not whether the Constitution was intended to protect some types of privacy—it clearly was—or whether privacy values should be important—they certainly should be—but whether we want to permit the justices to employ undefined and undefinable 'penumbras' to fasten on the nation their personal views of privacy rights."[67] Other conservatives, such as Robert Bork and Gary McDowell, have joined these views.

Justice Douglas thought that his constitutional role as a Supreme Court justice required judicial activism. In the second volume of his autobiography, *The Court Years,* he cheerfully accepted the "activist" label:

My view always has been that anyone whose life, liberty or property was threatened or impaired by any branch of government—whether the President or one of his agencies, or Congress, or the courts (or any counterpart in a state regime)—had a justiciable controversy and could properly repair to a judicial tribunal for vindication of his rights. . . . Courts sit to determine questions on stormy as well as on calm days. The Constitution is the measure of their duty.[68]

It is also helpful to remember that Douglas came out of a tradition of Legal Realism, which took seriously the role of the judge as one who must exercise power in deciding cases. He viewed his judicial role as that of a doer, not a debater. To Justice Douglas, his job description was "decider of cases and controversies." The work of a Supreme Court justice did not call for a constitutional scholar endlessly debating interpretivist versus noninterpretivist theories. Justice Douglas saw himself as required to call the cases as he saw them—in or out—rather than to articulate a seamless logical structure of constitutional adjudication.

But Douglas also valued his judicial independence and derided "the picture of timid judges looking anxiously at public opinion polls to see how far they should go in sticking to or abandoning the literal constitutional requirements."[69] It was emphatically the Constitution which Douglas saw himself enforcing as he insisted that government respect the constitutional right of privacy.

IV. Natural Right of Privacy

Douglas saw nothing wrong, or schizophrenic, about describing the right of privacy as also a natural right existing outside of the Constitution. In *The Right of the People,* Douglas sharply distinguished his views about natural rights from those

invoked by the *laissez-faire* theorists of the late nineteenth and twentieth centuries to protect the nation's economy against governmental control. . . . The natural rights of which I speak are different. They have a broad base in morality and religion to protect man, his individuality, and his conscience against direct and indirect interference by government. Some are written explicitly into the Constitution. Others are to be implied. The penumbra of the Bill of Rights reflects human rights which, though not explicit, are implied from the very nature of man as a child of God.[70]

Toward the end of his life, Douglas connected such natural law beliefs with the role of the Supreme Court: "The Court is really the keeper of the conscience. And the conscience is the Constitution."[71] Over and over again, Douglas repeated his views about the natural right of privacy in articles, in speeches, in books, and in judicial opinions.

Some constitutional scholars, particularly those influenced by the neutral-principles approach associated with Herbert Wechsler,[72] have objected to this extraconstitutional, natural law dimension of what purports to be a constitutional right.[73] For example, Robert Bork has long argued that characterization of privacy as a natural right precludes its consideration as a constitutionally derived right. According to Bork, enforcement of a natural right of privacy under the Constitution was unacceptable because it lacked what he considered to be a disciplined explanation. For Bork, the only legitimate explanations must be based on neutral principles and imbued with judicial restraint. Because Douglas's natural law views about the right of privacy did not explain why the Constitution should protect the right of privacy and not the right to pollute, it lacked what Bork called "craftsmanship" and merely enforced Douglas's own personal morality.[74] The real objection of Bork and of many of Douglas's other natural law critics has been that Justice Douglas used natural law to provide content for the constitutional aspect of the right of privacy. These critics often do not deny a natural human preference for privacy, but they do deny that this natural privacy preference translates into constitutional guarantees.[75]

In contrast, Douglas saw an organic interconnection between the natural and legal world, between the Constitution and basic human rights. Responding to a question about his active public and private life, Douglas characteristically noted, "We're all human. . . . The person who goes there and stays 10, 20, 30 years should be very active in life. Otherwise, he'll end up a dried husk unrelated to anything that's going on in the world."[76] Douglas's broad view of humanity, and of judging, insisted that judges are, and ought to be, part of a larger humanity. He saw the constitutional right of privacy as an instance of a broader natural right of privacy, which people from all parts of the world and all walks of life share as an attribute of their humanity.

V. Individual Right of Privacy

Privacy was of primary concern to Douglas as an individual right, although he also argued that the Constitution protects privacy of association.[77] Douglas identified his views about the individual right of privacy with those of Louis Brandeis, whom Douglas described as "a revolutionary symbol . . . [who]

wanted to put the individual and the individual's privacy first, and to establish only the controls that would keep the individual from being regimented."[78]

Douglas's views about the individual as the starting point for the right of privacy also derived from the classical liberalism associated with John Stuart Mill. Mill described "a sphere of action in which society, as distinguished from the individual, has, if any, only an indirect interest; comprehending all that portion of a person's life and conduct which affects only himself." Even the three categories of privacy which Douglas presents in his concurrence to the abortion cases derive from what Mill had described as "the appropriate region of human liberty. . . . First, the inward domain of consciousness; . . . liberty of expressing and publishing opinions. . . . Secondly, the principle requires liberty of tastes and pursuits; of framing the plan of our life to suit our own character. . . . Thirdly, . . . freedom to unite. . . . The only freedom which deserves the name is that of pursuing our own good in our own way."[79]

Critics of the individualistic quality of the right of privacy have pointed out that the right of privacy is antimajoritarian at best and downright antisocial at worst. Some feminists and others interested in Critical Legal Studies have considered the individual right of privacy to be at odds with more inclusive communitarian values. For example, Elizabeth Schneider has noted that "CLS scholars argue that rights are 'permeated by the possessive individualism of capitalist society.'"[80] Douglas's individual right of privacy is indeed the very paradigm of a bourgeois right embodying anticommunitarian "possessive individualism." Since Justice Douglas was a man of practical action, he would probably not have been much interested in probing the legitimacy of rights theories in legal philosophy. He simply believed that the individual comes before the community and argued that joining into a community was not possible without a strong sense of the individual self.

That Douglas also supported communitarian values was evident in *The Right of the People,* where he noted with approval that

joining is an innate American habit. Men like Emerson fought it; but the habit grew and grew and became distinctly American. It is indeed the source of much of the power of self-help that appears and reappears in all phases of our life. This "passion for joining," as Professor Schlesinger once put it, has roots not only in our habits but in the First Amendment. Joining is one method of freedom of expression; it is a form of free inquiry; it is an exercise of the right of free assembly.[81]

But Douglas also insisted, "Our Society is built upon the premise that it exists only to aid the fullest individual achievement of which each of its members is capable. Our starting point has always been the individual, not the state."[82]

Critics from the other end of the political spectrum also have objected to Douglas's emphasis on the individual for the different reason that an unconfined right of privacy undermines conventional morality. For example, Charles Krauthammer, agreeing with Robert Bork, postulated that if privacy "were truly a constitutional right, then heroin laws — shooting up is an even more 'private' act than sex since it requires only one consenting adult — should be struck down tomorrow."[83] Such critics have simply misunderstood Douglas's views about the right of privacy. Although Justice Douglas did see the right of privacy as protection for unconventional and nonconformist individuals, he did not consider it to be absolute. For example, dissenting in *Wyman v. James,* a case involving the warrantless search of a welfare mother's home, Douglas explained that the right of privacy does not insulate the individual absolutely: "Isolation is not a constitutional guarantee; but the sanctity of the sanctuary of the *home* is such — as marked and defined by the Fourth Amendment."[84]

Only in the intimate realm of belief and expression, which Douglas saw as absolutely protected under the First Amendment, did Douglas consider the individual right of privacy to be absolute. The individual was, for Douglas, at the center of the regime of privacy protected under the Constitution from government interference: "Our society — unlike most in the world — presupposes that freedom and liberty are in a frame of reference that makes the individual, not government, the keeper of his tastes, beliefs, and ideas."[85] Douglas had earlier called for "a spirit of liberty . . . which accepts in our daily living and behavior the attitudes of toleration of unorthodox opinions and respect for the dignity and privacy of each human being, which our Bill of Rights reflects."[86]

VI. Political Right of Privacy

For Douglas, the right of privacy also had an important political function: to force the government to respect the individual's right to be let alone. Douglas described this political dimension of the right of privacy as having as its purpose "to keep the government off the backs of people."[87] For example, dissenting in a case involving the army's surveillance of protesters opposed to the Vietnam War, Douglas insisted:

The Constitution was designed to keep government off the backs of the people. The Bill of Rights was added to keep the precincts of belief and expression, of the press, of political and social activities free from surveillance. The Bill of Rights was designed to keep agents of the government and official eavesdroppers away from assemblies of people. The aim was to allow men to be free and independent and to assert their rights against government.[88]

Douglas feared that an intrusive government threatened to overwhelm the citizenry.

Douglas's critics have objected to this political dimension of the right of privacy as an aspect of Douglas's judicial activism. For them, the right of privacy was just another mechanism for Douglas to enforce his own liberal political agenda. For example, Dinesh D'Souza has attacked the right of privacy as an effort by a liberal judiciary "simply to read its favored social vision into the Constitution, pretending that it was always there but previously latent. . . . Where does this privacy right that overpowers democratically elected state legislatures hark back to?"[89] Robert Bork has frequently pointed to the political dimension of the right of privacy as illegitimate "interest voting," which, according to Bork, results in the usurpation of legislative power by the judiciary. "Where objective constitutional law is not possible, the proper response is not 'political choice' but judicial restraint," which, Bork has argued, "grows out of a theory of the division of labor or competence in government and defines not only the occasions upon which the Supreme Court should defer to the will of representative institutions but also the occasions for, and the manner of, judicial intervention."[90] For Bork, Douglas's political right of privacy was grounds for double concern because it was a right operating both as a limitation on the power of legislatures and, at the same time, as an assertion of raw political power by the judiciary.

Justice Douglas repeatedly rejected such calls for judicial restraint in the enforcement of civil and political liberties. Enforcing the right of privacy was, in Douglas's view, a key task for the Supreme Court as the keeper of the Constitution. Since an important part of the Constitution's Madisonian design was to protect individuals from a too powerful government, enforcement of the political right of privacy was a legitimate and important responsibility of the Supreme Court.

VII. Conclusion

Looking back over the ongoing debate about Douglas's right of privacy, one cannot help but be reminded of one of Douglas's favorite quotations from Holmes regarding "the secret isolated joy of the thinker, who knows that, a hundred years after he is dead and forgotten, men who never heard of him will be moving to the measure of his thought."[91] Douglas used this quotation many times: early in his judicial career to describe Justice Brandeis,[92] and near the end of his life to describe himself.[93] It is certainly an apt description of the continuing controversy over privacy, in which most of the argument still moves to the measure of Douglas's ideas.

Echoes of Douglas's ideas about the right of privacy are everywhere – in politics, in legislation, in scholarship, and in modern notions of the role of government. For example, in his inaugural address, President Bush declared, "I don't seek 'a window on men's souls.' In fact, I yearn for a greater tolerance, and easy-goingness about each other's attitudes and way of life."[94] The Congress acted on Douglas's idea that the right of privacy is protected under the Constitution when, in enacting the Privacy Act, Congress found that the right of privacy is "a personal and fundamental right protected by the Constitution of the United States."[95] A unanimous Supreme Court protected this same right of privacy in holding that "rap sheets" on individuals compiled by the Federal Bureau of Investigation should not be disclosed.[96] Professor Laurence Tribe has devoted a key chapter of his treatise on *American Constitutional Law* to "Privacy and Personhood."[97] That chapter would not have been possible without Justice Douglas's concept of the right of privacy.

And there are echoes of Douglas's right of privacy even farther afield: in Hong Kong, even though there is no Chinese word for privacy,[98] legal scholars have urgently argued for its recognition.[99] In India, the Supreme Court recognized the right of privacy in a surveillance case, *Govind v. State of Madhya Pradesh.*[100] The European Court of Human Rights reflected Douglas's idea of the right of privacy in interpreting Article 8 of the European Convention on Human Rights when it decided a case involving the criminal prosecution of a homosexual man in Northern Ireland.[101]

In addition to these and many other echoes and reflections of Douglas's idea of a right of privacy, the measure of Douglas's thought also sets the pace for Douglas's critics. That his critics continue to argue about Douglas's penumbral, natural, individual, political, and above all, constitutional right of privacy demonstrates that they, too, move to the measure of Douglas's ideas about the right of privacy.

Notes

1. 381 U.S. 479 (1965). Five justices, including Douglas, joined in Douglas's opinion for the Court. Justice Goldberg's concurring opinion, in which Chief Justice Warren and Justice Brennan joined, states at the beginning, "I agree with the Court that Connecticut's birth-control law unconstitutionally intrudes upon the right of marital privacy, and I join in its opinion and judgment." *Griswold v. Connecticut,* 381 U.S., at 486 (Goldberg, J., concurring). Justice Clark joined the majority but did not specifically associate himself with any of the opinions. Justices Harlan and White agreed with the judgment but did not join the opinion of the Court. Justices Black and Stewart dissented.

2. For example, Justice Douglas's reading of the right of privacy was a key issue in the Senate Judiciary Committee's hearings on the nomination of Robert Bork to be an Associate Justice of the United States Supreme Court. The committee's eventual recommendation against confirmation was based in part on Bork's long-standing and energetic criticism of Justice Douglas's concept of right of privacy. "Nomination of Robert H. Bork to Be an Associate Justice of the U.S. Supreme Court," U.S. Senate Judiciary Committee Executive Report 100-7, 100th Cong., 1st Sess., Oct. 13, 1987. The portion of the report titled "A Critical Analysis of Judge Bork's Positions on Leading Matters" begins with "I. The Right to Privacy—The Right to be Let Alone." Ibid., p. 30. Judge Bork's criticism of Douglas's opinion for the Supreme Court in *Griswold v. Connecticut* is the first item discussed (p. 30).

3. L. A. Powe, Jr., "Evolution to Absolutism: Justice Douglas and the First Amendment," *Columbia Law Review* 74 (1974): 411.

4. James Simon, *Independent Journey: The Life of William O. Douglas* (New York: Harper and Row, 1980), p. 112. A number of interesting studies have explored Douglas's evolving sense of important constitutional rights and values, including the right of privacy. In addition to Professor Powe's article, "Evolution to Absolutism," Bernard Wolfman, Jonathan Silver, and Marjorie Silver have explored changes in "The Behavior of Justice Douglas in Federal Tax Cases," *University of Pennsylvania Law Review* 122 (1973): 235. An interesting Note by Sheldon S. Adler, "Toward a Constitutional Theory of Individuality: The Privacy Opinions of Justice Douglas," *Yale Law Journal* 87 (1978): 1579, provides a detailed description of many of Douglas's right of privacy decisions. There is no need to repeat this excellent work here.

5. I have discussed elsewhere Justice Douglas's "self-conscious inconsistency." Dorothy Glancy, "Getting Government Off the Backs of People: The Right of Privacy and Freedom of Expression in the Opinions of Justice William O. Douglas," *Santa Clara Law Review* 21 (1981): 1048. For a more critical view, see Ronald Dworkin, "Dissent on Douglas," *New York Review of Books,* Feb. 19, 1981, p. 8.

In Eric Sevareid's 1972 television interview with Justice Douglas, Douglas raised the subject of new members coming onto the Court (Powell and Rehnquist in that year): "It's very difficult to know what a new member will be like until he's there for five or ten years, because very few new members have been free and independent before. Now all the layers of prejudices of clients and what-not have been peeled off, and there the man is. And what does he basically think in the terms of constitutional values?" Transcript of CBS Reports, "Mr. Justice Douglas," Sept. 6, 1972, pp. 32–33. Douglas's remark was clearly self-descriptive.

6. *Skinner v. Oklahoma,* 316 U.S. 535, 541 (1942).

7. *Zap v. United States,* 328 U.S. 624, 630 (1945). This early opinion seems in some ways to foreshadow *Air Pollution Variance Board v. Western Alfalfa,* 416 U.S. 861 (1974), in which Douglas also upheld, without concern about the right of privacy, a warrantless inspection of smokestack emissions. He considered the emissions to be in plain view and subject to the open fields doctrine.

8. William O. Douglas, *An Almanac of Liberty* (Garden City, N.Y.: Doubleday, 1954), pp. vi, 353–55.

9. *Dennis v. United States,* 341 U.S. 494, 582–83 (1951).

10. Arthur Sutherland, "Privacy in Connecticut," *Michigan Law Review* 64 (1965): 283–84.

11. William O. Douglas, *The Right of the People* (Garden City, N.Y.: Doubleday, 1958), p. 113.

12. *On Lee v. United States,* 343 U.S. 747, 762–65 (1952). In *Goldman v. United States,* 316 U.S. 129 (1942), Douglas had joined the majority in refusing to overrule *Olmstead v. United States,* 277 U.S. 438 (1928).

13. Brandeis was for many reasons an important figure for Douglas. Douglas was appointed to fill Brandeis's seat on the Supreme Court, apparently at the suggestion of Brandeis himself. Simon, *Independent Journey,* pp. 189–91; William O. Douglas, *Go East, Young Man: The Autobiography of William O. Douglas* (New York: Random House, 1974), p. 449.

14. Samuel Warren and Louis D. Brandeis, "The Right to Privacy," *Harvard Law Review* 4 (1890): 193.

15. *Beauharnais v. Illinois,* 343 U.S. 250, 285 (1952).

16. *Public Utilities Commission v. Pollack,* 343 U.S. 451, 467 (1952). Douglas

emphasized the importance of allowing people to choose for themselves: "If people are let alone in those choices, the right of privacy will pay dividends in character and integrity. The strength of our system is in the dignity, the resourcefulness, and the independence of our people. . . . That system cannot flourish if regimentation takes hold. The right of privacy, today violated, is a powerful deterrent to any one who would control men's minds." Ibid., at 469.

17. Douglas, *The Right of the People,* pp. 87, 89.

18. *Poe v. Ullman,* 367 U.S. 497, 515, 517, 521 (1961). In *Poe,* Douglas also articulated views about marital privacy which he later made part of his opinion for the Court in *Griswold:*

> The regulation as applied in this case touches the relationship between man and wife. It reaches into the intimacies of the marriage relationship. If we imagine a regime of full enforcement of the law in the manner of an Anthony Comstock, we would reach the point where search warrants issued and officers appeared in bedrooms to find out what went on. It is said that this is not that case. And so it is not. But when the State makes "use" a crime and applies the criminal sanction to man and wife, the State has entered the innermost sanctum of the home. If it can make this law, it can enforce it. And proof of its violation necessarily involves an inquiry into the relations between man and wife. (Ibid., at 519–21)

19. 381 U.S. 479 (1965).

20. Bernard Schwartz, *The Unpublished Opinions of the Warren Court* (New York: Oxford University Press, 1985), pp. 234–37. Justice Black was amused, but not persuaded by Douglas's freedom of association theory. According to one of the justice's Conference notes, Justice Black objected to Douglas's freedom-of-association theory: "Right of association is for me right of assembly & rt of husband & wife to assemble in bed is new right of assembly to me." Ibid., pp. 234–37.

21. *Rochin v. California,* 342 U.S. 165, 179 (1951) (Douglas, J., dissenting).

22. Bernard Schwartz claims that Justice Brennan suggested basing the decision on privacy grounds, using the association cases as an analogous area of implicit constitutional protection. Schwartz, *The Unpublished Opinions of the Warren Court,* p. 238. Schwartz also notes that the circulated draft of the eventual opinion contained two sentences which Douglas omitted from the final version:

> After referring to the "notions of privacy surrounding the marriage relationship" toward the end of the opinion, the circulated draft stated, "We think that the enforcement of the aider-and-abettor statute in this marital setting likewise dilutes the right of privacy by demeaning it." And the draft's last sentence declared that marriage "flourishes only in the regime of privacy which we think the Bill of Rights creates." (p. 238)

23. *Roe v. Wade,* 410 U.S. 113 (1973); *Doe v. Bolton,* 410 U.S. 179 (1973).

24. Schwartz, *The Unpublished Opinions of the Burger Court* (New York: Oxford University Press, 1988), pp. 84–87.

25. In his memorandum directed to the Georgia statute challenged in *Doe v. Bolton,* Douglas suggested, in addition to his right of privacy rationale, two additional constitutional difficulties with the Georgia statute. First, the Georgia statute did not provide a woman applying for an abortion with a right to a hearing, thereby

violating procedural due process guarantees against deprivations of the liberty involved in the abortion decision. Second, Douglas was concerned that the statute's regulatory mechanism would result in the denial of equal protection, particularly to poor women seeking abortions. To resolve the latter problem, Douglas suggested the need to remand the case to the district court for findings regarding the actual application of the specific regulatory measures required under the Georgia statute. Since a constitutionally protected liberty, the right of privacy, was at stake, strict scrutiny should apply in evaluating the practical impact of the statute.

26. Schwartz, *Unpublished Opinions of the Burger Court,* pp. 120–40.

27. To reverse Gertrude Stein's comment about Oakland, California, there really is a there there. Gertrude Stein, *Everybody's Autobiography* (New York: Random House, 1937), p. 289.

28. Harry Jaffa, "Judge Bork's Mistake," *National Review,* Mar. 4, 1988, p. 38.

29. Dinesh D'Souza, "The New Liberal Censorship," *Policy Review* #38 (Fall 1986): pp. 8, 13.

30. Robert Bork, Foreword to Gary L. McDowell, *The Constitution and Contemporary Constitutional Theory* (Center for Judicial Studies, 1985), p. x.

31. "An Interview with Judge Robert H. Bork," *Judicial Notice* 3 (June 1986): 9. See also Robert Bork, "The Supreme Court Needs a New Philosophy," *Fortune,* Dec. 1968, p. 138; Robert Bork, "Neutral Principles and Some First Amendment Problems," *Indiana Law Journal* 47 (1971): 1; and Robert Bork, "The Constitution, Original Intent, and Economic Rights," *San Diego Law Review* 23 (1986): 823.

32. Douglas's use of "penumbra" to describe the right of privacy in *Griswold* was not the first time Douglas used the image. In his 1958 book, *The Right of the People,* Douglas explained his view that "The penumbra of the Bill of Rights reflects human rights which, though not explicit, are implied from the very nature of man as a child of God" (p. 89). Douglas also expressed a similar idea in his dissent in *Poe v. Ullman,* where he described the right of privacy that "emanates from the totality of the constitutional scheme under which we live." *Poe v. Ullman,* 367 U.S., at 521.

33. *Griswold v. Connecticut,* 381 U.S., at 509.

34. Thomas Emerson, "Nine Justices in Search of a Doctrine," *Michigan Law Review* 64 (1965): 230. Emerson's comment is part of an interesting sampling of legal scholars' initial reactions to the *Griswold* decision published in the *Michigan Law Review* in December 1965. All of the five distinguished constitutional law professors contributing to the commentary expressed uneasiness about the elusive quality of the penumbral right of privacy. Only Arthur Sutherland resisted outright criticism on this ground. For example, Paul Kauper objected to the "accordion-like qualities of the emanations-and-penumbra theory." Paul Kauper, "Penumbras, Peripheries, Emanations, Things Fundamental and Things Forgotten: The *Griswold* Case," *Michigan Law Review* 64 (1965): 253. Robert McKay complained that the "meaning [of the right of privacy], if it was ever clear, has become diluted and uncertain through overgenerous application to a wide variety of situations." Robert McKay, "The Right of Privacy: Emanations and Intimations," *Michigan Law Review* 64 (1965): 272. Robert Dixon described *Griswold* as "longer on yearning than on substantive content." Robert Dixon, "The *Griswold* Penumbra: Constitutional Charter for an Expanded Law of Privacy?" *Michigan Law Review* 64 (1965): 197.

35. "The Supreme Court, 1964 Term," *Harvard Law Review* 79 (1965): 164.

36. Richard Epstein, "Substantive Due Process by Any Other Name: The Abortion Cases," *Supreme Court Review* 1973: 170.

37. William H. Rehnquist, "Is an Expanded Right of Privacy Consistent with Fair and Effective Law Enforcement?" *Kansas Law Review* 23 (1974): 21.

38. Louis Lusky, *By What Right?* (Charlottesville: Michie, 1975), pp. 336–40. Lusky admitted in a footnote, "Perhaps my unwillingness to stand unprotesting while the term privacy is ruined for descriptive use is a consequence of my own struggle to sharpen the term." The footnote cites Louis Lusky, "Invasion of Privacy: A Clarification of Concepts," *Columbia Law Review* 72 (1972): 693; also at *Political Science Quarterly* 87 (1972): 192.

39. Paul Brest, "Fundamental Rights," *Yale Law Journal* 90 (1981): 1064, n. 2.

40. Simon, *Independent Journey,* pp. 348, 349.

41. *Griswold v. Connecticut,* 381 U.S., at 484.

42. *Doe v. Bolton,* 410 U.S., at 215 (Douglas, J., concurring).

43. Warren and Brandeis, "Right to Privacy," p. 193.

44. Vern Countryman, "Scholarship and Common Sense," *Harvard Law Review* 93 (1980): 1407, 1409, n. 14. See also, Kenneth L. Karst, "Invidious Discrimination: Justice Douglas and the Return of the 'Natural-Law-Due-Process Formula,'" *UCLA Law Review* 16 (1969): 749.

45. *Black's Law Dictionary,* 5th ed. (1979), p. 1022, describes the "penumbral doctrine" as referring to implied powers of the federal government and attaches it to the early federal eminent domain decision in *Kohl v. United States,* 91 U.S. 367 (1875).

46. The idea of implied limitations on government powers was not Douglas's invention. Thomas Cooley's *A Treatise on Constitutional Limitations* (Boston: Little, Brown, 1868) argues extensively for them and even discusses an implied right of privacy (p. 210).

47. *Olmstead v. United States,* 277 U.S., at 469.

48. *Hanover Star Milling Company v. Metcalf,* 240 U.S. 403, 426 (1916). This is the earliest usage of the word "penumbra" in Supreme Court opinions. Holmes also used "penumbra" to refer to the leeway federal courts should accord state legislation in applying the Fourteenth Amendment's Due Process Clause. For example, in his dissent in *Schlesinger v. Wisconsin,* a substantive due process decision striking down as unconstitutional certain presumptions in a Wisconsin estate tax law, Holmes suggested that "the law allows a penumbra to be embraced that goes beyond the outline of its object in order that the object may be secured." *Schlesinger v. Wisconsin,* 270 U.S. 230, 241 (1926).

49. Compare William H. Allen, ed., *Dictionary of Technical Terms for Aerospace Use* (Washington, D.C.: National Aeronautics and Space Administration, 1965), pp. 200, 295; Dismore Alter et al., *Pictorial Astronomy* (New York: Crowell, 1974), p. 17; Jay Pasachoff and Marc Kutner, *University Astronomy* (Philadelphia: Saunders, 1978), p. 365; Lawrence Frederick and Robert Baker, *Introduction to Astronomy* (New York: Van Nostrand, 1976), pp. 129–33.

50. *Poe v. Ullman,* 367 U.S., at 521.

51. William Safire suggested a similar understanding in his amusing "The Penumbra of Desuetude," *New York Times Magazine,* Oct. 4, 1987, p. 16.

52. Douglas rejected a tort right of privacy. He consistently relied on First Amendment grounds in voting to overturn damage awards in tort actions for invasion of

privacy. *Time, Inc. v. Hill,* 385 U.S. 374, 401 (1967); *Cantrell v. Forest City Publishing Co.,* 419 U.S. 245, 255 (1974); *Cox Broadcasting Corporation v. Cohn,* 420 U.S. 469 (1975). In one of Douglas's last opinions before retiring from the Supreme Court, Douglas explained his resistance to protection of privacy through tort actions: "there is no power on the part of government to suppress or penalize the publication of 'news of the day.'" *Cox Broadcasting v. Cohn,* 420 U.S., at 501.

53. *Griswold v. Connecticut,* 361 U.S., at 510. Similar views are echoed in Epstein, "Substantive Due Process by Any Other Name," p. 159. See also Paul Brest, "The Fundamental Rights Controversy: The Essential Contradictions of Normative Constitutional Scholarship," *Yale Law Journal* 90 (1981): 1060.

54. Bork, "Neutral Principles and Some First Amendment Problems," p. 16.

55. Bork, Foreword to McDowell, *Constitution and Contemporary Constitutional Theory.*

56. "Excerpts from Questioning of Judge Bork by Senate Committee Chairman," *New York Times,* Sept. 16, 1987.

57. See, for example, Raoul Berger, "New Theories of 'Interpretation': The Activist Flight from the Constitution," *Ohio State Law Journal* 47 (1986): 1.

58. Transcript of CBS Reports, "Mr. Justice Douglas," pp. 28–30. Douglas contrasted his strict constructionist approach to that of judges who write "58 page opinions" because they do not stick to the Constitution. Ibid.

59. *Roe v. Wade,* 410 U.S., at 209, n. 2.

60. Henry J. Friendly, "The Courts and Social Policy," *University of Miami Law Review* 33 (1978): 33; Archibald Cox, *The Role of the Supreme Court in American Government* (New York: Oxford University Press, 1976), pp. 113–14.

61. John Hart Ely, "The Wages of Crying Wolf," *Yale Law Journal* 82 (1973): 920, 929.

62. John Hart Ely, *Democracy and Distrust* (Cambridge: Harvard University Press, 1980), p. 221, n. 4. Ely notes a similar view in his article "Wages of Crying Wolf," p. 928, n. 60.

63. Brest, "Fundamental Rights Controversy," p. 1063; Henry Paul Monaghan, "Of 'Liberty' and 'Property,'" *Cornell Law Review* 62 (1977): 405, 406, 420; Harry H. Wellington, "Common Law Rules and Constitutional Double Standards: Some Notes on Adjudication," *Yale Law Journal* 83 (1973): 221; Epstein, "Substantive Due Process by Any Other Name," p. 159.

64. William Cohen has suggested that Douglas "wrote a compromise opinion for the Court in *Griswold.*" William Cohen, "Justices Black and Douglas and the 'Natural-Law-Due-Process Formula': Some Fragments of Intellectual History," *U.C. Davis Law Review* 20 (1987): 393.

65. *Doe v. Bolton,* 410 U.S., at 212, n. 4. (Douglas, J., concurring).

66. Justice Douglas explained, "Well I've always thought that on a constitutional decision, that *stare decisis,* that is, established law, was really no sure guideline because what did the guys do—the judges who sat there in 1875—know about, say, electronic surveillance? They didn't know anything about it. . . . Why take their wisdom?" Transcript of CBS Reports, "Mr. Justice Douglas," pp. 27–28.

67. Bruce Fein, "Courts Have Made Hash of Privacy Since *Roe vs. Wade,*" *Washington Post,* July 19, 1987; Berger, "New Theories of 'Interpretation,'" p. 1. In 1957, reacting similarly to what he felt to be undue judicial activism, Representative Hoffman proposed the impeachment of Douglas, along with all eight of his fellow

justices, "on the theory that the Court is attempting to overthrow the Government through fallacious reasoning, rendering decisions which make constitutional provisions void." Michael Kammen, *A Machine That Would Go of Itself* (New York: Random House, 1987), p. 328. This was the first of several unsuccessful attempts to impeach Douglas.

68. William O. Douglas, *The Court Years, 1939-1975: The Autobiography of William O. Douglas* (New York: Random House, 1980), pp. 55-56.

69. William O. Douglas, "Law and the American Character," *California State Bar Journal* 37 (1962): 753, 771.

70. Douglas, *Right of the People,* p. 89. See Cohen, "Justices Black and Douglas," p. 381. Compare Cox, *Role of the Supreme Court,* pp. 31-32, for a general discussion of the connection between natural law and doctrines of judicial review.

71. Transcript of CBS Reports, "Mr. Justice Douglas," p. 42.

72. Herbert Wechsler, "Toward Neutral Principles of Constitutional Law," *Harvard Law Review* 73 (1959): 1.

73. For example, Raoul Berger, *Government by Judiciary* (Cambridge: Harvard University Press, 1977), p. 257; Bork, "Neutral Principles and Some First Amendment Problems," p. 1; Alexander Bickel, *The Least Dangerous Branch* (New Haven: Yale University Press, 1962).

74. Bork, "Supreme Court Needs a New Philosophy," pp. 169-70; "Excerpts from Questioning of Judge Bork." See also Bork, "Constitution, Original Intent, and Economic Rights," p. 823.

75. For example, Richard Posner, "The Uncertain Protection of Privacy by the Supreme Court," *Supreme Court Review* 1979:173.

76. Transcript of CBS Reports, "Mr. Justice Douglas," p. 18.

77. Douglas frequently discussed privacy of association in connection with *NAACP v. Alabama,* 357 U.S. 449 (1958) (opinion by Harlan, J.). See, e.g., *Uphaus v. Wyman,* 364 U.S. 388, 401-08 (1960) (Douglas, J., dissenting); and *Laird v. Tatum,* 408 U.S. 1, 16, 24-29 (1972) (Douglas, J., dissenting). But he was interested in the issue earlier in connection with such cases as *Joint Anti-Fascist Refugee Committee v. McGrath,* 341 U.S. 123, 174-83 (1951) (Douglas, J., concurring).

78. Douglas, *Go East, Young Man,* pp. 448-49.

79. John Stuart Mill, *On Liberty* (New York: Appleton-Century-Crofts, 1947), ch. 1, ll. 433-36, 443-68. Joel Feinberg has suggested that Douglas's right of privacy "would have disappointed Mill." Joel Feinberg, "Autonomy, Sovereignty, and Privacy: Moral Ideals in the Constitution?" *Notre Dame Law Review* 58 (1983): 445, 488.

80. Elizabeth Schneider, "The Dialectic of Rights and Politics: Perspectives from the Women's Movement," *New York University Law Review* 61 (1986): 595, citing Staughton Lynd, "Communal Rights," *Texas Law Review* 62 (1984): 1417-18. See also Drucilla Cornell, "Toward a Modern/Postmodern Reconstruction of Ethics," *University of Pennsylvania Law Review* 133 (1985): 373.

81. Douglas, *The Right of the People,* pp. 91-92.

82. Ibid., p. 161.

83. Charles Krauthammer, "Who's Afraid of Pluralism?" *Washington Post,* Sept. 18, 1987.

84. *Wyman v. James,* 400 U.S. 309, 335 (1971).

85. *Paris Adult Theater I v. Slaton,* 413 U.S. 49, 73 (1973) (Douglas, J., dissenting).

86. William O. Douglas, *A Living Bill of Rights* (Garden City, N.Y.: Doubleday, 1961), p. 65.

87. The image of getting government off the backs of people may have come from Leo Tolstoy. In a political tract regarding the Moscow census, *What To Do?* (1887), Tolstoy personified the wealthy class saying to ordinary people, "I sit on a man's back, choking him and making him carry me, and yet assure myself and others that I am very sorry for him and wish to lighten his load by all possible means — except by getting off his back." *The Viking Book of Aphorisms* (New York: Viking, 1962), p. 297. I have explored elsewhere some of the half-dozen cases in which, beginning in the mid-1960s, Douglas used this phrase. Glancy, "Getting Government Off the Backs of People," p. 1048, n. 7.

88. *Laird v. Tatum,* 408 U.S. 1, 28 (1972) (Douglas, J., dissenting).

89. D'Souza, "New Liberal Censorship," p. 13.

90. Bork, "Supreme Court Needs a New Philosophy," p. 141.

91. The quotation is from Holmes's otherwise rather gloomy lecture to Harvard undergraduates on "The Profession of the Law," Feb. 17, 1886. Julius J. Marke, ed., *The Holmes Reader* (New York: Oceana, 1964), p. 67.

92. William O. Douglas, "The Lasting Influence of Mr. Justice Brandeis," *Temple Law Quarterly* 19 (1945): 361, 370.

93. Douglas, *The Court Years,* p. vii.

94. *Weekly Compilation of Presidential Documents* 25, Jan. 20, 1989, pp. 99, 101.

95. Public Law 93-579, §2(a)(4) 88 Stat. 1896, codified as 5 U.S.C. 552a. Senator Sam J. Ervin, Jr., who introduced the legislation, was an avid follower of Douglas's thinking about the right of privacy. See Sam J. Ervin, Jr., "Justice, the Constitution, and Privacy," *Vital Speeches* 39 (1973): 677.

96. *United States Department of Justice v. Reporters Committee for Freedom of the Press,* 109 S. Ct. 1468 (1989).

97. Laurence H. Tribe, *American Constitutional Law,* 2d ed. (Mineola, N.Y.: Foundation Press, 1988), pp. 1302–1435.

98. Harold Traver, "Privacy and Density," *Hong Kong Law Journal* 6 (1976): 325, 326.

99. Raymond Wacks, *Civil Liberties in Hong Kong* (Hong Kong: Hong Kong University Press, 1988).

100. *Govind v. State of Madhay Pradesh,* 1975, *All India Reporter (Supreme Court),* 1378 (India 1975).

101. *Dudgeon Case,* 45 Eur. Ct. H.R. (Ser. A) (1981).

COMMENTARY:
THE AFFIRMATIVE DIMENSIONS OF DOUGLAS'S PRIVACY

Elizabeth M. Schneider

DOROTHY GLANCY has discussed the various strands of Mr. Justice Douglas's views on the right of privacy. As she observes, there are many different aspects of his understanding of the right of privacy. In this comment, I explore a theme that Professor Glancy has only briefly touched upon, the expansive nature of Justice Douglas's views of the right of privacy. I discuss what I call the affirmative dimensions of Douglas's understanding of privacy, focusing on his concurring opinion in *Roe v. Wade,*[1] examine his views in light of more recent concerns with the right of privacy, and discuss some of the implications of his approach today.

Justice Douglas first developed his concept of a constitutional right of privacy in his opinion for the court in *Griswold v. Connecticut.*[2] In *Griswold,* the Court confronted a constitutional challenge to Connecticut's birth control statutes, which prohibited the use of contraceptives and counseling concerning the use of contraceptives, brought by doctors who had been convicted under the statutes. Douglas perceived the harm in this statute as an intrusion into the privacy and intimacy of the marital relationship. He looked to the varied constitutional sources of a right of privacy. He saw marriage as a "relationship lying within the zone of privacy created by several fundamental constitutional guarantees,"[3] the penumbras of a First Amendment-based right of association, the Third Amendment, the Fourth Amendment, and the Ninth Amendment. However, even though the constitutional sources for the right are defined broadly, the right itself is grounded in the particularity of the marital relationship. Douglas developed the right of privacy based on the associational aspects of marriage as an important relationship that requires protection, and grounded it in a recognition and appreciation of human intimacy and connection as an important value.

However, it is in his concurring opinion in *Roe v. Wade* and *Doe v. Bolton*[4] that Justice Douglas developed his most eloquent and expansive articulation of the concept of privacy. Justice Blackmun based the right of a woman to decide whether or not to carry a pregnancy to term on a right of privacy, that "whether founded on the Fourteenth Amendment concept of personal liberty and resting upon state action, or as the District Court determined, on the Ninth Amendment reservation of rights to the people, is broad enough

179

to encompass a woman's decision."[5] Justice Douglas's opinion was similarly ambiguous with respect to the doctrinal basis of the privacy right. He mentioned rights under the Ninth Amendment, as including "customary, traditional and time-honored rights, amenities, privileges and immunities that come within the sweep of 'the Blessings of Liberty' mentioned in the preamble to the Constitution."[6] He concluded that many of these rights come within the meaning of the term "liberty" as used in the Fourteenth Amendment.

Douglas developed three different dimensions of these rights of privacy and liberty. First, he described the "autonomous control over the development and expression of one's intellect, interests, tastes and personality,"[7] which he saw as absolutely protected by the First Amendment against government interference. Second, he saw "freedom of choice in the basic decisions of one's life respecting marriage, divorce, procreation, contraception and the education and upbringing of children."[8] Third, Douglas described "the freedom to care for one's health and person, freedom from bodily restraint or compulsion, the freedom to walk, stroll or loaf."[9] These rights, although fundamental, are subject to some control by the police power, subject to regulation on a showing of a compelling state interest.

Douglas then applied these dimensions of privacy and liberty to the situation of women who face state prohibitions on abortion; they ground and illuminate the harm that women face. He concluded that a woman is *free* to make the basic decision whether to bear an unwanted child, for "childbirth may deprive a woman of her preferred lifestyle and force upon her a radically different and undesired future."[10] He described in moving detail the harm that women face: "For example, rejected applicants under the Georgia statute are required to endure the discomforts of pregnancy; to incur the pain, higher mortality rate and aftereffects of childbirth; to abandon educational plans; to sustain loss of income; to forgo the satisfactions of careers; to tax further mental and physical health in providing child care; and in some cases to bear the lifelong stigma of unwed motherhood, a badge which may haunt, if not deter, later legitimate family relationships."[11]

It is significant that Douglas developed these aspects of privacy and liberty in the context of women's rights to reproductive control. In *Roe,* Douglas expressed a vision of a privacy right as something far more tied to an affirmative concept of liberty than a right to be let alone, or even as protection from intrusion into the marital bedroom, as he did in *Griswold*. This view of privacy as an aspect of liberty is an expansive concept that has a number of different dimensions. First, there is the dimension of autonomy over the development and expression of one's "intellect, interests, tastes and personality." Then there is the decisional dimension — "freedom of choice in the basic decisions of one's life respecting marriage, divorce, procreation and contraception." There is also freedom *from* intrusion, restraint, and compulsion and freedom *to* care for oneself and express oneself. We see the interrelated dimensions of privacy: autonomy, decisional privacy, what some have called restricted-access privacy, and affirmative self-expression as aspects of the *liberty* that Douglas describes as part of the Fourteenth Amendment. Liberty-freedom is the larger concept, within which these aspects of privacy are subsumed. Although Professor Glancy has suggested that these aspects of privacy discussed in Douglas's concurring opinion are derived from Mill's classic liberalism that focuses on the individual, it is critical that Douglas articulated this affirmative vision in the context of women's reproductive choice. His expression of what I call the liberty aspects of privacy emerges in the context of the reality of women's experience with abortion.

Much has been written about the internal process by which the Supreme Court arrived at its decision in *Roe.*[12] Justice Douglas wanted to write the majority opinion on privacy grounds, but Chief Justice Burger assigned the opinion to Justice Blackmun. Justice Blackmun's first drafts focused only on vagueness and overbreadth, and only after reargument (that Douglas opposed) and much prodding by Justice Douglas did Justice Blackmun take a position that affirmed a woman's right to choose whether to terminate a pregnancy in conjunction with her doctor. At the first argument, the justices asked a substantial number of questions about whether abortion was an issue to be left to the legislature, while at the reargument they were already talking about abortion as a woman's right and balancing it against the state's interest in the fetus.[13] *Roe* was, however, the culmination of an enormous educational process concerning women's rights to abortion that had gone on around the country for several years before, with the growth of the women's movement. In many cities across the country, women were coming forward in courtrooms and meeting places to tell their stories. Women forced the courts to confront the fact that millions of women every year had abortions at tremendous physical and psychic costs. The Supreme Court was being educated by this climate of national discussion.[14]

Justice Douglas's affirmative view of privacy and liberty in his concurring opinion in *Roe* was a product of this educational process. Indeed, his opinion was directly responsive to the range of arguments presented in the briefs submitted in *Roe,* particularly the feminist amicus briefs. The feminist briefs in *Roe* argued broadly that reproductive choice was central to women's equality both in allowing women to become full persons and in achieving full participation in society.[15] The briefs also linked the rights to reproductive control with women's autonomy and ability to be sexual and emphasized the disproportionate impact of criminalization on the poor. They presented to the Court a full factual and legal picture of the range of harms that women suffered as a result of abortion restrictions. For example, the amicus brief submitted by Nancy Stearns of the Center for Constitutional Rights for New Women Lawyers presented arguments concerning abortion restrictions as an affirmative infringement of women's liberty, sex discrimination, and as involuntary servitude under the Thirteenth Amendment.[16] This brief in particular focused on the practical impact of criminalizing abortion on women's lives, and was filled with rich, textured descriptions of the harms that women suffered as a result of prohibitions on abortion and the central role that reproductive choice had for women's lives.[17] Douglas's opinion, more specifically than the majority opinion in *Roe,*[18] echoed these themes, in particular the harms to women's liberty and freedom, and reflected the factual concreteness of the feminist briefs.

To the extent that Justice Blackmun's majority opinion primarily emphasizes individual decisional privacy, Justice Douglas's concurring opinion goes further in making an explicit link to liberty and in developing the more affirmative dimensions of autonomy, self-determination, and self-expression. It also presages concerns with privacy as too narrow a grounding for the right to abortion that feminist theorists have subsequently expressed. Douglas's affirmative view of privacy as a dimension of liberty and his grounding of the abortion right on liberty in his opinion in *Roe* resonates with critiques developed by feminist legal scholars of the privacy right as the doctrinal basis for the abortion decision.[19]

Feminist theorists have seen as problematic the articulation of a right of privacy, as opposed to liberty, as the doctrinal basis for the abortion decision in *Roe*. Feminists have argued that the abortion right should have been grounded on the concept of liberty rather than privacy, as it is women's freedom and autonomy that is at stake. Although feminist theorists have understood that there are many dimensions to privacy — decision making, autonomy, self-determination, and human and sexual self-expression[20] — privacy seemed to rest on a division of public and private which has been oppressive to women and has reinforced male dominance by, for example, perpetuating the appropriateness of the absence of law in the private sphere and denying legal relief to women from economic and physical abuse from husbands.[21] Privacy reinforces the idea that the personal is separate from the political, and that the problem of lack of reproductive choice is procedural, not substantive; privacy also implies something that should be kept secret.[22] The right of privacy has been viewed by feminists as a passive right, which says that the state can't intervene, whereas the right to liberty was viewed as a right that emphasized the harms that women suffered if they could not get abortions and seemed to imply that the state had an affirmative obligation to ensure that women exercise their freedom.[23]

Douglas's concurring opinion suggests the radical potential of the concept of privacy — articulating it as not only the right to be left alone but as affirmatively linked to liberty and the right to autonomy, self-expression, and self-determination. The notion of women as agents of our own lives is an important and powerful concept that transcends the common experience of the concept of privacy. Unfortunately, this radical potential of the concept of privacy has not been actualized by more recent decisions of the Court. Indeed, the Supreme Court's subsequent decision in *Bowers v. Hardwick*[24] suggests the limits of privacy as a doctrinal basis. In *Bowers,* it was not just the right of privacy, the right to seclusion, or decisional choice that was challenged, but the right to sexual autonomy and personal and emotional self-realization. The affirmative dimensions of Douglas's understanding of privacy and liberty are thus directly in issue in *Bowers,* but the majority there refused to protect the decisional choice as a matter of privacy out of rejection of the sexual choice — homosexual sodomy — that underlies it. Only Justice Blackmun's moving dissent in *Bowers* carries on Douglas's vision. As Rhonda Copelon has observed, Blackmun's dissent suggests that privacy means not simply that the state should not interfere with cloistered sexuality but that the Constitution should affirmatively protect different forms of sexual intimacy because sexual and familial self-definition is central to personal authenticity and self-realization.[25]

Douglas's opinion in *Roe* also reveals important dimensions of Douglas's method of judging. A growing feminist literature on judging suggests the importance of a judicial capacity to stand in another's shoes, really listen to another's experience, and open oneself to understand that experience.[26] Justice Douglas was unusual in the degree to which he was willing to open himself up to different experiences. In various contexts, with Native Americans for example, or in international situations, with racial minorities, and with women, Douglas sought to get beyond the limits of his own experience. As others have noted, Douglas looked to human experience as the source for decision making. Douglas was a judge, curious about experience that differed from his own, who sought to understand that experience. His openness to appreciating and understanding difference may have been crucial to his ability to explore and articulate the various strands of privacy and liberty that he develops in his concurring opinion in *Roe,* for it reveals an effort to seek to understand women's experiences with abortion. In this vein, the only opinion that Douglas wrote that related to women's issues other than *Griswold* and *Roe* was *Kahn v. Shevin.*[27] There he showed the same effort to understand and empathize with women's experiences by detailing the serious economic discrimination that women suffer. Although well meaning, this opinion, which upheld Florida's tax exemption for widows on the grounds that women suffer economic discrimination, has been viewed as naive and wrong. *Kahn* may have resulted from the same empathic impulse as *Roe,* but sex discrimination scholars have been unanimous in criticizing *Kahn.*[28]

In early 1989, at the abortion demonstration in Washington seeking to convince the Supreme Court not to overturn *Roe v. Wade,* I was reminded of the affirmative dimensions of Douglas's opinion in *Roe.* I saw many signs and slogans which captured, as Douglas's opinion did, the centrality of reproductive choice for women and the interrelated dimensions of the privacy and liberty claim: freedom, autonomy, decisional choice, and sexual expression. Douglas understood, as did few other judges, that the "loam of life" is the basis for legal ideas, and that there is what I have elsewhere called a "dialectical relationship between rights and politics."[29] Justice Douglas had an open, evolving understanding of the relationship between law and social change. Particularly at this historical moment, as the Supreme Court undoes *Roe v. Wade,* it is important to affirm his unique judicial capacity to grasp the centrality and transformative potential of women's reproductive choice for women's lives.

Notes

The ideas in this comment have been generated and enriched by the important work of Sylvia Law, Rhonda Copelon, and Nancy Stearns on reproductive freedom.

1. 410 U.S. 113 (1973).
2. 381 U.S. 479 (1965).
3. Ibid., at 485.
4. 410 U.S. 179 (1973).
5. *Roe v. Wade,* 410 U.S., at 153.
6. Ibid., at 210 (Douglas, J., concurring).
7. Ibid., at 211.
8. Ibid., at 213.
9. Ibid., at 214.
10. Ibid., at 214–15.
11. Ibid.
12. See Carl Bernstein and Robert Woodward, *The Brethren* (New York: Simon and Schuster, 1979), p. 278; Bernard Schwartz, *The Unpublished Opinions of the Burger Court* (New York: Oxford University Press, 1988), pp. 83–151; Melvin I. Urofsky and Philip E. Urofsky, eds., *The Douglas Letters: Selections from the Private Papers of Justice William O. Douglas* (Bethesda: Adler and Adler, 1987), pp. 180–87; James F. Simon, *Independent Journey: The Life of William O. Douglas* (New York: Harper and Row, 1980), pp. 438–42. For a discussion of the experience with *Roe* and *Doe* from a feminist perspective, see Janice Goodman, Rhonda Copelon Schoenbrod, and Nancy Stearns, "*Roe* and *Doe:* Where Do We Go From Here?," *Women's Rights Law Reporter* 1 (1973): 20; Lynne Henderson, "Legality and Empathy," *Michigan Law Review* 85 (1987): 1574, 1620–38; Sylvia Law, "Rethinking Sex and the Constitution," *University of Pennsylvania Law Review* 132 (1984): 956; Rhonda Copelon, "Unpacking Patriarchy: Reproduction, Sexuality, Originalism and Constitutional Change," in Jules Lobel, ed., *A Less Than Perfect Union: Alternative Perspectives on the U.S. Constitution* (New York: Monthly Review Press, 1988).
13. Goodman, Schoenbrod, and Stearns, "*Roe* and *Doe,*" p. 25.
14. Ibid.
15. The discussion in this section is drawn from Copelon, "Unpacking Patriarchy."
16. Brief *Amicus Curiae* on Behalf of New Women Lawyers, Women's Health and Abortion Project, Inc., National Abortion Action Coalition, in *Roe v. Wade, Doe v. Bolton,* Nos. 70–18 and 70–40, Supreme Court of the United States, Oct. Term 1971. I worked on this brief as a law student intern with Nancy Stearns at the Center for Constitutional Rights.
17. Ibid.
18. Lynne Henderson suggests that none of the opinions in *Roe* reflected a wom-

en's narrative or perspective. Henderson, "Legality and Empathy," pp. 1620–38, and n. 11.

19. See generally Copelon, "Unpacking Patriarchy," Law, "Rethinking Sex," Goodman, Schoenbrod, and Stearns, "*Roe* and *Doe*." This section draws on all these sources.

20. Copelon, "Unpacking Patriarchy." For an insightful discussion of the various dimensions of privacy and the particular link between decisional privacy and liberty for women in the area of reproductive freedom, see Anita L. Allen, *Uneasy Access: Privacy for Women in a Free Society* (Totowa, N.J.: Rowman and Littlefield, 1988).

21. See generally Nadine Taub and Elizabeth Schneider, "Perspectives on Women's Subordination and the Role of Law," in David Kairys, ed., *The Politics of Law* (New York: Pantheon, 1982).

22. Copelon, "Unpacking Patriarchy"; Henderson, "Legality and Empathy."

23. Goodman, Schoenbrod, and Stearns, "*Roe* and *Doe*," p. 27.

24. 478 U.S. 186 (1986).

25. Copelon, "Unpacking Patriarchy," p. 320.

26. Martha Minow, "Foreword: Justice Engendered: The Supreme Court, 1986 Term," *Harvard Law Review* 101 (1987): 10; Henderson, "Legality and Empathy"; Judith Resnik, "On the Bias: Feminist Reconsiderations of the Aspirations of our Judges," *Southern California Law Review* 61 (1988): 1877; Patricia A. Cain, "Good and Bad Bias: A Comment on Feminist Theory and Judging," *Southern California Law Review* 61 (1988): 1945.

27. 416 U.S. 351 (1974).

28. See generally Herma Kay, *Sex-Based Discrimination* (St. Paul: West, 1988), pp. 78–80; Barbara Allen Babcock, Ann E. Freedman, Eleanor Holmes Norton, Susan C. Ross, *Sex Discrimination and the Law: Causes and Remedies* (Boston: Little, Brown, 1975), pp. 123–25.

29. Elizabeth Schneider, "The Dialectic of Rights and Politics: Perspectives From the Women's Movement," *New York University Law Review* 61 (1986): 589.

Part Four

Douglas as Environmentalist

INTRODUCTION:
DOUGLAS AS ENVIRONMENTALIST

Ralph W. Johnson

WILLIAM O. DOUGLAS will be remembered as a dedicated wilderness advocate, environmentalist, and supporter of Indian self-determination and treaty rights. The three chapters in Part Four present a comprehensive view of Douglas's considerable achievements as an environmentalist.

Professor Ralph W. Johnson, in "'In Simple Justice to a Downtrodden People,'" gives us a perspective on Douglas's views by analyzing all the Indian cases where Douglas wrote majority, concurring, or dissenting opinions, and placing them in the context of national Indian law and policy. He tells how Douglas's judicial opinions affected and were affected by that context. Douglas's early views on Indian issues were quite at odds with his later opinions. In 1939 he signed a decision by Justice Black stating that assimilation and gradual takeover of Indian reservations by the states was national policy, and was the correct policy. But Douglas soon changed his mind, subsequently decrying state intervention in tribal affairs as dangerous to the Indian's welfare, and holding steadily in favor of Indian tribal sovereignty, self-determination, and independence from state laws.

Justice Douglas sought to uphold treaties and agreements with Indian tribes, arguing presuasively that these documents should be construed in favor of the Indians, and as the Indians understood them. There was one occasion, however, when this position and another strongly held Douglas priority came into conflict. First, he believed that states were powerless to interfere with Indian treaty rights without clear authority from Congress, and second, he believed that the salmon runs of the Pacific Northwest should not be destroyed by overfishing, either by Indian or non-Indian. Faced with this conflict, Douglas chose the second priority. Johnson explains why fish protection won out.

Professor Johnson notes that in his judicial opinions Douglas belongs to the group of justices, including former Justices Hugo Black and Frank Murphy and current Justices Marshall and Brennan, who have nearly always favored the Indian side in Supreme Court litigation.

Professor William H. Rodgers, Jr., weaves a story about Douglas's environmental opinions in "The Fox and the Chickens: Mr. Justice Douglas and Environmental Law." Douglas, Rodgers claims, was like the fox in his tactical flexibility, his versatility under stress, and his ability to make the best of a bad situation. Rodgers draws on decision theory to distinguish between maximizing styles and the style of "games" in which "the 'best' position for a player depends upon context and what the other players are doing." Rodgers groups Douglas with the "gamers." Rodgers tells us that one of Douglas's continuing themes, throughout judicial and private writings, was his faith that an informed public will insist upon protection of the environment and that Congress and other elective bodies, barring a corruption of process, can be depended upon to make the right choices for the welfare of the planet.

In his commentary, Professor Christopher D. Stone argues that Rodgers distinction between "gamers" and "maximizers," as applied to Douglas, is "untenable," and "a bit too fuzzy to follow." Stone claims that Rodgers has to "stretch—to be a little foxy with the opinions hmself—to make any case for Douglas's environmentalist impact at all." While Douglas made noises about giving standing to trees and other natural objects, he was, Stone writes, "predominantly homocentric—that nature should be conserved for human benefit, not for any rights of its own." In the end, however, Stone writes that, even if it were only for *Sierra Club v. Morton* alone, Douglas "would have instated himself as the leading judicial champion of the environment."

In "Justice Douglas and the Public Lands," Professor Charles F. Wilkinson describes Douglas's "passionate love" of the mountains, of the pleasure and solace he got from his mountain experiences, and how, when he retired from the Supreme Court and wrote his farewell to his fellow justices, he compared their experiences together to a long canoe trip on a wilderness river. Douglas consistently voted in favor of public control of public lands over the claims of corporate interests, demonstrating marked skepticism toward litigants seeking to establish private rights in federal lands and resources. The one area where Douglas believed state law should generally control over federal law concerned western water rights. Douglas reflected the standard westerner's view, hewing to the "states rights" position about water allocation on western rivers and streams. Nonetheless, Douglas evinced a powerful determination to protect the nation's rivers from excessive dam construction, especially in the West. One of Douglas's most innovative views in the public lands area, says Wilkinson, who differs from Stone, was that inanimate objects such as trees, mountain meadows, birds, and animals should have standing to sue. It should not be necessary to show injury to people to acquire standing.

T. H. Watkins, in his commentary to Wilkinson's chapter, illustrates Douglas's environmental activism by describing one highly publicized hike taken to encourage protection of the 189-mile-long towpath along the Chesapeake & Ohio Canal; and another to preserve the wilderness character of the 25-mile-long Pacific Ocean coastal strip of the Olympic National Park.

The three chapters present a comprehensive view of Douglas's considerable achievements as an environmentalist.

"In Simple Justice to a Downtrodden People": Justice Douglas and the American Indian Cases

Ralph W. Johnson

No FIELD OF federal Indian law really existed at the time William O. Douglas was appointed by Franklin D. Roosevelt to the Supreme Court in 1939. Thus he probably knew little about the subject, coming out of Columbia Law School, and having been a Securities and Exchange commissioner and a Wall Street lawyer. Indian law courses were not taught in law schools, no treatises or casebooks existed, and only rarely were law review articles published on native American issues.

It was also in 1939 that Dr. Felix S. Cohen, Associate Solicitor in the Department of Interior was appointed Special Assistant to the Attorney General to head the Indian Law Survey of the Department of Justice.[1] Cohen eventually amassed forty-six volumes of federal laws and treaties, culminating in publication of his monumental *Handbook of Federal Indian Law* in 1942 under the auspices of the Department of Interior. This treatise virtually created the field of American Indian law, bringing organization and clarity to a heterogeneous mass of disorganized laws, regulations, and cases.

Cohen conceptualized the idea of sovereignty, self-determination, and the rules of construction about treaties. His book had an immediate effect on the Supreme Court, being cited and quoted first by Douglas.[2] The *Handbook* has also had an enduring impact on this new field of law, having been cited and relied upon innumerable times by the federal courts.

I. The 1887 Allotment Act

William O. Douglas was born eleven years after Congress enacted the 1887 Dawes Act (General Allotment Act),[3] the most disastrous law ever passed concerning native Americans. This Act, motivated by a mixture of Christian zeal, Adam Smithian notions of human motivation, paternalism, and the non-Indian's land-grabbing greed, was designed to break up Indian reservations by allotting small acreages to individual Indians. The Indian allottee was to hold the allotment for twenty-five years, during which the allottee was supposed to learn the white man's legal and economic system. The allottee then could apply for a "certificate of competency," certifying that he was competent to handle property ownership; a patent (deed) would be issued,

191

conveying fee title to him from the federal government. The land then became subject to state and local taxes. The idea was to break up the communal lifestyle of the tribes and encourage Indians to become individual farmers and ranchers, like the whites.

In the early 1900s, when Bill Douglas was a growing boy, the government decided to speed up the ill-conceived allotment process by issuing "forced" fee patents to Indian allottees (in less than twenty-five years), whether or not they knew anything about the white man's legal system. In the next few years, thousands upon thousands of these forced-fee patentees lost their land on tax foreclosure sales, because they could not read the tax foreclosure notices, did not understand the process, or had no money to pay taxes. Moreover, the government decided the Indians had too much land, so millions of acres of reservations were declared "surplus" and given to white settlers.

There is no evidence that Douglas, as a boy, was aware of these national Indian policy issues. Living in the towns of Cleveland and Yakima, Washington, near the large Yakima Indian Reservation, he did not have extensive contacts with the Indian community. But he did come to know a few of the Indian teenagers, hiked, speared fish, shared stories with them, and retained some friendships for life. By this time Douglas had developed a love of the outdoors, deriving from many hikes he took to strengthen his muscles after a childhood polio attack. After his father's death in 1910, Douglas lived with his mother in rather extreme poverty. He worked on the local farms in the summers, lived in a tent in 1916 when he first went to Whitman College in eastern Washington, and in 1922 hitchhiked and hopped freight trains from Yakima to New York City to attend Columbia Law School, arriving with fifty cents in his pocket.[4] Douglas's youthful poverty, combined with his mother's strong religious and moral training, no doubt contributed to his innate urge to champion underdog causes. His contact with the Yakima Indians, reinforced by a love of mountains and hiking, probably contributed to a disposition toward favoring Indians, a disposition later reflected in his judicial opinions.[5]

By 1920, when Douglas graduated Phi Beta Kappa from Whitman College, the damage from the Allotment Act had been done. The Indians had lost two-thirds of their land. Their ownership had dropped from 150 to 48 million acres of land. The allotment process gradually slowed to a trickle through the 1920s. In 1928 the *Meriam Report* told Congress of the devastating impact of the Dawes Act. By 1934, the year Douglas was appointed to the Securities and Exchange Commission, Congress was intensely aware of the adverse effect on Indians of the Dawes Act. Responding to this awareness, Congress finally enacted the Indian Reorganization Act,[6] stopping all further allotments, and giving a boost to tribal governments and tribal economic development.

II. Two Pre-Douglas, Pro-Indian Supreme Court Decisions

In the early years of this century, while Douglas was growing up in Yakima and the Dawes Act was wreaking havoc with Indian land ownership, the Supreme Court rendered two important decisions in favor of Indians. One of these decisions, *United States v. Winans,*[7] was often cited and quoted by Douglas in his own later Court opinions.[8]

In *Winans,* the Court was asked to interpret an 1859 treaty reserving to the Indians a right to fish at their "usual and accustomed" off-reservation fishing sites. One of these sites was on the property of a non-Indian by the name of Winans. Winans's original patent from the federal government said nothing about any Indian rights. Justice McKenna, for the majority, nonetheless held the Indians had a right to go across, and fish from, Winans's land. He said that the right of the Indians to fish at these off-reservation sites was "not much less necessary to the existence of the Indians than the atmosphere they breathed . . . the treaty was not a grant of rights to the Indians, but a grant of rights from them—a reservation of those not granted. [The treaty] imposed a servitude upon every piece of land as though described therein."[9]

In the second case, *Winters v. United States,*[10] Justice McKenna, for the Court, dealt with an important water rights issue. The Fort Belknap Reservation in Montana had been created in 1888 by an agreement with the United States, approved by Congress. The northern boundary of the reservation was the Milk River. In the early 1890s, upstream non-Indian farmers appropriated virtually all the water of the river for irrigation, claiming they *used* the water first and under western water law had a vested legal right to continue that use. They said their water right took priority over a later, 1898, attempt by the tribe to use water. The United States sued on behalf of the tribe to enjoin the non-Indian diversion. The Supreme Court held for the United States (and the tribe), saying that when the reservation was created in a desert area where the Indians were to become farmers, sufficient water was impliedly reserved to the tribe to carry out the purposes of the reservation. Moreover, the Indians' water right dated from the creation of the reservation, no matter when the water was actually put to use. This was a major victory for the Indians.[11]

III. Douglas's Early Assimilationist Views
and How They Changed

PRE-WORLD WAR II

Douglas's first case on native Americans was decided in 1939, before Cohen's book was printed, as mentioned previously. In *Board of Commissioners v. United States,*[12] the question was whether interest should accrue on county property taxes wrongfully but innocently collected from an Indian allottee. Justice Frankfurter, for the majority, held that *federal* law controlled the issue and did not provide for repayment of interest by the county. In a concurring opinion, Justice Black, joined by Douglas, said that Kansas *state* law controlled, and that state law did not require interest on tax refunds. The reasoning of this assimilationist concurring opinion sheds light on both Black's and Douglas's pre-Cohen views. Black, with Douglas concurring, said that "Congress . . . has . . . gradually evolved a policy looking to [the Indians'] eventual absorption into the general body of citizenry. This policy has progressively subjected Indians to the laws under which all other citizens must live in the Indians' state of residence, if not in conflict with specific protective measures of Congress. [Congress's failure to specifically require interest on this refund] is entirely consistent with the Congressional policy of steadily extending the operation of the States' laws over their resident Indians."[13]

WORLD WAR II AND AFTER

During the Second World War, national policy toward Indians took a backseat to wartime priorities. Following the war, a strong assimilationist view began to dominate (in spite of the views expressed by Cohen in his *Handbook*). When the Eisenhower administration took office in 1952, this policy was pushed with a vengeance. Now called the "termination" policy, it was designed to terminate Indian tribes as governing entities and to end the federal trust relationship to them. Under this policy, more than one hundred tribes were terminated, including the large Menominee and Klamath Tribes. Congress enacted House Concurrent Resolution 108 formally pronouncing termination as the national policy. It also enacted Public Law 280,[14] authorizing states to impose state jurisdiction over reservations either with or without Indian consent.

During the 1950s termination era, the Department of Interior found Cohen's examination of the original treaties of 1942 embarrassing. Its carefully prepared legal and moral arguments articulating the self-determination of Indian tribes were now out of style. The response of the Department of Interior was simple: rewrite Cohen's treatise and discredit the original under the guise of a revision. The 1958 edition deleted all of Cohen's reasoning on sovereignty and self-determination. When the supply of the original Cohen book ran out, it was not reprinted. Only the 1958 book was available. The termination era lasted about ten years and by 1960 was waning. During this time, Douglas's own views were changing, going in the opposite direction, away from termination/assimilation and toward self-determination. The first inklings of this change in attitude can be seen in cases on "takings" of Indian lands.

Two important cases were decided on the takings issue during Douglas's tenure. In 1945, the Court decided *Northwest Band of Shoshone Indians v. United States.*[15] Justice Reed for the majority ruled that the Shoshone Indians were not entitled to compensation for the taking of aboriginal title, partly because of the difficulty of proving the boundaries of such claimed lands, and partly because the 1863 Treaty of Box Elder did not constitute a "recognition" by the United States of the Indian title. The Court rejected the argument that Shoshone control over these lands, requiring tribal permission for United States transportation and communication facilities, implied recognition of Indian title. The tribe had argued that all doubts about the meaning of the treaty must be resolved in the Indians' favor. The Court surprisingly rejected this long-standing rule[16] and said that the rule means no more "than that the language should be construed in accordance with the tenor of the treaty."

Justice Douglas dissented, arguing that compensation should be paid the Shoshones.[17] The "right of occupancy is considered as sacred [to the Indians] as the fee simple is to the whites."[18] In addition, he said, the United States "recognized" the Indian title by acceding to the Indian permit system for traveling on and using the Indian land, and by the Box Elder Treaty. He noted that Pokatello, the Indian leader who "signed the treaty, had no counsel . . . at his elbow when the treaty was drafted. [The treaty] was written in a language foreign to him. He was not a conveyancer. He was not cognizant of the distinctions in title. He neither had nor gave deeds to his land. . . . But he knew the land where he lived and for which he would fight. If the standards of the frontier are to govern, his assertion of ownership and its recognition by the United States could hardly have been plainer."[19] Douglas argued for the standard rule of treaty construction, that treaties should be "construed, not according to the technical meaning of its words to learned lawyers, but in the sense in which they would naturally be understood by the Indians. . . . The faith of this nation having been pledged in the treaties, the honor of the nation demands, and the jurisdictional act requires, that these long unsettled grievances be settled by this court in simple justice to a downtrodden people."[20]

The seminal case on compensation for aboriginal title is *Tee Hit Ton Indians v. United States.*[21] The Tee Hit Ton Indians of Alaska sued for Fifth Amendment compensation for the taking of timber on Indian aboriginal land. Justice Reed for the majority denied compensation, saying the federal government need only compensate Indians for title that was "recognized" by treaty or statute. The Court then analyzed the Alaska Organic Act of 1884 and decided that neither that statute nor any other constituted a "recognition" of Indian title. The Court added a philosophical note, probably reflecting the fact that national Indian policy during the 1950s was termination-oriented, saying, "Every American schoolboy knows that the savage tribes of this continent were deprived of their ancestral ranges by force and that, even when the Indians ceded millions of acres by treaty in return for blankets, food, and trinkets, it was not a sale but the conquerors' will that deprived them of their land."[22]

Douglas dissented, supported by Warren and Frankfurter, on the ground that Congress *had* recognized the Tee Hit Ton's possessory interest in the land and timber in the 1884 Organic Act for Alaska. Douglas said he did not need to rely on the special canons of construction for this interpretation of the statute. He found the meaning plain from the statute itself. He did say, however, that in enacting the Organic Act, "Congress did the humane thing of saving to the Indians all rights claimed: it let them keep what they had prior to the new Act. That purpose is wholly at war with the [intent of the Act] now attributed to the Congress."[23]

In 1959 Justice Black, who with Douglas had gradually changed from an assimilation viewpoint to a self-determination position, wrote an opinion[24] that, according to Professor Charles F. Wilkinson, "opened the modern era of federal Indian law"[25] and permanently changed the dialogue about Indian sovereignty. This case, Wilkinson says, is a "leading example of the special rules that the Court has recognized during the modern era in order to protect tribal government in Indian country."[26] Douglas joined in the majority opinion.

The opinion is significant. Plaintiff, the operator of a non-Indian federally licensed general store on the Navajo Reservation, brought suit in state court against an enrolled Navajo to collect for goods sold on credit. The U.S. Supreme Court reversed a state court ruling and held that the tribal court had exclusive jurisdiction over the case. In the course of the opinion, the Court made one of the most widely quoted statements in the field of Indian law, now known as the "infringement" doctrine, establishing a new test for deciding when state law might be excluded from the reservation. "Essentially, absent governing Acts of Congress, the question has always been whether the state action infringed on the rights of reservation Indians to make their own laws and be ruled by them."[27] By joining Black in this opinion, Douglas once again expressed his increasing conviction that self-determination was the right policy toward native Americans.

In 1960 the Court decided *Federal Power Commission v. Tuscarora Indian Nation*.[28] Justice Whittaker for the majority held that the condemnation power under the 1920 Federal Power Act authorized condemnation of fee patent land—not trust land—owned by the Tuscarora Indian Tribe. The Court in dicta said that "general acts of Congress apply to Indians as well as to all others in the absence of a clear expression to the contrary." Black, joined by Douglas and Warren, dissented, arguing that the federal government had encouraged the Indians to continue their traditional way of life, and while it "may be hard for us to understand why these Indians cling so tenaciously to their lands and traditional tribal way of life, some things are worth more than money. . . . great nations, like great men, should keep their word."[29]

Douglas's early assimilationist views were further rejected in later cases. However, now his "self-determination" views were supported by official

United States policy.[30] In *Menominee Tribe v. United States*,[31] Douglas, for the majority, held that a 1954 Act terminating the Menominee Tribe did not terminate tribal hunting and fishing rights, because the Act did not explicitly say these rights ended. Douglas wrote, "We decline to construe the Termination Act as a backhanded way of abrogating the hunting and fishing rights of these Indians. While the power to abrogate those rights exists, the intention to abrogate or modify a treaty is not to be lightly imputed to the Congress."[32]

Likewise in *DeCoteau v. District County Court*,[33] Douglas, in a vigorous dissent to a majority opinion that found disestablishment, expressed his anti-assimilationist views by saying, "This tribe is a self-governing political community, a status which is not lightly impaired."[34] He then claimed that the majority decision "tears the reservation asunder. It is the end of tribal authority for it introduces such an element of uncertainty as to what agency has jurisdiction as to make modest tribal leaders abdicate and aggressive ones undertake the losing battle against superior state authority." He then quoted from *United States v. Kagama*,[35] where the Court said, "They [the Indians] owe no allegiance to the states, and receive from them no protection. Because of the local ill feeling, the people of the states where they are found are often their deadliest enemies." Douglas's early view favoring assimilation through gradual imposition of state law on reservations had clearly changed.[36]

IV. 1968–1970, A Time of Change

INDIAN LAWYERS

In 1968 the American Indian Law Center at the University of New Mexico, under the distinguished directorship of Oneida Indian Robert L. Bennett, republished Cohen's original *Handbook*. At the same time, the center started a hugely successful annual summer program (now continued under Sam Deloria), which attracted to New Mexico twenty-five or thirty aspiring Indian law students, college graduates all, for a six-week orientation to law school courses. These students would later enroll and graduate from law schools throughout the nation, from Harvard, Yale, and Georgetown in the East to Stanford, Berkeley, and University of Washington in the West. The program continues to this day.

By 1970, Fred Hart, professor of law at the University of New Mexico, and Monroe Price, professor of law at UCLA, began to teach this subject.[37] Within a few years, federal Indian law became a recognized subject in several law schools. In 1973 Professor Price authored the first-ever casebook in the field.[38] By the early 1970s, law schools throughout the western United States were teaching the subject, turning out law graduates familiar with the unique and large body of law in this field.

In 1968 Congress enacted the Indian Civil Rights Act[39] and strongly encouraged Indian tribal courts to upgrade the quality of their court systems. This caused the newly formed National American Indian Court Justices Association to launch a training program for Indian court judges.[40] Since 1980, this program has been conducted by the Indian Justice Center in Sacramento, California. In addition, Congress mandated that the original Cohen treatise be revised and updated, and appropriated $500,000 for that purpose. A task force created to carry out this goal gathered a large amount of material, but the book was ultimately written and edited by a group of academic scholars teaching in the field of Indian law.[41]

Prior to the Indian Claims Commission Act of 1946, virtually no private lawyers knew enough about Indian law to represent Indian tribes or individuals in court adequately. Passage of this Act created a specialized bar to handle these multiyear, multimillion dollar claims by tribes for lost lands. These lawyers were specialists, however, and largely confined their interests to the huge claims under the 1946 Act. Not until the 1960s did the characteristics of lawyering for Indians change significantly. Lawyers in the Office for Economic Opportunity (War on Poverty Legal Service Program) became knowledgeable in Indian law. By 1969 some forty Legal Services lawyers were working on Indian law questions on reservations throughout the nation.[42] The civil rights movement also spun off lawyers who became seriously interested in Indian law questions. The University of New Mexico's Indian law student program succeeded in encouraging Indians to become lawyers, and most of them returned to their communities and became proficient in Indian law. Of enormous significance was the creation of the Native American Rights Fund (NARF) in 1970, as a spin-off of California Indian Legal Services, under the able leadership of David H. Getches. It continues its tradition of excellence under John Echohawk, a member of the first graduating class of the New Mexico program. This organization of about twenty lawyers had, and still has, a major impact on the quality of legal representation of Indian tribes throughout the nation. Over the past several years, NARF has participated in an average of seventy cases at any one time; the cases are distributed over about twenty-five states. NARF lawyers have made numerous arguments, oral and written, to the Supreme Court.

These events happened during the last decade of Douglas's tenure on the Court. Although it is not possible to trace directly the impact of each event on Douglas's thinking, or vice versa, it is not unreasonable to believe they did have an impact.

THE FISHING RIGHTS CASES

Charles Wilkinson has described the changes in litigation for Indian tribes that occurred in the 1960s and 1970s: "For decades before, Indian law decisions had been rendered fitfully by the Supreme Court. The tribes and the federal government instituted few cases to establish or expand tribal powers. After *Williams* the pace of decisions began to accelerate. . . . Twelve Indian law cases were handed down during the 1960s, and the extraordinary number of thirty-five Indian law decisions were reported by the Supreme Court during the 1970s, easily the most active decade in Indian law in the Court's history. Thirty-two decisions in the field have already been rendered during the first seven terms of the 1980s."[43]

This was the milieu in which Douglas wrote several important Indian fishing rights decisions. These Douglas decisions highlighted conflicts that existed in his mind, which affected his judicial decisions on Indians. As a committed conservationist, especially regarding the salmon and steelhead runs of the Pacific Northwest, he was deeply concerned that these beautiful anadromous fish might be destroyed by dams, by development, or by human predatory activities. In his personal life as well as in his judicial decisions, he sought to protect these fish and their environment. Of course, if a salmon run were wiped out, the loss would fall on Indians as well as non-Indians. Douglas felt constrained to interpret Indian treaty fishing claims in such a way as to protect the salmon and steelhead runs.

A second philosophical priority held by Douglas concerned the Bill of Rights of the federal Constitution, especially the equal protection concept that was read into the Fifth Amendment in 1954.[44] Douglas wanted to protect Pacific Northwest Indian off-reservation fishing rights, which by treaty were held "in common" with non-Indians, but he was worried about the relationship of his "in common" Indian right and the equal protection concept. He voiced that worry in his opinions, without suggesting how the issue might be resolved, thus creating confusion about the relationship of these concepts and in particular providing, unintentionally, an opportunity for the Washington Supreme Court to adopt an erroneous interpretation of equal protection as applied to treaty rights.

Six fishing rights cases involved the 1850s Pacific Northwest treaties that reserved to the signatory tribes the right to fish for salmon and steelhead at their traditional off-reservation fishing sites "in common with the citizens of the Territory." Douglas participated in three of these decisions, writing majority opinions in two. These fishing rights decisions reflect three Douglas priorities, all in some conflict. First, Douglas wanted to conserve the salmon and steelhead runs. Second, he wanted to hold in favor of the Indians. Third, he wanted to assure that constitutional rights such as equal protection were assured.

In 1942, three years after Douglas was appointed, the Court decided *Tulee v. Washington*.[45] Justice Black for the Court, including Douglas, reversed the state Supreme Court and held the state could not require Indians to purchase state fishing licenses to exercise their off-reservation treaty fishing rights.[46]

The first Douglas opinion of this series was *Puyallup Tribe v. Department of Game of Washington*.[47] The question was whether the Indians could use set nets at river mouths to fish for salmon under their off-reservation treaty right, or whether the state could prohibit such equipment as "necessary for conservation."[48] Douglas opined that, while the Indians had treaty rights *to fish* under the in-common clause, the *manner* in which they fished and its purpose were not mentioned in the treaty. He said, "we see no reason why the right of the Indians may not also be regulated by an appropriate exercise of the police power of the State. . . . But the manner of fishing, the size of the take, the restriction of commercial fishing, and the like may be regulated by the State in the interest of conservation, provided the regulation meets appropriate standards and does not discriminate against the Indians."

It seems unlike Douglas to rule that state law can be used to control Indian treaty fishing rights. Under well-established rules of Indian law, states do not have that power unless Congress clearly delegates it to them,[49] and no such delegation exists. Two reasons might be given for this unusual Douglas holding. (1) Douglas wanted to protect the fishery resource from destruction, by either Indians or non-Indians. If destruction occurred, neither group would get fish. (2) The second reason requires more explanation. The attorneys for the Puyallup Tribe were apparently so overconfident they would win the case no matter what, they had entered into a remarkably ill-advised, and disastrous, stipulation. The stipulation provided that the tribe "had fished contrary to state fishing conservation laws and regulations since 1960; that if permitted to continue, the [tribe's] commercial fishery would virtually exterminate the salmon and steelhead fish runs; . . . and that it is necessary for proper conservation of the salmon and steelhead fish runs . . . that the [state agencies] enforce state fishery conservation laws and regulations to the fishing activities of the defendants at their usual and accustomed grounds."[50]

It seems plausible that Douglas was influenced by this damning stipulation. His apparent frustration over this issue caused him to write five years later, in his majority opinion in *Puyallup II*, "that the police power of the state is adequate to prevent the steelhead from following the fate of the passenger pigeon; and the treaty does not give the Indians a federal right to pursue the last living steelhead until it enters their nets."[51]

The Douglas ruling that the state could regulate off-reservation Indian treaty fishing is further flawed. One must realize that by 1968 the state of Washington had established a pattern of opposition to and discrimination against Indian off-reservation treaty fishing rights.[52] (Until 1974, the tribes, under policies established by Washington's Attorneys General — John O'Connell, 1964–1968, and Slade Gorton, 1968–1980 — were limited to harvesting between two and four percent of the fish.) Thus to be effective, judicial standards for guiding such regulation would have to be clear and specific. These were not. Douglas had created a judicial quagmire. Neither the "appropriate standards" nor the guides for nondiscrimination are revealed. Nor is the phrase "necessary for conservation" defined.

The other concern raised by Douglas's *Puyallup I* opinion arises from a clause he added to the last sentence of his opinion: "We only add that any ultimate findings on the conservation issue must also cover the issue of equal protection implicit in the phrase 'in common with.'"[53] As to the Equal Protection Clause and the "in common" language of the 1850s treaties, the Indian tribes had given up claims to most of the state of Washington in return for these off-reservation fishing rights. No equal protection issue was involved. However, Douglas's language subsequently provided the excuse for the Washington Supreme Court to hold that the Equal Protection Clause of the Fourteenth Amendment prohibited the state from allocating 50 percent of the fish to treaty tribes, who constituted less than one percent of the population.[54] The Ninth Circuit later rejected the Washington Supreme Court's reasoning, saying that the state court had "unwittingly misconstrued the basic concepts of Indian law and failed to understand a long line of United States Supreme Court decisions beginning with *United States v. Winans*";[55] on review, the U.S. Supreme Court likewise rejected the state's equal protection argument, doing so without discussion. The Douglas dictum that was the basis of the Washington Supreme Court's error is at least partially understandable in view of the fact that the U.S. Supreme Court had not yet articulated its analysis of equal protection as applied to Indians. The seminal case here is *Morton v. Mancari*,[56] in which the Court held that a statutory preference for hiring and promoting Indians in the Bureau of Indian Affairs did not violate the Equal Protection Clause, because the Indian Commerce Clause[57] gives Congress authority to legislate specially about Indians, and legislation about Indian tribes applies to political groups, not to a racial class.[58] Such legislation does not, therefore, receive strict scrutiny, but is only subject to "rational basis" review.[59] *Morton v. Mancari* was decided in 1974, a year before Justice Douglas retired, and he joined in the Blackmun decision, indicating his acceptance of the Court's equal protection analysis as applied to Indians.

In *Puyallup II*,[60] the other Douglas fishing rights opinion, the Court was asked to approve a state ban on all Indian net fishing for steelhead in the Puyallup River on the ground that the ban was "necessary for conservation." The regulation allocated the entire steelhead run exclusively to hook-and-line sports fishermen, nearly all of whom were non-Indian. For the Court, Justice Douglas struck down the ban because it discriminated against treaty Indians. Douglas said the steelhead runs must be fairly apportioned between Indian and non-Indian fishermen.[61]

Resolution of this Puyallup dispute, and most other Indian off-reservation fisheries issues, was finally achieved in 1979 when the Supreme Court affirmed,[62] with slight modification, Federal District Court Judge George Boldt's 1974 decision that the "in common clause" meant that treaty tribes were entitled to catch up to one-half the harvestable (after spawning escapement) salmon and steelhead at their traditional off-reservation sites.[63] The state could still regulate Indian off-reservation fishing when necessary for conservation, but such regulation would not be necessary if a tribe had courts, police, and biologists and was otherwise capable of self-regulation. Although Douglas had retired from the Court by 1979 when the Supreme Court resolved the matter, I have no doubt he would have joined its decision. By limiting the treaty Indians to 50 percent of the "harvestable" fish, i.e., after spawning escapement, the decision met his concern to conserve the fish while at the same time upholding the off-reservation treaty rights of the Indians. And, as already noted, by that time the equal protection issue had long been put to rest.

A different fishing rights question arose in *Kake v. Egan*.[64] The Alaska native Village of Kake sought to enjoin a state ban on Indian fish traps. Justice Frankfurter for the Court held that the Village of Kake had no reservation, nor any treaty or statutory right, that exempted it from state fish trap laws, thus the state ban applied to the Village of Kake. Douglas concurred in part, but dissented from the Court's decision to allow the village one more year of fish trap use before submitting to the state ban. Douglas said fish traps were so "efficient" they could easily destroy the salmon runs and that they were a "lazy man's" device to catch fish. He said it was not apparent "why the Indians [could] not fish in the manner of all other fishermen," and he objected to giving "a part of the public domain to this favored few."[65] Once again, as in *Puyallup I* and *II,* Douglas expressed his overriding concern about conservation of salmon, a priority even dearer to his heart than the Indian claim.

V. Other Indian Cases Decided by Justice Douglas

Justice Douglas wrote majority, concurring, or dissenting opinions in other Indian cases, involving (1) the Supremacy Clause of the U.S. Constitution, (2) ownership (state or tribal) of the bed of a river bounding a reservation, (3) whether a reservation has been disestablished, and (4) whether a state tax applies on an Indian reservation.

THE SUPREMACY CLAUSE

States have usually been less tolerant toward Indians than has the federal government.[66] The state of Washington has been unusually hostile toward Indians, partly because of a racist attitude similar to that of southern state courts toward Black Americans before 1960, and partly due to the Indians' persistent, and since 1974 successful, claim to a large percentage of the harvestable salmon and steelhead in Washington waters. This issue is of great economic importance to the state. The hostility has spilled over into other areas of state/tribal relations.

In *Antoine v. Washington*,[67] the Washington Supreme Court upheld the conviction of a Colville Indian for the hunting and possession of a deer on ceded land during the state's closed season. The United States Supreme Court reversed. Justice Brennan, for the Court, said that when the tribe ceded the land to the United States in 1891, it reserved the right to hunt "in common" with others. The Court said that under the normal canons of construction, the wording of treaties and agreements with Indians is not to be construed to their prejudice, and in any event there was no ambiguity here, that is, the cession clearly reserved to the Indians the hunting right. Second, under the Supremacy Clause federal legislation ratifying the executive agreement with the Indians prevails over contrary state legislation.[68]

Douglas, in a concurring opinion,[69] emphasized that the agreement with the Colville Tribe could not be construed as merely "a grant of such rights as other inhabitants had."[70] To hold thus would be to discriminate against the Indians without any showing of a conservation need. Nor could the state require these Indians to obtain a state hunting license in order to exercise their treaty hunting right. Lastly, Douglas wanted to make clear that, under the rules of construction favoring Indians, the hunting right applied to private as well as federal lands. The cession did not clearly prohibit hunting on private land.[71]

TITLE TO RIVERBEDS

The question of who holds title to the bed of a river running through or alongside Indian reservations has often been an issue between the tribes and the states. In the most recent case before the Supreme Court, *Montana v. United States,*[72] the Court held that Montana owned the bed of the Big Horn River where it ran through the Crow Reservation. The Crow Tribe, the Court said, had not traditionally relied on fishing as a means of livelihood, and thus the bed of the river was not, prior to statehood, conveyed to the tribe. Instead, it was presumptively held by the United States for the future state under the equal-footing doctrine. The leading case on this issue prior to *Montana* was decided during Douglas's tenure.

In *Choctaw Nation v. Oklahoma,*[73] Justice Marshall for the majority upheld a tribal claim to title to the bed of the Arkansas River where it ran through land patented in fee simple, pursuant to treaty, to the Choctaw, Chickasaw, and Cherokee Tribes. The patent described the lands by metes and bounds. Nothing was said about the riverbed. The state claimed title to the riverbed under the equal-footing concept, arguing that the title to the bed was reserved for the future state unless a "very plain" pre-statehood conveyance could be found. However, the Court ruled that, in view of the history of removal of these tribes from their homeland in the East, the ambiguity of the patent, and the canons of construction concerning Indian treaties and patents, the tribal claims to the riverbed should be upheld.

Justice Douglas concurred, arguing that to hold that these lands were to be preserved for a future state under the equal-footing doctrine would be to "indulge a cynical fiction without any basis in fact."[74] "Only the continuation of a regime of discrimination against these people, which long plagued the relations between the races, can now deny them this just claim."[75]

THE DISESTABLISHMENT CASES

At least since *Lone Wolf v. Hitchcock,*[76] it has been settled that Congress has the power to abrogate Indian treaties and to disestablish Indian reservations if it so chooses. Several important disestablishment cases were decided during Douglas's tenure on the Court. In *Seymour v. Superintendent* and *Mattz v. Arnett,*[77] the Court held that reservation status survives the mere opening of the reservation to settlement by non-Indians, even when the moneys paid for the land by the settlers are placed in trust by the government for the Indians' benefit.

The Court's attitude seemed to change with the decision in *DeCoteau v. District County Court.*[78] The question was whether the Lake Traverse Indian Reservation in South Dakota, created by an 1867 treaty between the United States and the Sisseton and Wahpeton bands of Sioux Indians, was terminated and returned to the public domain by an Agreement of 1889 and an Act of Congress in 1891. Justice Stewart for the majority repeated the rule of construction that, to find disestablishment, the congressional intent "must be clear" to overcome the general rule that doubtful expressions are to be resolved in favor of the weak and defenseless people who are the wards of the nation, dependent upon its protection and good faith. Stewart then held, however, that this reservation had been terminated because the Indians were willing to convey their lands to the government for a specific sum. The Court also noted that South Dakota had exercised jurisdiction over the unallotted lands of the area in question for some eighty years.

Justice Douglas, joined by Brennan and Marshall, dissented. Douglas argued that the agreement and statute were designed to allow the sale of unallotted lands on the reservation and said, "There was not a word to suggest that the boundaries of the reservation were to be altered." He noted that the standard rule of construction favoring Indians was not necessary here because "there is no doubtful language in the Agreement or the Act." The majority's decision, he said, would "tear the reservation asunder. Most of the tribe lives on the disestablished portion. The local office of the BIA is on this portion; and a tribal constitution of 1966 perpetuates the concept of tribal jurisdiction over the contested area. The tribe has a police force that covers the area, and a garbage collection service. And the tribe is a major employer of persons in this area."[79] Lastly, Douglas noted that the majority decision would create a crazy quilt or checkerboard pattern of jurisdiction, which defeats the right of tribal self-government guaranteed by the 1867 treaty.

THE APPLICATION OF STATE TAXES

Three noteworthy state tax cases were decided during Douglas's tenure on the Court. In *Warren Trading Post v. Arizona Tax Commission,*[80] Justice Black for the Court, including Douglas, struck down a state tax on the gross income of a federally "licensed trader" on the Navajo Reservation.

The Court ruled that federal regulation of licensed traders was so comprehensive that "no room remains for state laws imposing additional burdens on traders." This is a "specific" preemption case, where the Court found a specific statutory and regulatory scheme that preempted state law.

In *Mescalero Apache Tribe v. Jones,*[81] Justice White, for the majority, upheld a state gross receipts tax on an off-reservation ski resort operated by the tribe on land that the tribe leased from the Forest Service under the Indian Reorganization Act. The Court struck down a use tax on personalty, that is, ski lifts, that the tribe had purchased from out of state and that were installed as permanent improvements. The majority said that on-reservation activities of Indians are generally exempt from state taxation, whereas off-reservation activities are generally taxable unless a specific exemption can be found. The use tax was struck down because of Section 5 of the Indian Reorganization Act, which exempted from state taxation "lands" held under the Act. The Court said this included ski lifts permanently attached to the land.[82] Douglas, joined by Brennan and Stewart, dissented from the part of the opinion upholding the state gross receipts tax. He argued that Section 5 of the IRA, construed in light of the Indian law canons of construction, should exempt the tribe from the state tax. Douglas also argued that the "instrumentality" doctrine should exempt the tribe from state taxes.

The third tax case is the most significant. In *McClanahan v. Arizona State Tax Commission,*[83] Justice Marshall for the Court, including Douglas, struck down a state tax on income earned by a reservation Indian, from reservation sources. The Court rejected the instrumentality doctrine, but nonetheless struck the tax on the ground of general preemption, that is, looking at the treaty, federal statutes encouraging Indian self-government, federal policy encouraging tribal self-determination, and the like.

The special significance of the case is indicated in the Court's statement about sovereignty and preemption: "Finally, the trend has been away from the idea of inherent Indian sovereignty as a bar to state jurisdiction and toward reliance on federal preemption. . . . The modern cases tend to avoid reliance on platonic notions of Indian sovereignty and to look instead to the applicable treaties and statutes which define the limits of state power. The Indian sovereignty doctrine is relevant, then, not because it provides a definitive resolution of the issues in this suit, but because it provides a backdrop against which the applicable treaties and federal statutes must be read."[84] By this language the Court changed permanently the analytical approach to application of state law on reservations from a sovereignty approach to a preemption approach with sovereignty as a backdrop. Instead of a bright, or fairly bright, sovereignty line drawn around the reservation, the Court engaged in a preemption analysis, a balancing exercise, to determine if state law applies on the reservation. The result is that if only Indians are involved the trend is to bar state law. If only non-Indians are involved, the trend is to apply state law. If a mixture of Indians and non-Indians are involved, then the Court makes a detailed, balancing study, and determines whether state law applies. The Court has also retained the "infringement" doctrine, from *Williams v. Lee,*[85] to test whether state laws apply on the reservation.

FREEDOM TO BE "INDIAN"

In *New Rider v. Board of Education,*[86] the Supreme Court denied certiorari from a court of appeals decision upholding a "hair length" rule of a junior high school. Douglas dissented. Petitioners, Pawnee students at a public school in Oklahoma, sought to wear their hair parted in the middle with a long braid on each side in the "old traditional way." This violated the school rule, and they were suspended indefinitely. School officials had claimed that to allow the Indian students to have long hair would be "disruptive" in that "an integrated school system cannot countenance different groups and remain one organization." Douglas, arguing that certiorari should be granted, responded:

They were in fact attempting to broadcast a clear and specific message to their fellow students and others — their pride in being Indian. . . . The effort to impose uniformity on petitioners is especially repugnant in view of the history of white treatment of the education of the American Indian. In the late 1800's . . . the Bureau of Indian Affairs began operating a system of boarding schools with the express policy of stripping the Indian child of his cultural heritage and identity: 'Such schools were run in a rigid military fashion, with heavy emphasis on rustic vocational education. They were designed to separate a child from his reservation and family, strip him of his tribal lore and mores, force the complete abandonment of his native language, and prepare him for never again returning to his people.'[87]

VI. Conclusion

Justice Douglas wrote fourteen majority, dissenting, or concurring opinions in Indian cases during his thirty-six years on the United States Supreme Court, out of a total of fifty-two Indian cases that came before the Court during his tenure. Douglas belongs to the group of justices, including former Justices Hugo Black and Frank Murphy and current Justices Marshall and Brennan, who have usually viewed the law as favoring the Indian side in Supreme Court litigation.

Douglas began his Supreme Court career believing that gradual assimilation of Indian tribes under state law was the correct policy. After the publication of Cohen's *Handbook of Federal Indian Law,* and after Douglas had read and heard arguments in more Indian cases, he changed his position, becoming an ardent supporter of tribal self-determination and a firm believer that agreements with Indian tribes should be construed in favor of the Indians, and should be upheld.

In the fishing rights cases, Douglas continually expressed concern that neither Indians nor non-Indians be permitted to destroy the salmon or steelhead runs. Everyone would lose if that occurred. Further, he expressed his concern that the "in common" language of the Pacific Northwest off-reservation treaty fishing rights be analyzed in light of constitutional equal protection principles. Douglas left the Court before it confronted these issues. It seems likely, however, that he would have joined in the decision that disposed of them. He had joined in the 1974 Blackmun decision, *Morton v. Mancari,* which provided the answer to the equal protection puzzle. As for protecting the fishery resource, the 50 percent allocation of *harvestable* fish to treaty tribes, mandated by the *Passenger Fishing Vessel* case, resolved the fishery protection question, so there is reason to believe that Douglas would have joined in the allocation aspects of that decision.

Indian decisions have continued to pour forth from the Court, now at the rate of more than thirty per decade, compared to the fifty-two decisions in Douglas's thirty-six years on the Supreme Court. It is interesting but fruitless to speculate on whether Douglas's views would have had an impact on later decisions that the Indians lost, such as *Oliphant v. Suquamish Indian Tribe,*[88] where the Court denied tribal courts criminal jurisdiction over non-Indians, or *Montana v. United States,* where the Court denied the Crow Tribe ownership and regulatory power over the bed of the Big Horn River where it runs through the reservation and gave title to Montana under the equal-footing doctrine.

Douglas was a man not rigid in his views, able to change them in light of new information, yet steadfast in devotion to basic principles of human rights. He was convinced that the Indians should be treated with "utmost good faith," and that their treaties and agreements with this nation should be honored.

Notes

The title phrase is from Douglas's dissent in *Northwest Band of Shoshone Indians v. United States,* 324 U.S. 335, 362 (1945). The author is indebted to Professor David H. Getches for insights offered on an early draft and to Anne Johnson for helpful editorial and organizational suggestions.

   1. Cohen received a Ph.D. in philosophy at Harvard in 1929 and an LL.B. from Columbia Law School in 1931. At the request of Professor Nathan Margold, Solicitor for the Department of Interior under Harold L. Ickes, Cohen helped draft the Indian Reorganization Act of 1934 (Wheeler-Howard Act). He resigned from the Department of Interior in 1948. Over the next few years he practiced law and taught courses at Yale Law School and New York City College. In 1948 he was given the Department of Interior's Distinguished Service Award. He died in 1953. During Cohen's life, his scholarship covered a remarkable array of topics, especially concerning the nature of law and philosophy. He wrote five books and more than thirty law review articles.

   2. *United States v. Santa Fe Pacific Railroad Co.,* 314 U.S. 339, 349 (1941).

   3. Act of Feb. 8, 1887, 24 Stat. 388. Apache Chieftain Geronimo was captured one year before the Dawes Act was passed, in 1886.

4. In 1924, when Douglas was a second-year law student at Columbia, Congress enacted a bill bestowing citizenship on all Indians born in the United States. Act of June 2, 1924, 43 Stat. 253. Historically, even though the Indians were here first, they were legally aliens. Prior to 1924 about two-thirds of the Indian population had become citizens under special statutes. The 1924 act bestowed citizenship on the other one-third. The Supreme Court has held that citizenship does not affect the Indians' treaty rights. See, for example, *Puyallup Tribe v. Department of Game of Washington,* 391 U.S. 392, 398 (1968) *(Puyallup I).*

5. Robert H. Keller, Jr., "William O. Douglas, the Supreme Court, and American Indians," *American Indian Law Review* 3 (2975): 333–60. "Twenty-eight times the court decided in favor of Indian claims, with Douglas voting with the majority in every instance. In the 19 cases decided against Indians, Douglas dissented 11 times, thereby giving him a record of 39 out of 47 decisions in favor of the Indian position. He has written 14 opinions: five for the Court, three concurring, six dissenting." Ibid., p. 333. This excellent article by Professor Keller should be studied by anyone desiring more insight into Douglas's attitude toward Indians and the background for his thinking.

6. 48 Stat. 984, 25 U.S.C. 461, et seq.

7. 198 U.S. 371 (1905).

8. See *Northwest Band of Shoshone Indians v. United States,* 324 U.S., at 354; *Antoine v. Washington,* 420 U.S. 194, 211 (1975); *Puyallup Tribe v. Department of Game of Washington,* 391 U.S., at 397; *Choctaw Nation v. Oklahoma,* 397 U.S. 620 (1970).

9. *United States v. Winans,* 198 U.S., at 374.

10. 207 U.S. 564 (1908).

11. Unfortunately, the Indian tribes around the nation have generally not had sufficient financing to develop their water resources. The United States, as trustee for the tribes, could have assisted with this financing, but miserably failed in its trust duty to develop these resources. Only recently, when most western water is already committed to non-Indian projects, has the United States tried to develop Indian water, usually over powerful political objections of non-Indian users. At present, some fifty lawsuits are pending to establish and quantify Indian reserved water rights around the nation.

12. 308 U.S. 343 (1939).

13. Ibid., at 353–54.

14. See 18 U.S.C.A. 1162, 28 U.S.C.A. 1369, 25 U.S.C.A. 1321, 1322, 1323, 1326.

15. 324 U.S. 335 (1945).

16. See *United States v. Winans,* 198 U.S. 371 (1905); *Jones v. Meehan,* 175 U.S. 1 (1899).

17. Justices Frankfurter and Murphy also dissented, but in a separate opinion. Their arguments are consistent with those of Justice Douglas, but their dissent is more scholarly and less pejorative.

18. *Northwest Band of Shoshone Indians v. United States,* 324 U.S., at 358.

19. Ibid., at 360.

20. Ibid., at 361–62.

21. 348 U.S. 272 (1955).

22. Ibid., at 289, 290. Similar statements appear elsewhere. "The Indian nations did not seek out the United States and agree upon an exchange of lands in an arm's

length transaction. Rather, treaties were imposed upon them and they had no choice but to consent." *Choctaw Nation v. Oklahoma,* 397 U.S., at 630 (1970).

A statement in 1916 by the Washington Supreme Court is also illustrative. When Douglas was eighteen years old, that state prosecuted and convicted Yakima Indian Towessnute for fishing, under his off-reservation treaty rights, without a state fishing license. The court said, "The premise of Indian sovereignty we reject. The treaty is not to be interpreted in that light. At no time did our ancestors in getting title to this continent ever regard the aborigines as other than mere occupants, and incompetent occupants, of the soil. . . . Only that title was esteemed which came from white men, and the rights of these have always been ascribed by the highest authority to lawful discovery of lands, occupied, to be sure, but not owned by anyone before. . . .

"The Indian was a child, and a dangerous child, of nature, to be both protected and restrained. In his nomadic life he was to be left, so long as civilization did not demand his region. When it did demand that region, he was to be allotted a more confined area with permanent subsistence. . . .

"These arrangements [for treaties and reservations] were but the announcement of our benevolence which, notwithstanding our frequent frailties, has been continuously displayed. Neither Rome nor sagacious Britain ever dealt more liberally with their subject races than we with these savage tribes, whom it was generally tempting and always easy to destroy and whom we have so often permitted to squander vast areas of fertile land before our eyes." *State v. Towessnute,* 89 Wash. 478, 481–82, 154 P. 805, 807 (1916).

In 1942, shortly after Douglas's appointment, Justice Black (with Douglas signing) held that the State of Washington could not require Indians to acquire state fishing licenses when exercising their off-reservation treaty fishing rights. *Tulee v. Washington,* 315 U.S. 681 (1942). This can be compared to the tone of the Northwest Ordinance, adopted by the Continental Congress in 1787: "The utmost good faith shall always be observed towards the Indians, their lands and property shall never be taken from them without their consent; and in their property, rights and liberty, they never shall be invaded or disturbed, unless in just and lawful wars authorized by Congress; but laws founded in justice and humanity shall from time to time be made, for preventing wrongs being done to them, and preserving peace and friendship." *Documents of United States Indian Policy,* ed. Francis Paul Prucha (Lincoln: University of Nebraska Press, 1975), p. 10.

23. *Tee Hit Ton Indians v. United States,* 348 U.S., at 294.

24. *Williams v. Lee,* 358 U.S. 217 (1959).

25. Charles F. Wilkinson, *American Indians, Time and the Law* (New Haven: Yale University Press, 1987), p. 1.

26. Ibid., p. 2.

27. *Williams v. Lee,* 358 U.S., at 220.

28. 362 U.S. 99 (1960).

29. Ibid., at 140–42.

30. In 1970 President Richard Nixon, in his address to Congress, said: "This policy of forced termination is wrong, in my judgment. . . . Because termination is morally and legally unacceptable, because it produces bad results, and because the mere threat of termination tends to discourage greater self-sufficiency among Indian groups, [the future policy should be one of self-determination]." H.R. Doc. No. 363, 91st Cong., 2d Sess. (1970).

31. 391 U.S. 404 (1968).

32. Douglas also relied on language in an earlier act of Congress (P.L. 280, 1953) that specifically exempted Indian hunting and fishing rights whenever states, pursuant to P.L. 280, imposed their jurisdiction over tribes. He said these two acts must be considered *in pari materia*. It escapes me entirely, as it did Stewart in his dissent in *Menominee,* as to why these two statutes should be read together. They had nothing to do with each other. Douglas, by reading them together, merely demonstrates the depth of his desire to hold in favor of the Indians.

33. 420 U.S. 944 (1975).

34. Ibid., at 964.

35. 118 U.S. 375 (1886).

36. In *Choctaw Nation v. Oklahoma,* 397 U.S., at 641, n. 6 (1970), Justice Douglas, concurring, said

> The story of the exploitation of Indians by state and local agencies has been recently summarized by William Brandon: "Termination is truly a word of ill omen to tribal Indians. Its meaning in Indian affairs is the termination of 'Federal responsibility,' the responsibility of the Federal Government to act as trustee for Indian lands, rights, and resources; the responsibility to protect Indian groups in these rights and possessions — protect them particularly against states, counties, cities, or other local powers that might divest them of their rights and possessions — and to provide certain services such as education and health. (*Progressive,* January 1970, p. 38)

37. I started teaching Indian law in 1969 — because a group of some fifteen Indian students and tribal leaders staged a crowded sit-in in my small law school office and to my mystified amazement insisted I teach Indian law, a subject I knew nothing about at the time. I became so fascinated with the field, I have never left it.

38. Monroe E. Price, *Law and the American Indian* (Indianapolis: Bobbs-Merrill, 1973).

39. 25 U.S.C. 1301–41. In 1966 Congress passed the Tribal Federal Jurisdiction Act, 28 U.S.C. 1362, permitting tribes access to federal courts for cases which the United States Attorney declined to pursue. This act was a "major turning point in tribal nationalism." Daniel H. Israel, "The Reemergence of Tribal Nationalism and its Impact on Reservation Resource Development," *University of Colorado Law Review* 47 (1976): 624.

40. At the request of the association, I organized this program for several years, until 1980.

41. Felix S. Cohen, *Handbook of Federal Indian Law,* 1982 ed. (Charlottesville, Va.: Michie-Bobbs Merrill). The board of authors and editors includes Rennard Strickland, editor-in-chief; Charles F. Wilkinson, managing editor; Reid Peyton Chambers, Richard B. Collins, Carole E. Goldberg-Ambrose, Robert N. Clinton, David H. Getches, Ralph W. Johnson, and Monroe E. Price.

42. Monroe E. Price, "Lawyers on the Reservation: Some Implications for the Legal Professor," *Law and the Social Order* 1969: 161.

43. Wilkinson, *American Indians,* pp. 1–2.

44. *Bolling v. Sharpe,* 347 U.S. 497 (1954).

45. 315 U.S. 681 (1942).

46. The Court stated that "while the treaty leaves the state the power to impose

on Indians, equally with others, such restrictions of a purely regulatory nature concerning the time and manner of fishing outside the reservation as are necessary for the conservation of fish, it forecloses the state from charging the Indians a fee of the kind in question." Ibid., at 684. Elsewhere, the Court noted that revenues from fishing licenses provide support for general state institutions, and are regulatory as well as revenue producing. Ibid., at 681.

47. 391 U.S. 392 (1968).

48. State experts testified that fishing with set nets at the mouth of the river could confuse the fish and delay the upstream movement of the run, thus causing harm far beyond the actual fish caught by the Indians. Ibid., at 401.

49. Under established rules of federal Indian law dating from *Worcester v. Georgia*, 31 U.S. 515 (1832), states cannot abrogate Indian treaty rights unless Congress delegates them such power. No such delegation exists here, and Douglas provides no theory on which to base his exceptions. See *Missouri v. Holland*, 252 U.S. 416 (1920); *Menominee Tribe v. United States*, 391 U.S. 404 (1968). See also Ralph Johnson, "The States Versus Indian Off-Reservation Fishing: A United States Supreme Court Error," *Washington Law Review* 47 (1972): 207.

50. *Puyallup Tribe v. Department of Game of Washington*, 391 U.S., at 402, n. 15. This stipulation is in sharp contrast to the Finding of Fact by Judge George Boldt in *United States v. Washington*, 384 F.Supp. 312, 338, n. 26, (W.D. Wash. 1974), where he said:

> With a single possible exception testified to by a highly interested witness . . . and not otherwise substantiated, notwithstanding three years of exhaustive trial preparation, neither Game nor Fisheries [Departments] has discovered and produced any credible evidence showing any instance, remote or recent, when a definitely identified member of any plaintiff exercised his off-reservation treaty rights by any conduct or means detrimental to the perpetuation of any species of anadromous fish.
>
> Unfortunately, insinuations, hearsay and rumors to the contrary, usually but not always instigated anonymously, have been and still are rampant in Western Washington. Indeed, the near total absence of substantial evidence to support these apparent falsehoods was a considerable surprise to this court.

51. *Department of Game of Washington v. Puyallup Tribe*, 414 U.S. 44 (1973).

52. See, for example, *State v. Towessnute*, 89 Wash. 478, 154 P. 805 (1916); *Department of Game v. Puyallup Tribe, Inc.*, 86 Wash. 664, 548 P.2d 1058 (1976). After a federal district court and the Ninth Circuit Court of Appeals, 520 F.2d 676 (9th Cir. 1975), had interpreted the 1850s treaties to allocate 50 percent of the harvestable salmon and steelhead to the Pacific Northwest Treaty tribes, state officials continued to thwart federal court orders, prompting the Ninth Circuit to say that "except for some desegregation cases . . . the district court [that decided on the 50 percent allocation] has faced the most concerted official and private efforts to frustrate the decree of a federal court witnessed in this century." *Puget Sound Gillnetters Association v. United States District Court*, 573 F.2d 1123, 1126 (9th Cir. 1978). The Supreme Court affirmed the 50 percent allocation. *Washington v. Washington State Commercial Passenger Fishing Vessel Association*, 443 U.S. 658 (1979).

53. *Puyallup I*, 391 U.S., at 403. This same hint about equal protection was contained in the Douglas opinion in *Department of Game of Washington v. Puyallup*

Tribe (Puyallup II), 414 U.S. 44, 45 (1973). There the Court adverted to *Puyallup I,* saying, "The case was remanded for determination of . . . 'the issue of equal protection implicit in the phrase "in common with" as used in the Treaty.'"

54. *Washington State Commercial Passenger Fishing Vessel Association v. Tollefson,* 89 Wash.2d 276, 571 P.2d 1373 (1977).

55. *Puget Sound Gillnetters Association v. District Court,* 573 F.2d, at 1128–29, n. 5. See *United States v. Winans,* 198 U.S. 371 (1905).

56. 417 U.S. 535 (1974). See also *United States v. Antelope,* 430 U.S. 641 (1977).

57. Art. I, §8, cl. 3 of the United States Constitution provides that Congress shall have power "to regulate commerce with foreign nations, and among the several States, and with the Indian Tribes." In *United States v. Sandoval,* 231 U.S. 28 (1913), and later cases, the Court has indicated this clause empowers Congress to legislate specifically about Indians, at least those who are members of tribes.

58. Also, the fact is that a legion of federal statutes would have to be declared invalid if the Equal Protection Clause banned legislation about Indian tribes.

59. See also *Washington v. Confederated Bands and Tribes of the Yakima Indian Nation,* 439 U.S. 463 (1979).

60. 414 U.S. 44 (1973).

61. *Puyallup Tribe, Inc. v. Department of Game (Puyallup III),* 433 U.S. 165 (1977) was decided after Douglas was off the bench. It upheld a state regulation that apportioned 45 percent of the natural steelhead run to the Puyallup Indian Tribe.

62. *Washington v. Washington State Commercial Passenger Fishing Vessel Association,* 443 U.S. 658 (1979). The opinion was by Stevens; Powell, with Stewart and Rehnquist, dissented.

63. Judge Boldt ruled that, in addition to their 50 percent entitlement, the tribes could catch fish for ceremonial and subsistence purposes. In addition, their 50 percent allocation did not include on-reservation catches. The U.S. Supreme Court reversed as to these add-ons.

64. 369 U.S. 60 (1962). In an unusual procedure, Douglas did not file his dissent until two weeks after the majority opinion appeared. His dissent appears with the majority opinion in the *U.S. Reports,* but not in the *S. Ct. Reports.*

65. Ibid., at 81, 83.

66. See *United States v. Kagama,* 118 U.S. 375 (1886).

67. 420 U.S. 194 (1975).

68. In 1871, Congress banned further treaties with Indian tribes. Ch. 120, Sec. 1, 16 Stat. 544, 566 (codified at 25 U.S.C. 71). Like treaties, agreements and statutes are the "supreme law of the land," creating rights and liabilities that are virtually identical to those established by treaties. See Cohen, *Handbook,* p. 127; Charles Wilkinson and John M. Volkman, "Judicial Review of Indian Treaty Abrogation," *California Law Review* 63 (1975): 615–17.

69. *Antoine v. Washington,* 420 U.S. 194, at 207 (1975).

70. Ibid., at 211.

71. "Doubtful expressions, instead of being resolved in favor of the United States, are to be resolved in favor of a weak and defenseless people, who are wards of the nation, and dependent wholly upon its protection and good faith." Ibid., quoting from *Choate v. Trapp,* 224 U.S. 665, 675 (1912). Justice Rehnquist, who almost never held in favor of Indians, and Justice Stewart, who usually held against them, dissented on the ground that no federal legislation could be found ratifying the hunt-

ing rights of the Colvilles. They thought the legislation in question merely appropriated money for the tribe, but was not intended to ratify hunting rights on ceded land.

72. 450 U.S. 544 (1981).

73. 397 U.S. 620 (1970).

74. Ibid., at 641.

75. Ibid., at 645.

76. 187 U.S. 553 (1903).

77. *Seymour v. Superintendent,* 368 U.S. 351 (1962); *Mattz v. Arnett,* 412 U.S. 481 (1971).

78. 420 U.S. 444 (1975).

79. Ibid., at 463.

80. 380 U.S. 685 (1965).

81. 411 U.S. 145 (1973).

82. The majority specifically rejected the "instrumentality" doctrine as a basis for striking down state taxes.

83. 411 U.S. 164 (1973).

84. Ibid., at 171.

85. 358 U.S. 217 (1959).

86. 414 U.S. 1097 (1973).

87. Ibid., at 1101, quoting S. Rep. No. 91-501, p. 12.

88. 435 U.S. 191 (1978).

The Fox and the Chickens:
Mr. Justice Douglas and Environmental Law

William H. Rodgers, Jr.

As any amateur biologist or conservationist is wont to do, let me begin with questions of taxonomy. Since we are talking here about judging, in particular the work of a single judge, my taxonomy will be drawn from decision theory.

Two versions of decision theory should be distinguished. First, there are the many variants of benefit-cost analysis that presuppose some summing up of the goods and bads by the decision maker and the deliberate selection of a "best" outcome.[1] All kinds of assumptions are at work here, not the least of which is the reduction and expression of values in terms (such as dollars) that facilitate policy comparisons. The ideal decision, according to these methodologies, is static, comprehensive, definitive and correct. My term for these steadfast pursuers of the ideal "best" outcomes is *maximizers*.

To be contrasted with benefit-cost analysis is game theory, where choice of the "best" is not formal and definitive but is uniquely dependent upon what the other players do.[2] Game theory's "best" is context-specific, provisional, and fluid. The key is to recognize that there is no definitive right answer: the best position for a player depends upon context and upon what the other players are doing. Observers of natural systems are offered repeated lessons in the dynamics of game theory. To mention a simple example, the red squirrel developed a "chattering" strategy as a defense against its principal predator, the great horned owl, who is inclined to depart from the scene upon being discovered.[3] This was a good strategy for the moment, but it is not a good strategy when the predator becomes a human, armed with a rifle, and attracted rather than repelled by chattering. My term for practitioners of decision making that is sensitive to the conditional best is *gamers*.

I. Methods: Of the Fox

A metaphorical and hyperbolic expression of the gaming point of view is summed up by the lifestyle of the fox — a remarkably opportunistic, adaptive, flexible, and suspicious creature, and one, it deserves emphasis, with no noticeable respect for human property boundaries.

Some elaboration may be useful. The fox has suffered a history of persecution going back to the fourteenth century B.C.,[4] and has long endured a consistently poor reputation among humans in a position to pass judgment. Foxes are exterminated as vermin, killed to limit their depredations (or at least avenge them), and pursued for sporting and commercial purposes. That many fox species and populations have continued to thrive despite high casualty rates and relentless pressures is a testament to their extraordinary adaptability and opportunism. Foxes are highly flexible in their patterns of basic biological behavior — territorialism, reproduction, social behavior, and diet: during certain times of year foxes can switch from bird food to earthworms to blackberries and other fruit. Foxes are extraordinary gamers, with a capacity to make the best of a bad situation — displaced by civilization, they have been known to take up residence in the auto plant; to turn the bad into a good — eat the bait and leave the poison; and to exploit unexpected opportunity — pouncing on mounds of loose soil expecting to find a mole.[5] One thing the fox isn't is a rigid subscriber to a fixed plan and a deferential bystander to established authority.

With the methodology of the fox established, it is time in this allegory to move Mr. Justice Douglas into the role of the fox. While the evidence is indirect, the Douglas disclosed in his writings and judicial opinions distinctly shows *gamer* rather than *maximizer;* Douglas was intuitively but fully aware that legal move *A* brings countermove *B,* which is sidestepped by defensive maneuver *C,* that is avoided by thrust-and-parry *D,* and so on. This awareness of the unintended consequence, the second- or third-level impact, and the ironic turnabout was fed by his understanding of the subtleties of ecological causation:

We have entered an era of "managed" wildlife that has serious impacts on our ecological balance. Thus the Park Service eliminated rattlesnakes in its Saguaro National Monument in Arizona. Why? To attract visitors. And why was that important? So that superintendents who served there would be identified with popular places and would be likely to be promoted. What was accomplished? A great increase in the kangaroo rat population that ate the young shoots and threatened the existence of the saguaros.[6]

And the gaming habits of thought were transferred readily to predictions of institutional and organizational behavior. It was Douglas as skeptic who wrote that "when we resolve to preserve [botanical and zoological] sanctuaries as parks, we put them in real danger. They have been preserved to date only because very few people frequented them. But the desire to maximize visitors puts them in jeopardy."[7]

Douglas as fox is illustrated by his treatment of two of the prominent methodological issues of contemporary environmental law — deference to agency choice and exclusivity of remedy.

THE FOX'S VIEW OF DEFERENCE

On the issue of deference, a maximizer who believes there is some best decision to be found out there is likely to believe also that there is an agency or organization that is best equipped to identify that decision. Surely the ill-informed, the casual, and the common cannot be expected to identify that which is best for society. Deference to some responsible entity thus seems to be an indispensable feature of the maximizer point of view.

Mr. Justice Douglas, of course, was intuitively suspicious of agency claims of expertise, calling it "the talismanic quality which is often given great credence. It often is only the accustomed way of doing things."[8] He also was a scathing critic of bureaucracies gone wrong—in the Soviet Union as well as in the United States,[9] at the international as well as the national level, and across the spectrum of U.S. domestic agencies—the National Park Service, Corps of Engineers, Bureau of Reclamation, Soil Conservation Service, Atomic Energy Commission, U.S. Forest Service, Bonneville Power Administration, Tennessee Valley Authority. There were occasional departures from these habits of thought, for example, in *Best v. Humboldt Placer Mining Co.,*[10] where he gave deference to the agency determination of a "valuable" mineral deposit on the implicit assumption that the agency would be more protective of the federal lands than would the federal judges. But Douglas routinely found reasons for not deferring to the environmentally destructive activities of federal military, transportation, and energy authorities.[11]

Yet Douglas as justice never found it necessary to challenge the deference proposition frontally. As any fox would know, the issue of deference always can be reformulated in terms not of whether to defer but to whom. Douglas was forever suspicious of the authorities making the choice, but openly deferential to those who could be trusted for their independence of judgment. In this connection, the National Environmental Policy Act, which took effect in 1970, emerged as an important weapon in the strategy of judicial review. The significance of NEPA is that it lays bare differences among agencies and multiplies the authoritative sources from which an otherwise "deferential" court can choose. Mr. Justice Douglas grasped NEPA's broad possibilities immediately, and in the few opportunities afforded him used NEPA to credit the views of established environmental opposition, as voiced by the Council on Environmental Quality, over those of the line agency defending the environmentally destructive policy choice.[12] One suspects that Douglas would have dissented from each and every entry in a long line of Supreme Court NEPA decisions deferring not to the extra-agency critics but to the intra-agency architects of the choices under attack as environmentally repulsive.[13]

THE FOX'S VIEW OF REMEDIAL EXCLUSIVITY

The maximizer view is that an Act of Congress represents some kind of comprehensive toting up of costs and benefits. A judge has little opportunity within this definitive package to find a right not explicitly mentioned nor discover a remedy not expressly prescribed.[14]

Every fox believes, however, that there is more than one way to accomplish the goal, and Mr. Justice Douglas was very much a fox when it came to identifying the remedies available in environmental cases. Under this view, congressionally prescribed remedies presumptively are not exclusive, and the courts are free to supplement, improve, extend, and refine to achieve the broad goals of pollution abatement.[15] This offers a dynamic perspective of the legal system: Congress is a source not so much of the last word but the first word; courts are not only rule followers but justice dispensers; the agencies will respond, react, and evade at a pace to match any rate of rule codification; and empirical reality is a concept sufficiently elusive to lie outside of the exclusive domain of any single branch of government.

II. Attitudes: Toward the Chickens, Noise, and Wilderness

It is time to meet the chickens in our parable, and they turn out to be Causby's chickens. One of the better known Douglas opinions on environmental law is *United States v. Causby,*[16] in which the Court held that sporadic overflights by military airplanes could effect a "taking" of private property that included the chickens that had died in panic and fright. It was Causby, the human, who had standing to bring an action to challenge the encroachment upon the chickens. So the rights of the chickens themselves weren't directly at issue.[17] The author of the opinion, however, had a more sympathetic view of the biological requirements of chickens than the dissenters, who thought the chickens should make way for the noise rather than the other way around: "The farmer's chickens have to get over being alarmed at the incredible racket of the tractor starting up suddenly in the shed adjoining the chicken house. These sights and noises are a part of our world."[18]

Causby's chickens are not the strongest example of the Douglas view of environmental rights. In the short run, and necessarily in the long run too, the chickens are very dead, and Causby enjoys only a liability right for the damage. This is not a powerful first page in a brief for the liberation of the chickens. Indeed, what security would a human acquire in the knowledge that his accidental demise would bring legal retribution in the form of a forced payment to a chicken with whom he had had some previous encounter?

A more instructive view of Causby's chickens, it seems, can be acquired by focusing on the instrument of their demise — the noise, which was perceived by Douglas as a social abomination of the first order. By conventional accounts, noise is a pollutant of little moment. The Noise Control Act of 1972 has gone nowhere in particular, and has given rise to scant regulation or administrative development. Noise victims, after all, can do much to protect themselves; the offense is difficult to control, temporary, and the intrusion is largely aesthetic. Noise injuries are almost always nonlethal to humans, although Douglas himself offered a celebrated illustration of health hazards in his meetings with sonic boom while astride a nervous horse traversing a precarious mountain trail.[19]

Mr. Justice Douglas detested the pollutant noise, particularly when it appeared in his wilderness retreats: "Wilderness is a therapist—a physician, indeed a preeminent one. The noise of civilization is one of man's worst enemies. Like a bacillus hostile to man, it produces disease—not directly but through the fatigue and the wariness that it creates. Tension caused by noise is enervating."[20] His views are captured nicely by a quotation of his choice from an unnamed emperor in the third century B.C.: "Criminals should not be hanged, but flutes, drums and the chime of bells should be sounded without letup until they drop dead, because this is the most agonizing death man can conceive."[21] And he was able to convey a sense of outrage when describing noise as a deep invasion of privacy: "Come with me to an isolated cabin in deep snow country and hear the snowmobiles roaring. They are now so numerous that it sounds as though a power saw is running full blast during all the daylight hours—right outside your study."[22]

It was the omnipresent pollutant noise that was invoked by Douglas in *Village of Belle Terre v. Boraas,*[23] as a justification for upholding an ordinance restricting land use to one-family dwellings:

The regimes of boarding houses, fraternity houses, and the like present urban problems. More people occupy a given space; more cars rather continuously pass by; more cars are parked; noise travels with crowds.
    A quiet place where yards are wide, people few, and motor vehicles restricted are legitimate guidelines in a land-use project addressed to family needs. . . . The police power is not confined to elimination of filth, stench, and unhealthy places. It is ample to lay out zones where family values, youth values, and the blessings of quiet seclusion and clean air make the area a sanctuary for people.[24]

The Douglas advocacy of a Wilderness Bill of Rights is a stronger example yet of his predilection to view environmental quality as an indispensable entitlement and not mere social convenience.[25] To Douglas, those who canoe or hike or backpack or ride horses or climb mountains deserve protection no less than that extended to racial or religious minorities:

Though these actual participants constitute a minority, they have rights that the majority should respect. The Bill of Rights, which makes up the first ten Amendments to our Constitution, contains in the main guarantees to minorities. . . . When it comes to Wilderness we need a similar Bill of Rights to protect those whose spiritual values extend to the rivers and lakes, the valleys and the ridges, and who find life in a mechanized society worth living only because those splendid resources are not despoiled.[26]

One can find in Douglas's writings an inchoate version of a constitutional right to environmental protection in some form and theory, like that developed for the right of privacy, protection of minorities, or the free exercise of religion. His vision of spiritual values would have added a distinctly discordant note to the deliberations of the Supreme Court in the 1987 Term in *Lyng v. Northwest Indian Cemetery Protective Association,*[27] in which the Court held that the Free Exercise Clause does not bar the government from authorizing timber harvesting and road construction in the Chimney Rock area of the Six Rivers National Forest, which had been used traditionally for religious purposes by members of three Indian tribes. Douglas would have resisted with all of his energy and ingenuity the Court's premise that the government need not honor any "religious servitude" as it went about the business of wrecking special places found on public lands.[28]

One suspects he also would have been sympathetic to arguments, derived from recent discoveries in molecular biology, that some environmental resources represent nonreplicable sources of information protected by First Amendment values of free speech.[29] Placement of environmental resources in the realm of information is reinforced by reference to First Amendment theory. Surveys of free speech theory are intuitively pertinent to the preservation of environmental values, both in the emphasis upon rewards for the individual, such as self-realization, and especially for the group, such as advancing knowledge, discovering truth, opening the doors to diversity, achieving a more adaptable and stable community. The metaphor of book burning has power in the context of environmental destruction. Examples can be found at the retail level — the official decision to fill the reservoir while archeologists worked desperately to save parts of history from the rising flood waters; and in wholesale — the consequences in the losses of human knowledge from the destruction of the tropical rain forest and the species dependent upon it. These examples call to mind the sacking of the library of Alexandria, and posterity will despise us for it. Douglas would have noticed.

III. General Property Theory

CORE RIGHTS

The rights to be free of noise and to enjoy wilderness suggest one leg of a tripartite property theory espoused by Mr. Justice Douglas that could be put to use in the service of environmental protection. The recognition of rights in creatures, places, or things, or in humans empowered to protect them, is an important component of any protectionist strategy. Typically, environmental conflict arises in the context of the passive commons open to exploitation by all but especially by those with a facility and capacity to move quickly and destructively. Giving would-be "savers" entitlements in the affected resources is an obvious counterweight to this tendency. Indeed, one could say that the prominent goal of contemporary strategies of environmental protection is to multiply the opportunities to say "No," or at least "Not yet," to unwelcome polluting or damaging initiatives. More and stronger victims' rights is the obvious and much pursued panacea.

PUBLIC TRUST CONSTRAINTS

The opposite side of the coin of a strategy that aims to expand our rights is to diminish theirs. In the environmental context, this means that developmental "property" rights that are recognized do not include the right to destroy, pollute, and ruin. The doctrine that serves most prominently to roll back extravagant expectations of this sort is the public trust doctrine.[30] It works by disavowing ownership claims to the resource commons on the theory that what you thought was "yours" was really "ours," and that there is no obligation to compensate for the difference. Just as some private wealth is immune from public confiscation, the trust doctrine protects some public wealth from private confiscation. As might be expected, Mr. Justice Douglas was a strong subscriber to public trust theory, although the doctrine in his time assumed the disguise of the navigation servitude,[31] which treats the waters of the United States as "public property" not subject to private claims protected by the takings clause.

LEGISLATIVE PREROGATIVE

The recognition of rights to protect and the repudiation of options to neglect are but two legs of a conservationist theory of property. A third leg is the recognition of the legislature's freedom to reallocate wealth and expectations to advance the cause of environmental quality. Mr. Justice Douglas's better known contributions on this subject are his opinions in *Berman v. Parker*,[32] equating the "public use" constraints of the Fifth Amendment with the scope of a sovereign's police power, and *Village of Belle Terre v. Boraas,* upholding a one-family dwelling ordinance over objections of exclusionary purpose and effect. Read together, *Berman* and *Belle Terre* accord legislative bodies considerable freedom to guess and to experiment in the choice of restrictions and exclusions that can advance the overall quality of life for the community.

HOPE FOR THE BEST

Mr. Justice Douglas's consideration of the Causby chickens and other ventures into property law have been described here as a robust and hopeful conservation strategy. And so it is if the doctrine laid out presumes an absolutist protection of certain natural assets (the Douglas views on wilderness), the disavowal of private acquisition of public natural and cultural assets (his views on the public trust doctrine), and an acknowledgement of the authority of the legislature to choose freely the means to build a better life (*Berman*), without compensating for social and economic inconveniences imposed upon those affected by the choice (the public trust, *Village of Belle Terre*).

Legal doctrine is, however, notoriously malleable, and under the insidious influence of neutral principle the Douglas conservation strategy can be reformulated and reduced to three central components: some core property rights that cannot be taken, some social property rights that can be redefined away as sentiments change, and elbow room for the legislature to make the choices. As applied, of course, the core property can turn out to be not the people's interest in protecting nature's creatures but the human right to tear up the land in search of oil shale;[33] the social property can come to mean not the gain from polluters' overreaching but the future tort claims of members of the public caught up in a nuclear disaster;[34] and the autonomy enjoyed by the legislature can be turned not to the cause of gentle and benign social configurations but to destructive highways, cruel urban renewal, and pie-in-the-sky water development.

So the Douglas property theory requires something more, and for want of a better word I will call it optimism. Throughout his writing, Douglas presents consistent themes that an informed public will insist upon protection of the environment and that Congress and other popular bodies, barring a corruption of process, can be depended upon to make the right choices for the welfare of the planet.[35] Part of this optimism, no doubt, is attributable to Douglas's faith in a dynamic world where bad laws, unwise precedents, and foolish utterances can be undone at the next sitting; the more awful the choice, from this perspective, the more short-lived it is likely to be. Part of this optimism is attributable to the Douglas faith in structure and process; a court's insistence on a dotting of the *i*'s and a crossing of the *t*'s — with NEPA again the prime example in environmental law — can lead to choices that can serve the natural environment. Part of it, however, also is attributable to a personal populist philosophy that insists that the "correct" environmental choice — measured abstractly as a matter of science — will coincide with the preferences of the general population. Mr. Justice Douglas may have been wrong, of course, but if he was, the prospects of containing global ecological disaster are even more bleak than they are usually depicted to be.

IV. Conclusion

Does Douglas the optimist contradict the fox in his psyche that is forever suspicious of motives, attentive to change, and provisional of purpose? Those foxes still pounce on the loose mounds of soil, hoping for the best — a vole or a mole — until they experience the worst — a snare or a trap.[36] A hearty skepticism serves nicely as an operational norm, but the reflective side of ourselves needs more. And optimism serves spendidly as a personal philosophy; a thousand disappointments and a lifetime of losses doesn't preclude a happy ending, because in the long and evolutionary view, the end never comes.

Notes

1. E. J. Mishan, *Economics for Social Decision: Elements of Cost-Benefit Analysis* (New York: Praeger, 1973); Edith Stokey and Richard Zeckhauser, *A Primer for Policy Analysis* (New York: W.W. Norton, 1978); Deborah Lee Williams, "Benefit-Cost Analysis in Natural Resources Decision-Making: An Economic and Legal Overview," *Natural Resources Law* 11 (1979): 761.

2. Robert Axelrod, *The Evolution of Cooperation* (New York: Basic Books, 1984); Manfred Eigen and Ruthild Winkler, *Laws of the Game: How the Principles of Nature Govern Chance* (New York: Knopf, 1981); Robert H. Frank, *Passions Within Reason: The Strategic Role of the Emotions* (New York: Norton: 1988). Examples of the application of game theory to environmental law include Donald J. Elliott, Bruce A. Ackerman, and John C. Millian, "Toward a Theory of Statutory Evolution: The Federalization of Environmental Law," *Journal of Law, Economics, and Organization* 1 (1985): 313; William H. Rodgers, "The Evolution of Cooperation in Natural Resources Law: The Drifter/Habitue Distinction," *University of Florida Law Review* 38 (1986): 195; Rodgers, "The Owl and the Crows: The Role of Deception in the Evolution of the Environmental Statutes," *Florida State University Journal of Land Use and Environmental Law* 4 (1989): 377.

3. William H. Rodgers, Jr., "The Lesson of the Red Squirrel: Consensus and Betrayal in the Environmental Statutes," *Journal of Contemporary Health Law and Policy* 5 (1988): 101.

4. See David MacDonald, *Running With the Fox* (New York: Facts on File, 1987).

5. "Generations of fox trappers have exploited the fox's habit of investigating scraps of loose soil—a habit which may have its origins in checking on likely cache sites." Ibid., p. 69.

6. See William O. Douglas, *The Three Hundred Year War* (New York: Random House, 1972), p. 8.

7. Ibid., p. 10.

8. See ibid., p. 182.

9. See ibid., pp. 7, 37: A study of the operations of TVA "reveals that socialism is no cure-all. . . . Socialist TVA has such an ugly demeanor that farmers whose land is sought for another needless dam are beginning to wait with rifles for the arrival of the TVA agent" (p. 38).

10. 371 U.S. 334 (1963).

11. *United States v. Causby,* 328 U.S. 256 (1946) (military); *United States v. Students Challenging Regulatory Agency Procedures (SCRAP),* 412 U.S. 669, 199 (1973) (Douglas, J., dissenting in part) (transportation); *Udall v. Federal Power Commission,* 387 U.S. 428 (1967) (opinion by Douglas, J.) (energy) (pre-NEPA case requiring assessment of alternatives and effects of the High Mountain Sheep hydroelectric project on the Snake River).

12. See *Aberdeen & Rockfish R.R. v. Students Challenging Regulatory Agency Procedures (SCRAP),* 422 U.S. 289, 328 (1975) (SCRAP II) (Douglas, J., dissenting

in part); *Warm Springs Dam Task Force v. Gribble,* 417 U.S. 1301 (1974) (Douglas, J.) (On Application for Stay).

13. See, for example, *Robertson v. Methow Valley Citizens Council,* 109 S.Ct. 1835 (1989); *Metropolitan Edison Co. v. People Against Nuclear Energy,* 460 U.S. 766 (1983); *Baltimore Gas & Electric Co. v. Natural Resources Defense Council, Inc.,* 462 U.S. 87 (1983); *Weinberger v. Catholic Action of Hawaii,* 454 U.S. 139 (1981); *Vermont Yankee Nuclear Power Corp. v. Natural Resources Defense Council, Inc.,* 435 U.S. 519 (1978).

14. William H. Rodgers, Jr., *Environmental Law: Air & Water* (St. Paul, Minn.: West, 1986), vol. 2, §4.6, p. 85 (on the "remedy restriction" strategy of the Supreme Court). Compare Richard I. Goldsmith and William C. Banks, "Environmental Values: Institutional Responsibility and the Supreme Court," *Harvard Environmental Law Review* 7 (1983): 1 (discussing Supreme Court's failure to protect environmental values); and Richard E. Levy and Robert L. Glicksman, "Judicial Activism and Restraint in the Supreme Court's Environmental Law Decisions," *Vanderbilt Law Review* 42 (1989): 343 (identifying a prodevelopment pattern in the environmental decisions of the Supreme Court since 1976).

15. *Illinois v. Milwaukee (I),* 406 U.S. 91 (1972); *United States v. Standard Oil Co.,* 384 U.S. 224 (1966); *United States v. Republic Steel Corp.,* 362 U.S. 482, 491–93 (1960).

16. 328 U.S. 256 (1946).

17. Compare *Sierra Club v. Morton,* 405 U.S. 727, 741 (1972), in which Douglas dissented, citing Christopher D. Stone, "Should Trees Have Standing? Toward Legal Rights for Natural Objects," *Southern California Law Review* 45 (1972): 450; and Christopher D. Stone, *Earth and Other Ethics: The Case for Moral Pluralism* (New York: Harper and Row, 1987).

18. See *United States v. Causby,* 328 U.S., at 270, n. 2 (Black, J., dissenting) (quoting District Judge Madden).

19. See Douglas, *Three Hundred Year War,* p. 97.

20. William O. Douglas, *A Wilderness Bill of Rights* (New York: Little, Brown, 1965), p. 33.

21. Douglas, *Three Hundred Year War,* p. 96.

22. Ibid., p. 99.

23. 461 U.S. 1 (1974).

24. Ibid., at 9.

25. Douglas, *A Wilderness Bill of Rights,* passim; James H. Caragher, "The Wilderness Ethic of Justice William O. Douglas," *University of Illinois Law Review* 1986: 645; Stanley Mosk, "William O. Douglas," *Ecology Law Quarterly* 5 (1976): 229; Matthew O. Tobriner and Michael A. Willemsen, "In Memoriam: William O. Douglas," *Ecology Law Quarterly* 8 (1980): 405.

26. Douglas, *A Wilderness Bill of Rights,* p. 86.

27. 107 S.Ct. 1319 (1988).

28. See Ibid., at 1327: the Indians' rights "do not divest the Government of its right to use what is, after all, *its* land."

29. William H. Rodgers, Jr., "A Constitutional Law of the Environment," in American Law Institute/American Bar Ass'n., *Blessings of Liberty: The Constitution and the Practice of Law* (ALI/ABA, 1988).

30. Rodgers, *Environmental Law,* vol. 1, §2.20; see William H. Rodgers, Jr., "Bringing People Back: Toward a Comprehensive Theory of Taking in Natural Resources Law," *Ecology Law Quarterly* 10 (1982): 205, 237, 239–41.

31. Compare Rodgers, *Environmental Law,* vol. 2, §4.14 (Section 404 – "Navigational Servitude"), with *United States v. Twin City Power Co.,* 350 U.S. 222 (1956) (opinion by Douglas, J.); *United States v. Grand River Dam Authority,* 363 U.S. 229 (1960) (same); *United States v. Gerlach Live Stock Co.,* 339 U.S. 725, 756 (1950) (Douglas J., concurring in part and dissenting in part); *General Box Co. v. United States,* 351 U.S. 159, 168 (1956) (Douglas, J., dissenting); and *United States v. Union Pacific R.R.,* 353 U.S. 112 (1957) (opinion by Douglas, J.) (finding reservation of mineral resources by United States in disposition of public lands).

32. 348 U.S. 26 (1954).

33. See *Andrus v. Shell Oil Co.,* 446 U.S. 657 (1980) (opinion by Burger, C. J.) (protecting speculative oil shale claims as valid existing rights not subject to public leasing requirements).

34. See *Duke Power Co. v. Carolina Environmental Study Group, Inc.,* 438 U.S. 59 (1978) (opinion by Burger, C. J.) (upholding constitutionality of the Price-Anderson Act, which limits liability of the nuclear industry for damages resulting from an accident).

35. Douglas, *Three Hundred Year War,* pp. 147, 183–84, 198–200.

36. MacDonald, *Running with the Fox,* p. 69.

William O. Douglas and the Environment

Christopher D. Stone

I F JUSTICE DOUGLAS was a great judge, and he may well have been, he was not a great judge in the way in which others — Holmes or Brandeis, say — were great judges. Those two we remember for a legacy of landmark cases that win our minds with carefully argued principle, well backed with precedent, and frequently adorned with powerful metaphor. Neither Holmes's opinion in *Abrams v. United States* ("the market place of ideas")[1] nor Brandeis's in *Whitney v. California* (explicating "clear and present danger")[2] were positions of the Court when written. But they were written in a way that appealed to and eventually won over majorities. Felix Frankfurter and John Marshall Harlan contributed to a sensitive examination of the Court's institutional competence.

I sometimes think that in Douglas's case, we are simply presented with a man whose dominance has to be accepted as a given; and if we cannot find a conventional theory of judging to explain why he remains dominant, well, then (Douglas certainly would say), it is up to us theorizers to reconsider our theories. Certainly Douglas will be more remembered overall for the positions he took, for what he was, rather than for the persuasiveness of what he said, or for any particular institutional sensitivities. Yet, what Douglas did and said over a thirty-six year Supreme Court career was marked by flashes of moral judicial brilliance that illuminated the history we were living. Douglas's reputation for being complex if not paradoxical persists. You can find people who will say he did not care about "the law." Yet I can still remember, from the days I practiced on Wall Street, hearing lawyers call Douglas "the smartest *lawyer* on the bench" — ordinarily in a tone that added, "what a shame he went wrong." Douglas was widely believed to be withdrawn from his colleagues, irascible with his subordinates, and impatient with conventional notions of role constraints. No court watcher doubts that a judge's temperament enters into his decisions. Douglas, however, may have taken his temperament to be legitimating.

It would be unwise, and it certainly would not honor the man, to flatten away all these rough facets of Douglas's life and career with uncritical adulation. They are what make Douglas interesting. But how do we even begin to approach so complicated a subject?

Rodgers takes two stabs at finding a point of entry. First, he draws upon decision theory, or says he does, to draw a distinction between maximizing styles (the classic illustration is utilitarianism) and the style of games, in which "the best position for a player depends upon context and upon what the other players are doing." Rodgers groups Douglas with the gamers.

Now, one might be tempted to go back over Douglas's most memorable decisions and see if this works. In *Griswold v. Connecticut,*[3] for example, one might rejoin that Douglas was not gaming but maximizing something, specifically, privacy. I am not inclined to press the point, however, because Rodgers's whole distinction strikes me as untenable, anyway. A maximizer of happiness, or minimizer of budget expenditures, has to account for how various people will respond to each alternative strategy. Just try working through a standard utilitarian critique of the death penalty, or of anything else. Good maximizers have to be wily reactors. And reciprocally, most of the players in game theory literature *are* supposed to be maximizing something, collecting more chips or capturing more cities. In the Prisoner's Dilemma, the classic nonzero-sum game, both of the prisoners are trying to get the hell out — to increase their benefits in the least costly way. Thus, the first line along which Rodgers wants us to walk, that between maximizing and game-winning styles, is a bit too fuzzy to follow.

I suspect that Rodgers himself has an uneasy awareness that his game metaphor is heading for defeat, and it is for that reason that he steers us toward the one about Douglas as fox. In doing so, Rodgers is not the only contributor to find himself fetching about for an animal simile, further evidence that we all find Douglas so hard to grasp in familiar human terms.

Rodgers finds foxes to be "extraordinary gamers, with the capacity to make the best of a bad situation." Of course, do not forget the other, maximizer's, side of that coin: that wiliness is the foxes' gene-game strategy for maximizing the number of foxes in succeeding generations. Douglas, Rodgers says, was like a fox in that he "was intuitively [!] but fully aware that legal move *A* brings countermove *B,* which is sidestepped by defensive maneuver *C* . . . and so on." Sure, but who on any bench — or in any introductory civics class — ever doubted that? Moreover, I do not find Douglas's memorable decisions to be marked by any distinctive foxiness about causal chains, anyway. Think, again, of *Griswold,* or of *Skinner v. Oklahoma,*[4] or of Douglas's splendid dissents in *Wisconsin v. Yoder*[5] and *Sierra Club v. Morton.*[6] To me, these all bear the evidence of allegiance to some deeply felt principle, come hell or high water.

On the other hand, in flushing foxes out into the room, Rodgers may have put us on the right scent. While what the fox is for Rodgers is not what Douglas is for me, Rodgers's analysis recalled to mind what may be the oldest fox quote extant, that from a fragment of the Greek poet Archilochus: "the fox knows many things, but the hedgehog knows one big thing." This is the passage that Isaiah Berlin enlisted as the dominant trope for his admired examination of Tolstoy, *The Hedgehog and the Fox*.[7] There, focusing on literary and artistic figures, Berlin characterized the hedgehogs as those who seek out single, universal principles with which to give unity to all experience. The fox types, by contrast,

lead lives, perform acts, and entertain ideas that are centrifugal rather than centripetal, their thought . . . [moves] on many levels, seizing upon the essence of a vast variety of experiences and objects for what they are in themselves, without, consciously or unconsciously, seeking to fit them into, or exclude them from, any one unchanging, all-embracing, sometimes self-contradictory and incomplete, at times fanatical, unitary inner vision.[8]

In some of the ways in which Berlin reads Archilochus, I think it is clear Douglas was a fox; I am not so certain he was a greater judge for it.

What is the Douglas legacy in the specific subject matter at hand: Douglas as environmentalist on the U.S. Supreme Court? In the public mind, no member of the U.S. Supreme Court, and few government figures in any area, were so closely identified with Nature as William O. Douglas. One is therefore struck to realize how little judicial legacy Douglas left for contemporary environmental law or theory. That is not the message Rodgers intended to send, but that is the message that comes across. I say that because he really has to stretch — to be a little foxy with the opinions himself — to make any case for Douglas's environmentalist impact at all.

Rodgers, for example, tries to squeeze out of Douglas's opinion in *United States v. Causby*,[9] the takings by overflight case, a suggestion that Douglas "had a more sympathetic view of the biological requirements of chickens than the dissenters." I had always thought Douglas right in *Causby*, but could not for the life of me recall any pronature sentiment. A rereading of the case shows that Rodgers's token of Douglas's environmentalism is based entirely upon a footnote in Black's dissent quoting with approval the trial judge's remark that chickens learned to get along with tractor noise, so they could therefore learn to live with airplanes; because Black was dissenting, we are asked to infer that Douglas felt otherwise! The truth is that there is not a scintilla of credible evidence that Douglas viewed the farmer's chickens any different than he did the farmer's corn: as property, the value of which the government was diminishing.

It is telling, too, that Rodgers, in his gracious attempt to honor Douglas as a judicial environmentalist, has to point to *Village of Belle Terre v. Boraas*.[10] Douglas's opinion there, in which he upheld a zoning ordinance that excluded living units of more than two unrelated persons, does, as Rodgers says, refer to "a quiet space where yards are wide" and "clean air" and a few such suburban amenities. But let us not forget — Thurgood Marshall, in his powerful dissent won't let us forget — that the challengers to the zoning ordinance were trying to raise serious questions of freedom of association, behind which loomed an equally large social issue, a lack of housing for the poor. Douglas's supposed promotion of a really rather shallow environmentalism permitted him to gloss this all over in what is really a rather shallow opinion. Indeed, Marshall in his dissent points out that only the term before, Douglas, in *United States Department of Agriculture v. Moreno,*[11] had scored a food stamp program that penalized households of "unrelated persons" as an infringement of First Amendment association rights. Someone less the fox than Douglas might have felt obliged to explain, to put the two cases into a unifying perspective.

There are a scattering of other decisions that we would regard today as pitching government action versus environmental concerns. In addition to *Causby,* there is *United States v. SCRAP,*[12] and *Udall v. Federal Power Commission.*[13] As Rodgers says, one can find in these opinions evidence of Douglas's nondeference toward the government side. But of course one can find Douglas exhibiting a pattern of nondeference toward the government in a number of areas: his mood in taxpayers suits has been well if not kindly chronicled by Bernard Wolfman.[14]

Of course, part of the reason Douglas did not build a stronger environmental record on the Court is that there were not many environmental cases coming his way. The National Environmental Policy Act was not passed until 1969, toward the end of his career. However, I think it is also worth noting — in putting Douglas in honest perspective — that Douglas's environmentalism, while it drew from several roots, was predominantly homocentric. In more familiar terms, Douglas was basically a conservationist of the persuasion that Nature should be conserved for human benefit, not for any rights of its own. It is easy to be misled into supposing he envisioned something more. Douglas indeed wrote a book titled *A Wilderness Bill of Rights.* I do not read it quite the way Rodgers does, however. The rights Douglas supports are not rights for the environment, but for environmentalists.[15] This is not so surprising. For example, Douglas, as avid sportsman, appears never to have felt any tension between loving nature and gunning down its denizens for trophies.

Nature had, as part of its beauty, a *utility* for Douglas. He liked the wilderness because it served him psychically. Douglas as a child suffered from polio, and overcame it by hiking in the woods. "Wilderness," he was to write, "is a therapist — a physician, indeed, a preeminent one."[16] Most important, and here Rodgers hits it right on the head, wilderness provided one of the things Douglas valued most consistently: quiet. Indeed, for Douglas the allure of Nature was as much a repulsion away from civilization, with its mechanization, bureaucracy, growing masses — and noise.

This outlook managed to tincture Douglas's views with a distinctly elitist cast. James Simon reports of a trip to the Cascades: "To Douglas's dismay, any TV watching, beer guzzling suburbanite could jump into his car and in a few hours behold the vistas that Douglas had sometimes trekked for days to discover." In Douglas's words, "'Potbellied men, smoking black cigars, who never could climb a hundred feet were now in the sacred precincts of a great mountain.'"[17]

The point is that Douglas did not leave American law a legacy of well-thought-out environmentalist principles. In part, that is because Douglas as a justice did not concentrate on a reasoned elaboration of principles in any field. It is a shame, because the law still lacks a theoretical foundation solid enough to guide us into today's environmental dilemmas, the way we have theories to advance us into, even if not *through,* the First Amendment. For example, in the wake of the *Exxon Valdez* oil spill, can there be legal damage to the environment per se, or can the courts take cognizance only of damage to people that results through changes in the environment? This has become a significant question, and one on which we need judicial direction. Perhaps to wish for some foundational basis from Douglas is to expect too much. Yet, from whom else might we have had any such expectation? Then, again, it is not really clear from Douglas's off-the-bench writings that he was hospitable to a far-reaching environmentalism that would recognize the rights of nature per se.

Not, at least — and only then, perhaps — until his dissent in *Sierra Club v. Morton.*[18] Even there, the standing of nature, as he endorsed it, is principally rested on functional grounds (that is, he recognizes the power of the idea as a sort of legal fiction for getting environmentalists into court). As the opinion proceeds, however, there are also traces not only of his love for Nature but of a sense that the idea of nature's standing contained the potential to challenge, and not merely, as a convenient legal fiction, to serve, homocentric pragmatism. One feels Douglas was pointing toward a new — for the courts — level of consciousness. For me, and for many environmentalists of various stripes, Justice Douglas, if it were only for that opinion alone, would have instated himself as the leading judicial champion of the environment.

Notes

The author would like to acknowledge the research assistance of Karen Chang.

1. 250 U.S. 616, 630 (1919) (dissenting opinion).

2. 274 U.S. 352, 357 (1927) (concurring opinion).

3. 381 U.S. 479 (1965).

4. 316 U.S. 535 (1942), striking down on equal protection grounds — a landmark usage — a state statute providing for the sterilization of anyone convicted three or more times of a felony offense involving moral turpitude.

5. 406 U.S. 205 (1972) (dissenting opinion).

6. 405 U.S. 727, 741 (1959) (dissenting opinion).

7. Isaiah Berlin, *The Hedgehog and the Fox* (New York: Simon and Schuster, 1953).

8. Ibid., pp. 1–2.

9. 328 U.S. 256 (1946).

10. 416 U.S. 1 (1974).

11. 413 U.S. 528 (1973).

12. 412 U.S. 669, 699 (Douglas, J., dissenting in part).

13. 387 U.S. 428 (1967).

14. Bernard Wolfman, Jonathan L. F. Silver, Marjorie A. Silver, *Dissent Without Opinion* (Philadelphia: University of Pennsylvania Press, 1975).

15. James F. Simon has it right, that for Douglas, "protection of environmentalist [sic] was given the same place as protection of speech and religion . . . and for many of the same reasons." *Independent Journey: The Life of William O. Douglas* (New York: Harper and Row, 1980), p. 332.

16. William O. Douglas, *A Wilderness Bill of Rights* (Boston: Little, Brown, 1965), p. 33.

17. Simon, *Independent Journey,* p. 330.

18. 405 U.S. 727, 741 (1972).

Justice Douglas and the Public Lands

Charles F. Wilkinson

J USTICE WILLIAM O. DOUGLAS grew up with the federal lands as a young man, and he loved them. Later in life, the field of public land and resources law and policy became one of his most noteworthy spheres of judicial decision making, professional writing, and personal activism. The world views of adults germinate from miscellaneous personal experiences: seemingly disconnected playground tussles, dinner table debates, madcap excursions, rooted friendships, and the smells and sights of discrete places are the loam for our opinions, philosophy, and character. Since the professional work of all judges is to some extent the product of this process — for Justice Douglas quite dramatically so — it is well worth our while to examine some of the formative experiences that were the loam of Douglas's views and actions in relation to the public lands.

I. The Formative Experiences

Douglas, who was born in 1898 in Minnesota but whose family migrated to California when he was three, was a westerner, where the great bulk of the public lands are located. His family soon moved from California to Cleveland, Washington, then to nearby Yakima, and he grew up in a state where half of all land is owned by the United States. Throughout his life, Douglas was stirred by the sagebrush plains of the Yakima region, by the lowslung, brooding hills that flank the Columbia River just east of the gorge, and by the green and white Cascades that rise up above Yakima to the west.

Douglas's descriptions of the shaping events in his life were often framed in terms of the public lands. When he was just six, Douglas lost his father, whom he idolized. At the funeral in Yakima, the young boy was lost in melancholy and terror during the indoor services at the church. Once the small congregation moved outside to the cemetery, however, the Cascades brought some measure of solace and the beginning of a larger understanding:

Then I happened to see Mount Adams towering over us to the west. It was dark purple and white in the August day and its shoulders of basalt were heavy with glacial snow. . . . As I looked, I stopped sobbing. My eyes dried. Adams stood cool

233

and calm, unperturbed by the events that stirred up so deeply. Suddenly the mountain seemed to be a friend, a force for me to tie to, a symbol of stability and sovereignty.[1]

Douglas was healed by the public lands in another, even more direct and literal, way, and the episode tells us a great deal about the development of his intense, dogged personality and the construction of his approach toward nature. Douglas had contracted polio when he was three, but by the time he had reached eleven, neither his mother's massages nor his weight-lifting regimen had brought strength to his legs, nor had his status as a straight-A student gained him the respect of his classmates. Douglas took to the out-of-doors, making strenuous hikes up the public domain foothills around Yakima. Then he engaged in excursions deep into the wild lands of the Cascades. Douglas credits those hikes with conquering his infantile paralysis.

These boyhood experiences made Douglas a wilderness devotee. "I took my early hikes into the hills to try to strengthen my legs, but they were to strengthen me in more subtle ways. As I came to be on intimate terms with the hills, I learned something of their geology and botany."[2] Throughout the remainder of his life, he worked hard at being a naturalist, and a great part of his writing dealt with the subject. He commonly evoked natural images. As a young lawyer at the Cravath firm, he lamented the senior partner who cloistered himself in his law office and "never had the time to get to know the flight of the whistling swan or the call of the loons across northern waters."[3] He articulated his devotion to country in terms of his feel for the Cascades, saying he "had a passionate love not only for the mountains but for our nation and its institutions as well."[4] When finally he left the Court, he wrote his farewell to his fellow justices by treating their explorations of the nation's laws as a metaphorical wilderness journey:

I am reminded of many canoe trips I have taken in my lifetime. Those who start down a water course may be strangers at the beginning but almost invariably are close friends at the end. There were strong headwinds to overcome, and there were rainy as well as sun drenched days to travel. The portages were long and many and some were very strenuous. But there were always a pleasant camp in a stand of white bark birch and water concerts held at night to the music of the loons; and inevitably there came the last camp fire, the last breakfast cooked over last night's fire, and the parting was always sad.

And yet, in fact, there was no parting because each happy memory of the choice parts of the journey — and of the whole journey — was of a harmonious united effort filled with fulfilling and beautiful hours as well as dull and dreary ones. The greatest such journey I've made has been with you, my Brethren, who were strangers at the start but warm and fast friends at the end.

The value of our achievements will be for others to appraise. Other like journeys will be made by those who follow us, and we trust that they will leave these wilderness water courses as pure and unpolluted as we left those which we traversed.[5]

The young Douglas knew the outdoors not only as a hiker and as a worker picking fruit, fighting fires, and logging, but he also spent time reading the literature of the public lands of the West. Although he had read John Muir, he had a special place for Gifford Pinchot, Chief of the Forest Service under President Theodore Roosevelt. Pinchot's advocacy of balanced use of the forest reserves, and doubtless his dashing style, captivated the young Douglas. He described Pinchot as "the most enduring influence in my life" and gave serious thought to becoming a forester.[6]

Another strand of childhood experience, not directly tied to the public lands, seems to have mattered in building Douglas's views toward the federal lands. From the beginning, he identified with the dispossessed. He grew up near the Yakima Indian Reservation and held deep sympathies for Indian people. He learned a healthy disrespect for the church, which catered more to Yakima's wealthy establishment than to its poor. Perhaps most of all, he was profoundly moved by the International Workers of the World—the Wobblies. He worked with them, rode the rails with them, and was filled with outrage when a roundup of Wobblies was herded through Yakima by rail in sealed boxcars: "there were no toilets, no food, no water, just sealed boxcars with those poor bastards inside. . . . I thought of all of the pompous members of the Establishment of Yakima who should have been in those cars."[7]

Douglas saw environmental issues in general, and public lands issues in particular, in those terms. Growing up at the end of "The Great Barbeque" of the public domain enjoyed by the railroads, the big timber companies, and the giant ranches, Douglas doubtless viewed public land law and policy as a David and Goliath confrontation and favored, as his hero Gifford Pinchot so often put it, "the little man." His commitment to the dispossessed would later appear in his Court opinions as a preference for public control of the public lands over the claims of corporate interests.

A last formative experience came much later, during law school at Columbia and, even more notably, during his teaching days at Columbia and Yale.[8] As a Columbia law student, Douglas was influenced by Dean (later Justice) Harlan Fiske Stone, whose work contributed to Legal Realism, and, even more specifically, by Professor Underhill Moore, for whom Douglas served as a research assistant. At the time, Moore was exploring the ways in which law could be more fully understood through principles of economics, anthropology, and psychology. After two years in private practice with the Cravath firm, Douglas returned to Columbia, now as a faculty member, and became committed to the then-burgeoning school of Legal Realism, which held that the law is better comprehended through extralegal societal forces than through legal rules. The influence of Legal Realism—a tendency on some occasions to eschew black-letter law in favor of results flowing from interdisciplinary sources of authority, real-world assessments of agency behavior, and perceived imbalances caused by powerful economic forces—is evident in the Douglas public lands opinions.

Thus Douglas had a mature and comprehensive philosophy of public land policy and law by the time he assumed his place on the Court in 1939. He cared deeply about the West and understood its spareness, aridity, and concentration of public lands in much the same terms as Bernard DeVoto and Wallace Stegner, both of whom had grown up in essentially the same West as had Douglas. Douglas was able to speak, for example, of the high desert and "the sharpened perception" caused by the sparse vegetation in terms of "the old relationship between scarcity and value."[9] He thought in terms of whole natural systems, and well appreciated the interrelationships among plants, animals, soils, and water. He knew the history of the region and how the public lands of the West had long been up for grabs. And he loved, and knew, great rivers and wilderness.

II. Public Lands Writing and Activism

The full extent of Douglas's personal commitment to these issues can be appreciated only through a sense of his writing and political activism during the Court years. One commentator has observed that Douglas "is the only Justice whose out-of-court literary output comes close to matching his pages of opinions."[10] Much of his work product was related to the environment, and much of that bore upon the public lands.

Douglas had worked hard to comprehend environmental policy and philosophy. He grew disenchanted with Pinchot's policies, if not his persona, and inveighed against multiple use, which according to Douglas, means that "every canyon is put to as many uses as possible."[11] In *A Wilderness Bill of Rights,* he engaged in a serious intellectual attempt to translate abstractions about wilderness into hard and fast rights.[12] He dealt with transcendent philosophical issues. In addition to thinking in terms of whole ecosystems, Douglas thought in terms of geologic time: he wrote that "peaks that have come and gone four times should halt a man in his steps."[13]

Douglas's literary style is not equal to that of a Leopold or a Stegner, but he did write as well as Muir, and he deserves to be taken seriously as a naturalist and an environmental philosopher. He had breadth: in addition to his writings on natural systems in several foreign countries,[14] he wrote of numerous western places, including Alaska, Oregon's Hart Mountain and Wallowas, Idaho's Silver Creek, and, of course, the Cascades. He had depth. He told of salmon (his ineptitude in attempting to spear salmon with a young Indian guide is hilarious[15]), coyotes, porcupines, sagebrush, blueberries, periwinkles, ouzels, chinook winds, hellgrammites, mosquitoes, and many another denizen of the West in compelling and elucidating ways. Douglas may not be in the front rank of enviornmental writers, but he is close to it. In a time when ecology had not yet become fashionable, Douglas was able to articulate the web of life in a legitimately useful and influential way.[16]

Douglas, of course, supplemented his judicial career not only with the out-of-court written word but also with a controversial series of political actions. As with his outside writing, much of this direct political activism was dedicated to public lands controversies. Douglas regularly engaged in protests, hikes, and speeches in opposition to public lands policies; he counted dozens of such activities between 1954 and 1968.[17] Perhaps the most successful were his hikes to protest a proposal to turn the Chesapeake & Ohio Canal near Washington, D.C., into a highway: ultimately, the highway plans were dropped and the canal was added to the National Park System, dedicated to Justice Douglas. In recognition of his many activities, the Sierra Club honored him by granting him its highest honor, the John Muir Award, in June 1975. In response to the impeachment charges brought against him, Douglas argued that outside activities keep " a judge from becoming a prisoner within the narrow confines of 'the law.'"[18] Right or wrong, Douglas lived out that maxim, probably to a considerably greater extent than anyone ever to sit on the Court.

III. Judicial Opinions

Douglas's public lands opinions while on the Supreme Court can be grouped into several categories. These include opinions upholding federal authority to protect the environment, opinions protecting rivers, those refusing to recognize private rights on public lands, and one opinion recognizing the rights of natural systems.

FEDERAL POWER TO PROTECT THE ENVIRONMENT

Justice Douglas believed that Congress possessed nearly unfettered authority to protect the public lands and resources. This view emerges from a number of his opinions, including those upholding a broad construction of the Rivers and Harbors Act of 1899;[19] allowing the Secretary of Interior broad authority to determine the validity of hardrock mining claims;[20] and arguing for a sweeping reading of the recently enacted National Environmental Policy Act.[21] This line of reasoning, while it evidences Douglas's proenvironment and profederalist stance, is to be expected: as a New Dealer, Douglas was in the forefront of the Court's post-1937 recognition of broad federal power, which was expressly recognized in the context of public land law shortly after Douglas left the Court.[22]

Douglas's upbringing as a westerner, however, came to the fore and caused him to argue against expansive constructions of federal land and resources laws in one area—western water law. Thus in *Arizona v. California,* one of the leading natural resources cases ever handed down, Douglas delivered a table-thumping dissent against the majority's finding that Congress had delegated to the Secretary of Interior the authority to apportion equitably the waters of the Colorado River among the states of Arizona, California, and Nevada: "The decision today, resulting in the confusion between the priority of water rights and the public power problem, has made the dream of the federal bureaucracy come true by granting it, for the first time, the life-and-death power of dispensation of water rights long administered according to state law."[23]

Douglas hewed to a states' rights line in other leading water cases involving the public lands. In *Federal Power Commission v. Oregon,*[24] Douglas argued in dissent that the United States must obtain its water rights under state law rather than through a federal reservation of water. This case involved the Pelton Dam, and Douglas was in fact taking the environmental side, since the state of Oregon staunchly opposed the Pelton Dam, on the Deschutes River, because of its negative effects on the salmon and steelhead runs. Much more often, however, western state water law has favored extractive interests. In 1971, Justice Douglas wrote for the majority in the *Eagle County* case, holding that the McCarran Amendment of 1952 waived the sovereign immunity of the United States and granted to state courts the power to adjudicate federal reserved water rights.[25] In *Eagle County* and its companion case,[26] Douglas engaged in perhaps his clearest departure from the environmental position by holding that reserved water rights of the national forests will be decided by state courts.

RIVER PROTECTION

Leaving aside the cases deferring to western state water law, the Douglas opinions evidence a powerful determination to protect the nation's rivers, especially in the West. It should be noted that western river policy is usually tied directly to public lands policy. The homesteading program faltered in the late nineteenth century because farmers lacked the wherewithal to put water on the arid land; without irrigation water, potential farmland in most areas west of the 100th meridian would lie barren. The Reclamation Act of 1902 began the era of the big dams that stored tens of millions of acre feet of water in western canyons, allowing homesteading of the public domain to proceed. Of course, from William O. Douglas's standpoint, the dams drowned canyons, barricaded the salmon and steelhead runs on those rivers with anadromous fish runs, and, more often than not, ultimately favored establishment interests such as big-city developers and agribusiness rather than the heralded yeoman farmer whom the reclamation program was originally designed to serve.

Douglas regularly handed down opinions protecting rivers. As noted, he wrote against the Pelton Dam and supported extensions of the 1899 Rivers and Harbors Act, the precursor of the Clean Water Act. In a number of cases, he argued against the recognition of private rights in western rivers and their beds on the ground that the creation of vested property rights would restrict subsequent public use of the rivers.[27] On two occasions, Douglas quoted Justice Holmes's dictum that "a river is more than an amenity, it is a treasure."[28]

The most enduring of Douglas's river protection opinions is *Udall v.*

Federal Power Commission,[29] where the justice joined with another fiery westerner, Interior Secretary Stewart Udall, in restraining the discretion of the Federal Power Commission to license dams on western rivers. A private utility had applied to build the proposed High Mountain Sheep Dam in the Columbia River system on the Snake River just below the Snake's confluence with the Salmon River. In March 1961, just a few months after taking office, Udall had requested postponement of the FPC licensing proceeding, pending more definitive research of the dam's potential impact on the salmon and steelhead runs. Eight dams had already been built on the mainstream Columbia below High Mountain since 1933, and numerous studies showed that anadromous fish were in serious decline on the Columbia, one of the world's greatest salmon-producing rivers. The FPC went ahead with its permitting process and granted the license.

Given the nascent state of administrative law and environmental law in the mid-1960s, one might have expected a routine affirmation of the FPC's decision based on notions of judicial deference to agency discretion. However, in a Douglas opinion that was a precursor of modern judicial review of agency decisions affecting natural resources, the Court remanded the case to the FPC for further consideration of the impacts on the salmon resource.

The opinion in *Udall v. Federal Power Commission* was trailblazing in a number of respects. Although the Federal Power Act delegated broad authority to the FPC—in concept it is much like the multiple-use provisions applicable to federal land agencies—Justice Douglas focused on Section 10's reference to "recreation purposes" and concluded that the agency had not sufficiently analyzed the impact of the dam on recreational fishing.[30] The opinion also looked to very general statutory language in the 1965 Anadromous Fish Act, which referred to "the conservation and enhancement of anadromous fishing resources"; the Fish and Wildlife Coordination Act, which stated that "wildlife conservation shall receive equal consideration and be coordinated with other features of water-resource development programs"; and the Federal Power Act, which stated that the Commissioner must act "in the public interest."

All of these statutory provisions could be viewed as window dressing, but Douglas, in order to mandate further review by the FPC, emphasized the economic and recreational values of salmon and the complexity of the Columbia River system and its ecology—apparently the first use of the word "ecology" in a Supreme Court opinion. To be sure, there have been many cases since in which the Court has reviewed similar statutes and dismissed challenges to agency action with a bow to administrative discretion, but *Udall v. FPC* has stood as a bright model of vigilant judicial review in complex natural resources litigation.

PRIVATE RIGHTS IN THE PUBLIC LANDS

One of the most consistent themes in the Douglas public lands opinions is his skepticism toward litigants seeking to establish private rights in federal lands and resources. In two condemnation cases, *Grand River Dam Authority v. Grand Hydro*[31] and *United States v. Gerlach Live Stock,*[32] he disagreed with majorities that found compensable interests in cases involving navigable watercourses. In *Grand River,* Justice Douglas argued that the value of land for use as a power site should not be considered in determining just compensation. In *Gerlach,* he believed that riparian water rights were not compensable. His reasoning in the two cases, relying upon the United States' prior and paramount navigation servitude on navigable watercourses, was that private parties can obtain no interests in navigable waters as against the federal government. In both *Alabama v. Texas*[33] and *United States v. Louisiana,*[34] he issued vehement dissents to majority opinions upholding state claims to offshore lands under the Submerged Lands Act of 1953. In *Alabama v. Texas,* in concluding that the Act's transfer to individual states of submerged lands out to the three-mile line was unconstitutional, he said:

Thus we are dealing here with incidents of national sovereignty. The marginal sea is not an oil well; it is more than a mass of water; it is a protective belt for the entire Nation over which the United States must exercise exclusive and paramount authority. The authority over it can no more be abdicated than any of the other great powers of the Federal Government. It is to be exercised for the benefit of the whole. . . .

Could Congress cede the great Columbia River or the mighty Mississippi to a State or a power company? I should think not. For they are arteries of commerce that attach to the national sovereignty and remain there until and unless the Constitution is changed. What is true of a great river would seem to be even more obviously true of the marginal sea. For it is not only an artery of commerce among the States but the vast buffer standing between us and the world. It therefore would seem that unless we are to change our form of government, that domain must by its very nature attach to the National Government and the authority over it remain nondelegable.[35]

Douglas's tendency to favor public ownership probably reached its zenith in *United States v. Union Pacific Railroad.*[36] The case involved an attempt by the railroad to drill for oil and gas on the right-of-way granted to it by Section 2 of the Union Pacific and Central Pacific Railroad Act of 1862. There was no express federal mineral reservation in Section 2, dealing with the right-of-way. However, Section 3 of the statute did provide for a reservation of minerals by the United States by specifying that "all mineral lands shall be excepted from the operation of this act." As the dissent demonstrated, there was good reason to believe that the mineral reservation language was not intended to apply to the right-of-way itself; rather, the provision in Section 3 may well have been intended only as a directive to the Secretary of Interior to make a determination of the mineral character of the alternate sections also granted to the railroad and, if known mineral land existed, to provide "in lieu" selections for those alternate sections containing minerals.[37] However, Justice Douglas, writing for the majority, concluded that the federal mineral reservation applied to the right-of-way as well as to the grant of alternate sections. He reasoned that any other construction would assume that the Thirty-seventh Congress was "profligate" and that Congress intended to "[endow] the railroad with the untold riches underlying the right-of-way."[38]

The fact, of course, is that Congress was in many ways "profligate" with the public lands during the nineteenth century and seemingly did intend to endow the railroads with untold riches. Such incentives, including about 131 million acres, seemed necessary at the time in order to promote the settling of the West. The following observation, although not made in regard to any of the railroad acts, probably reflects the mood of the time far better than Douglas's conclusions: "[If we do not open the West], these prairies with their gorgeous growth of flowers, their green carpeting, their lovely lawns and gentle slopes, will for centuries continue to be the home of the 'wild deer and wolf'; their stillness will be undisturbed by the jocund song of the farmer, and their deep and fertile soil unbroken by his ploughshare. Something must be done to remedy this evil."[39]

Douglas, intentionally or unintentionally, was a bad historian but he was a good judge. The statute was not clear as to the mineral reservation, and there was no legislative history directly on point. As a result, he relied upon a fundamental rule of construction in public land law: "If there are doubts, they are to be resolved for the government, not against it."[40] Because these were national resources, Douglas assumed that Congress was prudent and that it was careful to preserve the nation's assets.

In modern times, the Court has followed a similar approach,[41] citing *Union Pacific,* but did not do so in the notable opinion in *Leo Sheep Co. v. United States,* written by Justice Rehnquist.[42] Congress had granted odd-numbered sections near Seminoe Reservoir in Wyoming to the Union Pacific Railroad in 1862. The United States had retained the even-numbered sections, thus creating a "checkerboard" ownership pattern. The Leo Sheep Company had succeeded to the railroad's ownership of the odd-numbered parcels. The Bureau of Land Management built a dirt road to the reservoir, necessarily crossing the corners of some of Leo Sheep's sections. The principal question was whether the United States had impliedly reserved an easement, for which no compensation would be paid, across the odd-numbered sections to provide access for public recreation at Seminoe Reservoir.[43] The Court referred to the rule that grants from the United States should be construed in favor of the United States but refused to apply the maxim with "full vigor," because railroad grants are "quasi-public" and stand on a higher plane than "private grants."[44] Significantly, Justice Rehnquist's opinion did not discuss *Union Pacific,* where the Court had earlier applied the liberal rule in favor of the United States to the same statute. The Court then held that the implied easement had not been reserved on the primary ground that "the easement is not actually a matter of necessity in this case because the government has the power of eminent domain."[45]

Leaving aside the surprising failure even to cite *Union Pacific,* the specific result in the *Leo Sheep* litigation is perhaps supportable on a policy basis, because construing a general federal statute to imply the requested easement would have resulted in a cloud of some significance on millions of acres of private land in the West.[46] Nevertheless, my personal preference is that courts ought to proceed according to the implicit premise of Justice Douglas's opinion in *Union Pacific:* lacking clear legislative history, Congress should be presumed to have considered all of the ramifications of its decision and to have taken whatever prudent action is appropriate for the reasonable, long-term protection of the public lands and resources. Regardless of how one comes out on the merits, in a larger sense the *Leo Sheep* and *Union Pacific* opinions, written nearly a quarter of a century apart, provide fascinating insights into two of our most activist justices, both with deeply held views on the national resources, one believing that the public good usually is best achieved through the private sector, the other holding that the public good is usually furthered by public ownership.

THE RIGHTS OF NATURAL SYSTEMS

A last category of Douglas's public lands decisions, the recognition of the rights of natural systems, in fact contains just one opinion, his dissent in 1972 in *Sierra Club v. Morton.*[47] Nevertheless, the opinion, coming as it did near the end of the justice's long career and at the beginning of the modern era of public land law and policy, was the fullest embodiment of his philosophy of natural resources law and policy and deserves to be treated by itself.

The case involved a proposal by Walt Disney Productions to build an extensive ski complex in Mineral King Valley in the Sequoia National Forest in California's Sierra Nevada. The Sierrra Club sued to block the development, and the Court held that the Sierra Club lacked standing. The Club had alleged only that the case was a public action and that it, as plaintiff, could assert alleged damage to Mineral King on behalf of the public. The Court, on the other hand, held that a plaintiff in an environmental case must show more, namely that the plaintiff organization or its members had suffered some specific harm, even if the harm is to aesthetic values. It should be mentioned that many observers consider the *Sierra Club v. Morton* test to be quite liberal and relatively easy to meet for environmental plaintiffs; indeed, on remand, the Sierra Club was able to amend its complaint (for, of course, many of its members used Mineral King), and the Club was able to continue its litigative challenge to the Disney project.

Douglas, however, dissented and did so in one of the most expansive opinions ever written in the field of public land law. Douglas operated on several levels. In three lengthy footnotes, one running to two and one-half pages, he set out his view of the institutional personality of the Forest Service, taking it to task not for being "venal or corrupt"[48] but for being "notorious for its alignment with lumber companies."[49] Those real-world relationships, Douglas believed, required vigilant scrutiny by the public through the medium of the courts. Douglas made his sharply critical comments at exactly the time that Forest Service logging practices had come under heavy public and congressional criticism,[50] and he no doubt intended to add fuel to the fire.

Douglas's dissent was evocative, referring to the public interest in "priceless bits of Americana (such as a valley, an alpine meadow, a river or a lake)" and the importance of preserving public lands for "those who hike the Appalachian Trail into Sunfish Pond, New Jersey, and camp or sleep there, or run the Allagash in Maine, or climb the Guadalupes in West Texas, or who canoe and portage the Quetico Superior in Minnesota."[51] He finished the opinion by discussing Aldo Leopold's land ethic and by quoting from Leopold's *A Sand County Almanac,* perhaps the single greatest book on conservation thought ever written.[52]

These varied sources of evidence were marshalled to support an extraordinary conclusion in American law, that inanimate objects ought to have standing to sue — that regardless of whether the members of the Sierrra Club could show injury, Mineral King itself could show potential harm, and the valley ought to be an acceptable plaintiff:

The river, for example, is the living symbol of all the life it sustains or nourishes — fish, aquatic insects, water ouzels, otter, fishes, deer, elk, bear, and all other animals, including man, who are dependent on it and enjoy it for its sight, sound, or its life. Those people who have a meaningful relation to that body of water — whether it be a fisherman, a canoeist, a zoologist, or a logger — must be able to speak for the values which the river represents and which are threatened with destruction.[53]

Thus Douglas found authority in institutional behavior (the personality and actions of the Forest Service) and natural things (the qualities of valleys, rivers, and other natural objects). For legal authority, he looked to traditions of Anglo-American law, which in some instances recognizes inanimate objects such as ships or corporations as plaintiffs. His real legal authority, however, was the reasoning in a law review article by one of his former law clerks, Christopher Stone, "Should Trees Have Standing?"[54] And yet today, because of Stone's scholarship and because of Justice Douglas's popularization of Stone's concept, the question, "Should trees have standing?" personifies, for lawyers and nonlawyers alike, many of the root philosophical questions in the policy and jurisprudence of our natural resources.

IV. Conclusion

One issue in evaluating Justice Douglas's work in public land law is the influence of his judicial decisions. Three stand out as leading opinions. *Udall v. Federal Power Commission,* handed down in 1967, was one of the first "hard look" judicial review opinions in natural resources law. Although *Udall* preceded the well-known *Citizens to Preserve Overton Park v. Volpe*[55] by four years, the concept of "hard look" judicial review — engaging in a "thorough, probing, in-depth review"[56] of the basis of an agency decision in order to verify that the agency engaged in reasoned decision making — is the essence of Douglas's remand in *Udall v. FPC. Eagle County,* in 1971, set the stage for the adjudication of most federal and Indian water rights in state court. The dissent in *Sierra Club v. Morton,* in 1973, has had no effect at all on the law of standing. However, it was such a daring opinion, and conceptualized a point of view on large issues so well, that one can properly ascribe some considerable weight to it, although its influence is intangible and lies in the scholarship and the public mind rather than in the Supreme Court's opinions.

In all, Douglas wrote a sizable amount on federal public land and resources law, and he had some impact on the jurisprudence of the field, but ultimately his Court opinions have had considerably less influence during modern times than those of Chief Justice Rehnquist, who has written majority opinions in several close and important cases.[57]

There remains the question of Douglas's activism, both on and off the Court. Justice William O. Douglas is commonly criticized as being result-oriented, as bending results in cases to fit his own preconceived ideology. Much of what I have said is testament to that. The river wins in the Douglas opinions, with the rationale being based on congressional, federal agency, state, or tribal prerogatives, as appropriate and convenient. Other natural systems usually win, too. And Douglas had roughly the same truck with the Forest Service as he did with the Internal Revenue Service.

More, however, needs to be said.

Judges are well-educated, committed human beings, and obviously they have views, often deeply-held convictions, on the great public issues of their day. Equally obviously, most of them try to disengage themselves from those views when sitting on cases. Rather than basing decisions on those substantive views, judges consciously or unconsciously develop judicial methodologies, jurisprudential approaches toward deciding cases.

Much more often than not, however, a judge's judicial philosophy is not truly value-neutral. Political liberals will tend to view the Constitution as a dynamic document, evolving with the times, and may develop rules of construction and doctrines of procedure, such as those relating to standing, that favor the dispossessed and that tend to favor change and those interests that benefit from change. A political conservative is more likely to be a strict constructionist and to hew firmly to *stare decisis* and other approaches that tend to favor the status quo and those established interests that benefit from the status quo.

The truth is that it may go back to dinner tables. A young person who grows up poor, perhaps fatherless, may see and hear some angry table-thumping about the wrongs inflicted on some group, say, the Wobblies. As a judge, that person may favor the dispossessed and change and innovation. Young people who listened to deliberate, reasoned dinner table talk of commerce and banking and regularity are much less likely to venture out toward the edges of doctrine. They will pull back and protect the existing order and its beneficiaries by reading the new kind of remedy narrowly, by striking down the new idea.

So you can say that William O. Douglas was result-oriented or you can say that he was a practicing Legal Realist, an early-day critical legal theorist. This happens to be a time when Legal Realists and Crits are not appointed to the courts. But the winds, as they always do, will change. And when they do, my strong hunch is that William O. Douglas will be very, very au courant.

It is not clear to me that a sitting judge ought to psychoanalyze public agencies, write books taking white-hot positions on the great public issues of the time, or march alongside tight-jawed advocates to preserve a wetland, a canal route, or a sheer granite wall. But it gives a person pause to walk even a short part of a 189-mile narrow strip of land near the nation's capital called the Chesapeake & Ohio Canal Route National Historical Park and dedicated by the Park Service to Justice William O. Douglas. It gives a person pause the way the question, "Should trees have standing?" still rings in the ear and in the mind. And it gives a person pause a quarter of a century after the fulfillment of a great idea, the passage of the Wilderness Act of 1964, to contemplate how a Supreme Court justice's *Wilderness Bill of Rights* helped dignify and cement that great idea.

So questions remain as to exactly what a sitting judge ought to be and do. But the public should be grateful beyond the saying that we have one vivid and craggy model for what a judge can do in the field of public land law and policy if a judge is willing to push the system to its limits in pursuit of a fully formulated philosophy of what public resources can be, of how they ought to be conceptualized, of who ought to benefit from them, and of how they ought to be treated.

Notes

1. William O. Douglas, *Go East, Young Man: The Autobiography of William O. Douglas* (New York: Random House, 1974), p. 13.
2. Ibid., p. 36.
3. Ibid., p. 151.
4. Ibid., p. 95.

5. Douglas farewell speech, 423 U.S., at ix–x (1975).

6. Douglas, *Go East, Young Man,* p. 68.

7. Ibid., p. 85.

8. See, generally, Melvin I. Urofsky and Philip E. Urofsky, eds., *The Douglas Letters: Selections from the Private Papers of Justice William O. Douglas* (Bethesda: Adler and Adler, 1987), pp. xii–xiii.

9. Douglas, *Go East, Young Man,* p. 38.

10. Alan Westin, "Out-of-Court Commentary by United States Supreme Court Justices, 1790–1962: Of Free Speech and Judicial Lockjaw," *Columbia Law Review.* 62 (1962): 633, 658.

11. William O. Douglas, *My Wilderness: The Pacific West* (New York: Doubleday, 1960), p. 199.

12. See William O. Douglas, *A Wilderness Bill of Rights* (Boston: Little, Brown, 1965), pp. 85–169.

13. Douglas, *My Wilderness,* p. 103. See also Douglas, *Go East, Young Man,* p. 39.

14. Douglas's thinking on environmental issues was strongly influenced by five extensive Asian treks during the years 1949–1958. Todd G. Glass, "'Go East Young Man': The Asian Influence on the Environmental Philosophy of William O. Douglas," (rev. ed. Apr. 13, 1989) (unpublished manuscript).

15. Douglas, *Go East, Young Man,* pp. 71–72.

16. See, e.g., Douglas, *My Wilderness,* p. 76.

17. Urofsky and Urofsky, *Douglas Letters,* pp. 404–05. Douglas listed eighteen activities, but some (notably the C & O Canal hikes) were multiple entries, and Douglas was not sure that the listing was complete.

18. William O. Douglas, *The Court Years, 1939–1975: The Autobiography of William O. Douglas* (New York: Random House, 1980), p. 369.

19. *United States v. Republic Steel Corp.,* 362 U.S. 482 (1960) (construing "obstruction" to navigation broadly to include solid particles suspended in water despite the Act's exemption of liquid wastes discharged from sewers); *United States v. Standard Oil,* 384 U.S. 224 (1966) (1899 Act prohibits discharge of any refuse, including commercially valuable aviation gasoline).

20. *Best v. Humboldt Mining Co.,* 371 U.S. 334 (1963); *Hickel v. Oil Shale Corp.,* 400 U.S. 48 (1970).

21. *Sierra Club v. Federal Power Commission,* 407 U.S. 926 (1972) (dissenting to denial of certiorari) (arguing that Section 101 of NEPA was intended by Congress to establish an affirmative duty); *Life of the Land v. Brinegar,* 414 U.S. 1052, 1053 (1973) (dissenting to order vacating stay) (arguing that an environmental impact statement should not be prepared by a large corporation with a stake in the outcome).

22. *Kleppe v. New Mexico,* 426 U.S. 529 (1976) ("while the furthest reaches of the power granted by the Property Clause have not yet been definitively resolved, we have repeatedly observed that 'the power over the public land thus entrusted to Congress is without limitations'"). Ibid., at 539 (citations omitted).

23. *Arizona v. California,* 373 U.S. 546, 630 (1963) (Douglas, J., dissenting).

24. 349 U.S. 435 (1955).

25. *United States v. District Court In and For the County of Eagle,* 401 U.S. 520 (1971).

26. Ibid., at 527.

27. See *Grand River Dam Authority v. Grand Hydro,* 335 U.S. 359 (1948) (Douglas, J., dissenting); *United States v. Gerlach Live Stock,* 339 U.S. 725 (1950) (Douglas, J., concurring and dissenting in part); *Federal Power Commission v. Niagara Mohawk Power,* 347 U.S. 239 (1954).

28. *United States v. Standard Oil,* 384 U.S., at 230; *Udall v. Federal Power Commission,* 387 U.S. 428, 439 (1967).

29. 387 U.S. 428 (1967).

30. Ibid., at 449.

31. 335 U.S. 359 (1948) (Douglas, J., dissenting).

32. 339 U.S. 725 (1950) (Douglas, J., concurring and dissenting in part).

33. 347 U.S. 272 (1954) (Douglas, J., dissenting).

34. 363 U.S. 1 (1960) (Douglas, J., concurring and dissenting in part).

35. *Alabama v. Texas,* 347 U.S., at 282. Douglas's analogy of the beds of offshore lands to the beds of large navigable rivers such as the Columbia and Mississippi is inapt. The Court had long ago held that the beds of navigable watercourses passed to the states upon admission to the Union. See, e.g., *Martin v. Waddell,* 41 U.S. (16 Pet.) 367 (1842), and has uniformly followed the rule since; see, e.g., *United States v. Holt State Bank,* 270 U.S. 49 (1926).

36. 353 U.S. 112 (1957).

37. Ibid., at 133 (Frankfurter, J., dissenting). The Court had earlier held that minerals under patented land were not reserved by the government if minerals were subsequently discovered on such lands after the Secretary's initial determination of nonmineral character had been made. *Burke v. Southern Pacific Railroad,* 234 U.S. 669 (1914).

38. *United States v. Union Pacific Railroad,* 353 U.S., at 116.

39. *Congressional Globe,* 28th Cong., 2d Sess. (1844), p. 52 (remarks of Rep. Orlando B. Ficklin of Illinois).

40. *United States v. Union Pacific Railroad,* 353 U.S., at 116.

41. See *Watt v. Western Nuclear Co.,* 462 U.S. 36 (1983); *Andrus v. Charlestone Stone Products,* 436 U.S. 604 (1978).

42. 440 U.S. 668 (1979).

43. The United States also argued that an easement had been reserved by the doctrine of easement by necessity and that the right to cross private lands was a privilege recognized by the Unlawful Enclosures Act of 1885, 43 U.S.C. §§1061–66 (1976). The Court rejected both arguments. Ibid., at 681 and 685.

44. Ibid., at 682–83, citing *United States v. Denver & Rio Grande Ry.,* 150 U.S. 1, 14 (1893).

45. *Leo Sheep Co. v. United States,* 440 U.S., at 680.

46. See ibid., at 685.

47. 405 U.S. 727 (1972).

48. Ibid., at 745 (Douglas, J., dissenting).

49. Ibid., at 748.

50. See, e.g., Charles F. Wilkinson and H. Michael Anderson, *Land and Resource Planning in the National Forests* (Washington, D.C.: Island Press, 1987), pp. 138–45.

51. *Sierra Club v. Morton,* 405 U.S., at 750–52.

52. Ibid., at 752. Douglas also quoted at length from Leopold's *Round River.* Ibid., at 751.

53. Ibid., at 743.

54. Christopher Stone, "Should Trees Have Standing? Toward Legal Rights for Natural Objects," *Southern California Law Review* 45 (1972): 450. It was later reprinted as a book.

55. 401 U.S. 402 (1971).

56. Ibid., at 415.

57. See, e.g., *United States v. New Mexico,* 438 U.S. 696 (1978); *California v. United States,* 438 U.S. 645 (1978); *Leo Sheep Co. v. United States,* 440 U.S. 668 (1979).

COMMENTARY:
JUSTICE DOUGLAS TAKES A HIKE

T. H. Watkins

As MY FRIEND and colleague Charles Wilkinson has made abundantly clear in his chapter, Justice William O. Douglas was meticulously and consistently dedicated to interpretations of public land law that inclined sharply in the direction of preservation and protection over use and exploitation. If this was bias, an environmentalist will not be found complaining too much about it. Further, he was an equally vigorous spokesman for the wilderness in his nonlegal writings. The love of wild places expressed in his books and articles with a piety that was Thoreauvian in its intensity was a gift that came to us out of his youth. However, his understanding of the luminous saraband of life — the complex interrelationships that tie human life to all other forms of life on this small, fragile planet — was a gift not only of intuition but of an intellect forged by maturity and passion — and sometimes righteous anger. Taken together, these qualities alone made him a rarity in his time: a powerful servant of the public good who comprehended fully the fact that a healthy resource of untouched wild country was one of the chief barometers by which we can measure the social and economic health of the nation.

However, there was more to his activism than that. In this regard, Douglas was not merely a rarity; he was the next thing to unique. I don't know whether he actually knew Robert Marshall, the principal founder of The Wilderness Society, but he would have had no difficulty at all in agreeing with Marshall's conviction that "There is just one hope of repulsing the tyrannical ambition of civilization to conquer every niche on the whole earth. That hope is the organization of spirited people who will fight for the freedom of the wilderness."[1]

No one who knew Douglas would have described him as anything less than spirited, and he was in fact an early member of The Wilderness Society. And the Sierra Club. And of any number of other conservation organizations, some of them invented by himself.

He was, in short, an environmental activist in an age that preceded the term itself — a time before Earth Day, before the word "ecology" could be heard tumbling in ignorance from the lips of those attending suburban cocktail parties, before environmental impact statements, before Earth First! and the Monkey Wrench Gang, before Environmental Studies became an academic discipline, before any known president of the United States would be moved to describe himself deliberately and without shame as an environmentalist — and maybe even know what it meant.

William O. Douglas put his feet where his convictions lay. He understood, even before television took over our public lives, that while it might not replace the written word or the legal opinion, the visible statement had a value that could not be ignored. And so, on two particularly important occasions, Justice Douglas took a hike.

Douglas's first important perambulation with intent was to save the shadowed loveliness of the long towpath along the Chesapeake & Ohio Canal. This splendid corridor — 189 miles long and an average of 230 feet wide — ran alongside the remains of the 125-year-old C & O Canal through the valley of the Potomac River between Washington, D.C., and Cumberland, Maryland. It was the property of the federal government, having reverted to public ownership after the final demise of canal operations in the 1920s. In 1954, long-discussed plans to build an automobile parkway through the corridor came to the attention of the *Washington Post,* which on January 3 wrote an editorial supporting the idea.

Justice Douglas, who had spent many a happy hour tramping along the tangled wilderness path, did not support the idea. Indeed, he hated it, and on January 9, he issued a challenge to the chief of the *Post*'s editorial page, Robert H. Estabrook, and the author of the editorial in question, Merlo Pusey. The corridor, Douglas wrote in a letter to the editor, "is a refuge, a place of retreat, a long stretch of quiet and peace at the Capital's back door — a wilderness area where we can commune with God and with nature, a place not yet marred by the roar of wheels and the sound of horns." He continued,

I wish the man who wrote your editorial . . . approving the parkway would take time off and come with me. We would go with packs on our backs and walk . . . to Cumberland. I feel that if your editor did, he would return a new man and use the power of your editorial page to help keep this sanctuary untouched.

One who walked the canal its full length could plead its cause with the eloquence of a John Muir. He would get to know muskrats, badgers, and fox; he would hear the roar of wind in thickets; he would see strange islands and promontories through the fantasy of fog; he would discover the glory there is in the first flower of spring, the glory there is even in a blade of grass; the whistling wings of ducks would make silence have new values for him. Certain it is that he could never acquire that understanding going 60, or even 25, miles an hour.[2]

In an editorial that followed, the two editors accepted the challenge and the proposal swiftly took on the dimensions of a media event that lacked only the commentary of Dan Rather or Roger Mudd to be fully predictive of our times; Geraldo Rivera would not have been welcome. Hundreds of letters poured in to the offices of the *Post,* as well as to Douglas's chambers in the Supreme Court Building. Everyone, it seemed, wanted to take a hike with the justice. In the end, Douglas and the *Post* staff narrowed the number of participants down to a little over two dozen, which, as the justice noted, made it somewhat larger than the Lewis and Clark Expedition.

On Saturday, March 19, the hikers set off from Cumberland, with Douglas firmly in the lead, where he would remain for the entire trip, setting a pace that gave the twitches and the clammydamps to younger men and inspiring a stanza of his own in the official hymn of the expedition, "The C & O Canal Song":

> The duffers climbed aboard the trucks
>   With many a groan and sigh,
> But something faster passed them up—
>   The Judge was whizzing by.[3]

Most of those who made the trek did so as did most of the hikers in Martin Luther King's march to Selma a decade later—people came and went, joining the hike for a while, then retiring from the path. But not Douglas. Day after day for the next nine days, he led a pack of nine regulars in a brisk—some might even say, killing—pace. At both the beginning and the end of the trip, all three television networks did national stories on the event, as did all the radio networks. A reporter and a photographer for *Life* magazine joined the group. *Time* magazine sent a reporter. So did the Associated Press. Two newsreel accounts were sent to more than three thousand movie theaters across the nation. At the end of the trip, Interior Secretary Douglas McKay—a former car salesman and no fuzzy-haired preservationist—met and shook hands with the triumphant Douglas, promising to take under consideration any suggestions the justice and his marchers might have to make.

As it happened, they had many suggestions, and on March 31 the C & O Canal Committee, William O. Douglas, chairman, sent the Secretary a letter whose several points could be summed up in a single demand: keep the road out of the canal corridor and put the corridor under the protection of the National Park System. McKay's reply was just short of capitulation: "I was delighted to find that the suggestions presented by your committee so closely parallel those of this Department in so many particulars. Indeed, it appears that there is complete agreement on the major objectives to be achieved."[4]

At least the agreement was close enough, and the Canal Committee did its followup work so assiduously that on April 4, 1956, Douglas could write Harvey Broome of The Wilderness Society with uncharacteristic restraint that they had won: "A short while ago Secretary of the Interior McKay wrote me that he and National Park Service officials had decided not to build a highway on the old canal, and would seek legislation to make the canal property a National Historic Park. This was very good news."[5] So it was, and it got even better in 1961, when the canal corridor was finally and officially dedicated as a National Historic Park.

Even before that happy conclusion, Douglas was busily organizing yet another march, this one on the other side of the continent in Washington State. Once again, it was a highway he found offensive. This time, however, it was the wilderness character of an already established national park he was trying to protect — specifically, the Pacific Ocean strip of Olympic National Park that stretched twenty-five miles north from the little Indian village of LaPush to Ozette Lake. He began his agitation in fall 1956, first with a letter-writing campaign in which he described the strip as "the one remaining piece of thoroughly primitive beach on the whole coastline of the United States. . . . It is wild, raw, and beautiful." However, he said, local interests wanted a highway and had some Park Service people aligned with them. "Those in the Park Service that are against it," he wrote in an observation that has a chillingly familiar ring, "are keeping their mouths shut. So it looks as though the highway proposers in that part of the country are getting the green light."[6]

That situation did not last long. Once again, he organized a hike, this one in August 1958. Once again, there were newspaper reporters and television cameras and radio microphones in attendance. Once again, the sixty-year-old justice of the United States Supreme Court led the way with his stubborn steady stride, stringing hikers out behind him like ducklings swimming in the wake of their mother. Once again, at the end of the three-day hike, a committee was formed — the Olympic National Park Pacific Ocean Committee. Once again, Douglas was its chair. And once again, the sand kicked up in the face of the Interior Department in Washington, D.C., by a William O. Douglas committee caused bureaucrats to change their minds. The highway was never built, and today you can walk the unearthly beauty of that smooth-sanded, rock-ribbed, and mist-enclouded coast without having the ancient muttering of the ocean's waves or the peevish squawks of gulls be corrupted by the flatulence of internal combustion engines.

We owe William O. Douglas for that — and for the C & O Canal, and for a good part of most of the depressingly few conservation victories we have enjoyed since World War II. He was a public man who used his public influence and performed public acts to protect the public interest. Whom do we have today?

This year, we celebrate the twenty-fifth anniversary of the signing of the Wilderness Act of 1964, an act to the passage of which Douglas gave every ounce of his own energy and elicited the energy of countless others. Since then, more than ninety million acres have been added to the National Wilderness Preservation System — rings of safety that preserve us from the quantums of greed, shortsightedness, and unfettered technology. That is something to be proud of, but not to rest upon. As Douglas would be the first to point out, we are only halfway toward the preservation of everything that should be preserved.

The conservation community to which Douglas gave his heart and mind and feet has a long road ahead. We have to hike it without him now, and that is the hard part. The easy part — if there is an easy part — is that he has shown the way, and his antic spirit still illuminates the path.

Notes

1. Quoted in Stephen Fox, "We Want No Straddlers," *Wilderness* 48 (Winter 1984): 5–19.

2. Quoted in Jack Durham, "The C & O Canal Hike," *The Living Wilderness* 19 (Spring 1954): pp. 1–26.

3. Ibid., p. 7.

4. Quoted in ibid., pp. 22–23.

5. William O. Douglas to Harvey Broome, Apr. 4, 1956. Container 312, William O. Douglas Papers, Manuscript Division, Library of Congress, Washington, D.C.

6. William O. Douglas to Dr. Lorin W. Roberts, Sept. 28, 1956.

PART FIVE

Douglas as Internationalist

INTRODUCTION:
DOUGLAS AS INTERNATIONALIST

Thomas M. Franck

WILLIAM O. DOUGLAS'S weltanschauung, like his views on the environment, were basically monist and optimistic. He visualized the world as one, not only because its problems, for the most part, could only be dealt with globally, but because he believed in the fundamental, transcendent decency of all people in all nations. This made him a sort of twentieth-century John Stuart Mill, demanding unalloyed freedoms for all: freedom from external intervention by the big powers against the small and freedom for all to exercise autonomous self-determination. He believed people everywhere, regardless of station or education, were inherently capable of handling the responsibilities of freedom.

These absolutist libertarian views present conceptual problems today, as they did in J. S. Mill's time. For example, Mill's and Douglas's concept of nonintervention was attacked at its weakest point by President Godfrey Binaissa speaking at the U.N. General Assembly in 1979, shortly after the overthrow of the regime of Idi Amin. "Our people naturally looked to the United Nations for solidarity and support in their struggle against the fascist dictatorship," he told the delegates. "For eight years they cried out in the wilderness for help; unfortunately, their cries seem to have fallen on deaf ears," while Amin and his gang "continued with impunity to commit genocide against our people." Why did no one intervene, he demanded, replying sarcastically that "somehow, it is thought to be in bad taste."

The vast majority of the U.N. members have also lined up in opposition to Vietnam's intervention in Kampuchea, despite the acknowledged fact that this probably saved the remnants of the population of that nation from further decimation by the Pol Pot regime, which had already eliminated some two million of its citizens.

Are these not good examples of the need for intervention?

These "hard cases," Douglas might have argued, make bad law. Most interventions are not benevolent and do not aim so much at humanitarian rescue as at imperial expansion. But how important is motive? Presumably, having opposed the U.S. intervention in Vietnam, Douglas also would have been against the U.S. invasion of Grenada. Yet, even assuming the United States was acting with imperial, more than with humanitarian, intent, few would doubt that the Hudson Austin regime, which American forces over-threw, had begun to look and act much like the Idi Amin gang, or that Grenada is better off as a result of the U.S. action.

Insistance on an absolute principle has the merit of seeming to imbue that principle with justice. It has the disadvantage of inviting *reductio ad absurdum*. One may assume that Douglas would have opposed recent U.S. use of the Contras to intervene in Sandinista-ruled Nicaragua. But would he also have opposed Cuban, Venezuelan, and Costa Rican military and logistic support for the Sandinistas at the time they were seeking to overthrow the Samoza dictatorship?

It is not easy to accept J. S. Mill's purist view that intervention is always immoral. Perhaps Douglas did, but I think not. His was a result-oriented jurisprudence. I suspect he had some sympathy for what, in its current rein-carnation, is known as the Reagan Doctrine. This argues for intervention in support of good insurgents fighting evil regimes and also on the side of good regimes fighting evil insurgents, but against intervention on the side of repressive forces, whether governments or insurgents. Such a rule, like the just-war doctrines of yore, is far from being an absolute prohibition on intervention, but it makes a strong moral appeal. Its problem is in fitting the facts of an actual case to the theoretical categories. To this, Douglas may simply have responded that, after his decades on the bench, he could tell the black hats from the white. But, then, President Reagan thought so, too, when he compared the Contras to our founding fathers.

So one is damned if one is an absolutist and damned if one isn't.

Only J. S. Mill rejected all intervention. He believed that a nation's character and fiber could only be built by fighting its own domestic battle for freedom, and doing so without outside meddling. I am not sure that Douglas could have shared that austere, puritanical view. The experience of a world standing aside as Adolph Hitler began his genocide against the Jews of Germany altered perceptions and set in train a global move to legislate fundamental human rights. These are supposed to intervene to protect the citizens against his or her own government.

Multilateralism may well hold the key to the conundrum posed by absolutism and relativism in respect of intervention. In the world that shaped Douglas's views, unilateral intervention, often of a peculiarly self-serving kind, was going on all the time, and little good came of it. It was this actuality, rather than a theoretical conundrum, that shaped Douglas's views. As the world moves toward higher, more clearly enunciated principles of human rights, and as these are increasingly interpreted not by states but by multi-lateral fact-finding institutions, Douglas, had he lived, might well have become a champion of such intervention.

There is one further factor to be taken into account in assessing the validity and relevance of Douglas's views on nonintervention in the last decade of the twentieth century. In the 1960s, dictatorships were everywhere riding a historic tide. Well-meaning observers, writing from the comfort of established ivory towers, even applauded the "mobilizational systems" of such totalitarians as Stalin, Nkrumah, Toure, Soekarno, and Mao. Today, however, the tide is running in the opposite direction. In such a global context, the only valid reason for intervention—Binaissa's reason—scarcely arises. Democratic values are becoming global values, and the need for military intervention by states seems far less in an era when student demonstrations in China and workers' collective actions in Poland are the engine of antitotalitarian reform. This would make Douglas happy, for now—perhaps more than then—he would be right in his monist assumption that nations have a right, even as do persons, to be let alone.

Douglas the Internationalist: Separation of Powers and the Conduct of Foreign Relations

Michael J. Glennon

WILLIAM O. DOUGLAS served as Associate Justice of the United States Supreme Court through some of the most momentous foreign policy crises that this nation has faced: World War II, the Korean War, the Cold War, and the Vietnam War. The opinions that he wrote in connection with these crises addressed nerve-center constitutional issues concerning the power to make war, to make national commitments, to recognize new governments, to conscript military manpower. I propose in these few pages to restrict my remarks to that set of opinions that Douglas wrote dealing with one recurring issue: the allocation of constitutional power among the executive, legislative, and judicial branches in matters touching upon the nation's foreign relations.[1]

It has become fashionable in some academic circles to critique Douglas opinions as coming to the right conclusions for the wrong reasons. Whatever the merits of these attacks, I don't propose to join in this enterprise. Rather, I intend to take Douglas on his own terms, or at least what I suppose to be his own terms, and to look at Douglas the person, and at the concatenation of his thoughts, his prejudices, his contradictions—to trace how Douglas's attitudinal patterns are reflected in his opinions in general and, in particular, to examine his evolving ambivalence toward presidential foreign affairs power—an ambivalence that faded as his distrust of the presidency grew.[2]

In writing about some jurists, this approach would represent a daunting endeavor, for many judges consider it somehow unbecoming to express opinions "off the bench" (at least on matters other than their impossibly heavy caseload). With respect to Douglas, on the other hand, the task is difficult for the opposite reason: his extracurricular writings are voluminous, amounting to some thirty-one books, including two autobiographical volumes that are blunt, ingenuous, and outspoken and provide more than ample evidence as to where he stood.[3] Other judges might, in addition, find such an undertaking an insult, believing, or pretending to believe, that beliefs expressed in out-of-court utterances have no bearing on how they decide cases.

Douglas operated under no such illusion. He related a statement that Chief Justice Hughes made to him shortly after his appointment to the

Court, a statement, he said, that he found "shattering" at the time but which "over the years turned out to be true."[4] Hughes's statement was this: "Justice Douglas, you must remember one thing. At the constitutional level where we work, ninety percent of any decision is emotional. The rational part of us supplies the reasons for supporting our predilections."[5] I take with a grain of salt Douglas's suggestion that he was "shattered" by that revelation, for Douglas was, of course, a Legal Realist.[6] While he served on the Columbia law faculty, his friends included many of the founders of the Legal Realism movement: Underhill Moore, Herman Oliphant, Hessel Yntema, Karl Llewellyn, Julius Goebel, and Walter Wheeler Cook. Their aim, Douglas wrote, was "to learn what the law should be, by learning the problems with which it must deal."[7] After moving to Yale, he continued, with other leading Realists, "trying to do what we were unable to do at Columbia—make the law more relevant to life."[8] He admired the first "Brandeis brief"—an amicus brief submitted by Brandeis to the Supreme Court in 1908 that "contained not a single citation of legal precedent, only citations to social and economic treatises."[9] So I expect that Douglas would make no apologies for allowing his policy predilections to influence his judicial decisions; indeed, he might well ask, with many contemporary scholars, how it could possibly be otherwise.

To an extent, all this provides an answer to those who enjoy savaging his opinions. Perhaps Douglas simply did not believe that it was worth the time to load down his opinions with burnished prose and convoluted footnotes. Precedents can be sidestepped, he knew; "the facts of a case are the essentials."[10] Complicated, overwrought opinions are not immunized from history's trash bin; they merely take a little longer to distinguish from the simple ones he favored. As Professor G. Edward White has put it, Douglas was "thus not constrained either by the function of his office or by doctrinal principles; he was constrained only by the rightness or wrongness of his political philosophy."[11]

For these reasons, Douglas the person is my starting point. He has, as I say, left us with a rich literature from which his unvarnished views can be mined.

I

Like many admirers of FDR, Douglas began with a sense of confidence in executive diplomacy but came in his later years to develop a profound distrust toward it. This growing ambivalence toward presidential foreign affairs power was fed, on the one hand, by Douglas's abiding distrust of unchecked power in any form, and, on the other, by his adulation of Franklin D. Roosevelt, perhaps the most powerful president of the twentieth century, and of course, the president who appointed Douglas to the Court.

"My view of the conduct of foreign affairs," Douglas wrote, "is that the

Constitution provides that it is Congress which has the power to declare war and that all diplomacy, short of that, is under the guidance of the President."[12] Douglas's constitutional philosophy thus closely correlated with his policy views: he had seen — indeed, participated in — enlightened presidential initiatives during the New Deal. "I saw FDR frequently at night," he wrote, adding that Roosevelt liked his martini-making. "After dinner we would often see a movie, usually alone, sometimes with others."[13] They played poker together.[14] Douglas helped write FDR speeches,[15] and FDR "used me as a sounding board."[16] Roosevelt even asked Douglas to join the White House staff during the summer of 1942 — while remaining on the Court![17] Douglas, later suspicious of friends of the management, was therefore at the outset of his career one of the most intimate friends of the management.

Yet Douglas, over time, watched the integrity of the presidency gradually decline to the point where, he wrote during the Nixon administration, it had become "a huge public relations forum, operating with Madison Avenue techniques. Nixon did not create that attitude; he merely exploited it."[18] Douglas over this period became increasingly suspicious of government: "I, as one of its targets, can say that the power of the federal government leveled against the lone individual is ominous and forbidding."[19] He believed that, during the 1960s, justices' telephones as well as the Court's conference room were bugged.[20] "Government has been recurringly lawless" in a number of respects, he wrote; "lying and deception have grown as practices of government officials — practices that do more to undermine us than the 'subversion' against which we have long inveighed."[21] Not surprisingly, Douglas's distrust focused frequently upon the agencies of the executive branch engaged in the conduct of foreign affairs. After the passing of Roosevelt, he believed, American policy makers had taken the wrong path:

America, in its actions, became more "imperialistic" than the British at their worst. . . . The slogans of American imperialism made good politics at home, and we were soon saturated with fears of communism. The Cold War made anti-communism an easy program to follow blindly. The blueprint drawn in the fifties became the inspiration for disastrous overseas operations in the 1960s and 1970s.

America became quickly regimented and we lost our perspective in world affairs. By the 1960s and 1970s we were "policing" the world; we had become the great moralists, using our Army and Navy and Air Force to let the people of the world know the kind of government we thought they *should not* have.[22]

Douglas thus distrusted the military. "An armament program leads irresistibly to war," he wrote:

The reasons are partly subconscious perhaps. In any event the pressures mount to use newly acquired weapons and manpower. The military are bent on flexing their muscles; a theatre of war is a place where promotions come fast.

The presence of a big whopping military establishment puts immeasurable pressures on Presidents, senators, congressmen, Cabinet officers. They begin to think more and more in military terms. The mass media are attracted to shining armor, like flies to honey. In time the nation is saturated with military news, military hopes, military thinking.[23]

Douglas also distrusted the Central Intelligence Agency. "What," he asked, "does the individual do to resist the corrupting influence of the CIA or to combat the all-powerful military-industrial complex that now commands our lives?"[24] He thought that the CIA had paid off members of the Saigon government and had organized and financed riots in the streets of Saigon.[25]

Nor did Douglas believe that the press could be counted upon to protect democratic institutions: "The American press . . . is by and large a mimic, not an original research group. It prints handouts from government and from industry and expresses its opinions on those items. But the basic facts are seldom mined; the press does not have the initiative or the zeal to ferret out the original from the false or pretended."[26] In fact, Douglas viewed the press as a principal culprit as the United States inched into the quicksand of Vietnam. He wrote: "Three American newspapers — the New York *Times,* the Washington *Post,* and the San Francisco *Chronicle* — prepared the American people for military intervention in Vietnam. . . . They dutifully reflected the official line."[27]

So Douglas concluded that Americans faced with injustice might easily find themselves, legally, with nowhere to turn. "Citizens are often caught in a pot of glue and are utterly helpless when it comes to obtaining relief from an injustice."[28]

His solution? An active and vigilant judiciary: "My view always has been that anyone whose life, liberty or property was threatened or impaired by any branch of government . . . had a justiciable controversy and could properly repair to a judicial tribunal for vindication of his rights."[29] Judges tended to be less beholden to the powerful — particularly, Douglas thought, those appointed by FDR. Douglas admired Roosevelt for naming "offbeat" individuals to appellate courts, judges "who would make the established order wince. . . . 'Let's find someone who will upset the fat cats,'"[30] Douglas quotes Roosevelt as telling him. An independent judiciary, Douglas believed, was in the end America's best hope of preserving a free government under the Constitution. This is the thread that runs throughout his foreign affairs/separation-of-powers opinions.

Douglas also believed in international institutions as a means of promoting justice. One proposal on which he collaborated closely with FDR was the creation of the United Nations. The two talked "many times"[31] about a strategy for selling it to the American people and discussed "the errors made by Woodrow Wilson regarding the League of Nations which I as a youth had fervently supported."[32] Responding later to criticisms of the UN, Douglas wrote that "whatever its shortcomings, it was a step toward a Rule of Law — man's only hope for escape from total annihilation."[33]

Yet Douglas did not consider international institutions a panacea, recognizing that they could operate unfairly. He condemned the Nuremberg trials, for example, in the belief that the international ban on aggressive war lacked precision and clarity (rendering the action ex post facto) and represented a kind of victor's justice—providing an incentive to strike first.[34]

Our initial question, therefore, is this: how does an internationalist with incipient misgivings about the use of presidential power—and who at the same time is a poker-playing, speech-writing, martini-mixing crony of the most powerful president in modern American history—resolve disputes concerning uses of that power in the international arena? The judicial opinions of William O. Douglas provide a case study.

II

UNITED STATES V. PINK

Douglas wrote his first major foreign relations opinion during his third year on the Court, 1942. *United States v. Pink*[35] was not a case, however, in which Douglas or the Court had a great deal of latitude, for many of the same issues had been ventilated before the Court five years earlier in *United States v. Belmont.*[36] Each case involved the validity of an executive agreement (the so-called Litvinov Assignment) made by Roosevelt with the Soviet Union upon the recognition of its government by the United States in 1933. In *Pink,* New York state courts dismissed an action by the United States to recover certain assets assigned to it under the agreement, claiming that the assignment was contrary to the public policy of the state. The Court, per Douglas, reversed, holding that the president is possessed of the sole power under the Constitution to determine which governments shall be recognized, and that the "power to remove such obstacles to full recognition . . . certainly is a modest implied power of the President who is the 'sole organ of the federal government in the field of international relations.'"[37]

Pink does not make the president omnipotent in the conduct of foreign affairs. For one thing, Congress was silent; the dispute in *Pink* was between the president and a state. The issue, therefore, was one of federalism, not separation of powers. The opinion does not intimate that the president has independent power to enter into any executive agreement he wishes, or that treaties and "sole" executive agreements are constitutionally interchangeable instruments. Indeed, Douglas does not hold that the settlement of foreign claims is itself an independent presidential power; rather, it is a power exercised by the president *incidental to* the exercise of an independent presidential power—the power of recognition.

Nonetheless, the theory of "incidental implied power" on which the finding of validity rests is not without problems, at least for someone with Douglas's concerns about the arbitrary use of power. What, precisely, are the limits to what the president can do "incidental to" the exercise of his recognition power? Could the president, for example, have jailed representatives of the

Taiwan government as an act "incidental to" his recognition of the People's Republic of China? Could he have paid unauthorized funds from the treasury to the PRC in settling PRC claims against the United States? And what of *other* independent presidential powers; can the president, when acting under his independent power, say, to negotiate a treaty, order the covert assassination of "hard liners" on the other side's negotiating team? Can he, as "incidental to" the negotiating function, expropriate a private aircraft to transport urgently needed documents?

Yet we ought not overstate the theory's defects. This hypothetical parade of horribles has no counterpart in real abuse, and Douglas's "incidental" power theory is a lot safer than the "package deal" rationale set out in Sutherland's opinion in *Belmont,* which upheld the Litvinov Assignment because it and the act of recognition "were all parts of one transaction, resulting in an international compact between the two governments."[38] (All of my hypotheticals are also part of one transaction that includes a presidential act falling within his independent powers.) Douglas, to his credit, moved the Court away from that dubious approach. Finally, Douglas's theory did not unsettle a justice with similar values, William Brennan, who relied upon it in the only opinion in *Goldwater v. Carter*[39] to reach the merits of the challenge to President Carter's termination of the mutual security treaty with the Republic of China. Termination of the treaty, Brennan wrote, "was a necessary incident to Executive recognition of the Peking Government, because the defense treaty was predicated upon the now-abandoned view that the Taiwan Government was the only legitimate political authority in China."[40] Brennan cited *Pink* but not *Belmont* as authority for this proposition, suggesting that he too found Douglas's approach more prudent.

KOREMATSU AND ENDO

The next major foreign affairs opinion Douglas wrote was not published. It was not published because he did not file it, and that he did not file, he later wrote, was "one of my mistakes."[41] The case was *Korematsu v. United States,*[42] the infamous Japanese-American detention case. Douglas did not file the concurrence because my "Brethren, especially Black and Frankfurter, urged me strongly not to publish."[43] The unpublished concurrence would have agreed "to the evacuation but not to evacuation *via* the concentration camps."[44] Because of the Court's approval, "grave injustices" were committed; "fine American citizens had been robbed of their property by racists — crimes that might not have happened if the Court had not followed the Pentagon so literally."[45] The Pentagon, he wrote, "advised us on oral argument that the Japanese army could take everything west of the Rockies if they chose to land."[46] Douglas, of course, did not live to see it, but it later came to light that the military had grossly misrepresented the nature of the threat, and Fred Korematsu's conviction was vacated on the grounds of governmental misconduct.[47]

The same day that *Korematsu* came down, the Court decided another case, with the majority opinion written this time by Douglas. The case was *Ex Parte Endo*.[48] It was not an opinion that turned upon the Constitution; rather, the Court construed the meaning of an executive order, holding that the applicable order[49] did not authorize the detention of a person absent evidence of disloyalty. *Endo* sets the tone that we came to expect in Douglas opinions; set against *Korematsu,* it veritably rings with concern for individual dignity and governmental integrity: "Loyalty is a matter of the heart and mind, not of race, creed, or color. He who is loyal is by definition not a spy or a saboteur. When the power to detain is derived from the power to protect the war effort against espionage and sabotage, detention which has no relationship to that objective is unauthorized." Douglas concluded, "We cannot assume that the Congress and the President intended that . . . discriminatory action should be taken against these people wholly on account of their ancestry even though the government conceded their loyalty to this country."[50]

Why did Douglas go along with the Court's seemingly very different approach in *Korematsu?* I see no reason to doubt Douglas's own explanation—that he simply "bowed to his elders" on the Court.[51] Douglas had been on the Court for only five years, and he had not yet split with Frankfurter on the incorporation controversy, the issue of judicial restraint, or other questions that would later divide them. Prior to his appointment to the Court, Frankfurter was of course a renowned civil libertarian; Douglas perhaps felt comforted that Frankfurter was not overtly disturbed by *Korematsu.* Yet it is curious that nowhere does Douglas ask whether his own close friendship with President Roosevelt had any bearing on his willingness to accord such deference, unusual at least by Douglas's evolving standards, to the administration's assertions concerning national security. Eight years later, when the Steel Seizure Case[52] came before the Court, Douglas was unimpressed by the executive's arguments. Douglas did not play poker with Harry Truman.[53]

STEEL SEIZURE

Truman "was a man of lesser stature than FDR,"[54] Douglas wrote, "not an idea man,"[55] who "seemed to like picking mediocre men"[56] and who had "an abysmal ignorance of what actually went on in the world."[57]

One alarm that Hugo Black and I felt was the manner in which Truman militarized the nation. Military men were everywhere; the White House thought largely in military terms when foreign affairs were up for discussion. The Truman Doctrine, announced in 1947, resulted in our sending a military mission to Greece to help that country against Communist guerrillas. I was in Greece at the time and saw what was happening and why that military mission served a real need. But the Truman Doctrine developed inexorably into a program of American military intervention, first in Korea, then in Vietnam and then the Dominican Republic. Truman had nothing to do with any but the Greek and Korean adventures, but he greatly conditioned the American mind to think in terms of military solutions to problems of Communism.[58]

It should hardly be surprising, therefore, that Douglas had no compunction about the Court's boxing Truman's ears when the president seized the steel mills in 1952. A nationwide strike had broken out in the steel industry. According to the *Youngstown* Court, "The indispensability of steel as a component of substantially all weapons and other war materials led the President to believe that the proposed work stoppage would immediately jeopardize our national defense and that governmental seizure of the steel mills was necessary in order to assure the continued availability of steel."[59]

Truman consequently issued an executive order directing the Secretary of Commerce to take possession of most of the mills and keep them running, arguing that the president had "inherent power" to do so. The companies objected, complaining in court that the seizure was not authorized by the Constitution or by any statute.

Congress had not statutorily authorized the seizure, either before or after it occurred. Congress had, however, enacted three statutes providing for governmental seizure of the mills in certain specifically prescribed situations, but the administration never claimed that any of those conditions had existed prior to its action. More important, Congress had in fact considered, and rejected, authorization for the sort of seizure Truman actually ordered.[60]

The Steel Seizure Case is remembered mostly for the concurring opinion of Justice Robert Jackson, hypothesizing three tiers of presidential power.[61] But Justice Hugo Black delivered the opinion of the Court. The president, Black wrote, had engaged in lawmaking, a task assigned by the Constitution to Congress.[62] The seizure was therefore unlawful, since the "President's power, if any, to issue the order must stem either from an act of Congress or from the Constitution itself."[63] Notwithstanding the elegant simplicity of Black's opinion, it has not withstood the test of time; this seems not to be the first instance in which a president did something that Congress might also have done.[64] Douglas's concurrence "squares with the theory of checks and balances espoused by"[65] Black in that it too views as dispositive the legislative character of the power exercised by the president in seizing the mills. Unlike Black's opinion, however, Douglas's concurrence is not conclusory; it presents a tightly reasoned syllogism explaining precisely why this particular power is not concurrent but, rather, is exclusively legislative:

- the seizure of the plants represented a taking;
- a taking requires just compensation;
- just compensation necessitates the raising of revenue; and
- the raising of revenue requires congressional action.

In addition to supplying a reasoned basis to accept Black's conclusion, Douglas proceeded to make two points that are as important today as they are timely. First, Douglas rejected the notion of prophylactic, "emergency" executive power — presidential power that fluctuates in breadth and expands to meet crises. "The emergency did not create power," he wrote; "it merely marked an occasion when power should be exercised. And the fact that it was necessary that measures be taken . . . does not mean that the President, rather than the Congress, had the constitutional power to act." In some nations, such power is entrusted to the executive; "we chose another course."[66]

Second, Douglas acknowledged that "we pay a price for this system"[67] of divided power. "The President . . . can move with force as well as with speed, [whereas] legislative action may . . . often be cumbersome, time-consuming, and apparently inefficient."[68] He quoted Brandeis: "The doctrine of separation of powers was adopted by the Convention of 1787, not to promote efficiency but to preclude the exercise of arbitrary power. The purpose was, not to avoid friction, but, by means of the inevitable friction incident to the distribution of governmental powers among three departments, to save the people from autocracy."[69] Douglas thus concludes that it is the Constitution, and not contemporary notions of efficiency, that must govern presidential conduct. It is a lesson too often lost in current-day Washington.

If Douglas retained a measure of respect for Harry S. Truman, he had none for Richard Nixon. Truman "stood up against McCarthy";[70] Nixon, in contrast, "eagerly promoted"[71] what Truman termed "the thought control business" represented by the Subversive Activities Control Act of 1950, which Truman vetoed. Douglas said he first met Nixon when Nixon was a law student at Duke University: "I had gone there to give a lecture to the law school. I talked about predatory practices in finance. . . . Some years later Nixon told me that I had been an inspiration to him, that my lecture had affected his life. I did not ask in what way, for the uneasy thought crossed my mind that predatory practices had inspired him."[72] Nixon had mastered the "art of deceit."[73] "His legislative record was said to be conservative, but, in fact, it was rather unprincipled in that it was so rubbery as to suggest an indifference to policy."[74] Nixon was "amoral. . . . Deceit, simulations, telling lies marked the character of the man. . . . The appetite of his ego was devastating. Nothing could stand in his way."[75] During the Nixon administration, "great issues of war and peace were decided through the manipulation of public opinion polls, through falsification of the issues, through the spreading of lies by the President."[76]

VIETNAM AND STANDING

Douglas's above reference, of course, was to the Vietnam War. At least nineteen challenges to the war reached the Supreme Court, but in none did the Court grant certiorari.[77] Douglas "thought the Court did a great disservice to the nation in not resolving this, the most important issue of the sixties to reach the Court."[78] He thus repeatedly dissented.

In *Mitchell v. United States*,[79] the defendant declined to report for induction into the armed forces and was prosecuted and convicted. His defense was that the war was a war of aggression. The Supreme Court denied his petition for certiorari. Douglas, dissenting, "intimate[d] no opinion on the merits,"[80] but, citing the 1945 Treaty of London[81] and a statement made by Justice Jackson while prosecuting at Nuremberg,[82] went on to write that it was an "extremely sensitive and delicate question" whether "the Treaty may be tendered as a defense in this criminal case or in amelioration of the punishment."[83] Douglas also believed that the Court should have taken up, *inter alia,* the questions whether the issue was justiciable, whether the defendant had standing to raise the question, and whether "the Vietnam episode is a 'war' in the sense of the Treaty."[84]

In *Mora v. McNamara,*[85] servicemen ordered to Vietnam sued for a declaratory judgment that United States military activity in Vietnam was "illegal." The Court again denied cert. This time, Douglas, in dissent, picked up the vote of Justice Potter Stewart. Douglas again insisted that he intimated no views on the merits of defendants' claims.[86] But he agreed with Stewart that the case presented "large and troubling questions"[87] that the Court ought to decide, among them—in addition to those detailed in *Mitchell*—whether it was constitutional to order defendants into combat in the absence of a declaration of war; whether United States treaty obligations were relevant; and whether the Gulf of Tonkin Resolution was relevant and, if so, whether it breached the delegation doctrine.[88]

His dissents in these and other cases reveal Douglas's growing reluctance to defer to the judgment of the executive in foreign relations matters and further spell out his vision of the judiciary's role as independent arbiter in resolving such disputes. In *First National City Bank v. Banco Nacional de Cuba,*[89] for example, Douglas (along with five other justices) rejected the so-called "Bernstein exception," under which the Court could not apply the act-of-state doctrine when the executive branch expressly represents to the Court that its application would not advance the foreign policy interests of the United States. Under the Bernstein exception, Douglas wrote, "the Court becomes a mere errand boy for the Executive Branch which may choose to pick some people's chestnuts from the fire, but not others."[90] He—properly, I think[91]—gave short shrift to the argument that such disputes are nonjusticiable. If the Steel Seizure Case was justiciable, he wrote, and Truman was constitutionally unable to seize property in violation of the Constitution, "I do not see how any President can take 'life' in violation of the Constitution."[92] The circuits, he pointed out, were in conflict, and the questions presented were not trivial: "Families and careers are disrupted; young men maimed and disfigured; lives lost. The issues are large; they are precisely framed; we should decide them."[93]

Douglas's final opinions on separation of powers cases involving foreign affairs and national security matters were written as the doors of the Supreme Court continued slowly and gradually to close to foreign policy disputes. The Court appended various labels to its abstention: political question, standing, ripeness. But the result was the same: as constitutional controversy raged and the American national security state emerged, the final arbiter of the meaning of the Constitution, the branch of our government whose task it is to say "what the law is,"[94] became, over Douglas's strenuous objections, a bystander.

Laird v. Tatum,[95] for example, arose following disclosures in 1970 that for five years the army had been surveilling lawful civil rights and antiwar activities of civilians and helping to compile a Pentagon index (available to several hundred government officials) of the names of 25 million participants and groups such as the American Civil Liberties Union, Southern Christian Leadership Conference, and the National Association for the Advancement of Colored People. Several persons on the list brought an action charging that the existence of the index chilled the exercise of their rights to free expression and privacy. The Court dismissed the action on the theory that they lacked standing: they could show no direct injury, and they did not contend that any of their activities had actually *been* "chilled."

The claim that the plaintiffs lacked standing, Douglas wrote in dissent, "is too transparent for serious argument."[96] The question was whether the Army surveillance "exercises a *present inhibiting effect* on [plaintiffs'] full expression and utilization of their First Amendment rights."[97] He continued: "One need not wait to sue until he loses his job or until his reputation is defamed. To withhold standing to sue until that time arrives would in practical effect immunize from judicial scrutiny all surveillance activities, regardless of their misuse or deterrent effect."[98]

"This case," Douglas concluded, "involves a cancer in our body politic. When an intelligence officer looks over every nonconformist's shoulder in the library, or walks invisibly by his side in a picket line, or infiltrates his club, the America once extolled as the voice of liberty heard around the world no longer is cast in the image which Jefferson and Madison designed, but more in the Russian image."[99]

Schlesinger v. Reservists Committee to Stop the War[100] involved an action seeking a declaratory judgment that simultaneous service in Congress and in the military reserves violated the Constitution's Incompatibility Clause.[101] At the time of the challenge in 1974, some 117 senators and representatives held reserve commissions. The Court dismissed the action, again, for lack of standing: the complaint was a "generalized grievance"[102] and plaintiffs suffered no injury distinct from that of the general public. They thus lacked a "personal stake" in the outcome.

Although Douglas tried to bring the case within the ambit of standing requirements, his attack on the increasingly narrow doctrine of standing was more persuasive. "It protects the status quo," he wrote in dissent, "by reducing the challenges that may be made to it and its institutions." He continued: "It greatly restricts the classes of persons who may challenge administrative action. Its application in this case serves to make the bureaucracy of the Pentagon more and more immune from the protests of citizens."[103]

"The interest of citizens is obvious," he concluded. "Who other than citizens has a better right to have the Incompatibility Clause enforced?"[104] Their "'personal stake' in this case . . . is freeing the entanglement of the federal bureaucracy with the Legislative Branch,"[105] an interest every bit as personal as the right to vote — which, in *Baker v. Carr,*[106] was held to constitute a sufficiently "personal stake" for standing purposes. "All that the citizens seek in this case is to have the Constitution enforced as it is written."[107]

Finally, in *United States v. Richardson,*[108] a challenge was brought to enforce, as against the CIA, the constitutional requirement that "a regular Statement and Account of the receipts and expenditures of all public money shall be published from time to time."[109] The plaintiffs contended that public reports of the Treasury Department contained no accounting of receipts and expenditures of the CIA. Predictably, the Court decided the case on standing grounds: the plaintiff had none, it said, because his challenge was not directed at a violation of the taxing and spending power.

Douglas, as before, dissented. Accepting the test applied by the Court, Douglas asked how a taxpayer can challenge the validity of expenditures under the taxing and spending power unless he knows how the money is being spent. The plaintiff has a sufficiently personal stake because "he only wants to know the amount of tax money exacted from him that goes into CIA activities."[110] He quoted pointed comments from the debates of the state ratifying conventions, indicating that "secrecy was the great evil at which Art. I, §9, cl. 7 was based."[111] The majority decision "relegates to secrecy vast operations of government and keeps the public from knowing what secret plans concerning this Nation or other nations are afoot."[112] The Court should recognize, Douglas warned, that an individual has a stake in the integrity of constitutional guarantees, rather "than turning him away without even a chance to be heard."[113]

These blunt arguments may appear out of the mainstream in the highly nuanced (and, I think, casuistic) debate over standing. But at least in foreign affairs matters, where governmental power is so great and the consequences of its abuse so treacherous, the Court does need to take a broader view, as Douglas urged. I have suggested elsewhere that we may have something to gain by examining how international law treats the issue; international law

distinguishes between obligations of nations toward each other and obligations towards the international community as a whole. Ordinarily, claims for violation of an international obligation may be made only by the state to whom the obligation is owed. Obligations towards the international community, on the other hand, are "by their very nature . . . the concern of all States. In view of the importance of the rights involved, all states can be said to have a legal interest in their protection; they are obligations *erga omnes.*"[114]

Similarly, all citizens can be said to have an interest in the government's obligations to society as a whole; when the breach of such an obligation is alleged, broader standing should be permitted. "The alternative is a complete absence of any legal remedy and continued, unchecked constitutional violation."[115] Where, as in many foreign affairs disputes, no one (under current doctrine) has standing to sue, and where the controversy concerns compliance with fundamental structural guarantees directed at ensuring governmental legitimacy, the Court should not insist on the same measure of concrete, personal, individuated injury that might otherwise be required.

In its results, this approach is not different from Douglas's. In a case such as *Richardson,* as the Court acknowledged, it is likely that *no* plaintiff will have standing to litigate the violation of the constitutional provision in question. And while it remains theoretically true, as the *Richardson* majority argues, that such a constitutional guarantee can be vindicated by political rather than judicial processes, the historical record is only too plain that that route can be ineffectual, just as it was in *Baker.*

<h1 style="text-align:center">III</h1>

Douglas's fitting description of Brandeis applies equally to himself. Douglas, too, "was not a philosopher. . . . [He] was a modern Isaiah. He was a mighty man of action who, having found the facts and determined the nature and contours of the problem, moved at once.[116] . . . [He] wanted to put the individual and the individual's privacy first, and to establish only the controls that would keep the individual from becoming regimented.[117] This line of thought ran through all of [his] opinions, through all his papers, through all his talk. [He] had spiritual links with Jefferson as he did with Isaiah, and he lived every day by the faith he acquired from them."[118]

Douglas, like Jefferson, had an abiding confidence in the ultimate reliability of democratic institutions. Douglas, like Isaiah, was willing to speak truth to power. But his hopes for this nation took shape in the cauldron of the New Deal White House, and a forward-looking and intelligent presidency, an institution of innovation and integrity, surely was central to those hopes.

So, in the end, his final, sad thought about Brandeis also is probably true of Douglas: "He would be saddened to death if he could see what has happened to his dream for this nation."[119]

<h2 style="text-align:center">Notes</h2>

I am grateful for the comments of my colleague, Professor Alan Brownstein, on an earlier draft of this chapter.

1. Foreign affairs cases that deal primarily with issues other than separation of powers, such as *Zschernig v. Miller,* 389 U.S. 429 (1968) (federalism); *New York Times v. United States,* 403 U.S. 713 (1971) (First Amendment–national security);

and *Kent v. Dulles,* 357 U.S. 116 (1958) (right to travel), are thus beyond the scope of this chapter.

2. For this reason, I resist the temptation to apply (or to invent) a label that would purport to summarize a comprehensive Douglas world view or to render coherent an often contradictory judicial philosophy. Perhaps at some point in his life he "put it all together," so to speak; perhaps he was, for example, a "liberal activist internationalist." But in response to any such label, one is compelled to ask *which* Douglas it describes—and why one particular snapshot of the man, frozen in time, should be taken as encapsulating the entire evolution of his thinking, on and off the bench.

3. These are William O. Douglas, *Go East, Young Man: The Autobiography of William O. Douglas* (New York: Random House, 1974); Douglas, *The Court Years, 1939–1975: The Autobiography of William O. Douglas* (New York: Random House, 1980).

4. Douglas, *The Court Years,* p. 8.

5. Ibid.

6. See Karl Llewellyn, "Some Realism About Realism—Responding to Dean Pound," *Harvard Law Review* 44 (1931): 1222, 1227.

7. Douglas, *Go East,* p. 160.

8. Ibid.

9. Ibid., p. 444.

10. Douglas, *The Court Years,* p. 180.

11. G. Edward White, "The Anti-Judge: William O. Douglas and the Ambiguities of Individuality," *Virginia Law Review* 74 (1988): 48.

12. Douglas, *The Court Years,* p. 270.

13. Ibid., p. 276.

14. Ibid., p. 245.

15. Ibid., p. 168.

16. Ibid., p. 273.

17. Ibid., p. 267. Douglas of course declined, but only after seeking the advice of Justices Roberts and Black, both of whom recommended against it.

18. Ibid., p. 353.

19. Ibid., p. 354. Douglas was referring to the efforts of President Richard Nixon. In one intriguing passage, Douglas contrasted his and Hugo Black's backgrounds with that of Louis Brandeis. "We two had been exposed to raw-boned experiences. Brandeis did not grow up with policemen shooting at him. Whether that happened in freight yards or in a ghetto, the experience leaves its mark on a man." Douglas, *Go East,* p. 449.

20. Douglas, *The Court Years,* p. 256.

21. Ibid., p. 446.

22. Douglas, *Go East,* pp. 402–03 (emphasis in original).

23. Douglas, *The Court Years,* p. 273.

24. Ibid., p. 148.

25. Ibid., p. 207.

26. Ibid., pp. 206–07.

27. Ibid., p. 207.

28. Ibid., p. 148.

29. Ibid., p. 55.

30. Ibid., p. 244.

31. Douglas, *Go East,* p. 401.

32. Ibid.

33. Douglas, *The Court Years,* p. 276.

34. Ibid., p. 29.

35. 315 U.S. 203 (1942).

36. 301 U.S. 324 (1937).

37. *United States v. Pink,* 315 U.S., at 229, quoting *United States v. Curtiss-Wright,* 299 U.S. 304, 320 (1936).

38. *United States v. Belmont,* 301 U.S., at 330.

39. 444 U.S. 996 (1979).

40. Ibid., at 1007 (Brennan, J., concurring).

41. Douglas, *The Court Years,* p. 39.

42. 323 U.S. 214 (1944).

43. Douglas, *The Court Years,* p. 280.

44. Ibid.

45. Ibid., p. 280.

46. Ibid., p. 279.

47. *Korematsu v. United States,* 584 F.Supp. 1406 (N.D.Cal. 1984).

48. *Korematsu v. United States,* 323 U.S., at 283 (1944).

49. Executive Order No. 9066.

50. *Ex Parte Endo,* 323 U.S. 283 (1944).

51. Douglas, *The Court Years,* p. 280.

52. *Youngstown Sheet & Tube Co. v. Sawyer,* 343 U.S. 579 (1952).

53. Unlike Franklin Roosevelt, whom every one tried to "do in" at the poker table, Truman had a "patronizing attitude" toward the others at the table, who would let him win. After Truman walked out of Douglas's house one night with $5,000 in winnings, Douglas "was so disgusted I never played another game of poker in my life." Douglas, *The Court Years,* p. 245.

54. Ibid., p. 290.

55. Ibid., p. 292.

56. Ibid., p. 248.

57. Ibid., p. 291.

58. Ibid., p. 292.

59. *Youngstown Sheet & Tube Co. v. Sawyer,* 343 U.S., at 583.

60. Justice Frankfurter described the consideration of those amendments at some length. See ibid., at 598–602 (Frankfurter, J., concurring).

61. Jackson wrote that "presidential powers are not fixed but fluctuate, depending upon their disjunction or conjunction with those of Congress." Ibid., at 635 (Jackson, J., concurring). "When the President acts pursuant to an express or implied authorization of Congress, his authority is at its maximum. . . . When the President acts in absence of either a congressional grant or denial of authority, he can only rely upon his own independent powers, but there is a zone of twilight in which he and Congress may have concurrent authority, or in which its distribution is uncertain. . . . When the President takes measures incompatible with the expressed or implied will of Congress, his power is at its lowest ebb." Ibid., at 635–38.

62. Ibid., at 587–89.

63. Ibid., at 585.

64. See Edward Corwin, *The Constitution and What It Means Today* (Princeton: N.J.: Princeton University Press, 1978), p. 198.

65. *Youngstown Sheet & Tube Co. v. Sawyer,* 343 U.S., at 631 (Douglas, J., concurring).

66. Ibid., at 629.

67. Ibid., at 633.

68. Ibid., at 629.

69. *Myers v. United States,* 272 U.S. 52, 293 (1926) (Brandeis, J., dissenting).

70. Douglas, *The Court Years,* p. 64.

71. Ibid.

72. Ibid., at 340.

73. Ibid., at 343.

74. Ibid., at 342.

75. Ibid., at 351.

76. Ibid., at 353.

77. Ibid., at 152.

78. Ibid.

79. 386 U.S. 972 (1967).

80. Ibid., at 974 (Douglas, J., dissenting).

81. The treaty provides: "The fact that the Defendant acted pursuant to order of his Government or of a superior shall not free him from responsibility, but may be considered in mitigation of punishment if the Tribunal determines that justice so requires." 59 Stat. 1544 (1945).

82. Jackson wrote, "If certain acts in violation of treaties are crimes, they are crimes whether the United States does them or whether Germany does them, and we are not prepared to lay down a rule of criminal conduct against others which we would not be willing to have invoked against us." U.S. Dept. of State, *International Conference on Military Trials,* Publication 3080 (Washington, D.C.: GPO, 1945), p. 330.

83. *Mitchell v. United States,* 386 U.S., at 973.

84. Ibid.

85. 389 U.S. 934 (1967).

86. Ibid., at 939 (Douglas, J., dissenting).

87. Ibid., at 935 (Stewart, J., dissenting).

88. Ibid., at 934–35.

89. 406 U.S. 759 (1972).

90. Ibid., at 773 (Douglas, J., concurring) (footnotes omitted).

91. See Michael J. Glennon, "Foreign Affairs and the Political Question Doctrine," *American Journal of International Law* 83 (1989): 814.

92. *Holtzman v. Schlesinger,* 414 U.S. 1316, 1318 (1973) (Douglas, J., on re-application to vacate stay).

93. *DaCosta v. Laird,* 405 U.S. 979, 981 (1972).

94. *Marbury v. Madison,* 5 U.S. 137 (1803).

95. 408 U.S. 1 (1972).

96. Ibid. (Douglas, J., dissenting).

97. Ibid., at 24 (emphasis in original).

98. Ibid., at 26. In fact, the employment opportunities of persons seeking sensitive federal positions were directly jeopardized, Douglas noted.

99. Ibid., at 28.

100. 418 U.S. 208 (1974).

101. U.S. Constitution, Art. I, §6, cl. 2, provides that "no person holding any office under the United States, shall be a Member of either House during his continuance in office."

102. *Schlesinger v. Reservists Committee,* 418 U.S., at 216.

103. Ibid., at 229 (Douglas, J., dissenting).

104. Ibid., at 234.

105. Ibid., at 232.

106. 369 U.S. 186 (1962).

107. *Schlesinger v. Reservists Committee,* 418 U.S., at 232.

108. 418 U.S. 166 (1974).

109. U.S. Constitution, Art. I, §9, cl. 7.

110. *United States v. Richardson,* 418 U.S., at 198 (Douglas, J., dissenting).

111. Ibid., at 199.

112. Ibid., at 201.

113. Ibid., at 202.

114. Michael J. Glennon, *Constitutional Diplomacy* (Princeton University Press, 1990), quoting *Case Concerning the Barcelona Traction, Light, and Power Co. (Belgium v. Spain)* [1970] I.C.J. Rep. 3, 32.

115. Ibid.

116. Douglas, *The Court Years,* p. 443.

117. Ibid., p. 448.

118. Ibid., pp. 448–49.

119. Ibid., p. 449.

Justice Douglas the Internationalist: The Connection Between Domestic Liberty and Foreign Policy

Jules Lobel

WILLIAM O. DOUGLAS is primarily remembered as a staunch defender of civil liberties. Professor Vern Countryman has written that Justice Douglas took a more hospitable view of individual freedom under the Constitution than any other justice before or since.[1] During his long tenure on the Court his opinions extended and protected Americans' rights to privacy, free expression, freedom of religion, equal protection, and due process of law.

Yet Justice Douglas had another, now relatively unremembered, intellectual and political passion besides his ardent support of domestic civil liberties. He was an internationalist, who wrote dozens of books and essays on foreign affairs and world peace.

Douglas said in his autobiography that the job of a Supreme Court justice only took four days a week,[2] a view his critics would say explained a lack of thoroughness displayed by his opinions. For Douglas, however, the perceived relative ease of the job left him free to travel, to explore the world, to write and argue his views about foreign affairs before a broad audience. His constant journeys to such distant lands as the Soviet Union, India, Nigeria, Afghanistan, Iran, Lebanon, Greece, and Israel led Justice Hugo Black to once refer to him as Marco-Polo Douglas.[3] When President Truman offered him the position of Secretary of Interior in 1947, Douglas refused, yet he said there was one position for which he would leave the Court — that of Secretary of State.[4]

Douglas's interest in foreign affairs led him to be a forceful advocate for world peace, world law, and cooperation between nations. The connection between Douglas's outspokenness on behalf of individual rights domestically and his belief in international law, federalism, and cooperation abroad might at first appear tenuous or even paradoxical. The man who was the supreme individualist in his view of the Bill of Rights,[5] who supported absolute individual autonomy over the development and expression of one's intellect, interests, tastes, and personality,[6] who his colleagues complained was uncollegial and uncooperative on the bench,[7] was a fervent supporter of international cooperation, of subordinating national sovereignty to the rule of law. An uncompromising justice who seemed to revel in dissent,[8] he urged international compromise and dialogue. For a person who began his autobiography with a quotation from a Persian poet, "Seek disharmony; then you will gain peace,"[9] the advocacy of international harmony as the path to peace might appear inconsistent. Uninterested in consensus-building on the Court, Douglas's interest in fostering a "grand alliance with Russia," based "on *consensus* with the Soviet-Sino bloc" might seem paradoxical.[10]

Yet there is an underlying unity between Douglas's approach to domestic constitutional issues and his views of world affairs. His glorification of individuality under our Constitution made him respect cultural, social, and political difference abroad and champion national self-determination. Peace abroad had to be premised on respecting the right of nations to engage in international dissent, just as domestic tranquility and order was based on a constitutional right to dissent.[11] His notion of the rule of law at home and abroad was not the positivist view of sovereign command, but a Legal Realist perspective based on the felt necessities of the age. Douglas claimed that "those who move to the measured beat of custom, mores or community or world mandates are obeying law in a real and vivid sense of the term."[12] Finally, his egalitarianism and advocacy of the "common people" in the United States[13] found expression in his attacks on U.S. foreign policy as supporting the rich against the poor.

Since the end of World War II and the onset of the Cold War, it has become fashionable to separate our domestic constitutional order from the conduct of U.S. foreign policy abroad. The struggle against the perceived communist threat abroad has led to the view that our foreign policy could not be conducted according to traditional American values. A 1954 Hoover Commission report argued that in combating communism, "there are no rules in such a game. Hitherto acceptable norms of human conduct do not apply."[14] National Security Council Document 68 of April 1950, which became a blueprint for U.S. foreign policy, asserted that "the integrity of our system will not be jeopardized by any measures, covert or overt, violent or non-violent, which serve the purposes of frustrating the Kremlin design."[15] The Kennedy administration's attempts to assassinate Fidel Castro, the secret and brutal war waged by the CIA in Laos, the Reagan administration's disregard of congressional restrictions in aiding the Nicaraguan Contras, the judiciary's refusal to review the constitutionality of allegedly unlawful executive conduct in conducting foreign policy, all stem from the view that foreign policy can be separated from domestic affairs and is not subject to legal restraint. Justice Douglas's writings, speeches, and judicial opinions forcefully illustrate the contrary—that civil liberties at home are directly related to a foreign policy that is just, peaceful, and law-abiding.

I

The case that best illustrates Douglas's internationalist perspective as well as the unity between his views on foreign and domestic affairs is *Holtzman v. Schlesinger,*[16] in which the plaintiffs claimed that the U.S. bombing of Cambodia was unconstitutional.

In the summer of 1973, one of the last dramas in our nation's involvement in the Indochina War—sometimes known as the Vietnam War—was being played out in the rice paddies of Cambodia and the courts of the United States. The last American serviceman had been withdrawn from Vietnam on March 28, 1973, pursuant to the Paris Peace Accords signed in January of that year. A few days later, the last known American prisoners of war were released. Yet the Nixon administration had continued and indeed escalated the bombing of Cambodia.[17] Congress had attempted, albeit with some ambiguity, to discontinue the continued air force operations over Cambodia.

Congresswoman Elizabeth Holtzman, later joined by several air force officers serving in Asia, brought an action in federal district court in New York to enjoin the continued United States air operations over Cambodia. District Judge Orrin Judd ruled that Nixon did not have congressional approval for his actions and ordered that the bombing of Cambodia cease. The United States Court of Appeals for the Second Circuit, acting with traditional judicial caution in foreign policy issues, stayed the district court's order until the appeal could be heard. The Supreme Court justices were by then quietly ensconced in their summer retreats, but Representative Holtzman appealed to Justice Thurgood Marshall, who heard appeals from Second Circuit decisions. While sympathetic to plaintiffs' claims "on the merits that continued American military operations are unconstitutional," Marshall refused to lift the court of appeals stay because of the need for the judiciary to act cautiously. The bombing continued while Holtzman sought out Justice Douglas in Yakima, Washington, to renew her request.

The odds were extremely low, indeed virtually unprecedented, that one Supreme Court justice would reverse a fellow justice's decision. Yet Justice Douglas's general perspective was that "I would rather create a precedent than find one."[18] Douglas reinstated the district court's order to stop the bombing of Cambodia.

The key to Douglas's decision to put a halt to the bombing lay in his view that

this case in its stark realities involves the grim consequences of a capital case. The classic capital case is whether Mr. Lew, Mr. Low, or Mr. Lucas should die. The present case involves whether Mr. X (an unknown person or persons) should die. No one knows who they are. They may be Cambodian farmers whose only "sin" is a desire for socialized medicine to alleviate the suffering of their families and neighbors. Or Mr. X may be the American pilot or navigator who drops a ton of bombs on a Cambodian village. The upshot is that we know that someone is about to die.[19]

The comparison between the bombing of Cambodia and a capital case illustrates the connection between international affairs and individual rights in Douglas's thought. The Cambodian case was not merely about some abstract principle of separation of powers. It involved real issues of life and death. Just as the government cannot take property without due process of law, so too Douglas did "not see how any President can take 'life' in violation of the Constitution."[20] There was therefore a basic connection between individual due process rights and a foreign policy based on the rule of law.

The *Holtzman* case also illustrates the basic themes of Douglas's internationalism: a respect for diversity and self-determination, a compassion for the poor and suffering, and a belief in the rule of law as a foundation of both American and international society. That the people who would die might be Cambodians who believe in a different system than ours did not dissuade Douglas from desiring to protect and speak for them. That the Cambodian farmers might seek to alleviate their suffering by the "sin" of socialized medicine or collective farming was for Douglas no reason for the United States to intervene to stop them; indeed, he believed that in many such cases the United States should support such efforts. Difference must be tolerated and protected, internationally and domestically. That the issue involved foreign affairs was not sufficient to discard the rule of law. Therefore, Douglas saw "no reason to balance the equities"—the rule of law was as clear and absolute here as it was in the First Amendment context: Congress, not the president, has the power to declare war.[21]

Douglas's decision in *Holtzman v. Schlesinger* was overturned the very next day by Justice Marshall, acting on behalf of the full Supreme Court.[22] The bombing of Cambodia was therefore in all probability not affected one whit; not even one bombing raid was prevented. Yet Douglas probably recognized that his decision would be quickly overturned: his position as a minority on the Court was "an appeal to the brooding spirit of the law, the intelligence of a future day."[23] Many might view Douglas's act as that of a judge gone crazy, as that of an old man who paid no interest to judicial caution, the political sensitivity of the issue, or well-established precedent. But for Douglas and those who believed that the courts had failed to play its proper role in adjudicating the momentous legal issues raised by U.S. policy in Indochina, it was an act of courage. As Douglas said in 1948, discussing the role of a dissenter: "We must expect of judges the fortitude and courage that we demand of all other servants who man our public posts. If they are true to their responsibilities and traditions they will not hesitate to speak frankly and plainly on the great issues coming before them."[24]

II

The themes of respect for diversity, the rule of law, and a compassion for the poor that underlay Douglas's internationalism and that are revealed by the *Holtzman* opinion were already a part of his political philosophy in the 1940s. In his autobiography, Douglas recounts his discussions with Franklin

Roosevelt about ridding the world of unilateral military action and creating a United Nations.[25] Douglas believed that the traditional methods of settling controversies between nations were outmoded.[26] He was alarmed that the Truman administration thought primarily "in military terms when foreign affairs were up for discussion."[27] He complained that Truman, like most American officials, was ignorant of the problems and issues facing the world.[28]

In a 1946 speech, he argued for a world government modeled after the federalism and processes of law contained in the U.S. Constitution.[29] Just as domestically we must find "a permanent solution to the problems of economic injustice, racial prejudice and class conflict," internationally we must develop ways to bring about "stable, peaceful relations" between "millions of human beings . . . with diverse cultures, races and languages."[30] Douglas believed that the establishment of the United Nations was "the greatest step yet taken toward world peace," but only "the first step" toward creating a system of law at the world level.[31]

While Douglas was a strong anti-Communist and in the 1940s briefly flirted with the idea that Communism was a monolithic evil, his main emphasis was always on the diversity of the world. He was a strong advocate of self-determination and supported a diverse world community — just as he believed that the Bill of Rights protected diversity in the United States. He once stated that "the American formula of government . . . is not made to order for everyone."[32] While Douglas was unequivocal about his faith in the western democratic tradition, he wanted democracy to result from a people's free choice, not from forceful imposition by another nation.[33] In a 1948 speech he counseled, "All peoples should be free at all times to work out their own destiny."[34] Thus the world law Douglas advocated was fundamentally founded on a respect for diversity and self-determination.

Another key theme in Douglas's internationalism, his compassion for the poor and his concern that law be based on justice and not the status quo, was also evident by the 1940s. In 1946 he urged that law is "more than a mode of settlement of disputes, more than a sheriff to enforce a decree. The aim of law in its civilized sense is justice."[35] Douglas recognized that the living conditions of most people of the world were bleak, burdened by poverty and disease. The answer was not the promise of "vague and remote democratic ideals."[36] Nor did the answer lie merely in anti-Communism. Douglas was very prescient in understanding what was to be the Achilles heel of American foreign policy for the next forty years. He counseled that "our greatest error would be to fashion our foreign policy merely in terms of anti-communism."[37] For "the real victory over communism will be won in the rice field rather than on the battle fields."[38] As early as 1948 he realized that we could not prop up "self-seeking, corrupt or fascist governments"[39] in the name of the struggle against Communism. What was needed were concrete programs of social reconstruction, programs of mass education, and rural reconstruction.[40]

Thus, internationally as well as domestically, the rule of law had to be founded upon justice, and justice "does not mean the preservation of the status quo. . . . Illiteracy, disease and poverty, wherever they appear," Douglas advised, "must be recognized as the enemies of justice."[41] Peace therefore was not merely the absence of war, it was the presence of law, of justice, and of mechanisms for orderly change.[42] Douglas's counsel for the United States as early as 1946 was to ally itself with the winds of change sweeping the world, not with the status quo.

III

While Douglas's basic internationalist assumptions were established in the 1940s, he became both clearer and more vociferous during the 1950s and 1960s. His increasing outspokenness was probably based on several interrelated factors. First, a series of journeys to foreign countries beginning in the late 1940s and continuing throughout the 1950s heightened his awareness of the gap between American views and the reality of the world around us.[43] Second, his growing disenchantment with American foreign policy — beginning with our China policy and culminating with the Vietnam War — led Douglas to play the role of critic and dissenter. While his writings and speeches in the 1940s glowingly speak of America's benevolent role in the world, by the 1960s he is excoriating American officials and foreign policy for not following his advice. Finally, it is possible that Douglas's abandonment of his quest for political office, a quest that had led him to figure prominently in vice presidential and presidential speculation in 1944 and 1948, freed him to become even more outspoken and radical in criticizing U.S. foreign policy.[44]

Douglas's travels made him even more appreciative that national self-determination, diversity, and individuality must be the cornerstone of international society. In 1951, he published the first in his series of travel-adventure books — *Strange Lands and Friendly People* — an account of two trips to Greece, Cyprus, Israel, Lebanon, Syria, Iraq, Iran, Pakistan, and India.[45] He argued that we must surrender the idea that the world can be shaped in our own image and replace that view with a notion of democracy imposed not from above but coming from within the peoples of the developing nations.[46]

Upon returning from a trip to Asia on August 31, 1951, Douglas publicly called for United States recognition of the People's Republic of China.[47] Prophetically predicting the future relations between China and the Soviet Union, Douglas believed that such a diplomatic move would help split the Chinese away from the Soviets.[48] Douglas perceived that Communism was not monolithic and that each Communist revolution must be treated individually and not simply as part of a Soviet conspiracy. In a letter to Truman, he predicted that the "intense nationalism" of Third World nations would be the "Achilles heel of Soviet imperialism."[49] Truman was deeply upset by

Douglas's public statements. Chairman Tom Connally of the Senate Foreign Relations Committee denounced the justice for "roaming all round the world and Asia making fool statements," and *U.S. News & World Report* magazine viewed Douglas's statement as removing him from the 1952 election campaign because, "Any man holding that view could not hope to get far."[50]

His global travels also led Douglas to emphasize the need for social justice as the foundation of an American approach to the Third World. He was struck by Third World poverty, dedicating the book *Strange Lands and Friendly People* to his mother, "who once knew poverty in the Middle East meaning of the word."[51] While Douglas met with such notables as the Shah of Iran and Jawaharlal Nehru, he generally avoided VIP treatment, spending much time with ordinary villagers, discussing their problems, views, customs, and conditions of life.[52] He urged that United States diplomats and officials go to the villages and not simply meet with government dignitaries in national capitals.[53] In his account of a 7,000-mile auto trip from Karachi, Pakistan, to Istanbul, Turkey, in the 1950s, Douglas criticized American visitors to Asia who see those countries from luxurious hotels, go to teas in embassies, see the social whirl of the capital, but "never get close enough to the villages to feel the heartbeat of the people."[54] In 1952 he wrote to Remsen Du Bois Bird, president of Occidental College in California, that getting education to Asian villages couldn't be done by "flying squadrons . . . of experts." In language that could have come from Mao Zedong, Douglas argued that "those who go out there among these people must be revolutionaries as well as technical experts."[55]

Douglas also began to recognize that U.S. foreign policy was guided more by fear than the encouragement of people's hopes and dreams of a better world. For Douglas, the same fears that led to McCarthyism and racial prejudice at home were hindering our foreign policy abroad. In an article for the *New York Times Magazine* entitled "The Black Silence of Fear," Douglas warned that "we are developing a tolerance only for the orthodox point of view on world affairs."[56] Orthodoxy was the "stronghold of the status quo."

These fears came from within. "Each of us projects into his personal relationships and into his community relationships," Douglas noted in a 1952 speech, "the conflicts he has within himself."[57]

If you do not believe in free speech, if you are afraid of new ideas, of course, you will be panicky and alarmed at people like Nehru of India, who believes in experimentation.

If you are suspicious that every one who has a new idea may be a secret Communist agent representing the Kremlin, of course, you will be suspicious of the peoples of the Middle East who are speaking and working and striving for a higher standard of living for themselves. And if you practice racial discrimination, if you do not believe that a man is entitled to the same opportunities, whatever his religion, whatever his race, whatever his creed, when you turn to the colored people of Asia, you will be confused and in trouble, because you who are not able to recognize equality at home will not be able to recognize equality abroad.[58]

Douglas was suggesting to the nation that it follow the course he took in achieving success — that of conquering irrational fears by remaining true to its basic principles.[59] In world affairs and in his own individual struggle, Douglas found "the germ of a philosophy of life: that man's best measure of the universe is in his hopes and his dreams, not his fears."[60]

The nation's greatest fear was a fear of revolution. Yet for Douglas, revolution was a basic part of our heritage. He argued that we be true to our great traditions of freedom and justice. "Revolutions are in the making . . . Let us make revolutions."[61] Douglas believed that "There are revolutions in the world which need management and direction. It will be shameful, if, when the history of the period is written, America is credited with suppressing these struggles, with aligning itself on the world scene with reaction, tyranny and oppression."[62]

The revolutions Douglas urged were political and economic revolutions, revolutions that would overthrow feudalism. It was a revolution that supported the peasant struggle. As he said in 1952, "you cannot go into those villages [in the Middle East and Asia] and be there a week without taking sides. You are either for the landlord or you are for the peasants. Before we go, let us make up our mind whom we are for."[63]

In 1955, Douglas, at the request of Joseph Kennedy, took Robert Kennedy to the Soviet Union. Douglas gleaned from the trip that the Russian desire for peace was real, and in his subsequent travel book entitled *Russian Journey* he called for a political truce accompanied by disarmament, friendship, and nonaggression, as opposed to the policy of military preparedness.[64] Robert Kennedy, fresh from uncovering purported Communists, in his role as counsel to the Senate Investigations Subcommittee, was crusadingly hostile, and more skeptical of the purported Soviet desire for peace.[65] Douglas later claimed, however, that the Russian journey began Robert Kennedy's transformation from violent and hostile anti-Communism to an ability to see the basic human aspirations of the Russian people.[66] In any event, the Russian journey confirmed Douglas's belief in the potential of law, and not military conflict, as mediating the Soviet–U.S. conflict.

Douglas's travels and experiences in the 1950s led him to a decisive break with Cold War internationalism.[67] His brand of internationalism led him to recognize the diversity of different cultures, to support the peasantry in the struggle against the old feudal system, to align the United States with revolutionary movements abroad, and to urge an accommodation with the Soviet Union and China. His development as an internationalist was tied to his increasing commitment to civil liberties at home. Indeed, one of his former law clerks has written that Douglas's journey to a more protective view of the First Amendment was influenced by his extensive travels.[68] For only by clearly practicing democracy at home could we influence the world abroad.

IV

The 1960s brought increasing disenchantment with U.S. foreign policy and a more fervent internationalism on Douglas's part. He began to understand some of the more radical implications of his long-held views, criticizing an imperial America, recognizing the validity and even need for democratic socialism in Third World countries, and excoriating our stifling of what he termed "international dissent." His increasingly absolutist positions on domestic civil liberties paralleled a more radical criticism of America's policy abroad.

Douglas grew more vociferous in his commitment to national self-determination. Writing in 1961 on "The Rule of Law in World Affairs," he argued, "One of our major errors was to think of the world as if it were made in our image: at times we even thought that the non-conformists should be remade in our image."[69] His criticism of the stereotypical American who looked at the world totally from a Western perspective grew. In one of his speeches, he quoted Professor John K. Fairbank of Harvard saying, "We actually need more screwballs and misfits, more people, for example, who look American but think Chinese."[70] Twenty-five years before the current spate of books and articles on the decline of America, Douglas warned that our smugness and complacency could lead America to become a "second-rate power in the world."[71]

Several years later, Douglas set forth his counter plan for American foreign policy in a book entitled *Democracy's Manifesto*. His counter plan recognized that socialism could be a viable option for Third World countries. He severely criticized our whole foreign aid effort as being narrowly focused on developing "pro-Western or pro-American nations." Instead, "our concern should be the development in each country of the kind of government that fits the needs and genius of the people. It may at times be a socialist regime."[72] He generally argued that our market and free enterprise systems, which serve "our ends well," are "misfits" in Third World countries. In those countries, it is the "plan system," rather than the free enterprise or American market system, that must be used "if the old feudal ways are to be renovated."[73] Douglas looked to Yugoslavia as a socialist country that had been able to remain independent of Soviet or Chinese domination and believed that there would be increasing diversity and revisionism among Communist countries if tensions with the West lessened.

His recognition of the need for "the plan" as opposed to pure free enterprise also led Douglas to urge concrete measures to redistribute wealth in feudal societies.[74] He argued forcefully for land reform, to be achieved either by breaking up large holdings into individual plots, reducing rents, or developing cooperatives. Pouring dollars into these societies would only help the elite unless the villages were transformed, unless they were "changed from places of squalor to healthy communities."[75] His constant theme, as it was throughout the 1950s, was that the revolution against feudalism was inevitable, irrespective of Communism. The key question for America was whether to continue on the side of the status quo, or to join the revolution. For Douglas, the first choice was untenable, for the "internal ferment in the villages of these feudal societies is producing more powerful forces than all of our bombs and all our wealth."[76] Our policy of maintaining the status quo was, according to Douglas, Communism's greatest political asset.

Douglas's increasing egalitarianism internationally was reflected domestically in a series of opinions he wrote in the 1960s and 1970s applying heightened scrutiny under the Equal Protection Clause to classifications based on wealth which impinged on fundamental individual interests.[77] In both domestic and international contexts, he was often willing to look beyond formalism to the real economic and social forces that denied equality.

The Vietnam War caused Douglas to become even more alienated from American foreign policy. He was an early and persistent critic of the war. While Douglas was a confidant of Lyndon Johnson, even being considered his new Secretary of State in a hypothetical cabinet before the 1960 election campaign, the Vietnam War severely strained their friendship.[78] LBJ was angered by Douglas's participation in a series of peace conferences in New York and Geneva seeking dialogue on the Vietnam War. Douglas for a time acted as a relayer to Johnson of peace proposals from Ho Chi Minh and the Russians that proposed negotiations, messages that Johnson usually rejected as a Russian trick.[79]

Douglas's criticism of the Vietnam War led to increasing cynicism about whether we really believed in our stated ideals. He spoke of American imperialism, albeit usually utilizing more subdued terminology. He feared that "there is deep in the subconscious of many of our people an urge to establish in the world a Pax Americana, though we will, I think, fail to reach such a goal."[80] He openly challenged the established notion that United States actions were motivated by the need to defend against a Communist threat, believing that "subconsciously we are not reacting to external threats, but to a desire to extend our own economic realm and our political zones of action."[81] That we represent only 6 percent of the world's population but consume more than 60 percent of its goods and resources primed us to believe it was our destiny to run the world.[82]

His book *International Dissent,* published in 1971, made the clearest connection between Douglas's internationalism and his view of domestic liberty. His transformation from a balancing approach to an absolutist First Amendment stance domestically was paralleled by an increasing recognition of the need for toleration abroad. Douglas hoped that we were sufficiently alive to our own First Amendment tradition to take the international position that whatever brand of politics a people select, we will not intervene. . . . We should make tolerance our standard and try to give our First Amendment international dimensions. . . . The growing world problem is to try to tolerate national idiosyncrasies in international affairs, just as we profess to tolerate individual idiosyncrasies under our Bill of Rights. Our contribution is not to change other systems but to foster a climate where diverse regimes can survive conjointly.[83]

For Douglas a "recurring reaction to international dissent echoes the reaction to domestic dissent,"[84] using force to suppress opposing viewpoints. Invasions of other nations such as the Russian invasion of Czechoslovakia and Hungary and our own invasion of the Dominican Republic "were aimed at suppressing 'dangerous ideas.'"[85] The answer for Douglas was a "free association with all the nonconformists of the world."[86]

Moreover, Douglas was afraid that racism at home was affecting our attitude toward people of color abroad.[87] Just as he saw our lack of toleration to different ideas at home as tied to intolerance for international dissent,[88] Douglas viewed racial discrimination domestically as infecting our foreign policy. In 1968 he wrote that, while "the Cold War was largely responsible for our Vietnam venture, there was another powerful influence operating insidiously. For our domestic political philosophy has long rested on an unstated premise of white supremacy."[89] He agreed with Martin Luther King, Jr., that Vietnam was related to the racial problems of our urban ghettoes. And he believed that racism explained our willingness to make the countries of Asia into battlegrounds against communism, causing millions of dead and wounded, while we did not use armed forces to wrest the white Eastern Europeans from the Communist orbit.[90]

The Vietnam War also made Douglas return to the other critical strand of his internationalism — the need for the rule of law to govern international affairs. Douglas's main thrust for a settlement in Vietnam was a multilateral approach, under which the nations involved would agree to abide by the decision of a multilateral tribunal.[91] Law was based on consensus as opposed to unilateral action. "In this atomic age the people of the world can afford no more delay in finding formulae for submitting disputes between nations to some court, committee, conference or arbiter for decision."[92] One approach Douglas suggested was to reconvene the Geneva Conference, with both parties agreeing to abide by the result.

Douglas also proposed that the Vietnam controversy be referred to the International Court of Justice.[93] He believed that the conflict was a "justiciable — as distinguished from a political — issue since it involves construction of the Geneva Accord of 1954, the United Nations Charter, and various treaties."[94] As was often the case, Douglas was prophetic. In 1985, the ICJ unanimously agreed with Douglas's view, albeit in the context of the Nicaragua case against the United States and not the Vietnam War.[95] The United States government, disagreeing with Douglas in 1968, again disagreed with him almost twenty years later and refused to accept the court's decision.

Douglas's view that such international disputes could be resolved judicially paralleled his position that the Supreme Court should decide the Vietnam War cases. Douglas dissented from the Supreme Court's denial of certiorari in various cases seeking to adjudicate the lawfulness of the United States involvement in the Vietnam conflict.[96] In the first of these cases, Douglas argued in dissent that the Court should decide whether the United States was waging an aggressive war in Vietnam. While not expressing any opinion on the merits, he noted that there was a considerable body of opinion that our actions in Vietnam constituted the waging of an aggressive war.[97] Douglas observed that under the Constitution, treaties are part of the supreme law of the land and quoted Justice Jackson's statement after the Nuremberg Trials that, "If certain acts in violation of treaties are crimes, they are crimes whether the United States does them or whether Germany does them, and we are not prepared to lay down a rule of criminal conduct against others which we would not be willing to have invoked against us."[98]

In *Massachusetts v. Laird,*[99] Douglas again dissented, writing a lengthy opinion that utterly demolished the government's argument that the case was a political question and nonjusticiable. He found it hard to distinguish the Steel Seizure Case, the Civil War *Prize Cases,* and the Vietnam War cases. The Prize Cases and Steel Seizure Case involved claims of a wrongful taking of property; in the Vietnam War cases, life and liberty were involved. As Douglas noted, "Certainly the Constitution gives no greater protection to *property* than to *life* and *liberty*."[100] In *Massachusetts,* he was joined in his dissent by Justices Harlan and Stewart.

In the Vietnam War cases, as in the Cambodia Bombing Case, Douglas was willing to adjudicate whether U.S. actions abroad comported with the rule of law. In doing so, he was acting consistently with his long-held view that the survival of earth depended on the establishment of a "co-operative regime" of law, based "on fair dealing – due process if you please – on all sides." That rule of law must be applied consistently to the United States, as well as the Soviet Union.

Thus, while Douglas continued to believe that America ought to be active in world affairs, for him the key question was *the substantive nature of that activity.* Douglas wrote dozens of books in which he repeated almost ad nauseam the same theme: America's activism in the world was misdirected. United States activism should seek social justice and tolerate diversity, not simply intervene militarily and politically to maintain the status quo. He continuously argued that the United States could not deal with the nations of Asia, Africa, and the Middle East without taking sides between the rich elite and the poor peasant. Douglas knew where he stood: for improving the life of the peasantry.

To argue, as Harold Koh does in his commentary, that Douglas's first principle was a faith in presidential and American activism is at best unhelpful, and in his later years probably inaccurate. Harry Truman, Lyndon Johnson, and Richard Nixon were activist presidents, yet Douglas criticized each one severely because their foreign policy activism was misdirected. His agreement with Franklin Roosevelt was based on a common understanding of the substantive goals and directions of foreign policy, not on the fact that both were activists. To the extent it is useful to label Douglas, a more appropriate label than Koh's "liberal constitutional internationalism" would be "egalitarian internationalist." Douglas was an internationalist because he believed in international cooperation based on international law. He was an egalitarian internationalist because he believed that international cooperation must be based on social justice, in which the United States played a key role in reducing the extreme poverty, disease, and lack of education afflicting a large part of today's world.

V

There is a sadness in discussing Douglas's career as an internationalist. It is a sadness that stems from the recognition that despite Douglas's foresightfulness in predicting the key role that nationalism, diversity, and unorthodoxy were destined to play in the latter part of the twentieth century, despite his forceful and articulate advocacy for diplomacy, law, and consensus-building, despite his urging the judiciary not to abandon its role in deciding legal issues involving foreign policy, we may be no nearer to adopting his approach as we enter the 1990s.

In Central America, our government still refuses to tolerate international dissent and unorthodoxy, seeing every revolutionary movement as part of a Soviet conspiracy. We still support the status quo and oppose revolutionary movements seeking social justice around the world. Anti-Communism still seems to be the cornerstone of our foreign policy, as does the maintenance and utilization of a strong military force. Our federal courts still refuse to adjudicate foreign policy disputes, and the executive branch has withdrawn from the jurisdiction of the World Court in a fit of pique over the court's decision in the Nicaragua case.

Yet Douglas's views on foreign affairs, like his dissents on domestic issues, continue to stand as an appeal to "the intelligence of a future day." Douglas's perspective on the connection between social justice abroad and at home, tolerance domestically and internationally, and respect for the rule of law in both contexts stands as a constant reminder to those who would attempt to divide the domestic and international legal orders. His epigraph in his autobiography that only by seeking disharmony can we attain peace is as relevant internationally as domestically.

While the establishment that rejected Douglas's views on foreign affairs throughout his life continues to reject them, there is a growing movement in cities and towns across the country in support of the brand of internationalism Douglas was urging. As Justice Douglas recognized, "only drastic changes in attitude" will allow America to base its foreign policy on cooperation and not on unilateral action.[101] While certainly no "drastic changes of attitude" have afflicted our foreign policy establishment, there are inklings of such changes in at least sections of our population. It is precisely in such drastic changes of attitude that hope lies for a future America that learns to accept disharmony and difference in the world, live with other people and cultures, and recognize its need to cooperate with other countries instead of lording over them.

Notes

1. Vern Countryman, "Scholarship and Common Sense," *Harvard Law Review* 93 (1980): 1407.

2. William O. Douglas, *The Court Years, 1939–1975: The Autobiography of William O. Douglas* (New York: Random House, 1980).

3. Poem from Black to Douglas, reprinted in Melvin I. Urofsky and Philip E. Urofsky, eds., *The Douglas Letters: Selections from the Private Papers of Justice William O. Douglas* (Bethesda: Adler and Adler, 1987), p. 107.

4. Douglas, *The Court Years,* p. 288.

5. Dorothy Glancy, "Getting Government Off the Backs of People: The Right of Privacy and Freedom of Expression in the Opinions of Justice William O. Douglas," *Santa Clara Law Review* 21 (1981): 1047.

6. *Doe v. Bolton,* 410 U.S. 179, 211 (1973) (Douglas, J., concurring).

7. G. Edward White, "The Anti-Judge: William O. Douglas and the Ambiguities of Individuality," *Virginia Law Review* 74 (1988): 42–44.

8. William O. Douglas, "The Dissenting Opinion," *Lawyers Guild Review* 8 (1948): 467.

9. William O. Douglas, *Go East, Young Man: The Autobiography of William O. Douglas* (New York: Random House, 1974), p. 396.

10. William O. Douglas, *An Anatomy of Liberty* (New York: Trident, 1963), p. 177.

11. William O. Douglas, *International Dissent, Six Steps Toward World Peace* (New York: Random House, 1971), p. 130.

12. William O. Douglas, *The Rule of Law in World Affairs* (Santa Barbara: Center for the Study of Democratic Institutions, 1961).

13. *Harper v. Virginia State Board of Elections,* 383 U.S. 663 (1966); *Douglas v. California,* 372 U.S. 353 (1963); *Griffin v. Illinois,* 351 U.S. 12, 19 (1956) ("There can be no equal justice where the kind of trial a man gets depends on the amount of money he has"); Kenneth Karst, "Invidious Discrimination: Justice Douglas and the Return of the Natural-Law-Due-Process Formula," *UCLA Law Review* 16 (1960): 716, 717. Douglas has consistently adopted the position of an egalitarian activist.

14. Quoted in Senate Report 755, 94th Cong. 2nd Sess. (1977), p. 9.

15. Quoted in Walter LaFeber, "The Constitution and U.S. Foreign Policy: An

Interpretation," in Jules Lobel, ed., *A Less Than Perfect Union, Alternative Perspective on the U.S. Constitution* (New York: Monthly Review Press, 1988), pp. 221, 222.

16. 414 U.S. 1316 (1973).

17. *Holtzman v. Schlesinger,* 361 F. Supp. 553, 558 (S.D.N.Y. 1973).

18. Douglas, *The Court Years,* p. 179.

19. *Holtzman v. Schlesinger,* 414 U.S., at 1317.

20. Ibid., at 1318.

21. Ibid.

22. 414 U.S. 1321.

23. Douglas, "The Dissenting Opinion," p. 468.

24. Ibid.

25. Douglas, *The Court Years,* pp. 275–76.

26. William O. Douglas, Address at Ohio University, June 9, 1946, reprinted in Douglas, *Being an American,* ed. Richard J. Walsh (New York: John Day, 1948), p. 176.

27. Douglas, *The Court Years,* p. 292.

28. Ibid.

29. Douglas, Address at Ohio University, pp. 168–69.

30. Ibid., pp. 173–74.

31. Ibid., p. 175.

32. Douglas, *Go East, Young Man,* p. 396.

33. James C. Duram, *Justice William O. Douglas* (Boston: Twayne, 1981), pp. 83, 85, 89.

34. William O. Douglas, "Democracy Charts Its Course," *University of Florida Law Review* 1 (1948): 133, 143.

35. Douglas, Address at Ohio University, p. 171.

36. Douglas, "Democracy Charts Its Course," p. 146.

37. Ibid.

38. Ibid.

39. Ibid., p. 467.

40. Ibid.

41. William O. Douglas, Address at the Herald Tribune Forum, Oct. 28, 1946, reprinted in Douglas, *Being an American,* p. 210.

42. Douglas, Address at Ohio University, p. 176.

43. Duram, *Justice William O. Douglas,* p. 81.

44. Douglas was offered the vice presidency by Truman in 1948 and was considered by Roosevelt for the position in 1944. He apparently sought the presidential nomination over Truman in 1948, but a draft-Douglas movement got nowhere. See James F. Simon, *Independent Journey: The Life of William O. Douglas* (New York: Harper and Row, 1980), pp. 262–75; Douglas, *The Court Years,* pp. 201–90. In 1951, Douglas finally put an end to the speculation of a political career and announced his desire to remain on the Court for the rest of his life. Simon, *Independent Journey,* p. 275.

45. William O. Douglas, *Strange Lands and Friendly People* (New York: Harper, 1951).

46. Duram, *Justice William O. Douglas,* p. 83.

47. "Douglas: A Different Kind of Judge . . . His Views on China Jar Demo-

crats," *U.S. News & World Report,* Sept. 14, 1951; Urofsky and Urofsky, *Douglas Letters,* p. 108, n. 1.

48. Letter from William O. Douglas to Harry Truman, Sept. 23, 1951, reprinted in Urofsky and Urofsky, *Douglas Letters.*

49. Ibid.

50. "Douglas: A Different Kind of Judge," pp. 50, 54.

51. Duram, *Justice William O. Douglas,* p. 82.

52. Simon, *Independent Journey,* p. 316. See also William O. Douglas, "Revolution Is Our Business," *Nation,* May 31, 1952, pp. 516, 518.

53. Simon, *Independent Journey,* p. 318.

54. William O. Douglas, *West of the Indus,* p. 502, cited in Duram, *Justice William O. Douglas,* p. 86.

55. Letter, William O. Douglas to Remsen Du Bois Bird, Feb. 6, 1952, in Urofsky and Urofsky, *Douglas Letters,* pp. 260–61.

56. William O. Douglas, "The Black Silence of Fear," *New York Times Magazine,* Jan. 13, 1952.

57. Douglas, "Revolution Is Our Business," p. 516.

58. Ibid.

59. Duram, *Justice William O. Douglas,* p. 99. For an excellent discussion of the role overcoming fear played in Douglas's own life and philosophy, see White, "Anti-Judge," pp. 20–22, 32–33.

60. Douglas, *Go East, Young Man,* p. 396.

61. Douglas, "Revolution Is Our Business," pp. 517, 518.

62. "Douglas: A Different Kind of Judge," p. 52.

63. Douglas, "Revolution Is Our Business," p. 518.

64. Duram, *Justice William O. Douglas,* p. 85.

65. Simon, *Independent Journey,* p. 323.

66. Douglas, *The Court Years,* p. 307. Douglas later suggested to Robert Kennedy that he become secretary of state in place of Dean Rusk. Ibid., p. 309.

67. Douglas would write in *Kent v. Dulles,* 357 U.S. 116 (1958), that the right to travel abroad was a fundamental constitutional right. His rationale was in part based upon the value of foreign travel in providing first-hand information on a host of important public issues, a rationale which certainly reflected Douglas's own experience. Ibid., at 126–27.

68. L. A. Powe, Jr., "Evolution to Absolutism: Justice Douglas and the First Amendment," *Columbia Law Review* 74 (1974): 407–08.

69. William O. Douglas, *The Rule of Law in World Affairs.*

70. William O. Douglas, *America Challenged* (Princeton: Princeton University Press, 1960).

71. Ibid., p. 3.

72. William O. Douglas, *Democracy's Manifesto* (New York: John Day, 1962).

73. Ibid., p. 15.

74. Ibid., p. 41.

75. Ibid., p. 39.

76. Ibid., p. 16.

77. See Karst, "Invidious Discrimination," and cases cited therein. See also *Lindsey v. Normet,* 405 U.S. 79, 81, 90 (1972) (Douglas, J., dissenting in part) (attacking

procedure as "landlord legislation," and arguing that "slum landlord, not the slum tenant is the real culprit").

78. Douglas, *The Court Years,* pp. 314, 329–30.

79. Ibid., pp. 325–26.

80. William O. Douglas, *International Dissent.*

81. Ibid., p. 46. By 1974, in his autobiography, Douglas openly articulated the view that America had "become more 'imperialistic' than the British at their worst." *Go East, Young Man,* p. 402.

82. Douglas, *International Dissent,* p. 47.

83. Ibid., pp. 130–31.

84. Ibid., p. 128.

85. Ibid.

86. William O. Douglas, *Towards A Global Federalism* (New York: New York University Press, 1968), p. 167.

87. Ibid., p. 3.

88. Ibid., p. 167.

89. Ibid., p. 165.

90. Ibid., p. 166.

91. Ibid., p. 12.

92. Ibid., p. 13.

93. Ibid.

94. Ibid., p. 16. Douglas was a long-time supporter of the court and critic of the Connolly Amendment that allowed the United States to evade World Court jurisdiction whenever the United States determined that the dispute fell within the domestic jurisdiction of the United States. Ibid.

95. Military & Paramilitary Activities in and Against Nicaragua (*Nicaragua v. United States*), 1984 I.C.J. 392 (Jurisdiction).

96. *Sarnoff v. Shultz,* 409 U.S. 929 (1972); *DaCosta v. Laird,* 405 U.S. 979 (1972); *Massachusetts v. Laird,* 400 U.S. 886 (1970); *McArthur v. Clifford,* 393 U.S. 1002 (1968); *Hart v. United States,* 391 U.S. 956 (1968); *Holmes v. United States,* 391 U.S. 936 (1968); *Mora v. McNamara,* 389 U.S. 934, 935 (1969); *Mitchell v. United States,* 386 U.S. 972 (1967).

97. *Mitchell v. United States,* 386 U.S., at 973.

98. Ibid.

99. 400 U.S. 886 (1970).

100. Ibid., at 899.

101. William O. Douglas, *Holocaust or Hemispheric Co-Op: Cross Currents in Latin America* (New York: Random House, 1971).

COMMENTARY:
THE LIBERAL CONSTITUTIONAL INTERNATIONALISM
OF JUSTICE DOUGLAS
Harold Hongju Koh

PROFESSORS GLENNON and Lobel have perceptively captured certain core truths about Justice Douglas's internationalism. Professor Glennon surveys Douglas's principal judicial opinions in the foreign affairs field and finds that, over three decades, Douglas grew increasingly suspicious of the presidency, the military, the CIA, and the press, while simultaneously embracing judicial activism, international institutions, and individual rights. Professor Lobel focuses primarily on the justice's nonjudicial writings, concluding that Douglas respected diversity, self-determination, and the rule of law as foundations for both American and international society.

I do not dispute either of these conclusions, which my colleagues have astutely identified and elegantly analyzed. Given recent accounts challenging the historical accuracy of Douglas's autobiographies, one could question Professor Glennon's methodological decision to "take Douglas on his own terms" or Professor Lobel's unadorned celebration of Douglas's internationalism.[1] Taken together, however, the two chapters cite most of the right cases and writings about Douglas's internationalism.

Yet just because my colleagues have hit all the right notes does not mean that either has found the precise *melody* that formed the leitmotif of Douglas's internationalism. Professor Glennon accurately sketches the various strands of Douglas's thought but does not suggest how they tie together to form a world view. Professor Lobel paints Douglas as having a world view, but does not convincingly explain why that world view was coherent. In short, although both of my colleagues agree that Douglas was an internationalist, neither has told us what *kind* of internationalist he was, or why his peculiar brand of internationalism should speak to us today, nearly a decade after his death.

Any balanced look back at Douglas's internationalism must acknowledge certain inconsistencies within it. For example, civil libertarians have trouble squaring Douglas's votes supporting the detention of Japanese-American internees with his stirring rhetoric in *Ex Parte Endo*.[2] Critics juxtapose Douglas's 1973 vote to stay the Cambodian bombing with his 1953 vote to stay the Rosenbergs' execution and claim that both were politically motivated. Nor is it clear why Douglas, who as a scholar prided himself on being the quintessential domestic Legal Realist, became the quintessential legal *idealist* in international affairs, eschewing both political and Legal Realist views.

Even accepting these inconsistencies, however, I would argue that William O. Douglas made an enduring contribution to American postwar internationalism — a contribution captured not by any particular opinion or book, but by an important principle for which Douglas consistently stood: what I will call *liberal constitutional internationalism.* In my judgment, that principle was both internally coherent and formed the basic leitmotif of Douglas's internationalism. Moreover, that principle cannot be dismissed today as naive or irrelevant. To the contrary, modern-day civil libertarians and international lawyers can fully embrace that principle even after — and indeed, because of — the Vietnam War and the Iran-Contra Affair.

What principles formed the core of Douglas's liberal constitutional internationalism? At both the domestic and the international levels, his world view rested upon three principles: first, a faith in presidential and American *activism;* second, a conviction that such activism must be checked by *political institutions;* and third, a growing belief that such activism should be restrained by judges protective of the primacy of *individual rights.*

Douglas grew up in the early twentieth century, a period that transformed both America and the world. When he took the bench in 1939, in the wake of the First World War and the Depression, the greatest perceived threat to liberty abroad was American isolationism. The greatest perceived threat to liberty at home was not governmental overreaching, but governmental passivity. In response to both threats, Douglas's friend and confidant Franklin Delano Roosevelt urged a policy of activism. Roosevelt believed that American activism and leadership abroad were not just good for the world but indispensable to the creation of the structure of international organizations that has dominated the postwar era. At home, FDR believed that an activist national government and presidency were necessary to rescue America from the paralysis that had beset it during the Depression.

As an architect of the New Deal and a one-time presidential aspirant, Justice Douglas strongly supported both American activism abroad and presidential activism at home. In 1948, Douglas wrote, "let us act decisively; otherwise, the very refusal to act becomes a policy — the most self-defeating policy in the world."[3] On the domestic front, Douglas had helped to build and legitimate the New Deal; in the international arena, he supported the creation of the postwar United Nations and Bretton Woods systems of international organization, a sort of New Deal writ large. To mediate between these two New Deals, Douglas favored a strong national government that could act largely unencumbered by the states in foreign affairs, if necessary, overriding state prerogatives through exercises of federal supremacy. Douglas's strong nationalist orientation in foreign affairs was exemplified not only by his 1942 decision in *United States v. Pink,*[4] but also by his 1968 pronational government decision in *Zschernig v. Miller,* which struck down an Oregon statute as "an intrusion by the State into the field of foreign affairs which the Constitution entrusts to the President and the Congress."[5]

The crucial language in *Zschernig* was Douglas's statement that "the field of foreign affairs [is one] which the Constitution entrusts to the President *and the Congress*."[6] For Douglas did not make the mistake that Justice Sutherland had made in *United States v. Curtiss-Wright Export Corp.* three years before Douglas came to the Court, concluding that the strong national power required to support America's new international role should be exercised exclusively by the president.[7] As Professor Glennon explains, in the 1952 Steel Seizure Case, Douglas tempered his first principle — presidential activism — with a second notion, that the Constitution imposes institutional restraints upon presidential power in foreign affairs.[8] In that landmark case, Douglas reiterated the constitutional principle that ours is a constitutional system in which separated institutions share foreign policy powers. "The fact that it was necessary that [emergency] measures be taken," he said, "does not mean that the President, rather than the Congress, had the constitutional authority to act. The Congress, as well as the President, is trustee of the national welfare. . . . In some nations . . . power is entrusted to the executive branch as a matter of course or in case of emergencies. We chose another course."[9]

In the international realm, Douglas similarly believed that institutional checks would ensure that American activism did not degenerate into disguised imperialism. Particularly in his later books, he argued that America's activist impulses in the international arena should be checked by international organizations such as the United Nations, by a system of global federalism, and by the rule of international law, particularly treaty law.[10]

Starting in 1944, Douglas became increasingly concerned that growing American activism abroad and presidential power at home might overwhelm a third treasured principle: the idea that "the Constitution was designed to keep government off the backs of the people."[11] In *Ex Parte Endo,* Douglas held that the president could not detain Japanese-Americans following evacuation when they had not been proved disloyal nor detained to protect the war effort against espionage and sabotage.[12] Eight years later, in the Steel Seizure Case, he joined a Court majority that rejected the president's claim that inherent emergency powers authorized him to take private property without paying just compensation. Almost contemporaneously, he sought to stay Julius and Ethel Rosenberg's executions, based in part on his view that McCarthyism and Cold War hysteria had taken precedence over the Rosenbergs' right to a fair trial.[13] In each of these cases, Douglas concluded that presidential activism, like America's global activism, should be checked not only by institutional checks but also by direct judicial protection of individual rights. In the international arena, as Professor Lobel recounts, these same commitments to judicial activism and individual rights led Douglas to champion an expanded role for the International Court of Justice in international affairs and to praise as virtues international diversity, egalitarianism, self-determination, and dissent.

In short, Douglas was the quintessential internationalist because he believed in an activist president and an activist American foreign policy. His internationalism was constitutional, because he believed that both forms of activism should be conducted by separated national and international institutions sharing powers. His internationalism was liberal because he concluded that the president and America should pursue activist foreign policies without intruding upon the rights of individuals at home or abroad. When executive activism collides with constitutionalism and liberalism, Douglas concluded, judges must intervene to protect both constitutional democracy and individual rights.

In his first years on the Court, Douglas lacked a principled tool to guide and legitimate this form of judicial intervention. Indeed, in his sweeping *Curtiss-Wright* opinion, Justice Sutherland had urged the opposite notion: that courts should broadly defer to actions that executive officials take pursuant to foreign affairs statutes.[14] However, in *Ex Parte Endo,* Douglas modified Sutherland's view, declaring that judges must strictly construe foreign affairs statutes to ensure that they do not trench upon individual rights. Judges, he stated, "must assume, when asked to find implied powers in a grant of legislative or executive authority, that the law makers intended to place no greater restraint on the citizen than was clearly and unmistakably indicated by the language [that the Chief Executive and Congress] used."[15]

With those words, Douglas began to articulate the "clear statement" principle: the notion that judges must find a clear statutory statement that Congress has authorized the executive act in question before condoning an executive invasion of an individual's constitutional rights. The clear statement principle brilliantly combined all three features of Douglas's internationalism: the concept that both congressional restraints and judicial protection of individual rights should serve as checks upon presidential and American overreaching in foreign affairs. Moreover, the principle preserved the principle of executive accountability in foreign affairs by demanding that governmental rules regulating vital individual rights would reflect specific legislative consent, not just self-interested bureaucratic discretion.

The clear statement principle received its clearest expression in *Kent v. Dulles*—a 1958 decision mentioned only fleetingly by professors Glennon and Lobel—in which Justice Douglas upheld an individual's constitutional right to travel abroad.[16] *Kent* obliged judges, rather than simply abstaining or deferring to executive actions in foreign affairs, to subject such actions to a form of strict scrutiny, and to demand a clear "showing of joint action by the Chief Executive and the Congress to curtail a constitutional right of the citizen. . . . Since we start with an exercise by an American citizen of an activity included in constitutional protection, we will not readily infer that Congress gave the Secretary of State unbridled discretion to grant or withhold it."[17]

In short, long before the Vietnam War, Justice Douglas had concluded that America's internationalism must be restrained both by constitutionalism — the checks and balances provided by congressional restraint and judicial review — as well as by liberalism — the Constitution's original vision of a limited government that stays off the backs of the people. Thus, I read Douglas's later opinions calling for judicial review of the legality of various aspects of the Vietnam War[18] and siding with the *New York Times* in the Pentagon Papers Case[19] as driven not so much by ideology or political grandstanding as by his peculiar vision of a constitutional legal process. Under this view, Douglas asserted, Congress, the courts, international organizations, and treaty commitments properly restrain presidential and American discretion; the perceived need for an activist American foreign policy did not entitle the president to intrude without justification upon the lives of either American citizens at home or Asian citizens abroad.

Douglas was not the only liberal constitutional internationalist of his generation. Other prominent proponents of his view included Senators J. William Fulbright and Jacob Javits, United Nations ambassadors Adlai Stevenson, Arthur Goldberg, and Eleanor Roosevelt, and historian Arthur Schlesinger, Jr. Like Douglas, each of these thinkers began in Franklin Roosevelt's day by supporting an activist America in the international arena, led by an activist president. Each believed, however, that America should answer to international institutions and treaties at the global level, and that the president should answer to Congress, the courts, and the Constitution at the domestic level. By the waning days of the Vietnam War, each of these liberal constitutional internationalists had evolved from a position of uncritical support for American presidential power to one that was skeptical of both an imperial America and an imperial presidency.

What relevance, if any, does Douglas's liberal constitutional internationalism have for us today? The historical precedent for the Iran-Contra Affair, I would argue, was not Watergate, as many people assume, but rather, the Vietnam War. Like Vietnam, the Iran-Contra Affair marked a recent period of both American and presidential activism notably antithetical to Douglas's core principles. Unlike Douglas's internationalism, which posited that America's activist impulses abroad should be checked by both international organizations and rules of international law, the Iran-Contra Affair — like Vietnam — was driven by a world view that rejected the notion that American or executive activism should be restrained by either. Unlike Douglas's liberal constitutionalism, which posited that the president must answer for his international acts to Congress, the courts, and the Constitution, this view asserts, in the words of Lt. Col. Oliver North, that: "this nation is at risk in a dangerous world. . . . We all ha[ve] to weigh . . . the difference between lies and lives."[20] Or in the tragic words of former President Reagan, "the American people will never forgive me if I fail to get these hostages out over this legal question."[21]

In short, the Iran-Contra Affair turned on its head Woodrow Wilson's view that we must "make the world safe for democracy." Instead, the president's men have recently told us that the world is too unsafe for constitutional democracy in the conduct of American foreign affairs: that in times of crisis, both the Constitution and international law must give way to the press of external events and we must trust the president to do what is best, notwithstanding contrary congressional will, judicial opinion, or individual right.

If William O. Douglas's internationalism taught us anything, it is that this proposition simply cannot be so. As an international observer, he taught us that liberal constitutionalism should rule globalism and not the other way around. As a Supreme Court justice, he taught us that efficiency is not all; our government is bound by a constitutional process of foreign policy decision making, in which separated institutions share foreign policy powers and judges ensure that the government respects individual rights. As he observed in the Steel Seizure Case, "The President can act more quickly than the Congress. . . . All executive power—from the reign of ancient kings to the rule of modern dictators—has the outward appearance of efficiency. . . . [But we] cannot decide this case by determining which branch of government can deal most expeditiously with the present crisis. The answer must depend on the allocation of powers under the Constitution."[22]

Unlike my colleagues, whose chapters mourn the passing of Justice Douglas's internationalist vision, I do not close on a pessimistic note. Even fifty years after Douglas first took the bench—at a time when liberalism has acquired a bad name and constitutional internationalism is oft treated as an oxymoron—Justice Douglas's liberal constitutional internationalism offers a respite from cynical realism that has recently afflicted our activist foreign policy. For all of his flaws, William O. Douglas taught us an enduring lesson about internationalism: that if international events threaten democracy, the solution is not to abandon democracy, but to reaffirm it. It is for this principle that his career as an internationalist should be applauded. It is for this principle that his career as an internationalist should be remembered.

Notes

I am grateful to my colleagues Bruce Ackerman and Myres McDougal for their contributions to this commentary, and to David Hayes and Ronald Slye for able research assistance.

1. See, e.g., James F. Simon, *Independent Journey: The Life of William O. Douglas* (New York: Harper and Row, 1980), pp. 234, 442–46; Melvin I. Urofsky and Philip E. Urofsky, eds., *The Douglas Letters: Selections from the Private Papers of William O. Douglas* (Bethesda: Adler and Adler, 1987), p. xx: Douglas "too often . . . claimed to be an 'expert' on a country just because he had spent a couple of weeks traveling around in rural areas"; G. Edward White, "The Anti-Judge: William O. Douglas and the Ambiguities of Individuality," *Virginia Law Review* 74 (1988): 27: "Accuracy was clearly not a primary concern of Douglas' in writing about any portion of his life."

2. Compare *Korematsu v. United States,* 323 U.S. 214 (1944), and *Hirabayashi v. United States,* 320 U.S. 81, 105 (1943) (Douglas, J., concurring), with *Ex Parte Endo,* 323 U.S. 283 (1944) (Douglas, J.).

3. William O. Douglas, *Being an American,* ed. Richard J. Walsh (New York: John Day, 1948), p. 167. Douglas expressed similar views in *America Challenged* (Princeton: Princeton University Press, 1960).

4. 315 U.S. 203 (1942).

5. *Zschernig v. Miller,* 389 U.S. 429, 432 (1968). For a penetrating analysis of *Zschernig's* impact on the states by a state Supreme Court justice and former Douglas clerk, see Hans Linde, "A New Foreign-Relations Restraint on American States: *Zschernig v. Miller,*" *Zeitschrift fur Auslandisches offentliches Recht und Volkerrecht* 28 (1968): 594.

6. *Zschernig v. Miller,* 389 U.S., at 432 (emphasis added).

7. See *United States v. Curtiss-Wright Export Co.,* 299 U.S. 304, 320 (1936): "The very delicate, plenary and exclusive power of the President as the sole organ of the federal government in the field of international relations [is] a power which does not require as a basis for its exercise an act of Congress." For critiques of Justice Sutherland's opinion in *Curtiss-Wright,* see Harold Koh, "Why the President (Almost) Always Wins in Foreign Affairs: Lessons of the Iran-Contra Affair," *Yale Law Journal* 97 (1988): 1255, 1306–13; Michael J. Glennon, "Two Views of Presidential Foreign Affairs Power: *Little v. Barreme* or *Curtiss-Wright?*" *Yale Journal of International Law* 13 (1988): 12–17.

8. *Youngstown Sheet & Tube Co. v. Sawyer,* 343 U.S. 579, 629–34 (1952) (Douglas, J., concurring).

9. Ibid., at 629–30. For an elaboration of the notion that ours is a constitutional system in which separated institutions share foreign policy powers, see Harold Koh, *The National Security Constitution: Sharing Power After the Iran-Contra Affair* (New Haven: Yale University Press, 1990).

10. See generally William O. Douglas, *Toward a Global Federalism* (New York: New York University Press, 1968); Douglas, *International Dissent: Six Steps Toward World Peace* (New York: Random House, 1971); Douglas, *Holocaust and Hemispheric Co-op: Cross Currents in Latin America* (New York: Random House, 1971); Douglas, *The Rule of Law in World Affairs* (Santa Barbara: Center for the Study of Democratic Institutions, 1961).

11. *Laird v. Tatum,* 408 U.S. 1, 28 (1972) (Douglas, J., dissenting).

12. *Ex Parte Endo,* 323 U.S. 283, 302 (1944).

13. See *United States v. Rosenberg,* 346 U.S. 273, 310–21 (1953) (Douglas, J., dissenting).

14. See *United States v. Curtiss-Wright,* 299 U.S., at 320: "Congressional legislation . . . within the international field must often accord to the President a degree of discretion and freedom . . . which would not be admissible were domestic affairs alone involved."

15. *Ex Parte Endo,* 323 U.S., at 300.

16. *Kent v. Dulles,* 357 U.S. 116 (1958).

17. Ibid., at 128–29.

18. See, e.g., *Schlesinger v. Reservists Committee to Stop the War,* 418 U.S. 208, 229 (1974) (Douglas, J., dissenting); *Holtzman v. Schlesinger,* 414 U.S. 1316 (1973) (Douglas, J.) (opinion in chambers); *Laird v. Tatum,* 408 U.S. 1, 16 (1972) (Douglas,

J., dissenting); *Massachusetts v. Laird,* 400 U.S. 886 (1970) (Douglas, J., dissenting); *Mitchell v. United States,* 386 U.S. 972 (1967) (Douglas, J., dissenting).

19. *New York Times Co. v. United States,* 403 U.S. 713, 720 (1971) (Douglas, J., concurring).

20. See Oliver North, *Taking the Stand* (New York: Pocket Books, 1987), pp. 12, 256.

21. See "Shultz's Long War," *Newsweek,* Aug. 13, 1987, p. 16 (statement of Secretary of State Shultz, quoting President Reagan).

22. *Youngstown Sheet & Tube Co. v. Sawyer,* 343 U.S., at 629–30 (Douglas, J., concurring).

COMMENTARY:
DOUGLAS AS INTERNATIONALIST

Hans A. Linde

JUSTICE DOUGLAS'S VIEW of the world exemplified progressive thought in his generation. Son of midwesterners, growing up, not in Seattle, but on the eastern slopes of Mt. Adams, young Bill Douglas had no more reason to be an internationalist than Idaho's William Borah, Wisconsin's Robert La Follette, or Nebraska's George Norris. When Douglas came east to Columbia's law school, the business of America was business. Expertise in the laws of business brought him to Washington and eventually to the Supreme Court. Constitutional law for Roosevelt's appointees, except Felix Frankfurter, had appeared in the form of judge-made obstacles to progressive government action rather than as a source of individual liberty or equality.

In the agrarian and populist tradition of the West, progressive action meant domestic programs; internationalism meant the gold standard, hard credit, a big navy, the imperialism of the Spanish-American War and its consequences in Cuba and the Philippines, and the chauvinism of the same Theodore Roosevelt who asserted presidential "stewardship" over public lands in the progressive cause of conservation. But Woodrow Wilson, not Theodore Roosevelt, represented progressive government while Douglas went to high school.

Wilson took the country into war to make the world safe for democracy and made creation of the League of Nations his most insistent demand for the peace treaty, only to have the Senate refuse American participation in this uniquely American venture. Postwar Republican administrations later substituted the Kellogg-Briand anti-war pact, proposed to join in the World Court, and negotiated a naval disarmament treaty, but American policy toward political, economic, and human crises turned profoundly isolationist. Only about a dozen years separated the Senate defeat of Wilson's dream and the Japanese invasion of Manchuria in 1931. Throughout the 1930s, while the New Deal struggled with the domestic Depression, progressives saw Mussolini's conquest of Ethiopia, Franco's victory with fascist support in Spain, Japan's invasion of China in 1937, Hitler's triumphs in Austria in 1938 and in Czechoslovakia, and the Ribbentrop-Molotov Pact in 1939, leading to World War II. To the progressives who came to Washington with Franklin Roosevelt, himself once Wilson's Assistant Secretary of the Navy, the "lesson" of America's failure to lead the League of Nations was as close and as vivid as the "lessons of Vietnam" seem today.

In constitutional terms, the lesson was to free presidential leadership from congressional parochialism, for instance by delegating power to negotiate trade agreements, and from state laws by letting the president dispose of the American property of Russian nationals in recognizing the Soviet Union and, later, by striking down reciprocal inheritance laws that might burden foreign relations. Professor Glennon's chapter in this volume reviews the evolution of Justice Douglas's views on presidential power from Roosevelt's Litvinov Agreement and Japanese relocation order through Truman's Steel Seizure Case to Johnson's and Nixon's Southeast Asian operations. But Douglas's interest in international affairs ranged far beyond the constitutional issues that were his professional task. Soon after the end of World War II, he began the summer travels in Asia that he chronicled in *Strange Lands and Friendly People, Beyond the High Himalayas, North From Malaya, and West of the Indus.* In addition, during twenty years he set out his vision for the world in speeches, articles, and books, together a flow of observations and reflections that would be prolific even for a writer who was not simultaneously producing a record number of judicial opinions.

Here one can only summarize the major themes that Douglas first sounded in the 1940s and elaborated over the following decades:

• The atomic bomb, he said, made war obsolete. Disarmament and a Rule of Law were the only alternative.

• Law means peaceful settlement of "conflicts" or "disputes" among nations, typified by adjudication in the World Court. A Rule of Law (he used the indefinite article) must rest on "*consensus.*" But it also must allow for change through international legislation. The United Nations is the embryonic legislature.

• Mankind, he asserted, shares a vision of basic human values, catalogued in the United Nations' Universal Declaration of Human Rights.

• The nation-state, he believed, was obsolete, but nationalism remained an essential evolutionary stage. Communism is another form of exploitation, but the central aim of nationalist revolutions is to end feudalism and foreign domination; they are unavoidable and should be encouraged. The United States should support postcolonial regimes with trade and financial and technical assistance.

Summarized in this way, these views were the conventional wisdom, not to say the pieties, of postwar American internationalism. To Douglas, however, they were not abstract propositions. Douglas was not primarily a theorist. His speeches and writings on world affairs are filled with contemporary examples, economic statistics, and quotations from statesmen, psychologists, scientists, and writers. He meant the propositions for concrete application.

They were, however, at best marginal to actual American policy, which relied far more on military power, anti-Communist alliances, and overt or covert interventions in nations around the globe, policy made by men like Acheson and Kennan, who, Douglas wrote, thought that "American foreign policy had suffered under regimes of legalism."[1] Summing up his disillusionment in the preface to his Stokes Lectures in 1968, Douglas wrote of "the bankruptcy of my generation," the "architects of the existing design, [whose] thinking has been warped and conditioned by one evil man (Stalin), and by another who was ignorant of the world and its problems (Truman), and by a third (Churchill) who was a romanticist but a true apostle of the Rule of Force and White Supremacy."[2]

Douglas, a political as well as a Legal Realist, could not be charged with "legalism." Because of his long experience with the American Constitution and government, it is interesting to examine his vision of international institutions. Like almost all Americans since Wilson, Douglas saw in the League of Nations and its successor, the United Nations, a rudimentary but promising extension of the American experience with federalism. He reports, in *Go East, Young Man,* that he helped organize a Woodrow Wilson Club at Whitman College and debated in support of the League, though subsequently he thought better of Charles Evans Hughes, his later Chief whom Wilson defeated in 1916, than of Wilson.[3] During World War II, Douglas encouraged Roosevelt's strategy of winning American acceptance of a United Nations system that would include a big-power veto. The system would progress politically independent of texts. Douglas cheered as "noble, principled, responsible action" Truman's reliance on Security Council support for the Korean "police action," after the Soviet Union, relying on the U.N. Charter to require its assent, boycotted the meetings.

Writing in 1963 in "The United Nations and the Rule of Law," Douglas invoked familiar images of action by the Security Council or the General Assembly as "legislation," with executive functions vested in the Secretary General, and the judicial function in the International Court of Justice, rather lamely assigning all specialized agencies to an "administrative function."[4] Surprisingly, considering modern American federalism, he did not see in agricultural, health, and development programs, conditioned on economic, ecological, and human rights reforms, a stronger instrument of progress than the political resolutions of the General Assembly. He hailed the shift of political action to General Assembly "recommendations" under the Uniting for Peace Resolution, sponsored by the United States in 1950 in order to circumvent future Soviet vetoes, as a "constitutional landmark in the development of international lawmaking" greatly strengthening "the legislative power of the United Nations."[5] The United States soon lost its enthusiasm for this view of the General Assembly, as scores of new African and Asian members pursued their own anti-Western agendas.

The American public could be expected to see the United Nations in the images of American federalism, but one wonders that experienced students and participants would see an analogy. First, the League of Nations and then the UN were conceived in response to war, primarily as institutions to keep and, if necessary, to enforce peace between member states by means of "police forces" that could defeat "aggressor" nations. International law meant legal rights and obligations among national governments, and the role of the World Court was to decide legal disputes between nations that otherwise might lead to war. Keeping peace and settling conflicts between the states as such is a minor part of American federalism, and when a true fighting issue came along, it failed. The genius of the Constitution was and is precisely to legislate and adjudicate directly for private citizens and interests throughout the states rather than for the states as entities. Thus members of Congress, even when senators were still elected by state legislatures, always have been separate, often competing, servants of their constituents, not ambassadors extending their states' foreign policies into an intergovernmental forum.

During the fifty years since Douglas's appointment to the Court, there have in fact been two competing analogues to American federalism, alternative visions for surmounting the nation-state. Each attracted one of Douglas's colleagues. The hope for evolution of the United Nations, through plans like that proposed by Grenville Clark and Louis Sohn, into a world federation won Wiley Rutledge's allegiance as well as Douglas's. Owen Roberts, instead, supported Atlantic Union, a genuine economic and political federation of democracies proposed in Clarence Streit's 1939 book *Union Now*. It offered American leaders of the 1950s, including Senators Kennedy, Kefauver, Nixon, and Washington's Scoop Jackson, a positive vision to sustain the American military and economic commitment to a non-Communist Western Europe. But when Western European leaders like Jean Monnet pursued that vision toward forms of integration to which military forces and peace-keeping institutions are largely irrelevant, the United States contented itself with benign talk of transatlantic "partnership," a cliché that could not withstand the wheat and chicken wars of the 1980s, let alone the economic stresses in store for the 1990s. The postwar era of faith that American leadership embodied ideals shared among western democracies ended in 1968 — in Vietnam and in Latin America.

Douglas at first relegated the development of partial federal systems to "regionalism," which (like the UN Charter) he again saw mainly as ways to settle disputes without having to take them to the United Nations. He became more enthusiastic as the European Communities developed not only effective institutions for a common market, deciding issues like those he knew under the Constitution's Commerce Clause, but also established an active European Court of Human Rights. But he treated these as advanced examples of forms about to be emulated in Africa and Latin America and in the United Nations.

In sum, in a choice between universality or closer supernational integrations, Douglas came down on the side of universality. He deplored excluding Communist China from the United Nations and Castro's Cuba from the Organization of American States. His heart was with the vast, poor nations of Asia, Africa, and Latin America, as Professor Lobel's essay spells out, rather than with the more radical restructuring among the advanced democracies. This again was in the mainstream of progressive American thought. The preoccupation of the foreign policy establishment with Europe and the containment of Communism led it foolishly to support French colonialism in Indochina for the sake of NATO—against Kennan's advice, however. The perception of a geopolitical threat of Communism led to direct American intervention in Vietnam, besides supporting military tyrannies to thwart revolutions abroad from Iran and Indonesia to Guatemala and Chile.

At times, Douglas's view of Third World nations only reversed the romanticism with which he charged the old imperialist, Churchill. Douglas was not naive about them; he recognized endemic corruption, authoritarianism, and racism among nonwhite peoples, and he stressed the priority of economic development. But he took as evidence of common political goals and human values the plans and statements signed by Western-educated elites. He saw the future in the idealized image of Nehru's India, with its American-style constitution and British judicial and administrative tradition. Later he shifted from optimism about peaceful postcolonial development and concentrated on opposition to overt and covert American intervention on the side of repressive and reactionary regimes.

Douglas did not resolve, in his advocacy of a rule of law, the intrinsic tension between legal rules for nonintervention and dispute settlement between equal sovereign states and legal institutions designed to improve economic conditions and protect human rights within a state. Is it proper to condition financial support for Brazil on effective steps to save the rain forests and the aboriginal tribes of the Amazon basin, or are Brazil and its neighbors right to attack such conditions as interference with their use of their own national resources? What is the correct rule when an enlightened, progressive democracy is overthrown by a tyrant? Should a postnationalist order among democracies, in Europe, in Latin America, or elsewhere, like the American Constitution, guarantee to its members a republican form of government? One wonders which rules of law Douglas would have wanted his country to apply toward the murderous rulers in Uganda or Cambodia, the genocidal tribal or ethnic warfare within the artificial boundaries of postcolonial Africa, or the medieval cruelty and religious fanaticism among his once "friendly people," who hold hostages for ransom, use poison gas against their minorities, torture their political opponents, send their children into martyrdom, and proclaim a rule of law that requires the assassination of blasphemous novelists.

If Douglas did not resolve the tension, however, neither does anyone else.

In practice, support for nationalism or supranationalism, calls for intervention or nonintervention, are political alternatives just as demands for federal action or for "states' rights" are in the American constitutional system. Douglas, to repeat, was not concerned with legal theory but with law in the service of progress. It was not important to have a consistent definition to distinguish law from other social processes. He thought the precise forms of legal structures secondary to their use in practice. He used "rule of law" to mean any effective alternative to the rule of force, diplomacy instead of war, negotiated consensus instead of conflict.

This eclectic view of law, too, only postpones rather than resolves the ultimate question. Douglas left no doubt which side should prevail in the conflicts between oligarchy and populism, between the few rich and the many poor, between colonialism and nationalism, between short-term exploitation of resources and long-term conservation, between human rights and oppression. But regrettably, the good and bad sides of these couplets in many countries do not line up as neatly as he might have wished. A view of law measured by outcomes cannot maintain consistency about legal processes. An openly dualistic view of law and force has been part of Communist doctrine from its beginnings through the Brezhnev era, whatever it may become in the future. When the oligarchs, the rich, or the dominant race fail to negotiate a consensus on sharing their wealth or their power, both progressives like Douglas and, on the opposite side, conservatives like Reagan also have drawn from our own revolutionary history phrases to distinguish justified from unjustified use of force.

At the end of his century, Douglas's internationalism has a fair chance again to become the conventional wisdom. Few will disagree with his diagnoses of the world's chief ills. As the threat of Soviet or Chinese aggression recedes, so may the preoccupation with nuclear weapons, which have not yet proved more dangerous to peace or stability than conventional armies or AK-47s and plastic bombs, and so may American reliance on military forces in the Third World. Economic power gradually shifts from landowning oligarchies to literate and professional elites, but the urbanization of poverty endangers both the resulting gains for democracy and nature itself.

The United Nations may again prove a useful instrument for collective pressure to settle localized conflicts, though not in its original image as a police force armed to enforce the rule of law against an aggressor. Beyond this, the irresistible need will be for agencies to deal with the global problems of the sea, the air, and the space beyond the atmosphere that ignore territorial lines, and to find ways to share the costs and the benefits. It will call for examining the whole range of institutional models, unitary or decentralized, regulatory as well as fiscal and managerial, in which the experience of American federalism made Justice Douglas an expert; but it will require more than expertise. It will require Douglas's vision.

Notes

1. William O. Douglas, *Toward a Global Federalism* (New York: New York Univ. Press, 1968), p. 1.

2. Ibid., p. xi.

3. William O. Douglas, *Go East, Young Man: The Autobiography of William O. Douglas* (New York: Random House, 1974).

4. William O. Douglas, *The Anatomy of Liberty* (New York: Trident, 1963), p. 143.

5. Ibid., p. 127.

Selected Bibliography
Notes on Contributors
Table of Cases
Index

Selected Bibliography

I. Books by William O. Douglas

An Almanac of Liberty. Garden City, N.Y.: Doubleday, 1954.

America Challenged. Princeton, N.J.: Princeton University Press, 1960.

The Anatomy of Liberty: The Rights of Man Without Force. New York: Trident Press, 1963.

Being an American. New York: John Day, 1948.

Beyond the High Himalayas. Garden City, N.Y.: Doubleday, 1952.

The Bible and the Schools. Boston: Little, Brown, 1966.

The Court Years, 1939–1975: The Autobiography of William O. Douglas. New York: Random House, 1980.

Democracy and Finance. Edited by James Allen. New Haven, Conn.: Yale University Press, 1940.

Democracy's Manifesto. Edited by R. Walsh. New York: John Day, 1962.

Exploring the Himalayas. New York: Random House, 1958.

Farewell To Texas: A Vanishing Wilderness. New York: McGraw-Hill, 1967.

Freedom of the Mind. American Library Association, 1962.

Go East, Young Man: The Early Years. New York: Random House, 1974.

Holocaust or Hemispheric Co-op: Cross Currents in Latin America. New York: Random House, 1971.

International Dissent: Six Steps Toward World Peace. New York: Random House, 1971.

A Living Bill of Rights. New York: Doubleday, 1961.

Mr. Lincoln and the Negroes. New York: Atheneum, 1963.

Muir of the Mountains. Boston: Houghton Mifflin, 1961.

My Wilderness: East to Katahdin. Garden City, N.Y.: Doubleday, 1961.

North from Malaya: Adventure on Five Fronts. Garden City, N.Y.: Doubleday, 1953.

Of Men and Mountains. New York: Harper, 1950.

Points of Rebellion. New York: Random House, 1969.

The Right of the People. Westport, Conn.: Greenwood Press, 1958.

Russian Journey. Garden City: N.Y.: Doubleday, 1956.

Stare Decisis (1949 Cardozo Lecture). New York: Association of the Bar of the City of New York, 1949.

Strange Lands and Friendly People. New York: Harper, 1951.

The Supreme Court and the Bicentennial: Two Lectures. 1978.

The Three Hundred Year War: A Chronicle of Ecological Disaster. New York: Random House, 1972.

Towards a Global Federalism. New York: New York University Press, 1968.

West of the Indus. Garden City, N.Y.: Doubleday, 1958.

We the Judges: Studies in American and Indian Constitutional Law from Marshall to Mukherjea. Garden City, N.Y.: Doubleday, 1956.

A Wilderness Bill of Rights. New York: Little, Brown, 1965.

II. Articles and Books About William O. Douglas

Ares, Charles. "Constitutional Criminal Law." *Columbia Law Review* 74 (1974): 362–66.

Ball, Howard, and Phillip Cooper. *Of Power and Right: Justices Black and Douglas and America's Tumultuous Years, 1937–1975.* New York: Oxford University Press, 1991.

Baude, P. "An Appreciative Note on Mr. Justice Douglas' View on the Courts' Role in Environmental Cases." *Indiana Law Journal* 51 (1975): 22–26.

Caragher, James H. "The Wilderness Ethic of Justice William O. Douglas." *University of Illinois Law Review* 1986: 645–68.

Cohen, William. "Protection of the Individual Against Himself." In *The William O. Douglas Inquiry Into the State of Individual Freedom,* ed. Harry S. Ashmore, pp. 27–35. Boulder, Colo.: Westview, 1979.

———. "Justices Black and Douglas and the 'Natural-Law-Due-Process Formula': Some Fragments of Intellectual History." *U.C. Davis Law Review* 20 (1987): 381–85.

———. "Justice Douglas and the Rosenberg Case: Setting the Record Straight." *Cornell Law Review* 70 (1985): 211–52.

Cooper, Phillip J. "William O. Douglas: Conscience of the Court." In *The Burger Court: Political and Judicial Profiles,* ed. Charles Lamb and Stephen C. Halpern. Urbana: University of Illinois Press, 1991.

———. "William O. Douglas on Law and Administration in the Modern Governmental Context." *International Journal of Public Administration* 5 (1987): 1–56.

Countryman, Vern. "The Constitution and Job Discrimination." *Washington Law Review* 39 (1964): 74–95.

———. *Douglas of the Supreme Court: A Selection of His Opinions.* Garden City, N.Y.: Doubleday, 1959.

———. *The Douglas Opinions.* New York: Random House, 1977.

———. *The Judicial Record of Justice William O. Douglas.* Cambridge, Mass.: Harvard University Press, 1974.

———. "Justice Douglas: Expositor of the Bankruptcy Law." *UCLA Law Review* 16 (1969): 773–838.

———. "Justice Douglas: Expositor of the Bankruptcy Law." *American Bankruptcy Law Journal* 51 (1977): 127–94, 247–75.

———. "Justice Douglas and Freedom of Expression." *University of Illinois Law Journal* 1978: 301–27.

———. "Justice Douglas and the Law of Business Regulation." *Banking Law Journal* 91 (1974): 312–19.

———. "Search and Seizure in a Shambles? Recasting Fourth Amendment Law in the Mold of Justice Douglas." *Iowa Law Review* 64 (1979): 435–60.

Dorsen, Norman. "Equal Protection of the Laws." *Columbia Law Review* 74 (1974): 357–62.

Duram, James C. *Justice William O. Douglas.* Boston, Mass.: Twayne Publishers, 1981.

Emerson, Thomas I. "Justice Douglas and Lawyers with a Cause." *Yale Law Journal* 89 (1980): 616–23.

———. "Government Secrecy and the Citizen's Rights to Know." In *In Honor of Justice Douglas: A Symposium on Individual Freedom and the Government,* ed. Robert H. Keller, Jr. Westport, Conn.: Greenwood Press, 1978. Pages 27–54.

Epstein, Leon D. "Justice Douglas and Civil Liberties." *Wisconsin Law Review* 1951:125–57.

Gazell, James A. "Justice Douglas and Judicial Administration: A Libertarian Approach." *Gonzaga Law Review* 14 (1979): 785–817.

Glancy, Dorothy J. "Getting the Government Off the Backs of People: The Right of Privacy and Freedom of Expression in the Opinions of Justice William O. Douglas." *Santa Clara Law Review* 21 (1981): 1047–67.

Glennon, Robert J., Jr. "'Do Not Go Gentle': More Than an Epitaph." *Wayne Law Review* 22 (1976): 1305–34.

Hopkirk, J. W. "W. O. Douglas — His Work in Policing Bankruptcy Proceedings." *Vanderbilt Law Review* 18 (1965): 663–99.

Irish, Marian D. "Mr. Justice Douglas and Judicial Restraint." *University of Florida Law Review* 6 (1953): 537–53.

Isenberg, Max. "Thoughts on William O. Douglas' *The Court Years:* A Confession and Avoidance." *American University Law Review* 30 (1981): 415–28.

Karst, Kenneth L. "Invidious Discrimination: Justice Douglas and the Return of the Natural-Law-Due-Process Formula." *UCLA Law Review* 16 (1969): 716–50.

Keller, Robert H., Jr. "William O. Douglas, the Supreme Court, and American Indians." *American Indian Law Review* 3 (1975): 333–60.

———, ed. *In Honor of Justice Douglas: A Symposium on Individual Freedom and the Government.* Westport, Conn.: Greenwood Press, 1978.

Louisell, David W. "The Man and the Mountain: Douglas on Religious Freedom." *Yale Law Journal* 73 (1964): 975–98.

Linde, Hans. "Justice Douglas on Freedom in the Welfare State." *Washington Law Review* 39 (1964): 4–46.

———. "Constitutional Rights in the Public Sector: Justice Douglas on Liberty in the Welfare State." *Washington Law Review* 40 (1965): 10–77.

Manning, Leonard F. "The Douglas Concept of God in Government." *Washington Law Review* 39 (1964): 47–73.

Morris, Arval A. "Citizen Access to the Federal Courts: Douglas v. The Burger Court." In Keller, ed., *In Honor of Justice Douglas.* Westport, Conn.: Greenwood Press, 1979. Pages 90–104.

Murphy, Jay W. "Justice William O. Douglas: Humanism: A Copernican Revolution in Law." In Keller, ed., *In Honor of Justice Douglas.* Westport, Conn.: Greenwood Press, 1979. Pages 3–26.

Note. "Toward a Constitutional Theory of Individuality: The Privacy Opinions of Justice Douglas." *Yale Law Journal* 87 (1978): 1579–1600.

Note. "Economic Predilections of Justice Douglas." *Wisconsin Law Review* (1949): 531–62.

Parrish, Michael E. "Justice Douglas and the Rosenberg Case: A Rejoinder." *Cornell Law Review* 70 (1985): 1048–57.

Powe, L. A., Jr. "Evolution to Absolutism: Justice Douglas and the First Amendment." *Columbia Law Review* 74 (1974): 371–411.

———. "Justice Douglas After Fifty Years: The First Amendment, McCarthyism and Rights." *Constitutional Commentary* 6 (1989): 267–87.

Richards, D. R. "Justice Douglas and the Availability of the Federal Forum to Civil Rights Litigants." *Baylor Law Review* 28 (1976): 221–34.

Rodell, Fred. "As Justice Douglas Completes His First Thirty Years on the Court: Herewith a Random Anniversary Sample." *UCLA Law Review* 16 (1969): 704–15.

Sevareid, Eric. "An Interview with William O. Douglas." In Keller, ed., *In Honor of Justice Douglas.* Westport, Conn.: Greenwood Press, 1979. Pages 148–169.

Simon, James F. *Independent Journey: The Life of William O. Douglas.* New York: Harper & Row, 1980.

Stickgold, Marc. "Nineteen Eighty: Being an Interview with William O. Douglas Shortly After His Death Together with a Brief Remembrance of His Life." *Golden Gate University Law Review* 10 (1980): 535–52.

Thomas, H. S. "Justice W. O. Douglas and the Concept of 'Fair Trial.'" *Vanderbilt Law Review* 18 (1965): 701–16.

Ulmer, S. Sidney. "Parabolic Support of Civil Liberty Claims: The Case of William O. Douglas." *Journal of Politics* 41 (1979): 634–39.

Urofsky, Melvin I. "Conflict Among the Brethren: Felix Frankfurter, William O. Douglas and the Clash of Personalities and Philosophies on the United States Supreme Court." *Duke Law Journal* (1988): 71–113.

———. "'Dear Teacher': The Correspondence of William O. Douglas and Thomas Reed Powell." *Law and History Review* 7 (1989): 331–386.

———. "William O. Douglas and His Clerks." *Western Legal History* 3 (1990): 1–20.

———, and Philip E. Urofsky, eds. *The Douglas Letters: Selections from the Private Papers of Justice William O. Douglas.* Bethesda: Adler and Adler, 1987.

Van Alstyne, William W. "The Constitutional Rights of Government Employees." *UCLA Law Review* 16 (1969): 751–72.

Way, H. Frank. "The Study of Judicial Attitudes: The Case of Mr. Justice Douglas." *Western Political Quarterly* 24 (1971): 12–23.

White, G. Edward. "The Anti-Judge: William O. Douglas and the Ambiguities of Individuality." *Virginia Law Review* 74 (1988): 17–86.

Wolfman, Bernard, Jonathan L. F. Silver, and Marjorie A. Silver. "The Behavior of Justice Douglas in Federal Tax Cases." *University of Pennsylvania Law Review* 122 (1973): 235–65.

———. *Dissent Without Opinion: The Behavior of Justice William O. Douglas in Federal Tax Cases.* Philadelphia: University of Pennsylvania Press, 1975.

Notes on Contributors

HOWARD BALL is dean of the College of Arts and Sciences at the University of Vermont. Author of *Justice Downwind: America's Nuclear Testing Program in the 1950's* and of a text on the Supreme Court, he and Phillip Cooper are coauthors of the study of Justices Black and Douglas, *Of Power and Right: Justices Black and Douglas and America's Tumultuous Years, 1937–1975* (1991).

WILLIAM COHEN, a former clerk for Justice Douglas, is C. Wendell and Edith M. Carlsmith Professor of Law at Stanford Law School and coauthor of Barrett, Cohen, and Varat, *Constitutional Law—Cases and Materials.*

DREW S. DAYS III is professor of law at Yale Law School and former assistant attorney general for civil rights in the U.S. Department of Justice.

NORMAN DORSEN is Stokes Professor of Law at New York University, coauthor of cases and materials on civil liberties and of materials on lawyers' ethics, and is president of the American Civil Liberties Union.

STEVEN B. DUKE, a former clerk of Justice Douglas, is Law of Science and Technology Professor at Yale Law School. He has written previously about Justice Douglas.

THOMAS M. FRANCK is Murry and Ida Becker Professor of Law at New York University School of Law and director of the Center for International Studies there. He is author of *Human Rights in Third World Perspective* and coeditor of *United States Foreign Relations Law: Documents and Sources.* He is also editor of *American Journal of International Law.*

DOROTHY J. GLANCY is professor of law at Santa Clara University's School of Law. She has written previously about Justice Douglas's views of privacy.

MICHAEL J. GLENNON is professor of law at University of California, Davis, School of Law, author of *Constitutional Diplomacy,* and coeditor of *United States Foreign Relations Law.*

ROBERT JEROME GLENNON, professor of law at the University of Arizona's School of Law, is author of *The Iconoclast as Reformer: Jerome Frank's Impact on American Law.*

319

DONALD W. JACKSON, a political scientist and lawyer, is professor of political science at Texas Christian University and former Judicial Fellow at the United States Supreme Court.

RALPH W. JOHNSON, professor of law at the University of Washington's School of Law, has edited and coauthored *Felix Cohen's Handbook of Federal Indian Law* and written about environmental matters.

SANFORD H. KADISH is Morrison Professor of Law at Boalt Hall College of Law, University of California, Berkeley. He has written extensively about criminal law and discretion in the law.

HAROLD HONGJU KOH, a former clerk to Justice Harry Blackmun, is professor of law at Yale Law School and author of *The National Security Constitution: Sharing Power After the Iran-Contra Affair.*

HANS A. LINDE, a former justice of the Oregon Supreme Court, was clerk to Justice Douglas and professor of law at the University of Oregon School of Law. He has written widely on constitutional law and on the role of state constitutional law in relation to federal constitutional law.

JULES LOBEL is professor of law, University of Pittsburgh School of Law, and editor of *Civil Rights Litigation Attorneys Fees Handbook* and of a volume on the Constitution.

L. A. POWE, JR., a former clerk to Justice Douglas, is Anne Green Regents Chair at the University of Texas Law School and author of *American Broadcasting and the First Amendment* and of previous work on Justice Douglas.

CHARLES REICH, formerly professor of law at Yale and the author of *The Greening of America,* is Marshall P. Madison Professor at the University of San Francisco School of Law.

WILLIAM H. RODGERS, JR., is Bloedel Professor of Law, University of Washington School of Law. He is the author of *Cases and Materials on Energy and Natural Resources Law* and of a several-volume set, *Environmental Law.*

ELIZABETH M. SCHNEIDER, a former staff attorney at the Center for Constitutional Rights, is professor of law at Brooklyn Law School and visiting professor at Harvard Law School (1991).

CHRISTOPHER D. STONE is Roy P. Crocker Professor at the University of Southern California Law Center. Coauthor of *Law, Language and Ethics,* he has also written on the environment: *Should Trees Have Standing* and *Earth and Other Ethics.*

NADINE STROSSEN is professor of law at New York Law School and is general counsel, American Civil Liberties Union. She has written extensively on church-state relations.

MELVIN I. UROFSKY is professor of history at Virginia Commonwealth University. He is author of *Louis D. Brandeis and the Progressive Tradition* and editor of *The Douglas Letters: Selections from the Private Papers of Justice William O. Douglas.*

SAMUEL WALKER is a historian in the School of Criminal Justice at the University of Nebraska at Omaha. He is the author of *Popular Justice: A History of American Criminal Justice* and *In Defense of American Liberties: A History of the ACLU.*

STEPHEN L. WASBY is professor of political science at State University of New York at Albany. He is the author of *The Supreme Court in the Federal Judicial System* and author and editor of works on civil liberties and civil rights.

T. H. WATKINS is editor of *Wilderness* magazine and a vice president of the Wilderness Society. He is a former senior editor of *American Heritage* magazine. He has published numerous books, including a history of the American public lands and a biography of John Muir. His biography of Harold L. Ickes is forthcoming.

CHARLES F. WILKINSON, Moses Lasky Professor of Law at the University of Colorado's School of Law, writes on natural resources law and policy relating to the American West. He is coauthor of *Federal Public Land and Resources Law* and *Land and Resource Planning in the National Forests.* Among his writings on Indian law and policy is *American Indians: Time and the Law.*

Table of Cases

Abbate v. United States, 359 U.S. 187 (1959), 145*n22*

Aberdeen & Rockfish R.R. v. Students Challenging Regulatory Agency Procedures (SCRAP), 422 U.S. 289 (1975) (SCRAP II), 223*n12*

Abington Township, School District of, v. Schempp, 374 U.S. 203 (1974), 103, 105*n3*

Abrams v. United States, 250 U.S. 616 (1919), 227

Adamson v. California, 332 U.S. 46 (1947), 124

Adderly v. Florida, 385 U.S. 39 (1966), 56*n8*, 70, 73–75

Adickes v. Kress, 398 U.S. 144 (1970), 117

Adler v. Board of Education, 342 U.S. 485 (1952), 80

Air Pollution Variance Board v. Western Alfalfa, 416 U.S. 861 (1974), 171*n7*

Alabama v. Texas, 347 U.S. 272 (1954), 240, 247*n35*

Alexander v. Louisiana, 405 U.S. 625 (1972), 56*n10*

Alexander v. United States ex rel. Kulik, 332 U.S. 174 (1947), 30*n91*

American Communication Workers v. Douds, 399 U.S. 382 (1950), 87*n9*, 87*n18*

Anastaplo, In re, 366 U.S. 82 (1961), 83–84, 87*n19*, 89*nn77–78*, 125*n2*

Anders v. California, 386 U.S. 738 (1967), 141

Anderson v. United States, 417 U.S. 211 (1974), 145*n16*

Andrus v. Charlestone Stone Products, 436 U.S. 604 (1978), 247*n41*

Andrus v. Shell Oil Co., 446 U.S. 657 (1980), 225*n33*

Antelope, United States v., 430 U.S. 641 (1977), 212*n56*

Antoine v. Washington, 420 U.S. 194 (1975), 202, 208*n8*, 212–13*n71*

Argersinger v. Hamlin, 407 U.S. 25 (1971), 237

Arizona v. California, 373 U.S. 546 (1963), 246*n23*

Arlan's Department Store of Louisville v. Kentucky, 371 U.S. 218 (1962), 95, 105*n3*

Bailey v. Richardson, 341 U.S. 918 (1951), 88*n61*

Baker v. Carr, 369 U.S. 186 (1962), 272–73

Baldwin v. New York, 399 U.S. 66 (1970), 147*n71*

Balint, United States v., 258 U.S. 150 (1922), 153*n5*

Ballard, United States v., 322 U.S. 78 (1944), 93, 98, 105*n6*

Baltimore Gas & Electric Co. v. Natural Resources Defense Council, Inc., 462 U.S. 87 (1983), 224*n13*

Barenblatt v. United States, 360 U.S. 109 (1959), 83–84, 89*nn77–78*, 125*n2*

Barker, United States v., 546 F.2d 940 (D.C. Cir. 1976), 145*n16*

Barsky v. Board of Regents, 347 U.S. 442 (1952), 81, 86

Bartkus v. Illinois, 359 U.S. 121 (1959), 145*n22*

Beauharnais v. Illinois, 343 U.S. 250 (1952), 71–72, 156–57

Bell v. Maryland, 378 U.S. 226 (1964), 113, 151

Belle Terre, Village of, v. Boraas, 461 U.S. 1 (1974), 219, 221–22, 229–30

Belmont, United States v., 301 U.S. 324 (1937), 265

Berman v. Parker, 348 U.S. 26 (1954), 221

Best v. Humboldt Placer Mining Co., 371 U.S. 334 (1963), 217, 246*n20*

Board of Commissioners v. United States, 308 U.S. 343 (1939), 193–94

Board of Education v. Allen, 392 U.S. 236 (1968), 104*n3,* 106*n27*

Bolling v. Sharpe, 347 U.S. 497 (1954), 210*n44*

Bouie v. City of Columbia, 378 U.S. 347 (1964), 138, 151

Bowers v. Hardwick, 478 U.S. 186 (1986), 182–83

Boykin v. Alabama, 395 U.S. 238 (1969), 141

Boyle v. Landry, 401 U.S. 77 (1971), 88*n53*

Brandenburg v. Ohio, 395 U.S. 444 (1969), 73, 125*n4*

Brown v. Board of Education, 347 U.S. 483 (1954), 110

Burke v. Southern Pacific Railroad, 234 U.S. 669 (1941), 247*n37*

Burton v. Wilmington Parking Authority, 365 U.S. 715 (1961), 118*nn16, 20*

Butler, United States v., 297 U.S. 1 (1936), 89*n70*

Byrne v. Karalexis, 401 U.S. 216 (1971), 88*n53*

California v. United States, 438 U.S. 645 (1978), 248*n57*

Camara v. Municipal Court of San Francisco, 387 U.S. 523 (1967), 48*n50*

Cantrell v. Forest City Publishing Co., 419 U.S. 245 (1974), 175*n52*

Cantwell v. Connecticut, 310 U.S. 296 (1940), 104*n2*

Case Concerning the Barcelona Traction, Light, and Power Co. (Belgium v. Spain) [1970] I.C.J. Rep. 3, 277*n114*

Causby, United States v., 328 U.S. 256 (1946), 223*n11,* 224*n18,* 229

CBS v. Democratic National Committee, 412 U.S. 94 (1973), 73, 75

Choate v. Trapp, 224 U.S. 665 (1912), 212*n71*

Choctaw Nation v. Oklahoma, 397 U.S. 620 (1970), 203, 208*n8,* 208–09*n22,* 210*n36*

Citizens to Preserve Overton Park v. Volpe, 401 U.S. 402 (1971), 244

City of Richmond v. Corson, 109 S.Ct. 706 (1989), 116

Civil Rights Cases, 109 U.S. 3 (1883), 109–12

Classic, United States v., 313 U.S. 199 (1941), 114–15, 137

Cleveland v. United States, 329 U.S. 14 (1946), 92, 95–96, 105*n6*

Cole v. Young, 351 U.S. 536 (1956), 89*n66*

Communist Party v. Subversive Activities Control Board, 367 U.S. 1 (1961), 73

Connolly v. General Construction Co., 169 U.S. 385 (1926), 146*n25*

Cox v. Louisiana, 379 U.S. 559 (1965), 87*n13,* 138–39, 146*n40,* 151

Cox Broadcasting Corporation v. Cohn, 420 U.S. 469 (1975), 175*n52*

Craig v. Harney, 331 U.S. 367 (1947), 143*n3*

Curtiss-Wright Export Co., United States v., 299 U.S. 304 (1936), 275*n37,* 299, 303*nn7, 14*

DaCosta v. Laird, 405 U.S. 979 (1972), 276*n93,* 295*n96*

Debs v. United States, 249 U.S. 211 (1919), 88*n37*

DeCoteau v. District County Court, 420 U.S. 944 (1975), 197, 204

DeFunis v. Odegaard, 416 U.S. 312 (1974), 5, 6n10

DeGregory v. New Hampshire, 383 U.S. 825 (1966), 75, 87n21

Dennis v. United States, 341 U.S. 494 (1951), 71–72, 77, 79–80, 83, 123, 156

Denver & Rio Grande Railway, United States v., 150 U.S. 1 (1893), 247n44

Department of Game of Washington v. Puyallup Tribe, 414 U.S. 44 (1973), (*Puyallup II*), 200–02, 211–12n53

Department of Game v. Puyallup Tribe, Inc., 86 Wash. 664, 548 P.2d 1058 (1976), 211n52

District Court In and For the County of Eagle, United States v., 401 U.S. 520 (1971), 238, 244

Doe v. Bolton, 410 U.S. 179 (1973), 105n18, 159, 172–73n25, 174n42, 175n65, 292n6

Dombrowski v. Pfister, 380 U.S. 479 (1965), 90n91

Dotterweich, United States v., 320 U.S. 277 (1943), 153n5

Douglas v. California, 372 U.S. 353 (1963), 140–41, 292n13

Dudgeon Case, 45 Eur. Ct. H.R. (Ser. A) (1981), 177n101

Duke Power Co. v. Carolina Environmental Study Group, Inc., 438 U.S. 59 (1978), 225n34

Durham v. United States, 214 F.2d 862 (D.C. Cir 1954), 143n4

Dyson v. Stein, 401 U.S. 200 (1971), 88n53

Eagles v. United States ex rel. Samuels, 329 U.S. 304 (1946), 30n91

Ehrlichman, United States v., 546 F.2d 910 (D.C.Cir 1976), 144–45n16

Elfbrandt v. Russell, 384 U.S. 11 (1966), 48n47, 74, 87n21, 125n4

Endo, Ex parte, 323 U.S. 283 (1944), 13–14, 267, 297, 299–300, 303n2

Engel v. Vitale, 370 U.S. 421 (1962), 95, 100–01, 103, 105n3, 106n27, 124, 144n2

England v. Louisiana State Board of Medical Examiners, 375 U.S. 411 (1964), 118n34

Erznoznik v. City of Jacksonville, 422 U.S. 205 (1975), 125n10

Estep v. United States, 327 U.S. 114 (1945), 17–19, 25, 54

Evans v. Abney, 396 U.S. 435 (1970), 118n37

Everson v. Board of Education, 330 U.S. 1 (1947), 103, 104n1, 124

Evitts v. Lucey, 469 U.S. 387 (1984), 141

Falbo v. United States, 320 U.S. 549 (1943), 16–17, 19

Federal Power Commission v. Niagara Mohawk Power, 347 U.S. 239 (1954), 247n27

Federal Power Commission v. Oregon, 349 U.S. 435 (1955), 238

Federal Power Commission v. Tuscarora Indian Nation, 362 U.S. 99 (1960), 196

Feiner v. New York, 340 U.S. 315 (1951), 87n26

First National City Bank v. Banco Nacional de Cuba, 406 U.S. 759 (1972), 270

Follett v. McCormick, 321 U.S. 573 (1944), 92, 98, 105n6

Fowler v. Rhode Island, 345 U.S. 67 (1953), 105n6

Frank v. Maryland, 359 U.S. 360 (1959), 48n49, 48n50

Freed, United States v., 401 U.S. 601 (1971), 137

Galvan v. Press, 347 U.S. 522 (1954), 80, 86

Garner v. Louisiana, 368 U.S. 157 (1961), 110

General Box Co. v. United States, 351 U.S. 159 (1956), 225*n31*
Gerlach Live Stock Co., United States v., 339 U.S. 725 (1950), 225*n31,* 240,
    247*n27*
Giboney v. Empire Storage & Ice Co., 336 U.S. 490 (1949), 125*n5*
Gibson v. Florida Legislative Investigating Committee, 372 U.S. 539 (1963),
    90*n91,* 125*n3*
Gillette v. United States, 401 U.S. 437 (1971), 30*n95,* 93, 99, 105*n6,* 106*n41*
Girouard v. United States, 328 U.S. 61 (1946), 105*n6*
Goldman v. United States, 316 U.S. 129 (1942), 171*n12*
Goldwater v. Carter, 444 U.S. 996 (1979), 266
Govind v. State of Madhay Pradesh, 1975 All India Reporter (Supreme Court)
    1378 (India 1975), 170
Grand River Dam Authority v. Grand Hydro, 335 U.S. 359 (1948), 240, 247*n27*
Grand River Dam Authority, United States v., 363 U.S. 229 (1960), 225*n31*
Grayned v. City of Rockford, 408 U.S. 104 (1972), 70
Greenwood v. Peacock, 384 U.S. 808 (1966), 115
Griffin v. California, 380 U.S. 609 (1965), 141
Griffin v. Illinois, 351 U.S. 12 (1956), 292*n13*
Griswold v. Connecticut, 381 U.S. 479 (1965), xii, 56*n7,* 69, 97, 111, 130, 155,
    158–61, 163–64, 170*n2,* 172*n22,* 173*nn32, 34,* 179–80, 228
Guest, United States v., 383 U.S. 745 (1966), 145*n16*
Gutknecht v. United States, 396 U.S. 295 (1970), 30*n95*

Hanover Star Milling Company v. Metcalf, 240 U.S. 403 (1916), 174*n48*
Harisiades v. Shaughnessy, 342 U.S. 480 (1952), 88*n62*
Harper v. Virginia Board of Elections, 383 U.S. 663 (1966), 67*n1,* 292*n13*
Harriss, United States v., 347 U.S. 612 (1954), 146*n28*
Hart v. United States, 391 U.S. 956 (1968), 295*n96*
Hayes, United States v., 589 F.2d 811 (5th Cir. 1979), 145*n22*
Heart of Atlanta Motel v. United States, 379 U.S. 241 (1964), 109, 113–14
Hickel v. Oil Shale Corp., 400 U.S. 48 (1970), 246*n20*
Hirabayashi v. United States, 320 U.S. 81 (1943), 7, 9–12, 80, 303*n2*
Holmes v. United States, 391 U.S. 936 (1968), 295*n96*
Holt State Bank, United States v., 270 U.S. 49 (1926), 247*n35*
Holtzman v. Schlesinger, 361 F.Supp. 553 (D.D.N.Y. 1973), 293*n17*
Holtzman v. Schlesinger, 414 U.S. 1304, 414 U.S. 1316 (1973), 56*nn11–12,*
    276*n92,* 281–82, 303*n18*

Illinois v. Milwaukee (I), 406 U.S. 91 (1972), 224*n15*
International Brotherhood of Teamsters v. Vogt, 354 U.S. 264 (1957), 125*n5*
International Minerals Corp., United States v., 402 U.S. 558 (1971), 146*n37*

Jackson, United States v., 390 U.S. 570 (1968), 147*nn57, 60*
Jackson v. Metropolitan Edison, 419 U.S. 345 (1974), 118*n38*
Johnson v. Robison, 415 U.S. 361 (1974), 93, 105*n6*
Joint Anti-Fascist Refugee Committee v. McGrath, 339 U.S. 123 (1950) and 341
    U.S. 123 (1951), 88*n61,* 176*n77*
Jones v. Mayer Co., 392 U.S. 409 (1968), 116–17

Jones v. Meehan, 175 U.S. 1 (1899), 208*n16*
Jones v. Opelika, 316 U.S. 584 (1942), 16

Kagama, United States v., 118 U.S. 375 (1886), 197, 212*n66*
Kahn v. Shevin, 417 U.S. 351 (1974), 183
Kake, Village of, v. Eagan, 369 U.S. 60 (1962), 202
Keith: see *United States District Court*
Kenosha v. Bruno, 412 U.S. 507 (1973), 116
Kent v. Dulles, 357 U.S. 116 (1958), 274*n1,* 294*n67,* 300
Keyes v. School District No. 1, Denver, 413 U.S. 189 (1973), 118*n40*
Keyishian v. Board of Regents, 385 U.S. 589 (1967), 125*n4*
Kleppe v. New Mexico, 426 U.S. 529 (1976), 246*n22*
Kohl v. United States, 91 U.S. 367 (1875), 174*n45*
Konigsberg v. State Bar of California, 366 U.S. 36 (1961), 83–84, 87*n19,* 89*nn77,*
    79, 125*n2*
Korematsu v. United States, 323 U.S. 214 (1944), 12–14, 25–26, 54–55, 80, 266,
    267, 303*n2*
Korematsu v. United States, 584 F.Supp. 1406 (N.D.Cal. 1984), 29*n60,* 275*n47*
Kovacs v. Cooper, 336 U.S. 77 (1949), 125*n8*

Laird v. Tatum, 408 U.S. 1 (1972), 176*n77,* 177*n88,* 271, 276*n98,* 303*n11,*
    303–04*n18*
Lambert v. California, 355 U.S. 225 (1957), 137–38, 150–51
Lamont v. Postmaster General, 381 U.S. 310 (1965), 74, 87*n21*
Landmark Communications, Inc. v. Virginia, 435 U.S. 829 (1978), 125*n4*
Lanzetta v. New Jersey, 306 U.S. 451 (1939), 146*n26*
Law Students Research Council v. Wadmond, 401 U.S. 154 (1971), 125*n4*
Lehman v. City of Shaker Heights, 418 U.S. 298 (1974), 122–23
Lemon v. Kurtzman, 403 U.S. 602 (1971) (*Lemon I*), 93, 104*n3,* 106*n27*
Lemon v. Kurtzman, 411 U.S. 192 (1973) (*Lemon II*), 104*n3,* 106*n27*
Leo Sheep Co. v. United States, 440 U.S. 668 (1979), 241–42, 248*n57*
Levy v. Louisiana, 391 U.S. 68 (1968), 67*n2*
Life of the Land v. Brinegar, 414 U.S. 1052 (1973), 246*n21*
Lindsey v. Normet, 405 U.S. 79 (1972), 294–95*n77*
Lombard v. Louisiana, 373 U.S. 267 (1973), 111–12
Lone Wolf v. Hitchcock, 187 U.S. 553 (1903), 204
Louisiana, United States v., 363 U.S. 1 (1960), 240
Lyng v. Northwest Indiana Cemetery Protective Association, 107 S.Ct. 1319
    (1988), 220, 224*n28*

McArthur v. Clifford, 393 U.S. 1002 (1968), 295*n96*
McClanahan v. Arizona State Tax Commission, 411 U.S. 164 (1973), 205–06
McCleskey v. Kemp, 107 S.Ct. 1756 (1987), 116
McCollum v. Board of Education, 333 U.S. 203 (1948), 100
McGowan v. Maryland, 366 U.S. 420 (1961), 99–102, 105*nn3, 6,* 106*nn26–27, 35*
Mapp v. Ohio, 367 U.S. 643 (1961), 129
Marbury v. Madison, 5 U.S. (1 Cr.) 137 (1803), 276*n94*
Martin v. Waddell, 41 U.S. (16 Pet.) 367 (1842), 247*n35*

Massachusetts v. Laird, 400 U.S. 886 (1970), 30*n94,* 290, 304*n18*

Mattz v. Arnett, 412 U.S. 481 (1971), 204

Menominee Tribe v. United States, 391 U.S. 404 (1968), 197, 210*n32,* 211*n49*

Mesarosh v. United States, 352 U.S. 1 (1956), 89*n66*

Mescalero Apache Tribe v. Jones, 411 U.S. 145 (1973), 205, 213*n82*

Metropolitan Edison Co. v. People Against Nuclear Energy, 460 U.S. 766 (1983),
    224*n13*

*Military & Paramilitary Activities in and Against Nicaragua (Nicaragua v. United
    States),* 1984 I.C.J. 392, 295*n95*

Milliken v. Bradley, 418 U.S. 717 (1974), 118–19*n40*

Minersville v. Gobitis, 310 U.S. 586 (1940), 15–16, 20, 25–26, 54–55

Missouri v. Holland, 252 U.S. 416 (1920), 211*n48*

Mitchell v. United States, 386 U.S. 972 (1967), 269–70, 295*nn96–97,* 304*n18*

Monell v. Department of Social Services, 436 U.S. 658 (1978), 116

Monroe v. Pape, 365 U.S. 167 (1961), 115–16, 135

Montana v. United States, 450 U.S. 544 (1981), 203, 207

Moose Lodge v. Irvis, 407 U.S. 163 (1972), 118*n39,* 119–20*n40*

Mora v. McNamara, 389 U.S. 934 (1967), 56*n12,* 220, 295*n96*

Morton v. Mancari, 471 U.S. 535 (1974), 201, 207

Murdock, United States v., 290 U.S. 389 (1933), 144*n14*

Murdock v. Pennsylvania, 319 U.S. 105 (1943), 92–93, 98, 105*n6*

Myers v. United States, 272 U.S. 52 (1926), 276*n69*

NAACP v. Alabama, 357 U.S. 449 (1958), 158, 176*n77*

Nashville Milk Co. v. Carnation Co., 355 U.S. 373 (1958), 48*n46,* 52

National Dairy Products Corp., United States v., 372 U.S. 29 (1963), 146*n28*

New Jersey Lottery Commission, United States v., 420 U.S. 371 (1975), 125*n10*

New Rider v. Board of Education, 414 U.S. 1097 (1973), 206

New Mexico, United States v., 438 U.S. 696 (1978), 248*n57*

New York Times v. United States, 403 U.S. 713 (1971), 273*n1,* 301

Northwest Band of Shoshone Indians v. United States, 324 U.S. 335 (1945),
    194–95, 207*n,* 208*nn8, 18*

Noto v. United States, 367 U.S. 290 (1961), 87*n19*

O'Brien, United States v., 391 U.S. 367 (1967), 30*n93,* 56*n12,* 72–73, 78

Oestereich v. Selective Service Board No. 11, 393 U.S. 233 (1968), 30*n95,* 56*n6*

Oliphant v. Suquamish Indian Tribe, 435 U.S. 191 (1978), 207

Olmstead v. United States, 277 U.S. 438 (1928), 162, 171*n12*

On Lee v. United States, 343 U.S. 747 (1952), 156–57

Papachristou v. Jacksonville, 405 U.S. 156 (1972), 123, 138–39, 151

Paris Adult Theater I v. Slaton, 413 U.S. 49 (1973), 176*n85*

Parker v. Levy, 417 U.S. 733 (1974), 146*n28*

Patterson v. McLean Credit Union, 109 S.Ct. 2363 (1989), 119*n63*

Pennsylvania v. Nelson, 350 U.S. 497 (1956), 86*n66*

Perez v. Ledesma, 401 U.S. 82 (1971), 88*n53*

Peters v. Hobby, 349 U.S. 331 (1955), 89*n66*

Pink, United States v., 315 U.S. 203 (1942), 265, 298
Pinkerton v. United States, 328 U.S. 640 (1946), 139–40, 152
Plessy v. Ferguson, 163 U.S. 537 (1896), 110
Poe v. Ullman, 367 U.S. 497 (1961), 158–59, 162, 172*n18*, 173*n32*
Poulos v. New Hampshire, 345 U.S. 395 (1953), 105*n6*, 106*n38*
Price, United States v., 383 U.S. 787 (1966), 119*n48*
Prize Cases, 67 U.S. (2 Bl.) 635 (1863), 290
Public Utilities Commission v. Pollak, 343 U.S. 451 (1952), 105*nn15, 18,* 122, 156–58
Puget Sound Gillnetters Association v. United States District Court, 573 F.2d 1123 (9th Cir. 1978), 211*n52,* 212*n55*
Puyallup Tribe v. Department of Game of Washington, 391 U.S. 392 (1968) (*Puyallup I*), 199–202, 208*nn4–5,* 211*n48*
Puyallup Tribe v. Department of Game of Washington, 433 U.S. 165 (1977) (*Puyallup III*), 212*n61*

Ragen, United States v., 314 U.S. 513 (1942), 144*n14,* 146*n28*
Raley v. Ohio, 360 U.S. 423 (1959), 137–39, 151
Regents of University of California v. Bakke, 438 U.S. 265 (1978), 116
Reitman v. Mulkey, 387 U.S. 369 (1969), 118*n36*
Republic Steel Corp., United States v., 362 U.S. 482 (1960), 224*n15,* 246*n19*
Reynolds v. United States, 98 U.S. 145 (1878), 106*nn34, 37*
Richardson, United States v., 418 U.S. 166 (1974), 272–73
Robertson v. Methow Valley Citizens Council, 109 S.Ct. 1835 (1989), 224*n13*
Rochin v. California, 342 U.S. 165 (1951), 159, 164
Roe v. Wade, 410 U.S. 113 (1973), 65, 69, 159, 163–64, 179–84
Rosenberg et ux v. United States v., 346 U.S. 273 (1953), 20–25, 54, 299
Ross v. Moffitt, 417 U.S. 600 (1974), 141
Roth v. United States, 354 U.S. 476 (1957), 71, 125*n5*
Runyon v. McCrary, 427 U.S. 160 (1976), 119*n63*

Saia v. New York, 334 U.S. 558 (1948), 125*n8*
Samuels v. Mackell, 401 U.S. 66 (1971), 88*n53*
Sandoval, United States v., 231 U.S. 28 (1913), 212*n57*
Santa Fe Pacific Railroad Co., United States v., 314 U.S. 339 (1941), 207*n2*
Sarnoff v. Shultz, 409 U.S. 929 (1972), 295*n96*
Scales v. United States, 367 U.S. 203 (1961), 74, 87*n19*
Schlesinger v. Reservists Committee to Stop the War, 418 U.S. 208 (1974), 271–72, 303*n18*
Schlesinger v. Wisconsin, 270 U.S. 230 (1926), 174*n48*
Schneiderman v. United States, 320 U.S. 118 (1942), 31–32*n131*
Scott v. Illinois, 400 U.S. 367 (1979), 147*n75*
Screws v. United States, 325 U.S. 91 (1945), 114–16, 134–36, 138, 144*n15,* 149–50
See v. Seattle, 387 U.S. 541 (1967), 48*n50*
Seeger, United States v., 380 U.S. 163 (1964), 30*n92,* 99, 105*n3*
Seymour v. Superintendent, 368 U.S. 351 (1962), 204
Shelley v. Kramer, 334 U.S. 1 (1948), 111–12
Sherbert v. Verner, 374 U.S. 398 (1963), 94, 102–03, 105*nn6, 20*

Sicurella v. United States, 348 U.S. 385 (1954), 30*n92*
Sierra Club v. Federal Power Commission, 407 U.S. 926 (1972), 224*n17,* 246*n21*
Sierra Club v. Morton, 405 U.S. 727 (1972), 56*n5,* 190, 228, 231, 242–44
Skinner v. Oklahoma, 316 U.S. 535 (1942), 111, 155–56, 228, 231*n4*
Sperling, United States v., 506 F.2d 1323 (2nd Cir. 1974), 147*n53*
Standard Oil Co., United States v., 384 U.S. 224 (1966), 224*n15,* 246*n19,* 247*n28*
Stanley v. Georgia, 394 U.S. 557 (1969), 87*n28*
State v. Stein, 70 N.J. 369, 360 A.2d 347 (1976), 146*n50*
State v. Towessnute, 39 Wash. 478, 154 P. 805 (1916), 209*n22,* 211*n52*
State of Washington, United States v., 520 F.2d 676 (9th Cir. 1975), 211*n52*
Students Challenging Regulatory Agency Procedures (SCRAP), United States v.,
     412 U.S. 669 (1973), 223*n11,* 230
Sullivan v. Little Hunting Park, 396 U.S. 229 (1969), 116–17
Sunal v. Large, 332 U.S. 174 (1947), 30*n91*

Tee Hit Ton Indians v. United States, 348 U.S. 272 (1955), 195–96
Terminiello v. Chicago, 337 U.S. 1 (1949), 73, 124, 126*n24,* 143*n3*
Tilton v. Richardson, 403 U.S. 672 (1971), 93, 104*n3,* 106*nn27, 29–30*
Time, Inc. v. Hill, 385 U.S. 374 (1967), 175*n52*
Tulee v. Washington, 315 U.S. 681 (1942), 199, 209*n22,* 210–11*n46*
Twin City Power Co., United States v., 350 U.S. 222 (1956), 225*n31*

Udall v. Federal Power Commission, 387 U.S. 428 (1967), 223*n11,* 230, 238–39,
     244, 247*n28*
Union Pacific Railroad, United States v., 353 U.S. 112 (1957), 225*n31,* 240–42,
     247*n37*
United States v.: see opposing party
United States Department of Agriculture v. Moreno, 416 U.S. 1 (1974), 230
*United States Department of Justice v. Reporters Committee for Freedom of the
     Press,* 109 S.Ct. 1468 (1969), 177*n96*
United States District Court, United States v., 407 U.S. 297 (1972) *(Keith),* 78–79
Uphaus v. Wyman, 364 U.S. 388 (1960), 176*n77*

*Vermont Yankee Nuclear Power Corp. v. Natural Resources Defense Council,
     Inc.,* 435 U.S. 519 (1978), 224*n13*

Wallace v. Jaffree, 472 U.S. 38 (1985), 144*n13*
Walz v. Tax Commission of City of New York, 397 U.S. 664 (1970), 92–93, 99,
     102, 104*n3,* 106*nn27–28, 30,* 107*n59*
Warm Springs Task Force v. Gribble, 417 U.S. 1301 (1974), 224*n12*
Warren Trading Post v. Arizona Tax Commission, 380 U.S. 685 (1965), 204–05
Washington, United States v., 384 F.Supp. 312 (W.D.Wash. 1974), 211*n50,* 212*n63*
Washington v. Confederated Bands and Tribes of the Yakima Indian Nation, 439
     U.S. 463 (1979), 212*n55*
*Washington v. Washington State Commercial Passenger Fishing Vessel Associa-
     tion,* 443 U.S. 658 (1979), 211*n52,* 212*n62*
Washington State Commercial Passenger Fishing Vessel Association v. Tollefson,
     89 Wash. 2d 276, 571 P.2d 1373 (1977), 212*n54*

Watt v. Western Nuclear Co., 462 U.S. 36 (1983), 247*n41*
Webster v. Reproductive Health Services, 109 S.Ct. 3040 (1989), 130
Weinberger v. Catholic Action of Hawaii, 454 U.S. 139 (1981), 224*n13*
Welsh v. United States, 398 U.S. 333 (1970), 30*n92*
West Virginia Board of Education v. Barnette, 319 U.S. 624 (1943), 103, 144*n11*
Wheeler v. Barrera, 417 U.S. 402 (1974), 92, 104*n3,* 106*n27*
Whitney v. California, 274 U.S. 357 (1927), 88*n38,* 227
Wilkinson v. United States, 365 U.S. 399 (1961), 83, 87*n19,* 125*n2*
Williams v. Lee, 358 U.S. 217 (1959), 198, 209*nn24, 27*
Williams, United States v., 341 U.S. 58 (1951), 144*n9*
Williams, United States v., 341 U.S. 70 (1951), 115
Williams v. United States, 341 U.S. 97 (1951), 145*n23*
Williamson v. Lee Optical of Oklahoma, 348 U.S. 483 (1955), 56*n3*
Winans, United States v., 198 U.S. 371 (1905), 193, 201, 212*n55*
Winters v. United States, 207 U.S. 564 (1908), 193
Wisconsin v. Yoder, 406 U.S. 205 (1972), 56*n9,* 93, 98, 105*n6,* 106*n41,* 147*n60,* 228
Worcester v. Georgia, 31 U.S. 515 (1832), 211*n49*
Wyman v. James, 400 U.S. 309 (1971), 168

Yates v. United States, 354 U.S. 298 (1957), 88*n50*
Younger v. Harris, 401 U.S. 37 (1971), 79, 88*n56,* 118*n34*
Youngstown Sheet & Tube Co. v. Sawyer, 343 U.S. 579 (1952), 267–69, 275*nn60–61,* 302, 303*n8*

Zap v. United States, 328 U.S. 624 (1945), 156
Zorach v. Clauson, 343 U.S. 306 (1952), 5, 91–92, 95, 99–102, 105*n3,* 106–07*n47,* 123–24
Zschernig v. Miller, 389 U.S. 429 (1968), 273*n1,* 298–99

Index

Abortion, 130, 159–60, 163, 180–84
Acheson, Dean, 307
Affirmative action, 116
American Bar Association, 140
American Civil Liberties Union, 271
American Law Institute, 75, 140
Amish, 93–94
An Almanac of Liberty, 156
The Anatomy of Liberty, 97
Anti-Communism. *See* Communism
Ares, Charles (clerk), 43, 47*n27*
Arnold, Thurman, 59
Association, freedom of. *See* Freedom of association
Atlantic Union, 308
Atomic Energy Act, 22–24
Atomic Energy Commission, 217

Barber, James David, on political styles, 45, 61
Balancing tests, 83–84
Bazelon, David, 143*n4*
Benefit-cost analysis, 215
Berlin, Isaiah, 228–29
"Bernstein exception," 270
Beyond the high Himalayas, 306
Bill of Rights, xii, 65, 74, 158–59, 163–64, 199, 279, 283
Big Horn River, 207, 302
Birth control. *See* Contraceptives
Black, Hugo, 4, 8–10, 14–15, 18, 20–25, 33, 36–37, 41–42, 44–45, 46*n8,* 47*n26,* 53, 58, 69, 71, 73, 77–78, 80–86, 113, 121, 125, 134, 149, 160, 163–64, 170*n1,* 172*n20,* 189, 194, 196, 199, 204, 206, 209, 229, 266–68, 274*n17,* 274*n19,* 279; and Douglas, 4, 10, 20, 27*n20,* 37, 41, 80–86, 121
Blackmun, Harry, xv, 35, 42, 159–60, 179, 181–83, 207

Boldt, George, 201, 211*n50*
Bonneville Power Administration, 217
Bork, Robert, 86, 160, 162–63, 165–66, 168–69, 170*n2*
Brandeis, Louis, vi, 47*n29,* 76, 134, 169, 171*n13,* 227, 262, 269, 273, 274*n19;* and privacy, 157, 161–62, 167–68
Brandeis brief, 262
Brennan, William, 4, 19, 27*n13,* 37, 41–42, 45, 48*n50,* 51, 53, 70, 74, 83, 112, 121–23, 137, 147*n74,* 159, 170, 189, 203, 205–06, 266
Brownell, Herbert, 22
Bureau of Indian Affairs, 201, 204
Bureau of Land Management, 241
Bureau of Reclamation, 217
Burger, Warren, 4, 19, 35, 181
Burger Court, 19, 129
Burton, Harold, 20, 22–23
Byrnes, James, 16

C & O Canal. *See* Chesapeake & Ohio Canal
Cambodian bombing, 55, 281–82, 290, 298
Campbell, James (clerk), 44
Cardozo, Benjamin, 134
Carter, Jared (clerk), 43
Cascade Mountains, 233–34, 236
Cases. *See* Table of Cases (p. 323) for case names and citations
Central Intelligence Agency, 264, 272, 280, 297
Certiorari, 21, 55; clerks' work on, 37, 39; denial of, 21, 55, 290. *See also* Dissent
Chesapeake & Ohio Canal, xi–xiii, 41, 191, 237, 245, 246*n17,* 250–52
Children, rights of, 55
China. *See* People's Republic of China
Church-state relations, 5, 91–104
Civil liberties. *See* particular topics

Civil rights, 66, 109–17; and civil suits, 115–17, 135–36; and criminal law, 114–15, 134–37, 149–50; demonstrations, 11–13, 74, 117, 139; and statutes, 66, 115–17, 134–37. *See also* Equal protection; Fourteenth Amendment

Civil Rights Act: of 1875, 109–10; of 1964, 109, 113

Civil War Amendments. *See* Fourteenth Amendment; Fifteenth Amendment

Clark, Tom, 20, 23, 40, 121, 170*n1*

Clean Water Act, 236

"Clear and present danger" test, 69, 71–72, 227

Clerks. *See* Law clerks

Cohen, Felix, 190, 193–94, 197, 207*n1; Handbook of Indian Law,* 191, 194, 197, 206

Cohen, William (clerk), 24, 38, 47*n27,* 75

Cold War, 20, 25, 121, 261, 280, 286, 299. *See also* McCarthyism

Columbia Law School, xv, 35, 192, 262, 305

Columbia River, 233, 239–40

Commerce Clause, 109, 113–14, 308

Communism, 78, 280, 285, 291, 307, 310

Communist party, 71–72, 77–78, 80, 156

Communists, 72, 74, 77–78, 82–83, 86

Congress, 78, 268, 271–72; and civil rights, 109–10, 113; and environment, 237; and Federal Rules, 147; in foreign relations, 299–300; and Indians, 191–93, 196, 201, 212*n68;* and remedies, 217–18. *See also* Deference; Separation of powers; and specific acts

Connally Amendment, 295*n94*

Conscientious Objectors, 16–19, 55, 99, 103

Contraceptives, 159, 179

Contras, 258, 280. *See also* Iran-Contra Affair

Corps of Engineers (U.S.), 217

Countryman, Vern (clerk), 39–40, 43–44, 54, 162, 279

Criminal law, 114–15, 133–43; and civil rights, 134–37

Criminal procedure, 129, 140–41. *See also* Criminal law

Critical Legal Studies, 85, 167, 245

Cuba, 258, 305

Dawes Act, 191–93

Death penalty, 22–24, 116

Decision theory, 215, 229

Deference, 9, 14, 230, 270; to agencies, 216–17; to military, 9–14, 55

Democracy's Manifesto, 287

Depression, 298, 305

Dissents, 12, 24, 70, 72, 76, 270, 279, 282; from cert. denial, 21, 55, 290

Dorsen, Norman, 42

Douglas, William O.: and absolutism, 91, 95, 102, 104, 257–59; as activist, 164–65, 244; as anti-judge, 58–59, 79; autobiography of, 167, 297; background of, xv, 8, 305; and Black, 4, 10, 20, 27*n20,* 37, 41, 80–86, 121, 125*n5;* and Brandeis, 157, 169; and Cambodian bombing, 55, 280–82, 290; changes in view of, 4, 25, 126*n22,* 155, 189, 206, 262; characteristics of, 8, 32*n133,* 34–37, 57–58, 60–61; on church and state, 5, 91–104, 123–24; and civil liberties, 55, 65–67, 91–104, 121–24, 155–70, 279; and civil rights, 109–17, 123; and civil rights statutes, 114–17; and clerks, 37–45, 52–54; and colleagues, 4, 7–8, 31–32*n131,* 33–37, 44–45, 51–54, 70, 279; and Columbia Law School, xv, 35, 208, 235, 262, 305; and Communism, 283, 285, 287; and Conscientious Objectors, 16–19, 55, 91, 103; and criminal law, xii, 114–15, 133–43; and deference to government, 9–14, 216–17, 230, 270; dissents by, xii, 2, 24, 70, 72, 76, 164, 195, 212*n64,* 242, 244, 270, 279, 282, 290; and doctrine, 75–76, 122; and environment, xi–xiii, 45, 65, 189–90, 215–23, 229–31, 233–45, 249–53; as example, 71, 79–80, 84–86; extrajudicial writings of, 65, 101, 231, 236–37, 261–69, 279–80, 297; and facts, 73–74, 76–78; and federal statutes, 114–17, 146*n37;* and fishing rights, 198–202, 206–07; on foreign relations, 261–73; formative experiences of, 233–35; and Frankfurter, 10, 21, 36, 44, 53–54, 57; as great judge, 227, 229; impeachment of, 78, 175–76*n67;* inconsistency in opinions of, 54, 100–04, 122–24; and Indians, 5, 65, 183, 189, 191–208, 235; as internationalist, 257–59, 261–73, 279–92, 305–10; and Japanese-American cases, 4, 7, 9–14, 297, 299; and Jehovah's Witnesses, 15–17; and Lyndon Johnson, 288; judicial style of, 25–26; as lawyer, 234–35; legacy of, 70–71, 73–76, 79–80, 84–86, 122, 129–30, 133–43, 229, 231, 244–45; and Legal Realism, xv, 58–60, 69, 75–76, 84, 121, 245, 262, 280, 298, 307; as loner, 7–8, 33, 51–52, 54; and loyalty, 9–26; on marriage, 97, 179; and military, 9–14, 263–64; and national security, 8–26; and New Deal, 8, 237, 273;

Douglas, William O. (*cont.*)
opinions of, criticized, 72–74, 100–01,
123–24, 160–61; and opinion-writing, 14,
66; parents of, 101; and penumbras, 160–
62; as philosopher, xi; political ambition
of, 70, 124, 284; political style of, 45, 60–
61; and precedent, 82, 164; on privacy, 94–
95, 97, 111–12, 155–70, 179–84; and property theory, 220–22; and public lands, 233–
45; on race relations, 5, 12; religious background of, 101; and Franklin D. Roosevelt,
262–64, 282–83; and Rosenberg case, 20–
25; and secretaries, 42; at Securities and
Exchange Commission, xv–xvi, 34, 44,
190, 192; on separation of powers, 261–73;
sources for opinions of, 93–94; on standing, 231, 244, 271–73; and taxpayers, 4–5,
230, 244; travels of, 70, 246*n14,* 279; and
Harry Truman, 275*n53;* and Vietnam War,
19–20, 55, 72, 168–70, 264, 284, 288–90,
298, 301; and water rights, 237–40; and
Whitman College, xv, 192, 307; and
women clerks, 47*n28;* and women, 183;
work patterns of, 25–26, 34–35, 45, 52–53;
and world peace, 279; worldview of, 257;
and Yakima Indians, 192; and Yale Law
School, xv–xvi, 34, 262. *See also* Columbia Law School; Liberty; Rule of law;
Securities and Exchange Commission;
Whitman College; Yale Law School; and
specific topics
Draft-card burning, 72, 78
Due process, 12, 20, 282
Due Process Clause, 123, 134, 137, 174

Earth Day, 249
Earth First!, 249
Eighth Amendment, 20. *See also* Death
penalty
Eisenhower, Dwight, 194
Electronic surveillance, 156–57
Emerson, Thomas, 70–71, 73, 77, 95, 160
Environment, xi–xiii, 45, 65, 189–90, 215–23,
229, 233–45. *See also* Land use restrictions
Equality, 65. *See also* Equal protection
Equal protection, 70, 199
Equal Protection Clause, 110–11, 113, 201, 288
Espionage Act, 20, 23, 30*n98,* 31*n108*
Establishment Clause, 91–93, 95–97, 100–01,
103, 123–24
European Convention on Human Rights, 170
European Court of Human Rights, 170, 308
Executive agreements, 265

Fair Housing Act of 1968, 116–17
Falk, Jerome (clerk), 39–40, 44, 47*n27,* 54
Federal Bureau of Investigation (FBI), 170
Federalist Society, 85
Federal Power Act, 196, 239
Federal Power Commission, 239
Federal Rules, 140–41
Feinberg Law, 80
Fifteenth Amendment, 114
Fifth Amendment, 9–12, 73, 83, 157–58,
162, 164, 195, 199, 221. *See also* Due pro-
cess; Self-incrimination
First Amendment, 40, 65, 69–94, 91–104,
122, 136, 157, 159, 161, 174–75*n52,* 180,
220, 230–31, 271, 273*n1,* 282, 287–88. *See
also* Church-state relations; Freedom of
speech
Fishing rights, 65, 193, 198–202, 206–07
Ford, Gerald, 78
Foreign relations, 261–73; judges' role in,
300
Forest Service (U.S.), 205, 217, 235, 243–44
Fortas, Abe, 59
Fourteenth Amendment, 66, 109–15, 159–
60, 164, 174*n48,* 179–80, 201. *See also*
Equal protection; Equality
Fourth Amendment, 14, 41, 156, 162. *See
also* Search and seizure
Frank, Jerome, 59
Frankfurter, Felix, 5, 7, 9–14, 18, 21–25,
27*nn14–15,* 33, 35–36, 41–42, 44–45,
47*n29,* 53, 57, 71, 73, 77, 82–83, 85, 121,
135, 137, 149, 151, 159, 194, 202, 208*n17,*
227, 266–67, 275*n60,* 305; and Douglas,
10, 21, 36, 44, 53–54, 57
Freedom of association, 159, 163, 229
Freedom of expression. *See* Freedom of
speech
Freedom of speech, 19, 55, 65, 70–75, 163,
220; and public forum doctrine, 74–75.
See also Draft-card burning; Obscenity
Free Exercise Clause, 92–93, 96–99, 103,
104*n1,* 220
Fulbright, J. William, 301

Game theory, 215
General Allotment Act. *See* Dawes Act
Ginsberg, C. David (clerk), 34, 41
Goldberg, Arthur, 121, 170*n1,* 301
Goose Prairie (Washington), xi, 36, 52–53
Greece, 279, 284
Grenada, 257–58
Griswold, Erwin, 72, 83

Grossman, Harvey (clerk), 41, 43
Gulf of Tonkin Resolution, 270
Gunther, Gerald, 42–44

Habeas corpus, 10, 18
Hankin, Lewis, 42
Harlan, John Marshall (the elder), 109–12, 114
Harlan, John Marshall (the younger), 40, 42, 53, 73, 83–84, 117, 170n1, 227, 290
Harvard Law School, 44, 75, 82, 192
High Mountain Sheep Dam, 239
Hitler, Adolph, 258, 305
Holmes, Oliver Wendell, 69, 76, 134, 162, 169, 227
Holtzman, Elizabeth, 281
Homosexuality, 170, 182–83
Hong Kong, 170
House Un-American Activities Committee (HUAC), 80, 82, 84
Hughes, Charles Evans, 15, 35, 46n10, 262, 307
Hutchins, Robert M., xiii

Impeachment, 78, 175–76n67
Incompatibility Clause, 271
India, 279, 284–85, 309. See also Nehru
Indian Civil Rights Act, 197
Indian Claims Commission Act, 198
Indian Commerce Clause, 201
Indian law, 191–207
Indian Reorganization Act, 192, 205, 207
Indians, 65, 183, 189, 191–207, 220, 235; Douglas's votes on, 5, 208n5; and fishing rights, 193, 198–202; as lawyers, 197–98; and reservations, 193, 196, 203–04; state jurisdiction over, 204–06, 210n32; taxation of, 204–06; and "termination," 194, 209n30, 210n36; and title to riverbeds, 203; treaties with, 193–95, 199–201, 204–05; tribes of, 194, 197, 202–03, 207; and water rights, 193. See also Fishing rights
Interior Department, 194, 207n1, 251–52. See also Secretary of Interior
Internal Revenue Service. See Taxpayers
International Court of Justice, 289–90, 299, 306, 308
International Dissent, 288–89
International Workers of the World. See Wobblies
Iran, 279, 284–85
Iran-Contra Affair, 299, 301
Israel, 279, 284–85

Jackson, Robert, 12–13, 16, 21–25, 36, 72, 77, 135, 149, 268, 270
Japanese-American Exclusion Cases, 7, 9–14, 80, 266–67, 297, 299–300
Japanese-Americans, 27nn17–18, 297, 299
Jefferson, Thomas, 271, 273
Jehovah's Witnesses, 15–17, 93–94, 98
Johnson, Lyndon, 61, 66, 288, 291, 306
Judd, Orrin, 280
Judicial activism, 85
Justices: interaction among, 7, 9–14; votes of, 3–5. See also specific names
Justiciability, 55, 271–73

Kennan, George, 307, 309
Kennedy, John F., 280, 308
Kennedy, Joseph, 286
Kennedy, Robert, 286
King, Martin Luther, Jr., 251, 289
Klitgard, Thomas (clerk), 47n27
Korean War, 261

Land use restrictions, 219, 221, 229
Latin America, 258, 305, 308–09
Law clerks, 38, 42–44. See also Douglas; specific names
League of Nations, 264, 308
Lebanon, 279, 284
Legal Realism, xv, 58–60, 75–76, 122, 262, 280, 298, 307. See also Yale Law School
Legal Services lawyers, 197–98
Leopold, Aldo, 236, 243
Liberty, xi–xiii, 8, 158, 179–83. See also Civil liberties; Privacy
Litvinov Assignment, 265–66, 306
Loyalty security program, 74, 80

McCarran Act, 80
McCarthyism, 69–71, 79, 85, 285, 299. See also Cold War
McKay, Douglas, 251
Madison, James, 96, 101, 270
Mann Act, 92
Marriage, 156, 180
Marshall, John, 86
Marshall, Thurgood, 42, 66, 70, 116, 189, 203, 205–06, 229–30
Meador, Daniel, 42, 44
Meiklejohn, Alexander, 75
Military, deference to, 9–14, 55
Mill, John Stuart, 167, 181, 257–58
Miller, Charles (clerk), 41, 43, 47n26
Mineral King Valley, 243
Minton, Sherman, 20, 33, 121

Model Penal Code, 139
Mormons, 93, 96–97
Muir, John, 235–37, 250
Murphy, Frank, 9–13, 14–17, 20, 25, 59, 121, 189, 206, 208*n17*

National Association for the Advancement of Colored People (NAACP), 271
National Environmental Policy Act (NEPA), 217, 222, 230, 237
National Park Service, 217, 251–52
National Park System, 237
National security, 8–26
National Wilderness Protection System, 252
Native American Rights Fund, 198
Native Americans. *See* Indians
Nehru, Jawaharlal, 285, 309
New Deal, 8, 69, 81, 237, 298, 305
Nicaragua, 258, 280, 289–90
Ninth Amendment, 179–80
Ninth Circuit, 38, 201, 211*n52*
Nixon, Richard, 45, 61, 79, 209*n30*, 263, 269, 291, 307
Noise Control Act, 218
North Atlantic Treaty Organization (NATO), 309
North from Malaya, 306
Northwest Ordinance, 208
Nuremberg, 265, 270

Obscenity, 71–72. *See also* Freedom of speech
Office for Economic Opportunity, 198
Olympic National Park, 190, 252
Organization of American States, 309

Pacific Northwest, xv, 189, 199, 207
Packer, Herbert, 137, 150
Pakistan, 284–85
Pelton Dam, 238
Penumbras, xii, 160–62. *See also* Privacy
People's Republic of China, 259, 266, 284, 286–87, 310
Pinchot, Gifford, 235
Points of Rebellion, 78, 85
Police misconduct, 114–16, 134–37, 149–50
Polygamy, 96–98
Powe, Lucas (clerk), 39
Powell, Lewis, 4, 36–37, 171*n5*
Precedent, 82, 164, 245
President, foreign relations power of, 261–73. *See also* specific names

Privacy, right to, xii–xiii, 55, 65, 94–95, 111, 129–30, 155–70, 179–84, 228; penumbral, 160–62
Privacy Act, 169
Process jurisprudence, 81–83
Public accommodations, 110–11
Public forum doctrine, 74–75
Public lands, 233–45

Race relations. *See* Equality; Racial discrimination
Racial discrimination, 5, 12, 66, 109–17
Radin, Max, 38
Reagan, Ronald, 258, 280, 310
Reagan Doctrine, 258
Reclamation Act, 238
Reed, Stanley, 11–12, 23, 33, 194
Rehnquist, William, 4, 35, 42, 51, 53, 66, 147*n75,* 161, 171*n5,* 212–13*n71,* 244; as law clerk, 21
Rehnquist Court, 129
Religion. *See* Church-state relations
Removal statute, 115
Reservations, 193, 196, 203–04, 235
The Right of the People, 97, 99, 102, 158–59, 165–67
Right to counsel, 140–42
Right to privacy. *See* Privacy, right to
Rivers and Harbors Act, 237–38
Roberts, Owen, 13, 27*n18,* 135, 149, 274*n17,* 308
Rodell, Fred, 59
Roosevelt, Eleanor, 301
Roosevelt, Franklin D., 9, 14, 41, 70, 191, 267, 275*n53,* 282–83, 291, 298, 305
Roosevelt, Theodore, 235, 305
Ruckershauser, Charles (clerk), 40–41, 54
Rule of Law, 81, 264, 289, 306, 310
Russia. *See* Soviet Union
Russian Journey, 286
Rutledge, Wiley, 12, 16, 20, 28*n29,* 121, 308

School desegregation, 114. *See also* Racial discrimination
School prayer. *See* Church-state relations
Search and seizure, 156–57, 168. *See also* Fourth Amendment
Second Circuit, 281
Secretary of Interior, 237, 239, 251, 279
Secretary of State, 279, 288
Section 20 (18 U.S.C. §242), 115, 134–36
Section 1981 (42 U.S.C. §1981), 117
Section 1982 (42 U.S.C. §1982), 116–17

Section 1983 (42 U.S.C. §1983), 115–17
Securities and Exchange Commission (SEC). *See* Douglas
Selective Service Act, 16, 19. *See also* Conscientious Objectors
Self-incrimination, xii, 140
Separation of powers, 261–73, 299–300. *See also* Congress
Sierra Club, 236, 243, 249
Simon, James, 155, 161, 230
Sit-ins. *See* Civil rights
Sixth Amendment, 147*n72*
Small, Marshall (clerk), 41, 43
Smith Act, 71–72
Snake River, 239
Southern Christian Leadership Conference, 271
Soviet Union, 77, 94, 157, 217, 265, 280, 284, 286–89, 306–07, 310
Sparrowe, Stanley (clerk), 40–41, 47*nn26–27*
Speech, freedom of. *See* Freedom of speech
Standing, 271–73
Steel Seizure Case, 267–70
Stewart, Potter, 19, 164, 205, 270, 290
Stone, Christopher (clerk), 243
Stone, Harlan Fiske, 7, 10, 12–14, 17–18, 33, 35, 54, 81, 134, 149, 235
Strange Lands and Friendly People, 284–85, 306
Submerged Lands Act, 240
Subversive Activities Control Act, 269
Sunday closing laws, 95–96
Supremacy Clause, 202–03
Supreme Court: interaction in, 7, 9–14; and opinion-writing, 51; roles, 152–53
Sutherland, George, 301

"Takings," 194–95, 218, 229
Taxation, of Indians, 204–06
Taxpayers, 4–5, 230, 244
Tennessee Valley Authority, 217
Third Amendment, 157
Third World, 70, 287, 309–10
Tolstoy, Leo, 177*n87,* 229
Torre, Gary (clerk), 43
Trautman, Donald, 42–43
Travel, right to, xiii, 294*n67*
Treason, 20, 25
Treaties. *See* Indians
Tribal Federal Jurisdiction Act, 210*n39*

Tribes, 192, 194, 196–97, 202–03, 207
Truman, Harry S., 20, 267–70, 279, 283–84, 291, 306–07
"Truman" Court, 20

Union Pacific and Central Pacific Railroad Act, 240–41
United Nations, 257, 264, 283, 289, 298, 301, 306–08, 310
Universal Declaration of Human Rights, 306
University of New Mexico, 197–98
University of Washington Law School, 38, 197

Vietnam War, 19–20, 55, 72, 169, 261, 264, 269–70, 284, 288–90, 301, 306, 308. *See also* Cambodian bombing
Vinson, Fred, 20–23, 73, 77

Warren, Earl, 4, 19, 33, 36, 42, 44, 58, 83, 86, 121, 170
Warren Court, 19–20, 69, 85–86, 129–30, 149
Washington (State), 201, 209*n22,* 252
Washington Supreme Court, 199, 201, 209*n22*
Watergate, 79, 301
Water rights, 238–39
West of the Indus, 306
White, Byron, 170*n1,* 205
White, G. Edward, 58, 79, 84, 262
Whitman College, xv, 192, 307
Wilderness. *See* Environment
Wilderness Act of 1964, 253
Wilderness Bill of Rights, 219, 230, 236, 245
Wilderness Society, 249, 251
Wilkinson, Charles, 196, 198–99, 210*n41*
Wilson, Woodrow, 305, 307
Wobblies, 235, 245
World Court. *See* International Court of Justice
World War I, 298
World War II, 261, 305–07. *See also* Japanese-Americans

Yakima (Washington), 233, 281
Yale Law School, xv–xvi, 34, 44, 59, 197, 207*n1,* 262

Zedong, Mao, 259, 285
Zoning. *See* Environment

Pitt Series in Policy and Institutional Studies
Bert A. Rockman, Editor

The Acid Rain Controversy
James L. Regens and Robert W. Rycroft

Agency Merger and Bureaucratic Redesign
Karen M. Hult

The Aging: A Guide to Public Policy
Bennett M. Rich and Martha Baum

The Atlantic Alliance and the Middle East
Joseph I. Coffey and Gianni Bonvicini, Editors

Clean Air: The Policies and Politics of Pollution Control
Charles O. Jones

The Competitive City: The Political Economy of Suburbia
Mark Schneider

Conflict and Rhetoric in French Policymaking
Frank R. Baumgartner

Congress and Economic Policymaking
Darrell M. West

Congress Oversees the Bureaucracy: Studies in Legislative Supervision
Morris S. Ogul

Democracy in Japan
Takeshi Ishida and Ellis S. Krauss, Editors

Demographic Change and the American Future
R. Scott Fosler, William Alonso, Jack A. Meyer, and Rosemary Kern

Economic Decline and Political Change: Canada, Great Britain, and the United States
Harold D. Clarke, Marianne C. Stewart, and Gary Zuk, Editors

Foreign Policy Motivation: A General Theory and a Case Study
Richard W. Cottam

"He Shall Not Pass This Way Again": The Legacy of Justice William O. Douglas
Stephen L. Wasby, Editor

Homeward Bound: Explaining Changes in Congressional Behavior
Glenn Parker

Imagery and Ideology in U.S. Policy Toward Libya, 1969–1982
Mahmoud G. ElWarfally

The Impact of Policy Analysis
James M. Rogers

Iran and the United States: A Cold War Case Study
Richard W. Cottam

Japanese Prefectures and Policymaking
Steven R. Reed

Making Regulatory Policy
Keith Hawkins and John M. Thomas, Editors

Managing the Presidency: Carter, Reagan, and the Search for Executive Harmony
Colin Campbell, S.J.

Organizing Governance, Governing Organizations
Colin Campbell, S.J., and B. Guy Peters, Editors

Party Organizations in American Politics
Cornelius P. Cotter et al.

Perceptions and Behavior in Soviet Foreign Policy
Richard K. Herrmann

Pesticides and Politics: The Life Cycle of a Public Issue
Christopher J. Bosso

Policy Analysis by Design
Davis B. Bobrow and John S. Dryzek

The Political Failure of Employment Policy, 1945–1982
Gary Mucciaroni

Political Leadership: A Source Book
Barbara Kellerman, Editor

The Politics of Public Utility Regulation
William T. Gormley, Jr.

The Politics of the U.S. Cabinet: Representation in the Executive Branch, 1789–1984
Jeffrey E. Cohen

The Presidency and Public Policy Making
George C. Edwards III, Steven A. Shull, and Norman C. Thomas, Editors

Private Markets and Public Intervention: A Primer for Policy Designers
Harvey Averch

Public Policy in Latin America: A Comparative Survey
John W. Sloan

Roads to Reason: Transportation, Administration, and Rationality in Colombia
Richard E. Hartwig

Site Unseen: The Politics of Siting a Nuclear Waste Repository
Gerald Jacob

The Struggle for Social Security, 1900–1935
Roy Lubove

Tage Erlander: Serving the Welfare State, 1946–1969
Olof Ruin

Urban Alternatives: Public and Private Markets in the Provision of Local Services
Robert M. Stein

The U.S. Experiment in Social Medicine: The Community Health Center Program, 1965–1986
Alice Sardell